The Foreign Self
Truth Telling as Educational Inquiry

Edited by François V. Tochon

Atwood Publishing
Madison, WI

The Foreign Self: Truth Telling as Educational Inquiry
Edited by François V. Tochon

© 2002 Atwood Publishing
2710 Atwood Ave.
Madison, WI 53704
888.242.7101
608.242.7101
www.atwoodpublishing.com
ISBN: 1-891859-41-2

Cover design by TLC Graphics, www.tlcgraphics.com
Wooden carved mask by Jonathon Bedford

Printed in the United States of America

Library of Congress Cataloging-in-Publication Data

The foreign self: truth telling as educational inquiry/edited by François Tochon.

    p. cm.
  Includes bibliographical references and index.
  ISBN 1-891859-41-2
  1. Language and languages. 2. Identity (Psychology) 3. Self-disclosure. 4.
  Language and languages--Study and teaching. I. Tochon, François Victor,
1954-
P106.F654 2002
401'.41--dc21

                                        2002025448

Table of Contents

Foreword

Gloria Ladson-Billings
University of Wisconsin, Madison

Almost twenty years ago I found myself sitting in a writing workshop. I was accompanying a group of pre-service teachers who were looking for new ways to teach writing and support student learning through writing. The workshop leader was a skilled and experienced teacher. For the first assignment the leader asked us each to do a "free-write" about a person we knew well. I chose to write about my husband. In my essay I described my husband as a kind, gentle man who loves people. I wrote what I thought was a flattering and truthful description. Shortly after I finished my essay the workshop leader announced, "Now I want you to write what you *really* think about the person." Initially, I thought I would have nothing else to write. I had already written everything I had to say about my husband. I sat for a few minutes and before long I began to jot down a few things. Before long I had a long stream of complaints about "Mr. Wonderful." He snored, he ate weird foods, he talked to every single person he met. The next thing I knew I was asking myself, "What in the world did you ever see in him?"

This experience in "truth telling" reminded me that our stories are multi-layered and complex and as Catherine Bateson (2000) tells us, "We live with strangers. Those we love most, with whom we share a shelter, a table, a bed, remain mysterious." Thus, knowing others and ourselves is a process that we engage in over and over and one of the sites of our discovery is through language. We write and speak others and ourselves into being. But what if one is asked to write oneself into existence in a language other than that which is familiar and comfortable? What does it mean to translate oneself across languages and cultures? Who do we become in this new language and culture? Can we tell the truth about ourselves in a language where the idioms sound strange and unfamiliar? This is exactly the task of millions of students who find themselves as second language learners and cultural others in US classrooms.

The title of this volume is *The Foreign Self: Truth Telling as Educational Inquiry*. The very notion of "the foreign" is complex and de-stabilizing. Foreign-ness is always relational. On some level we are all foreigners because we are strange and different in relation to some defined other. When we travel, whether it be across the country or around the world, we accept some notion of ourselves as foreigners. We realize that we may not know the norms, customs, or folkways of some new environment. However, this sense of the foreign generally is expected and accepted. What allows us to tolerate this sense of the foreign is that typically we have a home place—a sense of the familiar to which we can refer. Thus, traveling throughout Europe or Latin America or a new metropolitan area in the US we can (and do) remind ourselves that we understand this new place in relation to our home place. No matter how wonderful or how terrible we experience our foreignness in this new place, we recognize such a place as temporary and limited. Our sense of self, our identity, is constructed in relation to a place we have established as home.

However, there is another sense of the foreign that is not established in relation to our familiar and comfortable sense of place. This foreign self emerges in the midst of places that should be familiar or home-like. This is a foreign self that is strange and different not because of the difference between the self and the external world. This self is foreign because it does not recognize itself. The tension is an internal one like the one DuBois (1903) called, "double consciousness" or what novelist Ralph Ellison (1952) called the "invisible man." In both instances, we have what might be thought of as an alienated self. In DuBois' concept we consider the way in which individuals are forced to cope with two separate and warring identities in order to fit into mainstream or dominant world views. For students in the classroom this may mean the constant switching between the home self—comfortable and at ease with one's language, customs, and perspectives—and the school self—struggling to learn and perform normative behaviors.

In Ellison's view, this foreign self becomes invisible, "invisible...simply because people refuse to see me." In the classroom such a self disappears into the background, attempts to blend in to a hardly noticeable landscape to escape the scrutiny of the teacher and classmates who stand as constant reminders of one's foreign-ness. The result of this invisibility or double-consciousness is not merely a sense of standing aside or away from the mainstream. Rather it is a turning inward on oneself. It creates both an alienation and self-hatred that force one to attempt to re-make and refashion oneself in the image of the dominant group.

Most people can identify times in their lives when they struggled to maintain an authentic sense of self. Sometimes we were successful and other times we gave in to the social and cultural pull of the majority or mainstream society. However, some of us, by virtue of status characteristics—race, class, gender, language, ability, sexuality—live in this state of alienation and foreign-ness. For some, the self is foreign.

In this volume the authors engage in a process of telling and re-telling to reveal both authentic and foreign selves. Choi explores the dual experiences of an immigrant — both the joy of new opportunities in the U.S. and the very real barriers that foreign identities pose to people configured as others. Choi's examination of the power of language to create and re-create the foreign self infuses the chapter with the pain and pathos of coming to terms with exclusion and social dislocation.

In "Hail to the Email: Tales about Foreign Language Education in a Globalized Age," Carter and Raizler introduce the reader to the way technology configures language. By maintaining contact over time and space, the writers demonstrate how this new form of conversation that has the informality of speech and the formality of writing can become an important aspect of unraveling the foreign self. Both authors in this chapter share similar experiences of being foreign language teachers and non-native speakers in a foreign country. Thus, their conversations contain many layers and nuances that signal a new language in the context of the global environment.

Miller's chapter on sheltered English in a U.S. civics classroom raises questions about the intent and benefits of the technique known as sheltered English. Rather than reinforce and support the students' familiar selves through their native languages, American English slowly but surely reasserted itself as the dominant and preferred language. Thus, an American self is always, already inscribed on students as they enter in U.S. classrooms.

Thompson-Cooper's chapter calls in to question a prevalent practice among teacher educators—reflection. Her exploration of her own practice challenges the meaning and usefulness of reflection as a normal, taken for granted activity in the preparation of teachers. Do pre-service teachers have the experiential and professional background with which to make such an activity meaningful? What are we to make of their reflections? Does reflection equal a form of truth-telling or is it a trope, deployed by pre-service teachers to avoid real excavation of their thoughts and perspectives about teaching and the students (and their families) they teach?

Krauthamer-Maloney's chapter represents another form of truth-telling. In an introspective look at the nature of a classroom, the author challenges herself to examine the quality of the social relations that develop in a classroom over the course of a year. Although many of the students express their delight with having spent a year with their classmates, the author questions whether or not all students shared this community-building experience. Perhaps some students remember the year as foreign selves.

Hyo-Kyung Ahn's chapter is about the nature of text. Moving back and forth between the bland, black and white classroom texts and the colorful texts found at home, Ahn demonstrates how the visual becomes more than a representation, it becomes her reality. Her chapter helps us understand the way instrumental practices in language instruction (e.g. to pass an examination, to gain college entrance, to get a job) create a foreign self. Instead of experiencing the multiple and culturally grounded aspects of language, Ahn's bland textbooks represented a new language to her—French—as a sterile and disembodied subject. However, the colors of her parents' texts taught Ahn an important lesson about the power of the visual for supporting students' learning.

In his chapter, Weaver-Hightower presents another way we experience our foreign selves—through gender roles. Through an examination of the way men learn to be grooms, Weaver-Hightower explores how a particular kind of masculinity is taught and reinforced through the material and symbol systems that pervade the society. The work of learning masculinity involves incorporating prevalent notions of power and authority. The invisibility of the groom serves a different function than that of Ellison's invisible man. Instead of being unimportant and marginalized, the invisibility of the groom is more about transparency—an implicit and tacit presence in the fairy tale world of brides, princesses, and other maidens longing for male affirmation and validation. Ultimately, two foreign selves stand before the marriage altar—the fabricated identity of the male and the effaced, veiled identity of the female.

Finally, François Tochon uses communication within an encounter group to offer a methodological tableau on which to describe the research challenges such settings produce. The author is clear that he and his research team are not therapists, however, the work they do involves issues of privacy, confidentiality, and trust. Tochon provides the reader with narratives of the group. Then he explores the process of conducting such research by exploring both conventional (e.g. note-taking, member checking, replication) and non-standard (e.g. silent intervention, building objectivity through discussion, letter writing) research techniques.

This volume offers a unique and multi-faceted look at the way we become strangers to the very person we purport to know best. Although the literature is replete with discussions of identity, our identities are never stable. They shift and change with our circumstances. At the same moment we construct our identities, our identities are being constructed by others. Thus, any attempt at truth-telling on our parts will always be partial. Truth-telling is a social activity that is negotiated and re-negotiated in a myriad of ways. This volume illuminates that process in a novel and important way.

References

Bateson, M.C. (2000). *Full circles, overlapping lives: Culture and generations in transitions*. NY: Random House.

DuBois, W. E. B. (1903). *The souls of black folks*. Chicago: A.C. McClurg & Co.

Ellison, R. (1952). *Invisible man*. New York: Random House.

Introduction

François V. Tochon

Oneself as foreigner: the theme of this book links it to trends in phenomenology that describe the development of self-perception as experience unfolds. Paul Ricoeur, for example, has forged a methodology from narrative of experience in the three volumes of his *Time and Narrative* (1984, 1985, and 1988) and in *Soi-même comme un autre* (Oneself as Another, 1990), revealing thereby both his human and his social concerns. The book before you is in tune with this trend, but it engages as well with an interlinguistic and interethnic dimension that was not much developed in Ricoeur. Recall that Paul Ricoeur was Dean of the University of Nanterre at the time of the May, 1968, student revolt in Paris. He was involved in the existentialist movement and was a first generation phenomenologist.

What happens when, by virtue of being newly immersed in another culture and another language, we realize that we are being viewed in light of a set of presuppositions that make different beings of us? What a shock to one's identity to realize that one is no longer being viewed on one's own terms, but rather through an interpretive grid that makes us foreign to what we are. Pressures of this kind impose conformity to a social mold that was absent before, one whose presuppositions we will scrutinize through alternating phases of rejection and assimilation. For those who remain in their own country and their own culture, the experience of culture shock is rare. Even if your society as a whole is evolving and changing by reason of inevitable outside contacts, or even in situations of linguistic hegemony, shock is mitigated.

In this introduction, I will briefly review each of the chapters that follow in order to present the way each situates the self as foreigner and draw inferences about using expression of the truth about oneself as a method of research. But first, I'd like to offer a theoretical overview on the construction of the self to underpin an understanding of the way the processes of acculturation entail changes in identity in the course of which one becomes, oneself, momentarily, foreign.

Otherness as the Potential for Becoming Another Self

Our concepts of health and normality rest on implied norms that, in the last analysis, derive from our surrounding culture. Curricula are not exempt from this normative power. Individuals tend to submit to cultural norms, to become "normal," in other words, to "normalize" their behavior in line with the expectations they discern in their surroundings. School and university curricula thus form something like epistemic and cultural molds. A child's growth to adulthood involves learning a degree of conformity to the behavioral canons that are in force in his or her society. The late Pierre Bourdieu studied this social legacy and is one of the first scholars to have brought it into relief.

At certain ages, aberrant behavior is tolerated, but only to the extent that a society considers such aberrant behavior normal for a given age period. Thus these implicit rules broadly govern — with variations among social strata — what is normal and considered acceptable. When a given behavior is unacceptable yet persists, feedback and corrective measures come into play. If these are ineffective, they are soon replaced by ostracism, indeed by coercion. In punitive cultures, modest sums of money are dedicated to social normalization through education and much more significant ones to correctional redress when education has not fulfilled its role. At a talk given in Madison, Donaldo Macedo observed that, currently, the State prefers to pay $35,000 a year to imprison young people whose education would cost only $20,000 a year. Since this is how things are usually managed in our society, nobody pays attention except when a recession makes the expenditure painful.

Your individuality (what you view as yourself) depends heavily on your cultural setting; the very development of the brain depends on stimulation from the environment. We do not exist as distinct atoms. The self depends on its interrelation with its setting for its structuring. Well before R.D. Laing's "antipsychiatry" (1960) taught the importance of group influence, and family influence especially, on the developing psyche, Freud had provided a fully developed theory on the subject; it is still relevant. Even for non-Freudians and those skeptical about psychoanalytic theory in general, it's interesting to note that Freud's theory of the genesis of identity is one of the sturdiest conceptual structures of psychoanalytic thought and the one that has been subjected to the least scientific challenge. Aspects of this theory are very close to the social-interactionist principles of Vygotsky, for example. In Freud's later writings (post-1920), the sense of self is a layer of memory produced through social interaction. In education, reflection on the way one's sense of self is constructed on the basis of the influences and information one is subject to from childhood is essential. It is clear that academic content cannot be selected just any way. The way it's organized will give rise to a specific way of thinking and seeing reality. For example, we're accustomed to treating science, language, and culture separately from each other, even though linguistic anthropology has shown how closely scientific concepts are tied to language. Semiotics, or the study of signs, shows us that the means used by different disciplines to construct signification (Danesi, 1999) resemble each other. These means have a structural impact on the meaning one gives to one's identity (Rogers, 1998).

Freud wished to study the self scientifically; his concept of it changed over time. (I apologize to learned readers who may feel this brief overview to be a bit simplistic and crude. Theoretical and historical details cannot be reported here.) During the first stage of his research, Freud distinguished the unconscious, the preconscious, and the conscious, each of which was said to have a different function (Freud, 1926). The conscious was viewed as consisting of conscious perception in a waking state; the preconscious, found at the limits of consciousness, was said to be formed of memories of which we are unaware at the moment but that are accessible to memory; and the unconscious was seen as the product of drives and the storing away in memory of their repression. Freud had noticed that our psychic apparatus can operate in two modes: a primary mode, in yielding to drives, and a secondary one, in obedience to the system of the conscious-preconscious. During this phase of his research on identity, Freud defined the ego as the sum of the preconscious and the conscious, that is, of all our faculties of judgement and logical reasoning.

During this period in the history of psychoanalytic theory, the relationship of the ego to overall identity was not clear. The ego was not defined as the individual as a whole or even as one's psychic apparatus taken as a whole; it was understood as a part only. Studies on narcissism, on identification as constitutive of the ego, and on differentiation within the ego between certain ideal components, led the first psychoanalytic school to define the ego, in 1914-1915, as *object*, thus ensuring it would not be confused with the *subject*'s inner world as a whole. A milestone, reached around 1920, led to a whole new tri-partite conception: the id, the ego, and the superego. In current psychoanalytic definitions, the id consists of the set of unconscious drives, an individual's life force. Lying fallow during childhood, the id is progressively structured through contact with the outside world to produce the ego. In this light, the ego is understood to be much larger than it was initially thought to be. Whereas, previously, the unconscious had been understood to comprise everything that was repressed, it was now seen that some things could be unconscious without being repressed: A significant portion of the ego is unconscious. This portion is not latent in the same way as the preconscious. Thus, in the course of research, the ego proved to be broader than the conscious-preconscious system, and some of its mechanisms to be unconscious in a way specific to itself. The ego is a part of the id that has undergone change under the direct influence of the outside world, via consciousness-perception (Laplanche & Pontalis, 1973). Put simply, a child is probably born with no other perception of what she is than her own life force. Only little by little does she attain awareness that she is different, that she is differentiated from her parents, and realize that she is a distinct "someone."

It is here that Freud and Vygotsky meet in a truly exciting way: The ego emerges as the product of progressive differentiation of the id resulting from the influence of outside contacts. This differentiation has its point of departure within the system of perception, which could be compared to the cortical component of an incipient life form: The ego has developed out of the id, which, designed to choose among stimuli, is in direct contact with the outside world. Relying on its own conscious perception, the ego brings under its sway ever deeper regions of the id (Freud, 1938).

One can view the ego, again, as an organ that represents the reality it has internalized following on numerous interactions with the world. Sandwiched between the requirements of the world and the requirements of its own drives, it seeks to reconcile them, organize them, and make them compatible in a productive fashion. Since it represents reality (the influence of the surrounding world), the role of the ego is to cause the influence of the outside world to govern the id and its tendencies (Freud, 1923). The id is the "reservoir" of the libido. The libido is the energy derived from transformed sexual drives. (Note that in Carl-Gustav Jung, initially a disciple of Freud's, libido would come to be another word for life force and not necessarily synonymous with sexuality.) To sum up, the progressive emergence of the ego can be figured as a layer intermediate between the id and the world. (See Figure 1.)

In psychoanalytic theory, the superego is formed by the internalization of influences that prevailed in early childhood, influences dating from the beginnings of the life of the ego, that have had a structuring impact on it. The superego is the totality of parental requirements and interdictions. The superego plays the role of judge and censor in relation to the ego; it constitutes the ego's depths and determines how ideals, self-observation, and moral awareness are formed. What happens if the ego frees itself up from the superego? If the influences of the outside world are so different from parental influence that, over the course of new interactions, the ego develops in a direction incompatible with the deeply entrenched and partly unconscious structures and standards instilled during childhood? Your id will then experience conflict that it will either repress or externalize. The management of these internal conflicts, the management of external conflicts that emerge from the encounter with other ways of seeing and doing and with new norms, is something that is not much studied by a dominant culture, because it is quite simply unaware of them. It is unaware of them because those who are at home in it rarely or never experience them. How do we deal with daily life when the forms it takes clash directly with the principles we were handed during childhood, principles that are sometimes unconscious, implicit, that we acquired in the bosom of a different culture? What are we to do when the self becomes other, when the self becomes foreign to oneself? When your culture is different, can you achieve fulfillment at school? Will the culture imposed by academic curricula function as a meta-superego, a post parental normative framework, a collective parent you are expected to internalize?

In this introduction, I do not intend to give more than the briefest theoretical overview: My aim is to shed light on the questions presented in the book in order to highlight their significance. Clearly, one can challenge the theory according to which the ego is the prey of three tyrants: The id and its libido deliver the ego over to passion, while the authority of the superego generates constant guilt by reflecting the requirements of the outside world, which pass from rule enforcement to law enforcement, etc. A vision of this kind is certainly one of an atrophied, suffering ego, and says little about the healthy individual's autonomy: Does consciousness play no more than a passive, secondary role? The constraints represented by a homogeneous

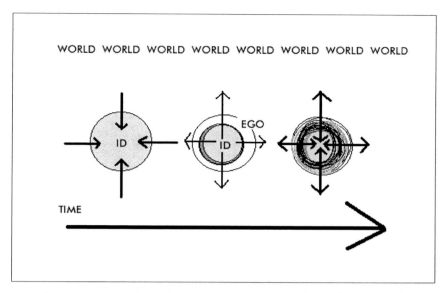

Figure 1: The ego is born of a progressive differentiation of the id from the world

superego in conflict with the ego, as well as the image of a dark, immutable libido, may reflect the repressed perceptions of a specific era (the end of the nineteenth century), and there are certainly more up-to-date perspectives that see our inner forces as having a positive power, whose impact can be liberatory rather than repressive. Freud did discern this approach, having come to acknowledge the existence of a desexualized, sublimated force. The superego could have an intuitive dimension, that of deep ethical understanding of the nature of human interaction. And does not the ego itself have its own force, which enables it to bring the other branches of the self into balance? If it is capable of encountering the id and the outside world, where does it draw its energy from? What is the place of the ego within the broader self constituted by an individual's total identity? These are all questions that have been asked by both neo-Freudian and non-Freudian schools and are far from being resolved.

The Swiss psychiatrist Carl Gustav Jung offered a series of interesting solutions that include an educational dimension, by virtue of their symbolic content. Jung's moment of glory was succeeded by oblivion for a while. Since the nineteen-sixties, however, many of his theories have been put before the North American public by writers such as the theorist on myth Joseph Campbell and the novelist Robertson Davies; in the last fifteen years he has enjoyed a clinical renaissance.

A key component of Jung's theory of personality is the notion of the *complex* (Jung, 1973a). This term has currency in pop psychology, but the meaning commonly associated with it is not that developed by Jung. According to Jung, the unconscious is populated by ideational-affective kernels that only need to be projected to replace the ego. In Jungian theory, a complex is by no means by definition negative. An individual with no complexes would be feeble-minded — such a person would lack a psychic life. Complexes are normal constituents of the psyche. They are unconscious, highly emotionally charged phenomena acquired over the course of the subject's personal life. They are the kernels of rational, affective, or symbolic representations of a situation, mini-egos (in the Freudian sense). Like the ego, a complex emerges from an experience that has left mental and emotional marks at the boundaries of the conscious and the unconscious, the intersection of the id and the world (see Figure 2). Jung's theory of complexes explains the existence of multiple "egos" and the fragmentation of identity associated with experiential adjustment and acculturation. It explains personality "code switching," when an individual has the impression of changing personalities along with languages or cultures. It explains why it is possible to have the feeling, from time to time or during certain periods of one's life, that one's new self is foreign — that one has become foreign to oneself.

Complexes are the product of experience. Jung defines human identity as having three "floors": a conscious in which the ego is the subject; an individual unconscious based on complexes and holding everything repressed by the conscious; and a collective unconscious, based on archetypes, that is shared by all humanity and that is the source of the great mythical images (see Matoon, 1994). The idea of the autonomy of the unconscious radically differentiates Jung's theories from Freud's. Today, we would be inclined to postulate the existence of several collective unconsciouses (rather than a single collective unconscious), of which different cultures are the vehicles. In Jungian theory, a complex can become autonomous. A person's role in society for example, assigns a mask to that person (the letter-carrier, the teacher, the senator, the insurance broker, and so on). This social mask (or *persona*) can become so significant that it replaces the ego. The ego becomes identified with the mask, the complex associated with its persona. Such is the case for a boss in the business world who thinks she's the boss at home and the teacher who thinks he's a teacher when he's with his children. The boss and the teacher mistake themselves for their roles; their public roles have devoured them. The same could be said of people who are devoured by social stereotypes — for example, the foreigner who's expected to behave in a certain way linked to her or his nationality. In cases like these, it's as if the persona were imposed from outside.

Jung defined another complex as well: Men often repress their feminine sides and women leave certain masculine potentials fallow. Since human beings incline to polarization on sexual issues, they tend to consciously externalize only one facet, either repressing the other, unconscious facet, or unwittingly playing it out in specific activities. Thus one's identity is polarized by complexes existing in binary opposition: alternately introverted or extraverted, depending on situations or settings; calm or impulsive; and so on. A consciously introverted person, then, has an extraverted unconscious. One's "declared sex" entails repression of other aspects of the self, other possibilities that remain buried and largely unexplored. If exces-

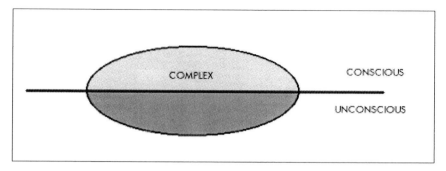

Figure 2: Complex: A partly unconscious organized cluster or representations
and memories with powerful affective value

sively strong personal or social pressures keep one part of the self hidden, that part is likely to find its way out through slips of the tongue or in other ways and eventually perhaps become an independent complex in competition with the ego. The way to obtain balance is to harmonize the polarities by becoming aware of them through dialogue with oneself, that is, to be honest and tell the truth about oneself. Speaking educationally, this constitutes a method of research; speaking individually, it constitutes a quest.

In a Jungian light, complexes consist of ways of relating to one's unconscious. They can be brought to consciousness; they then become a significant aspect of healthy identity building. Otherwise, they will remain autonomous: potential sources of disturbance that escape the control of the conscious and lead one to behave inappropriately in certain situations. Complexes tend to arrogate the role of the conscious. The more complexes an individual has, the more that person is in the grip of the unconscious and the less he or she is him or herself. Thus a delicate process of attaining a balance occurs when you assimilate the elements of another culture: To the extent that these are poorly assimilated, they can form autonomous complexes and become antagonistic to your central identity. Jung describes psychic health as the bringing to awareness of such unconscious, implicit, individual or collective contents, which produce an experience of seizure. With this coming to awareness, the ego acquires greater unity. Complexes emerge from social experience and constitute life lessons that need to be digested.

Academically speaking, perhaps curricula could be viewed as societal complexes, aggregates carrying heavy emotional and identificational loads and seeking to replace the ego. This, then, would be how scientists, artists, cultivated people, and educators are forged. In Jungian theory, the ego that, little by little, positions itself vis-à-vis the experiential clusters that constitute complexes acquires a new dimension, that of a broader identity that has assimilated the information in the complexes in order to comprehend it within a new unity. This process would appear to be important; it provides a solution to the conflict embodied in the title of this book: How can we assimilate the other face that we have and that, at the outset of acculturation, we reject? How can we manage things so that this foreigner, who lives inside us because we coexist with a different culture than that of our birth, can live in peaceful coexistence with older aspects of our identity? For example, a worker travels from the Midwest to New York and is faced with unaccustomed ways of seeing and doing things; or a Californian moves to the Midwest and feels completely out of place, with his or her habits of candor and openness. How are we to accommodate two sources of influence, two cultures, two languages: the old and the new?

The truth is, what's needed is a process of research — on the personal level, a search, a quest. This process begins when you tell yourself the truth about yourself. In one sense, it's a process that corresponds to what we may take to be most valuable in the term "education": The idea is to learn yourself as part of the very process of change, at the moment where the other is transforming you and you refuse to be transformed without being aware of it. In a Jungian framework, to acquire another language and another culture by immersion means to integrate experiences that have entered the ego's periphery half consciously, because they are not immediately assimilated into the ego, and take on independent life for as long as they remain unexamined with sufficient reflective intensity to determine their fate. Do these new mental and behavioral habits correspond to aspects of one's identity one wishes to develop, that one accepts as new constituents of one's identity? Or are they psychic constituents whose existence in others one can grasp, but that one wishes not to assimilate, in order to preserve coherence with one's prior psychic make-up?

For Jung, the ego is a complex of representations that constitute the heart of the field of consciousness and are continuous and identical with it to a high degree. Nevertheless, the ego is just one complex among others; it predominates because it is prior to the others and because of its capacity for incorporating other complexes that emerge from new experiences little by little, through reflection. The ego is not the totality of the psyche, so it's important to distinguish between the ego and the self: The ego is the object of consciousness, while the self is the subject of the person's overall identity, including individual unconscious. These two aspects of the self complement each other; they are not necessarily in conflict. Conflict can emerge from the momentary helplessness the ego may experience faced with new complexes or its own deepest self, if it seeks to assimilate outside influence too fast. The self is thus a superordinate entity in relation to the ego, a broader personality which is *also* what we are (Jung, 1973b).

Those who are educated in a bicultural setting can reach a point where they have a sense of having taken everything into consideration, of being able to assimilate fresh aspects of the other culture without necessarily causing harm to their psychic integrity, and without each new experience giving rise to new conflict. To attain this, it would appear to be necessary to develop great cognitive and emotional flexibility and malleability. This developmental process, which defines psychic growth, is characterized by increased familiarity with oneself — a self that is no longer the stranger in the house.

Psychologists who have researched this process of coming to awareness and growth have been largely inspired by the phenomenology of perception. For example, Maslow (1968) learned a great deal from the
existentialists. But there is such a thing as cheaply earned growth, paying in
money rather than paying a personal price. This has led many to be under-
standably wary of the pseudo-psychological approaches that have hooked
so many people. But another psychiatrist and philosopher who is coming
back into vogue is worth serious attention in connection with the issue we
are examining, the issue of the self as stranger and truth as a search or
quest: This person is R.D. Laing.

The influence that Laing once had on English-speaking readers and
educators may be compared to that of Sartre or Marcuse on the intellectu-
als of Continental Europe. He exerted this influence in the realms of both
politics and psychology, as may be seen from the titles of his best know
works, *The Politics of Experience* (1967) and *The Politics of the Family*
(1969). Laing melded phenomenology and psychiatry in order to free human beings from the straitjacket of social conformity. He redefined the concept of normality by suggesting that the self's experience contradicts the
normalness of socially accepted experiences. He thus restricts the concept
of normality to the end goal of dialogue with the unconscious, namely, acceptance of oneself, development of one's potential, and liberation from
alienation. True normality is found at the end of an inner voyage which he
sometimes defines as a descent into Hell, in the manner of Dante. This descent into oneself is one that every individual who wishes to be freed from
the pressure of society, the Other, must undertake. It is a process that re-
verses the false values one has adopted through conformity. For Laing, the
deepening of experience unveils the *self*. This term, borrowed by Jung from
Nietzsche (from whom Freud borrowed no more than the "id" through
Graddeck!) was taken up by Laing with its existentialist meaning of being-
in-itself, the ontological subject.

Following Heidegger, Laing broaches the possibility of pure experience. Indirectly, he engages with the dilemma of the phenomenologists:
Thought co-opts experience and is always situated post-experience rather
than inside it. For the phenomenologists, experience only comes into existence at the moment when it is put into words — that is, the moment when it
eludes us. For Laing, it's possible to confront experience, for example artistic experience, by plunging into it and with it, and living out the creative impulse to the limits, like Mary Barnes, a schizophrenic who found herself
through painting, following a phase of free self-expression with her own ex-
crement (Barnes & Berke, 1973). As Laing would say, anything but the
chemical straitjacket! His presupposition is that healing processes are natural and can't be dangerous. Society only fears them because it fears its own
unconscious, that is, what it truly is.

According to this logic, humanity is alienated from its authentic potential — it is peopled with those who are strangers to their true egos. Every human being is *potentially* a human being, but in a state of alienation.
Experience allows one to emerge from the vicious circle of dualities, because it is simultaneously inner and outer, passive and active. In the instan-

taneousness of self-in-action, experience is the intimate of behavior. On this view, behavior is a function of experience: The possibility for acting is the possibility for acting on the experience of others. Thus, the experience that consists of *being* the very means for the ongoing process of the emergence of Being from non-Being leads those who go through it to the other side of chaos and the void. Without the inner, the outer loses meaning: The two comprise an indissoluble whole. This indissolubility of the whole confronts the whole of the fragmentation we experience in society: our sexuality riven from our hearts, our hearts riven from our heads, our heads riven from our sexuality, without unity and without identity. The authors of the different chapters of this book went through this fragmentation, report on its existence, and try to find solutions for it. Later on, we will see that these solutions take the form of a search/quest for the truth. Truth is relative; you have to find your own. Below is a table that presents the way each chapter broaches the theme of "the self as foreign."

The Foreign Self	
Chapter, title, author(s)	Self as Foreigner
Chapter 1 Blending Oil into Water: Making the Invisible Visible and Giving a Voice to the Silenced Jung Euen Choi	Two Koreans are transplanted to an American setting and suddenly perceive their own foreignness in the face of surroundings featuring linguistic and cultural discrimination they really hadn't expected. They have the impression they've lost the status their maleness entitled them to in Korea and feel that they've lost a part of their identity. The author of the chapter is a woman. She analyzes their conversations and situates them by examining the cultural presuppositions that underlie identificational differences.
Chapter 2 Hail to the Email: Tales about Foreign Language Education in a Globalized Age Sabine Raizler & Gloria Carter	Sabine is Brazilian. She gives advanced workshops in English writing in an American arts college. She embarks on an email conversation with Gloria, an American teacher of German. In their messages, they examine the presuppositions that differentiate each one's language teaching from the other's by virtue of their social status. Before long, the conversation deals with questions about identity and politics, the domination of one culture by another, and the way such domination is internalized.
Chapter 3 Minority Languages in the Classroom: Promise becomes Possibility Elizabeth R. Miller	A support system with interpreters is offered to bilingual students in some classes. Hours of observation of these classes reveal an ambiguous reality. Analysis of the conversations brings out a second level of discourse, which conveys to the foreign students the supremacy of the host culture and the criteria by which they can overcome their cultural deficits if they wish to become "normal." Almost subliminally, they are taught that they are inferior and why they are inferior. Fortunately, among themselves, the foreign students make a counter-hegemonic space for themselves in their own tongue.

The Foreign Self	
Chapter, title, author(s)	Self as Foreigner
Chapter 4 Practicum Students' Confessions on Truth-telling in Reflections: Kurosawa's *Dreams* Mary K. Thompson-Cooper	Certain practicum students who have been asked to reflect on their experiences during their education make up case reports that seem to them to be more interesting and true to life. Their logs deliberately convey false images of them, the images they believe their supervisors want to see. With time, they seem to begin to believe in their made up identities, which they're obliged to play out to the end. The process of becoming a professional has incorporated this creation of social masks behind which they acquired self-confidence. Their selves are another.
Chapter 5 Finding the Truth in Our Inclusive Community Amy Krauthamer-Maloney	When an elementary school teacher decides to create a sense of community in her classroom to help children in special circumstances, all the children fall in with her plans. But there are signs that, under the appearances of a communitarian culture created by the teacher, differences persist. The children grasp that measures for achieving integration are targeted at certain children in particular, who have special rights. The children who don't have these rights are not jealous about the differences, because they realize they're not value enhancing. So long as the teacher is present, the class community functions like a little family. But the group identity is only on the surface; and the integration strategies are just another way to identify the differentness, the foreignness of certain pupils.
Chapter 6 Between Black-and-White and Blue-White-Red: Pictorial Illustrations and Color in the Foreign Language Textbook Hyo-Kyung Ahn	Is a foreign-language text book just another vehicle for conveying surrounding conformity, or does it free itself to present the other culture in form as well as substance? What is the role of the illustrations? Is learning French in Seoul a way of engaging in vivid travels of the imagination, a sort of inner liberation, or is it just a way of submitting to the standards that govern university entrance examinations? What audience does the textbook target? A future speaker of the foreign language who is open to difference and to some extent integrated into the target culture, or a technician who can give form to linguistic problems in order to feature in his or her native country's performance statistics? In some textbooks that seem to be designed to avoid the attainment of awareness of identity and cultural difference, the other is just another self.

The Foreign Self	
Chapter, title, author(s)	Self as Foreigner
Chapter 7 The Truth about Grooms (or, How to Tell Those Tuxedoed Men Apart) Marcus B. Weaver-Hightower	An engaged man getting ready for his wedding has to prepare himself for certain changes in identity. This change doesn't only alter his own self perception; others suddenly see him differently too. He thus enters a conceptual network of vague and ambiguous expectations that take him over. During the preparations for the wedding, he has no access to some of the tasks (for example the choice of flowers) and he realizes that everyone is behaving towards him, not according to what he is, but according to a stereotype he's supposed to fit. He suddenly discovers himself as another, a stranger whom he didn't know before, whose new roles he must come to terms with.
Chapter 8 Families of the Soul: The Truth on Method François V. Tochon	Most research reports seek to tell the truth about objects, not about the subjects who conduct the research. During a study conducted in a bilingual setting, on the relationship between families and daycare centers, the team of researchers went in quest of themselves. Recording their own conversations, members of the team started to write down their reflections, teasing out what was implicit in their interventions, their motives, and their potential biases. Conducting research on themselves, they both narrated and uncovered themselves as other: What is said differs imperceptibly from what is done, and reconstruction of what has been done brings to light the implications of social intervention when the desire to help the other risks constructing difference rather than making it possible to overcome it.

A Question of Method: To Tell the Truth?

It's hard to tell the truth. To tell it, one must know it and find it. How can we be sure of the truth? Do we know the truth about ourselves? The acknowledged bias of this book is that of viewing truth, not in a philosophical or an ethical light, but as a major issue in education and research on education. Truth is defined as a process rather than a product: Truth is understood to be a quest. The search for the truth allows one to define oneself, to deepen one's approach to questions of identity, and to discover one's other self in all its uniqueness.

This book as a whole deals with the boundary between truth and lies in education, and the role played by discourse and language in structuring this boundary. This theme is prominent in semiotics. If you define semiotics as the study of the ways meaning is constructed and of the signs meaning rests upon, the issue of truth and lies becomes central. More than a question of logic, this is a question of social negotiations.

Several chapters of this book deal with linguistic and ethnic barriers, but a deeper, more human question is posed over the course of these pages: How do we define reality? Do we all experience the same reality, or do we carry distinct realities within ourselves? If the latter is the case, is it possible for us to access the reality of others? What do others experience? What are the signs that manifest differences in perception of the real? And — of course — do we really want to know other perceptions, other representations, other realities? It is common to act on the assumption that we all share the same reality: Yet it takes just one extended period abroad to realize the effort needed to grasp the systems of logic of the other, systems that are interwoven with practice implicated in language itself.

Does this mean that not everything can be translated into English? Clearly not — many realities are untranslatable. One only accesses them by using another language, or by having the patience to listen and engage in dialogue long enough to grasp the nuances that reveal how one can think wholly differently about the most everyday practices. The culture you live in becomes transparent to you. It becomes visible when you have the opportunity to get outside it, for example through travel abroad on holiday. It also becomes visible in contrast with other ways of seeing, when these are offered through testimonials. This book can be viewed in such a light: as a set of testimonials about other ways of seeing. Definitions of reality can be so diverse that they turn us into translators, interpreters of cultural and social signs, seeking identity and recognition, confronted with our ignorance of others and our longing to be valued at our intrinsic worth and not according to appearances.

It's hard to orient yourself towards others. Each of us has our own set of needs, sufferings, and ceaseless activities. As a matter of principle, most of us very likely want to be open, not just to those who are like us but to those who are different, from empathy, curiosity, and respect, but also because we want to learn new ways of seeing. In practice, though, have we the time and the courage to make the changes needed to accomplish this? Are we capable of refusing to hand over the power to act to institutions and remaining true to our convictions through independent action? Can we struggle against conformity, the all-powerful reign of money in our society, the easy inaction that allows us to enjoy, without any objections, the privileges of xenophobia and implicit racism that continue to inform our society's major decisions?

Are we prepared to live a lie? Are we going to meekly agree to live with the fact that two-thirds of the planet is suffering from poverty, hunger, lack of hygiene and health care, and education? That international development programs are being cut, one after another, with the recession as a pretext? We spend seventeen billion dollars a year to feed our pets, when thirteen billion would suffice to eliminate hunger worldwide. How do we explain our impotence, our denial of the reality of other people, our irresponsibility?

One explanation that's been frequently cited for some years now is corporate power. Corporations are understood to be all-powerful both internationally and locally. For example, prison construction and prison management represent an industry that pulls in more money than the hospitality industry and is state subsidized. The costliest of jails are the high-security ones, with full-isolation cells, intended in theory for the most dangerous inmates. But once they're built, an effort is made to keep them full to ensure their profitability, and in the absence of dangerous inmates, ordinary ones are housed there. Can we live with the presence of teenagers and adults in high-security prisons that don't even satisfy internationally agreed on criteria for the treatment of war criminals? We all agree on the horror of terrorism, but does it justify treating foreign prisoners, however despicable, with such contempt for hygiene and minimum livable conditions that dozens of them are reduced to sewing together their own lips to protest the conditions inflicted on them?

Corporations and banks have so much power internationally — in particular the power to get around the law just by changing venues — that citizens feel swept aside and even governments seem to be at corporations' service. Proof of this is not far to seek; indeed, comments like these may even appear naïve when you have only to open your daily paper to see the evidence on the front page. Governments are tending more than ever to perpetuate the power of the extremely rich at the expense of the masses, bringing profound changes to what would appear to have been a decades-long illusion of democratic functioning, turning it into what looks like an oligarchy of wealth with international ramifications. It would seem that some industries deliberately engage in contact with the underworld of other nations to avoid taxation. Called before the courts, they're released by legal stratagems. While it's true that a hypothetical Society of Nations could control some of the excesses of this plague, isn't the problem really *inside ourselves*? For reasons of pride, nationalism, revenge, for fear of reprisals or through sheer impotence, we accept a war which, over a few months, has cost sums that could erase world hunger for several years. Aren't worldwide hunger and injustice among the key likely causes for international violence?

We develop comfortable convictions that enable us to avoid challenging the status quo. Up to a point, this can be explained in psychological terms: We avoid at all costs becoming foreign to ourselves. It's very disagreeable to see yourself differently. Becoming foreign to yourself requires a higher-level act of synthesis, an effort, a whole new kind of learning. It's not easy to tell yourself the truth about yourself. Material values have supplanted moral ones, we think of ourselves before thinking of others and the world we live in, and in this great wave of selfish freedom that allows us to demand our rights, we seek to forget that we have obligations, and our failure to fulfil them has an irreversible impact on the planet.

Comfort is lulling us to sleep in the face of passive acceptance of growing injustice. We have such a craving to own that we forget to be, to be one with our convictions and to give of ourselves. The survival of the status quo is based on the easiness of letting things be, the lies we entertain — the lies that say things can and will go on as they are. But we are facing troubled times, and profound change is not just necessary but inevitable. It will be imposed on us by the force of circumstance and possibly because of our own inertia and lack of courage in insisting that we be told the truth. In such a context, utterance of the truth is more than therapy, it's a quest for life.

How can we act conscientiously? Are we capable of learning to cooperate and to build a society that will better satisfy ideals of generosity and sharing? Will we live with the fact that other human beings endanger their lives to obtain resources that we then deny them and refuse to share? For example, most of us encounter immigrants daily. Do we realize that, in order to live among us, they were obliged to submit to a military-style examination entailing full nudity and often requiring forced vaccination or revaccination and the taking of fingerprints? The criminalization of immigration has become so commonplace that we don't even notice it anymore. We have to make an effort of awareness to grasp that no other country engages in such humiliating and costly practices in its treatment of a needed and often qualified work force. Accustomed as we are to work with concepts severed from experience, we are inclined to legislate on the basis of unexamined assumptions that betray our fear of foreigners, and we fail to see we are imposing unacceptable conditions on others.

Television has accustomed us to mingle reality and fiction and the ubiquity of advertising forces on us a non-stop conflict of values: We must constantly take our bearings anew and struggle to avoid being sucked in. In the conceptual universe we inhabit, it seems only natural to cry out for rights and use every means available to reach goals. There is no such thing as truth any more, only efforts to persuade. Intentions underlie all speech and every act, and we have been forced to learn to mistrust intentions, because they are most often selfish and revelatory of potential aggression. In a universe of this kind, all contact is ephemeral: It can't be deep, because everyone is trying to trick everyone else in some fashion or another.

The society we are building and living in appears to be founded on the selfish manipulation of resources and human beings such that they can be viewed almost exclusively in terms of potential profit and benefit. With this approach, means of communication are subject to the wish to put consciousness to sleep, to focus it on material, not reflective, goals, and to prohibit the expression of ideas, by any means whatsoever, whose impact can't be controlled and manipulated to profitable ends. Efforts to prompt reflection as an agent of change in society are quickly transformed into a series of standards of behavior. These then override the freedom conferred by independent inwardness, and prohibit (by virtue of the very labor intensiveness entailed in controlling reflection) the cultivation of values not subject to those in whose interest it is to suppress freedom of thought. Reflection is recommended at certain times, for certain purposes, and in a certain form. Reflection on the ways that reflection is imposed for purposes of control is forbidden.

When, in spite of everything, ideas about a different society do manage to circulate, they get co-opted into a logic of profits and benefits and bring consumers back round to approaches that yield the most profit for those in power. The concept of democracy has been derailed, and the ways that community is represented have become fictitious. The Internet is thought to allow direct representation of popular opinion, but there are filters that keep the information supplied there within standard parameters. Whole nations construct firewalls to filter out information coming in from outside.

In a sense, filters like these are simply huge curricula: They dictate how reality is to be perceived.

Human beings wind up trained to filter information in a certain way and have no freedom to think otherwise. Thoughts that exceed the principles taught in school are proscribed. No one wanders outside the Newtonian universe and non-Cartesian thinking is ridiculed. And yet, there's good reason to ridicule the primitivism of Newtonianism and Cartesianism themselves. As a result, neither schools nor universities convey knowledge essential to human beings, and this widespread self-censorship means the most important information must be acquired outside institutional walls. After all, it's not surprising that those who occupy the social institutions that use knowledge as power know their power derives equally from the dissemination of information *and* the hoarding of the kind of knowledge that would make a difference. If you understand the fit between information and awareness, you grasp that depriving other human beings of knowledge they need is a sure way to dominate them. For proof of this, you just need to go on-line regularly to read other countries' newspapers in other languages.

In contrast, freedom of thought and divergent expression tends towards greater potential good for one's fellows, but they are often discredited by the establishment. The credibility that derives from holding back incompatible knowledge paradoxically constitutes an effective instrument for preserving the status quo as regards power. Creativity is not given high marks unless it is politically conformist and yields financial spin-offs. Oil continues to be our dominant energy source, even though a Swiss inventor patented a water-based engine some forty years ago. The patent was bought out by a petroleum company. Bacteriophages are life-friendly anti-bacterial life forms whose existence was deliberately ignored because research on them appeared in Russian and not in English-language science journals. To acknowledge their usefulness would have conflicted with the corporate production of antibiotics, which better suit the logic of the marketplace. These two examples show society making two choices governed by essentially financial considerations. The consequences are obvious.

There is no need to provide a demonstration of the failure to link the economy to the ecosystem. The economy benefits an oligarchy, and the logic of capital prevails because the economy benefits banks and corporations that in turn reward their managers. The conditions stipulated by the World Bank in its effort to force the logic of the marketplace on the poorest countries of the world appears to drive those countries to their knees before the wealthiest ones, by giving corporations power over their citizens' most fundamental resources, such as drinking water. Foreign corporations buy water that had formerly been available cost free, and the poorest people on the planet are forced to pay monthly fees to be allowed to drink from wells that, in some cases, they themselves built. In many countries, the purchase of land by foreign corporations has been accompanied by the creation of small armies to eliminate the competition. And while you're at it, why not overthrow the local government and replace it with people who buy into your logic? Meanwhile, nobody tells.

When someone does tell, people don't listen. They don't dare acknowledge that it's about their own lives: The whole planet has now come under domination. This domination of human beings by human beings — to the extent they can still be called that — is perpetuated and made acceptable by the media. To say that information is filtered and made only selectively available is to state the obvious. Some people would have us believe that the suppression of information is a way of deploying power for the good of all. Recently, a TV journalist admitted that he fought for several years to be allowed to get two international news stories on every program, not just one, but two. The standard for every program was a local news story, a national story, and something on a lighter note — a humorous story when people are being killed daily in citizens' names.

Laws are passed to prevent citizens from acting. And so long as citizens are tied down by jobs and debts, they can't even dream of changing the things that tie them down. They're too caught up in the system to realize that it can only tie them down as long as they depend on it. A decision to make a break with a system that perpetuates injustice can be made within the space of a few days. But everyone is benefitted by the perpetuation of some aspect of injustice, at least in Western nations, because most of us benefit from the injustice our own society is producing worldwide. Of course, in speaking of making a break with the system, the idea is not to commit violence. Violence is produced by the system and benefits from it. Resistance can take the form of acting differently, just acting differently. Turning off the TV: beginning to position yourself in relation to some life goals, to act according to those goals, without making a parade of them, and to tell yourself the truth about yourself.

In this kind of context, education takes on a different meaning. There are educators (in a broad sense) and there's a school system. There are educators who need no system to educate. They have a message and their message is their life. For them, partnership is a way to start a new society. Rather than wasting time tearing down fast food places, like René Bovet, they may try learning to cultivate hydroponic plants in readiness for the consequences of the droughts that, without making headlines, have been shrinking harvests and food stores around the world for several years now. They realize that soon, when the banks have pushed their logic to an absurd extreme and citizens have come to see they were being treated with contempt, they'll be depending on their neighbors for their survival. Educators such as these will build up support networks based on an ideal of sharing.

Rather than investing for retirement in shares of transitory profitability, they'll have organized living spaces allowing for change in harmony. They will understand that it's going to be necessary to withdraw into a shell for a while, because we're entering on troubled times. By establishing a feeling of harmony with their environment, they'll begin to teach at a level that is not found in any school. Educating at the level of being necessitates being and acting in harmony with what you say — walking the walk you talk — and teaching through gestures and silence, rather than speech. To accept the task of educating at this level requires a powerful, difficult decision, and it's certainly harder to do it when the system is still in existence. But we must begin to think in terms of post-system logic, even if thoughts of this kind are different from the ones we're used to, in fact contrary to them. Thinking the system is going to persist indefinitely is an illusion we would like to entrench ourselves in. Teachers within the system can go from being transmitters of the approved conceptual filters to being makers of freedoms. They don't have to wait until there are no more schools.

Can semiotics, the science of signs and their situated meaning, contribute to the process of awareness raising? What does semiotics have to tell us about truth? That there is not one truth but many, and that they depend on point of view. Perspective testifies to intention. In the process of communication, as with any psychological act, intentions can be turned towards the self or towards others. A plural truth corresponds to various *fabulae*, ways of scripting experience. Truth can have to do with being or having and it can carry information or information's negation. It can be defined by what is obvious or what is veiled, beyond reach, in the background, behind the scenes, behind appearances, requiring effort to be uncovered. Truth is not necessarily accessible. It could be a part of those dichotomies whose paradoxical synthesis occurs in difference. It could require deciphering and rebuilding. Sometimes the discourse of truth serves to convey lies. Behind the façade, truth will be a light in the shadows.

We like to simplify life because we lack the time to grasp it in all its complexity for ourselves. Have we really chosen to be where we are, to be the way we are, and to take on these roles and these functions? We like easy answers because reflection causes us suffering: What's the good of reflecting on our errors, another self, the possibility of acting irreproachably? Reflecting on collective errors and the logic of responsibility? By way of displaying a positive attitude, we form a collection of euphemisms. Don't make waves. Say only what helps you preserve your own status. Simplify life, because, even in conditions of comfort, it's already semi-unlivable — what would it be like if we acknowledged our debt towards whole peoples for whom our micro-society is a predator? Doubtless they're lazier, maybe less intelligent, less gifted, is what we tell ourselves. And in fact, what they really may be is less aggressive, less prone to violent judgment, less domineering, and more enlightened about the relativity of human perception and the lies associated with money.

When things are going well, we pat ourselves on the back. When everything goes sour, a scapegoat is needed. A scapegoat provides an easy way to deny your own responsibility. We feel better when we've passed judgment on someone and punished them. We like this way of getting socially involved. We all agree on the baseness of the actions of one individual. This baseness then allows us to forget other disgraceful scandals in which we take part daily. If some corporations achieve success by building costly prisons in which to incarcerate those who think differently, so much the better. It's dangerous to be poor when legislation and judges' decisions seem dictated by money. Our society terrorizes and abuses the poor, but woe to those who challenge this! Measures are taken to crush even the most modest initiatives, and no one will contest the truth we want to proclaim, even though all who hear it know it's built on a set of lies that no one has the energy to expose.

The world we impose becomes our truth: a world based on the effort to overcome others, criteria that enable us to prove we're better, and notions of property and the legal extortion of money. "If you have no money, there are jails. And no one will fight on your behalf, because everyone needs money and you can't even afford to pay for your lawyer. True, the cost of your jail is higher than the cost of your education, but what can you do — that's the way things are. We would rather shell out money to be sure we're safe and prevent you from doing harm than educate you and have to face you in ruthless competition." Of course, nobody would admit to thinking that way.

In education, we know that reflection is necessary. Reflection has been introduced into our curricula. Reflection has become our truth, because truth requires reflection. But can reflection be imposed from the outside and as part of overloaded curricula? Students prefer to cut and paste other people's reflections, to ape them, to script fake but extraordinary reflections rather than build their own modest truth, small, real, personal truths that would attract no attention and only earn their authors mediocre grades. Thus, reflective curricula that form a part of teacher education paradoxically suck student teachers into lying. They're led to create reflective fictions of genius from whole cloth, because these will get them good grades. Professors as Pavlovians: Grades cause the ink to flow and the end of semester sees pseudo-reflections, extraordinary logs, experiences like you've never heard before, come down like leaves from the trees. Having attained the status of a criterion of professionalism, reflection has produced a new generation of black-belt teachers whose round-table discussions are driven by the wildest inspiration. Next to this, in-class experience is disillusioning and often disillusioned. But all the reflections deserve the best grades, regardless of whether they're real or invented. Semiotics deals with the fabrication of meaning, and one chapter of this book invites us to analyze such fictional truth. It plunges us into the world of the movies: Truth is always scripted. Students stage their reflections to make them more true-to-life than life itself.

In another chapter, a conversation examines the truth of language-teaching in the USA. Just recently, I heard a highly dedicated school superintendent express the following views: Everything significant from other languages has already been translated into English; most great Nobel Prize winners are found in the USA (the *Chronicle of Higher Education* reminds us that most are immigrants); all the important people from other countries come to teach in the USA; the USA is the most creative country on earth, as proven by the fact that the best computers are built here; the only useful language in the world is English; our students don't know English any more and the teaching of English is the only priority that deserves funding. This position has the merit of being clear even if it's simplistic and incorrect on the subject of language. The superintendent excused his inaccuracy by stating that he was chosen for his political views: "We're the best." It might be reasonable to wonder how the smartest country in the world chooses its politicians. Maybe reflective citizens don't dare state their convictions. Maybe they've got enough money not to have to worry about it, because power is on the side of wealth. The people I know who have no health insurance keep quiet.

Several chapters of this book follow this tendency to shine the light on facts that are little known, little noted, little noticed by people who are not going through immigration procedures or have never gone through them, who are not experiencing linguistic change, who are unaware of the dramas of identity associated with passage from one culture to another. When someone finds it hard to express oneself, those around who are functioning in their own mother tongue may conclude it's from lack of intelligence. But how can you show your intelligence without the words to express it? How can you show your true face when the conventions around you are different or don't allow it? How can you be accepted as a peer, an equal, when you haven't even been granted the right to express yourself, because mutual shyness and ubiquitous social judgement will make your self-expression an embarrassment to all? Here is an analysis of the methods used in the various chapters of this book to extract truth and use truth as a research method.

Truth Telling as Educational Inquiry	
Chapter, title, author(s)	Facets of Truth-Telling Methodology
Chapter 1 Blending Oil into Water: Making the Invisible Visible and Giving a Voice to the Silenced Jung Euen Choi	Informal interviews and conversations, some recorded and some not, were conducted on various occasions to allow for a participatory examination of what self-perception consists of when experience is under way and when it is reconstituted retrospectively. These life fragments were then reassembled as case studies.
Chapter 2 Hail to the Email: Tales about Foreign Language Education in a Globalized Age Sabine Raizler & Gloria Carter	Email messages were exchanged by two correspondents who sought to tell the truth about their perceptions of a problem. During a second stage, these messages were reread and rewritten, as the process of coming to awareness attained greater refinement and brought something closer to an authentic, mature perception of the situation analyzed.
Chapter 3 Minority Languages in the Classroom: Promise becomes Possibility Elizabeth R. Miller	Interactions were observed, videotaped, and audiotaped over a long enough period to allow for a grasp of their implications and to permit knowledge of the participants. Verbatim transcriptions then made it possible to "reread" the interactions and grasp what was implicit in them. This process of decipherment and encounter took place within a team including several observers. The task, then, was to reconstruct the meanings of the interactions by contrasting the double messages of the cultures involved.

Truth Telling as Educational Inquiry	
Chapter, title, author(s)	Facets of Truth-Telling Methodology
Chapter 4 Practicum Students' Confessions on Truth-telling in Reflections: Kurosawa's *Dreams* Mary K. Thompson-Cooper	The interviews that underlie this chapter were unstructured conversations in which the participants sought to tell the truth about a particular experience, specifically, in this case, their reflective practice. Once transcribed, the interviews were read several times over in an effort to identify a narrative link, a myth, or a story that illustrates well the interpretive hypothesis the researcher was beginning to formulate. In this instance, a film by Kurosawa was chosen. The interview texts are placed vis-à-vis excerpts from the movie to determine how they resemble them or differ from them, and in order to extract from them complex, nuanced truths in symbolic form.
Chapter 5 Finding the Truth in Our Inclusive Community Amy Krauthamer-Maloney	The researcher, a teacher, was a participant in the study. The teacher logged those events and interactions among her pupils that suggested a true community was being constructed over the course of the school year. She confronts the episodes, as experienced, with the concept of community she has internalized and notes the correspondences and differences. Her reports on them take the anecdotal form of sketches.
Chapter 6 Between Black-and-White and Blue-White-Red: Pictorial Illustrations and Color in the Foreign Language Textbook Hyo-Kyung Ahn	The author of this chapter tries to retrace the impressions she derived from reading language textbooks when she was a student and from reading a specific textbook now. She seeks to analyze the source of her impressions by examining the balance of colors, graphic items, and photographs, viewing all these as revelatory. She analyzes her own implicit assumptions and the affective and motivational processes that underlie the use of this or that graphic element, employing an experiential perspective for her analysis.
Chapter 7 The Truth about Grooms (or, How to Tell Those Tuxedoed Men Apart) Marcus B. Weaver-Hightower	The author of this chapter was the central participant in an event — in this instance, his wedding — and recounts how he felt as his change in identity unfolded. The small events that make all the difference are recounted in light of the emotion, the questioning, the awareness-raising, and the self-positioning they prompted, like an introspective journal whose exposure to others and publication should reveal the truth about oneself and one's experiences.

Truth Telling as Educational Inquiry	
Chapter, title, author(s)	Facets of Truth-Telling Methodology
Chapter 8 Families of the Soul: The Truth on Method François V. Tochon	Members of a research team engaged in participatory and semi-participatory observation of intervention processes that were preceded and followed by meetings where the research team reflected on their own modes of action. The group sought to understand how interactions unfold, with each intervener striving to be truthful in this process of elucidation. The group's sessions were tape-recorded and played back and gave rise to discussions by phone, by email, in letters, and during individual meetings, making it possible to plan upcoming action as a result of the emergent consensus. Over the course of these intervention sessions, preceded and followed by preactive and postactive reflection, several narratives of intervention were produced in which each writer was able to express a particular point of view, her or his own facet of the truth, the truth itself being approached only through the encounter between those various perspectives.

How can I close an introduction of this kind? Following the logic of disposable everything, we'll soon have to throw the earth to the poor, because it will be too polluted for the rich. Billionaires and their domestic leaders are fretting about escaping to Mars: NoahsArk v.1.1. The problem, at least to judge by the geometric and anthropomorphic structures NASA has observed there, is that someone appears to be there already. Maybe it's a great *Jurassic Park*. Humans are still the slaves of their reptilian brains. What you tell them figuratively can't be stated rationally without being discredited, because denial allays fear.

Blending Oil into Water: Making the Invisible Visible and Giving a Voice to the Silenced

Jung Euen Choi

> Language determines not only how we are judged by others but how we judge ourselves and define a critical aspect of our identity: who we are is partially shaped by what language we speak. Social considerations, therefore, could be instrumental in explaining how people come to learn a new language. (Bialystok & Hakuta, 1994, p.134)

Prologue

"Asshole means I am very angry."

It was about nine years ago when I first came to America. I was a freshman with little knowledge of English. Everything was new and foreign to me. The way I spoke with people, life in the dorms and much more were all new to me at that time. Because of my outgoing personality, I was doing pretty well with learning English and adjusting to my new life in America. Then — I had to learn the harsh reality of living in America as a "mute Asian girl."

One day I was eating lunch and talking with my Korean friend at the dormitory cafeteria. Only a few people and a large group of college football players were there to eat. The football players were loud and the noise was echoing all around the dining hall, which reminded me of the late lunchtime; or they must have been so loud because they were in a large group. If I were there with my Korean friends I could also have been that loud, I thought.

While my friend and I were talking, the group of football players sitting behind us was becoming louder and louder. Suddenly, my friend's face changed to express surprise and embarrassment. I did not know what she was reacting to until she said, "Jung-Euen, there is rice on your hair," and then I actually felt some rice on the back of my head. Where did the rice come from?

People sitting behind me were playing around with food and rice was one of the lunch-menu items that they were throwing at each other. The rice must have flown accidentally toward me and unfortunately landed on my hair.

I felt insulted when I found out that my hair was covered with rice. At first, I felt insulted about the fact that they were throwing rice at each other. Later, I felt ridiculed by their laughing and giggling and ignored because they did not offer an apology.

Why rice? Rice is my food, my culture and my identity. In my country, people appreciate rice. In my childhood I learned from my grandparents and my teachers at school that we should all be thankful to the farmers for growing rice for us—my holy food, rice.

Well, here in America, the grocery stores are so big and have all kinds of food in unimaginable amounts, so America must be a rich country. Because of this, I knew that my gratefulness and appreciation toward rice would not make any sense to them.

But, I would have liked to have had their apologies for throwing food at me, for whatever their reasons. I turned back and looked at them with my eyebrows up as they continued to laugh and giggle.

"I didn't do it!" was one of the first responses I got. They continued laughing, and indeed they cracked up, pointing and looking at my "funny" appearance. Rice was all over my hair. My holy food, rice...

The sense of honor toward rice, my food, my culture, I knew, was not often found in the western culture. Rice was rather seen as an "inferior" type of food. In my childhood, I still remembered watching a classic American movie in which the actress, Ingrid Bergman, was a missionary in the middle of the Korean War, giving out bowls of rice soup to the Korean orphans on the street. I remembered feeling shame as a child to see the watery bowls of rice that were depicted in the movie. I somehow must have sensed the embedded stereotypical viewpoint of how westerners relate war and poverty to rice. Yes, rice, low in nutritional value, and consumed in most of the poor countries, was my food, my sacred shameful food, and my culture. Shame, shame, shame...

Along with the feeling of being embarrassed about my culture, this stereotype about rice with the associated feeling of shamefulness, became mixed with the embarrassment of appearing "funny" in public. I should not allow you people to harass me, I yelled in my head in Korean. I started to feel upset and then angry. I kept looking at them, signaling to them that I was not pleased with their deeds. Offering them another chance to apologize to me, I looked at them for a while. Their giggling continued, and their laughter became even louder. I turned furious. How was it possible that they were showing no respect for me as a human being?

Just a simple apology and to be acknowledged as an equal was all that I wanted. I stood up from my seat and walked up to their table. Once more somebody said, "I did not do it, he did it," and more loud giggling was heard. Standing in front of the large group of football players with my face turned red, I could not find suitable words. I wanted to show them I was very angry. I was so furious that I felt that all the blood from my body was gushing up to my head. I was desperately trying to find words in my mind. English! Uh! If I had spoken fluent English!

I had to walk away with the tray in my hands. No, I cannot walk away like this! What do I do? What can I say? English! English! Ah! English! I turned my back and walked away from their table.

"Asshole!" I swore. This word was a word I could say with clear pronunciation. I said the bad word to myself, but loud enough so that they would hear it. This word meant: "I am very angry." When I was walking away from them with my food-tray, I was feeling terribly sad that the only word I could think of and was able to say was a swear word. I still heard them laughing at my back. Shame, shame, shame...

I still had the urge to straighten this out. It was not right! I could not go away like this! The thoughts in my mind that if I could only speak English, and if I was not a girl, not a small skinny girl from Asia made me feel frustrated from the unfairness. If only I had been able to deliberately articulate the unjust situation with sophisticated, polite, strong, and eloquent language—or at least if I had been with a large group of my Korean friends. Instead, I was a weak-looking Asian girl with little English, who had said a swearword. Shame, shame, shame...

I went to the staff office of the cafeteria to talk to the manager, who was a nice old lady at first. I explained to her what had happened at the dining hall, my English falling apart from outrage and anger. She said, "Oh, my dear, don't be so angry. Those kids are just a bit naughty today."

Right! They were a bit naughty that day, but I still could not stand their harassment. Because she was just trying to console me, I had to shape myself up to clearly say what I wanted her to do. She was playing the nice warm old-grandma-style woman until I said, "I cannot just go home like this." Her face suddenly turned cold and rigid.

I was at least expecting some kind of action taken by an authority figure to give notice of warning to those football players for their inappropriate behavior in the dining hall. However, I had to realize that the authority figure I was talking to had no sense of fairness. Indeed, she was siding with the white students. This was, of course, a very natural phenomenon in this white dominated community, which I had not yet realized.

My legs were shaking and my face was red. I felt the heat from both sides of my cheeks, which were flushed from outrage and tension. I was trying my best neither to lose more of my temper, nor at the same time, my ability to speak English. I did try to convey my intention to the woman that I would like her to go to them and at least chastise them for their inappropriate behavior in the dining room. The woman apparently did not like that I was being assertive. She might have judged me by my appearance. She must have regarded me as only a foreign student with little English. You know, foreign students or Asian students are usually quiet. She seemed to be surprised that I would not give up explaining my complaint to her with such little English and a heavy foreign accent. As I was making my points very clear, she could not pretend anymore as if she could not understand me—or my English. Then, she burst out with an irritated face saying, "So, what do you want me to do? You want those boys to have a bad record for their whole life?"

At that time I did not consider officially reporting them although, I was desperate to have her take action for what had happened in the dining hall. She walked up to them with the nice-old-lady voice again. "What are you boys doing, oh, don't be so naughty, you boys! Tell me what happened with this girl here." Then one of the boys said, "She swore at us, you know." "Oh, no! You apologize to them," said the old lady to me. I apologize to the boys? Oh, no, she was not listening to me. She could listen only to the voices of the white boys.

The boys were saying that it was an accident and they had not done anything. I had to intervene and make it clear what they had done wrong.

There were some people watching us.

I said, after taking a deep breath, "If I were a big football boy, as big as you and with many other friends of mine, would you have done the same? You guys did not apologize to me right away but laughed at me. It was very inappropriate and humiliating." At least, these were the words that I had in mind to tell them. Frankly speaking, I do not remember exactly what I said at the time. I only remember that I heard myself stuttering. I was trying neither to lose more of my temper, nor my ability to speak English. I really tried to speak "clear" English.

The "nice" old lady warned them not to throw food around. "No, no, no, my boys, don't do that again, O.K.?" And then, she told them to apologize to me for throwing food at me.

"Because I am a small girl from Asia, you guys did not pay proper attention to me," I continued. They hardly made a decent apology. My voice, my English was being swallowed by the constant chatting of the football players. They continued joking and talking as I was still standing there in front of them.

Yes, I knew that my language was not clear enough at that time, and I did not have much confidence to make such a speech in front of those American students. However, I was so outraged at their unfair treatment of me. Actually, I was surprised at myself that I went ahead and protested to a large group of huge, white American college football players. Later, my friends were saying how daring I was to stand up to such a large hostile group.

That day, I could not go to sleep for the bitterness, anger, sadness, and shame I still felt from the incident. Those big white boys might have just made fun of me even more when they saw me standing up for my ideas and opinion in mumbled and broken English. Still, the outrage was right there as a huge stone in my chest, and the fact that I could only find a swear word as a medium of language to express my emotion at that time made me feel sad and ashamed of myself. This feeling of shame, from not having access to a competent language level, broke my heart.

For a while, I had to learn what kind of reality I had to live in. Those football boys, whenever we ran into each other again on campus, continued verbally harassing me, saying "stinky, stinky Asian bitch." I did not take any further action against their harassment. It took me a while to make myself aware of the harsh reality in America of being an ENGLISH AS A SECOND LANGUAGE [ESL] student, and of being a female from a non-western, non-mainstream culture. My own voice still echoes in my mind, saying, "And only if I could speak English as good as, or even better than you ... Because I am a small Asian girl ... If I were, too, with a lot of my Korean friends ..." My culture, my ethnicity, my gender, my language, my voice, myself and my English ...

Introduction

The story above is a narrative of my own experience as an ESL student. Through this story, I would like to draw the attention of the readers to the interference of invisible factors in the process of language learning. Narrative forms give voice to the invisible variables of second language learning and thus, these variables may become visible.

The invisible variables became visible to me because I had a dual perspective as an ESL learner and teacher. I had to go through the process of acquiring English as a second language myself. Having gone through this process, I experienced various situations and moments which have been both barriers and stimulators to ESL learning. Years later, as I stepped into the realm of ESL education, I came to recognize some of the critical factors that greatly influence the success and failure of ESL learning. Of all factors in second language acquisition theory, it may be that the most significant is the interference of our personal identity into the process of language learning in terms of culture and emotion.

My daily life of learning English in America as an ESL student enabled me to approach the critical issues in ESL education more personally. These issues were once part of my way of life and invisible to me. However, as a prospective ESL educator, I feel I can see these issues more clearly than perhaps the other ESL educators who are native speakers of English.

What are they, those invisible factors or issues of successful language acquisition in ESL? I could not dissect all the parts of my stories and other ESL students' life stories to pick out and identify every invisible component that determines effective ESL education. However, by attempting to narrow the focus, I will seek to give the issues not only a voice but also a life.

In order to endow a visibility to these invisible variables, attempting to understand them in terms of culture would be a good start. Indeed, many scholars have worked on the topic of culture in order to offer an explanation of understanding what interferes in language acquisition. Furthermore, the investigation around the topic culture could be narrowed down to the differences between two distinct cultures.

Each culture has different norms, customs, and expectations. Accordingly, people of different cultures may have different ways of thinking and behaving. When two cultures meet, a mismatch of expectation may occur. Agar (1994) called this moment of intersection between two different cultures the "rich point." I saw relevance in his explanation with my own experiences of living in a different culture. For example, the "rich point" explained well what I had been through as an ESL student. My Korean identity and the Korean frame I held were often different from the frame of American culture. Thus, the fact that I was living in America with my Korean identity led me to experience the various moments of "rich point." The story I told in the prologue of this paper was also an incident of encountering "rich point" which was made evident through the problem of using a second language. It was really part of my daily life.

From the story in the prologue, I would call the incident of seeing rice flying around the dining hall as my personal experience of a case of a "rich point" which resulted in misunderstanding and lack of understanding. For the football boys, playing around with food or rice was not a big deal: it happens all the time, and it is fun, like a joke you would play as a kid. But for me, playing around with rice meant something very different. The symbolic value of rice was complicated. The fact that I am not from the generation of hunger and starvation or that no one from my direct or extended family are from the countryside may make this symbolic value of rice to be rather a remote experience for me. Nevertheless, the symbolic value of rice was taught to me through various indirect ways; for instance, by my grandparents, school textbooks, and Korean literature. And, at the time of the "rich point" when my Korean identity collided with the American ways, I took this cultural value of rice to be my own. My Korean culture taught me to hold respect for rice. In western culture, through the media, rice is seen as the symbol of "third world." There are different expectations according to different cultural frames. As a result of all these meanings taken together, I was offended by the act of playing around with rice. For the football boys it meant fun, for me, playing around with food was insulting. Thus, explaining ESL issues and trying to define the invisible factors with the concept culture seemed to be a good start. Like Agar, I wanted to base the causes and reasons of ESL issues on the topic of culture.

Language learning is not only about acquiring the systematic rules of the language. Rather, it involves more about learning new cultural ways of interacting with others while using the new language and new interpersonal skills. People learning English in America have to acquire American ways. True, I thought at first. Later, I found this point of view somewhat incomplete.

Therefore, I thought that starting my investigation with Schuman's (Bialystock & Hakuta 1994, p. 144) "acculturation model" would be logical. It provided me with a possible definition for what the invisible factors could mean. Schuman explains second language acquisition through two major variables: "social and affective aspects of an individual's interaction with a society." He stresses that while the other factors are still important, the "social and affective components" are the most significant factors which are linked to acculturation, thus determining successful second language acquisition.

"Social component" can mean many different things. I understood it as the cultural identity of the ESL learner. Diaz-Rico and Weed (1995) explained well how a person's cultural identity is closely related to the social aspects of second language acquisition. Because it is very important to the definition of what cultural identity means, I cite them at length:

> Any learning that takes place is built on previous learning. Students have learned the basic patterns of living in the context of their families. They have learned the value of some things and not others. They have learned the verbal and nonverbal behaviors appropriate for their gender and age and have observed their family members in various occupations and activities. The family has taught them about love, and relations between friends, kin, and community members.... Finally, they have learned to use language in the context of their homes and communities. They have learned when questions can be asked and when silence is required. They have used language to learn to share feelings and knowledge and beliefs. Indeed, they are native speakers of the home language.... The culture that students bring from the home is the foundation for learning. (p. 230)

Here, I understand culture to be the differences which influence the success or failure of second language acquisition. This point of view changed as I proceeded with my investigation, as I will discuss later in this paper.

For me, the "affective component" means the emotional aspect of the student's personal identity. For example, one of the significant emotional aspects would be how a student feels about himself or herself, thus, his or her self-esteem. Yule and Tarone (1991, pp. 133-134) note that the affective factors and self-esteem are inter-related in terms of the learning strategy of overcoming errors in their speech. In other words, self-esteem seems to be a key factor in second language acquisition when learning how to deal effectively with mistakes.

The emotional aspect of language learning later guided me to see why the cultural component is critical in the process. I labeled this process "invisible" for two reasons. These reasons are both articulated by Yule and Tarone (1991). First, there is not much known about the degree to which SLA is influenced by such factors. Second, not many ESL teachers are aware of the immense impact of such factors. It is said that affective components, for example, are difficult to observe and to differentiate from one another. As a result teachers "do very little, if anything, to investigate their students' affective state"(p. 133-134).

In the first half of the following discussion I will share how I changed my viewpoint about the topics through the research procedure of narrative inquiry. Because the basis for my investigation started with the focus on culture, I attended to the cultural and emotional aspects of language learning. Later, I discovered that the focus on the culture could not explain why some ESL learners succeed while others fail in ESL education. Thus, I had to change my assumptions about how I had initially planned to project the participants. I will therefore discuss three topics related to the methodology of narrative inquiry; participants, procedure, and interpretation. Reciprocity in the relationship between researcher and participants from the procedure of narrative inquiry will be the main topic.

In the second half I will draw upon the life stories of two Korean males who came to America to learn English and pursue higher education. By capturing the life stories of Korean males over 25 years old who have finished mandatory military service in Korea, I attempt to make some specific issues visible. Their stories and experiences provide me with knowledge about what they had to face in their everyday life, by which the practical, actual, and authentic ESL issues will be brought to light.

While it is difficult to pinpoint all the critical issues which I would like to present in this paper related to ESL education that emerge in the stories, it is important at least, to begin addressing these issues as at one time they were invisible. Through my own life stories as an ESL student, I attempt to give them voice. Yet, if I let the critical issues merely remain there, without proper labels, telling the stories will be in vain. If I cannot identify and explain each issue, even though they have been implied in the stories, they will remain as empty echoes that can neither receive proper attention, nor reform the status quo of ESL education.

Before and After:
How and Why I Had to Modify the Hypothesis

The hypothesis I had imposed around these ESL topics before carrying out this qualitative research of interviewing Korean males was that Korean males seem to have distinct difficulties in terms of acquiring cultural capital and the English language in the U.S. At this point, my focus lay on the cultural aspect of language learning, and I only attended to the differences of cultures as the sole important factor in language learning. I did not see the interrelated and inseparable state of culture and emotion in how they form personal identity. Therefore, I thought the focal point of the investigation should be on the cultural identity of the participants.

My presumption was that their Korean male cultural identity, which is based on the patriarchal nature and male dominance in Korean culture and society, was the most critical factor. This Korean male identity seemed to become intensified as Korean men spend time in and finish mandatory military services. This reality of the Korean male, that they had just finished their army duty in Korea, seemed to make great differences in interactional patterns and language learning behavior. For example, among Korean males, the concept of seniority is a central factor in how they interact with each other. The younger Korean male student will address the older Korean male not by the first name but by a semi-formal address, such as "Hyung" (older brother) or "Sun-bae-nim" (my senior). I speculated that this kind of interaction that was adherent to the hierarchy of age must be an extension of the behavior or socialization of the military rules where hierarchical order and rank are strictly kept. I wished to investigate their Korean cultural male identity by looking more closely at the several tendencies in their processes of language learning that mark their behavior as "Korean male." For this reason, I have chosen two participants who were Korean males who had finished their military services.

Through the narratives of these two Korean males, Min-yong Kim and Taek-kyu Park, I encountered practical and emotional difficulties that arose in the process of their acquisition of English due to their cultural and gender identity as Korean males. These experiences of Korean male students may imply certain patterns of issues and complexities that are related to the process of learning English.

My initial hypothesis needed modifications as I continued to investigate the tendencies of Korean males' category of behavior focusing on culture. Whether or not they have finished army duty might not be as great a factor as I had initially thought. The fact that they had finished army duty might be less significant in determining their Korean-male identity than the fact that they were going through emotional challenges. The emotional difficulties seemed to arise due to the problematic status of their personal identities.

I needed to change my initial hypothesis around new questions which arose as I went on with the research. What were the grounds for experiencing identity problems such as insecurity and troubled self-esteem in the process of second language acquisition? How was emotion and culture coherent to form language learner's personal identity? Why was the issue of emotion critical in understanding the notion of culture in Second Language Acquisition?

Korean male students tend to go through the experience of acute identity crises, which result in certain patterns in the process of learning English. Often, their identity crises become negative factors that discourage or inhibit successful language learning. For example, their new situations of learning a new language make them see themselves as "childish," "stupid," "inferior," or "powerless." These negative affective consequences reflect the difficulties in their new identity as ESL students in America. Their Korean male identity at home is very different from the ESL identity they hold in the United States. The discrepancy between the old identity and the new ESL identity is so great that they experience insecurity in their self-esteem. In America, because of such difficulties, Korean males often tend to have harsh experiences and find themselves in traumatic situations while trying to learn the new ways and language. Therefore, in their testimony emotion, was at the center of their themes. I came to recognize that culture, emotion, and personal identity, were interplaying in the process of language acquisition.

Thus, the shift in the viewpoint to investigate ESL issues with a modified hypothesis was made possible through employing narrative inquiry. As I tried to relate narrative inquiry with the given topics, I came to discover the emphasis on the emotional aspect of the language learning, and how it may be interrelated with the issues of language learners, identity, and culture. I came to see that the cultural component of SLA was meaningful because it was inseparable, from the learners' personal identity and emotional aspects in language learning.

Narrative Inquiry: Why Narrative Inquiry, Participants, Procedure, and Interpretation

The Application of Narrative Inquiry

As I have illustrated in the earlier part of this paper, my focus on the ESL issues were, with broader scope, the two invisible factors: Schumann's "affective component" and the "social component" of the learners (Bialystok, & Hakuta, 1994, p.144). I saw relevance in narrative inquiry for ESL issues because the importance of emotional and cultural identity in ESL learning can be presented more fully through narrative forms. In this context, there are three main reasons I chose narrative inquiry as the research method to investigate my topic.

First, narrative inquiry has the strength of attending to the emotional factors of an experience. Ellis (1997) talks about how powerful the emotional aspect of narrative writing can be. She investigates the feeling of jealousy through the Narrative Inquiry. In her project of investigating the experiences of emotional reactions toward jealousy she expresses frustration with the reality that in the social sciences "detailed lived experiences were secondary to abstraction" (p.124). She suggests that narrative forms have the power to invite vivid feelings and sensations into the reader's mind. "Didn't 'like a dentist's drill hitting a nerve' tell readers more about the jealous flash and get more reaction than 'extreme pain' or 'blended emotion' (p.124).

Ellis continues discussing the strength of storytelling, which carries emotional qualities, as she shares her own personal story about her relationship with Gene Weinstein, with whom she shared personal and professional relationships. Ellis shared the process of the time when Gene was dying of emphysema.

> Gene and I spent many hours each week talking about his illnesses, our relationship, and their intersection, as well as probing emotions and other aspects of sociological inquiry. In our conversation around the kitchen table, I learned more sociology than ever I learned in class. But when we left the kitchen table, the only knowledge that seemed respected was the abstract conclusion we had drawn, not the stories we had told. "You're so perceptive about what people are feeling, thinking, and what motivates them," Gene once said. "Too bad there isn't a way to turn that into sociology." (Ellis, 1997, p. 125)

I agree that personal narratives are charged with emotions, and thus, may tell us more about the truth than numbers in the scientific studies. Likewise, the emotional aspect of ESL learning cannot be discussed readily by such scientific inquiries. It is possible only through qualitative inquiry and storytelling that these invisible variables become tangible. By listening to personal narratives, the emotional experiences of ESL learning situations can be finally placed at the center of the ESL issues as one of the most tangible topics.

The second motivation for me to take up the method of narrative inquiry is that it reveals the relationships between individual and culture and the power dynamics that play within the culture. In the Personal Narrative Group, it is clearly stated that "cultural models, power relations, and individual imagination" have to be taken into consideration when interpreting narrative forms (Personal Narrative Group, 1989, p. 102). Because I initially searched for the critical impact of cultural identities of the ESL learners in their language learning situations, this quality of narrative form to look closely on "cultural models" and "power relations," is relevant to my research.

Since I believe that the cultural identity of the ESL learner determines the success of ESL education, it is meaningful to me to learn what kind of a cultural identity the ESL learner holds. Thus, it is necessary to bring cultural identity into light. Narrative inquiry is well-suited to meet the goal of this task.

Lastly, narrative form focuses on the self and the identities of people. The explanation by Gergen and Gergen (1997) about the self and identity helps me to explain why I think narrative inquiry fits my purpose of research method: "The individual is capable of making him or herself intelligible as an enduring, integral, or coherent identity" (p. 173). This aspect of narrative inquiry, bringing out the various aspects of identity issues, will serve well to uncover the reality that ESL learners have to face in their day-to-day life in language learning situations. Thus, I have chosen narrative inquiry to explore the ESL issues in terms of emotion, culture, power relations, and learner's identity.

There are two reasons why I have presented my own personal stories along with my research participants' stories. First of all, my previous experience as an ESL student has served as a lens for me to view ESL issues. Following Pamphilon (1999) who developed various aspects of the "zoom model," I, in particular, have applied the "interactional-zoom" to my analysis. According to him the persona of the researcher is significant and to be shared in the research process. I cite his work at length for it underlines the significance of the interrelated relationship between the researcher and the research process:

> Within a postmodern analysis, it is crucial to acknowledge whom it is that is speaking, the site from which they speak and the position available to them as speakers within that relationship. This is relevant to both the narrator's position and the position of the researcher ... I believe that we must begin to take risk by, self-consciously, but not self-centeredly, writing ourselves into the text. ... The interactional-zoom asks the researcher to address and not hold aside his or her own subjectivity. (Pamphilon 1999 p. 405-406)

I find it important to tell my stories because it is through them that it will be transparent to the readers where I started with my hypothesis and my position in carrying out the interviews. Also, in the process of retelling the stories of the participants and analyzing the data, my initial and ultimate perspectives play a large role. Through telling my own stories, I am able to display why and how I came to take a certain perspective on the issues I raised in the beginning of this paper. As a Korean female ESL student in an American educational institution, these specific and multi-layered "I"s have become another tool for me in approaching ESL topics.

In the article, *When We Are Capable of Stopping, We Begin To See*, Frankenberg (1996) articulates how her racial identity of being white became visible to her as she became aware of her own racial privilege as a white woman. The more she realized the advantage of living a white life, the more she learned about the differences and disadvantages of living a non-white life, which as a whole made her critically review her racial identity in a broader socio-cultural context (pp. 3-17) .

The scope of Frankenberg's interpretation is relevant to my approach in narrative inquiry. Just as Frankenberg was able to recognize her differences through her own whiteness, I came to see my own Koreaness and femaleness in ESL learning situations. I came to see that I was different from others in the same situation while Frankenberg could see "others" as she recognized her own differences of being a white female (p. 8). As a result, I became aware of my own Koreaness and femaleness. Because of this self-consciousness of Korean femaleness, I could more readily view the Korean maleness in the ESL learning situations. At the very end, I came to question the ESL student identity itself within a wider range of socio-cultural perspectives. For this reason, I find it necessary to tell my stories and their stories together. In other words, this close connection to my experience and the Korean males' stories allows me to investigate specific situations, experiences, and cases of personal difficulties of acquisition of the new culture and language.

By employing this method, I hope to have brought each difficulty of these Korean males' language learning experiences into light. First of all, the narrative form allows the untold stories to come alive and be revealed. Once visible, then, it is easier to give proper attention to the issues. Okely regards self-awareness as the medium for critical thought. Becoming aware of certain facts, which would make us puzzled and uneasy, says Opie, will make the significant determinant visible: They (the acknowledgment of discomfort and noncomprehension) force us to identify and question our own values, stereotypes, and truth. They draw attention to the paradoxical, the contradictory, as well as the compatible (Pamphilon, 1999, pp. 406-407).

Then, the silenced invisible factors should become visible by being given voice through narrative inquiry: "The personal account makes excluded voices "hearable" within dominant discourse — it is compelling in part because it reveals in vivid detail" (DeVault, 1997, p. 226).

The Participants

I have chosen two participants who are Korean males, over 25, who have recently completed military services, who were ESL students, and as well, they are both from my church community. The reason why I chose these two Korean men, Min-yong and Taek-kyu, was because of the assumption I had in my mind prior to my research.

Why did I approach Min-yong and Taek-kyu? It has to do with the earlier hypothesis, that I assumed an association between their challenges in an ESL learning situation and their experiences of having been in the army. As I explained above, I had presumed that the distinct difficulties that the Korean men have in the process of learning English in America was due to the cultural identity of being Korean males who have finished army duties. For this reason, I had in mind to investigate the cultural aspects of Korean maleness of Korean male ESL students who had finished the military services.

To protect their identities, both of the participants' names are pseudonyms. I have known Min-yong for a long time, but not Taek-kyu. It was I who approached them about participation in the interviews for my research. My old friend Min-yong agreed easily as I explained the purpose of the research and what I was looking for through the interview. However, it made less sense to Taek-kyu, at first, to participate in the interview since I had known him for only a couple of months. Both of the participants, as I understand it, agreed to take part in the interview session mainly because of the relationship we shared (that of friendship through our church community).

Also, Taek-kyu, and later Min-yong too, both wished to remain anonymous as they thought they had been and were sharing personal and emotional experiences of their life. For me it made sense that a Korean man would not wish to show the "weaker/softer side" of the personality. My father was like that and so was my brother. Admitting to one's own weaknesses and emotional difficulties and telling others about it is regarded as "not manly" in Korean culture. There is an expression in Korean slang that describes such incidences of embarrassment: "Being sold of one's front." This means to lose face, and both Min-yong and Taek-kyu wished not to lose face as Korean men.

Taek-kyu Park was 28 years old and had come to the United States about four months prior to the time of the interview. Taek-kyu was taking ESL classes at WESLI (Wisconsin English as a Second Language Institute) when he was taking part in the interview session with me. His current situation of learning English was a rather fresh and a completely new experience. His testimony reflected the urgent and immediate issues of learning English as a second language in the U.S.

He had just finished his mandatory army service in Korea. He left school to serve in the army when he was in his sophomore year of college. Military duty is mandatory for all Korean men, and 26 months of duty is required in the Korean military. As he had finished the army duty, he had a several-month gap before he could go back to college. He came to the United States to study English for a while, and it was possible for him not only because his sister and her family were living in Madison, but also because his parents were able to support him financially for ESL education in America.

The reason he had chosen to study English during his free time after military service and before returning to school was due to the competition in Korea for English proficiency. Everybody who wants a decent job has to be able to speak English. Proficiency in English is the sole access and resource for Koreans these days to get a secure job which will promise more access to a privileged life and financial resources — a common dream of many Koreans these days.

Korean students who come to the United States to learn English or go to college are mostly from well-to-do families. It is often the case that the parents provide financial support for their studies and living expenditures, which implies that these families are upper-middle class in the Korean society. Not only do the parents have a higher education level, but the rest of the family members usually have access to higher education and a high living standard. For this reason, I could assume that Take-kyu was from such a privileged family in Korea.

Generally, the sons in Korean families are given more frequent chances to study abroad. It is perceived that the successes of the sons determine the future of the rest of the family members. This cultural favoritism toward sons to distribute more resources to support their accomplishments is even more evident when the son is the oldest child in the family. The oldest son has more responsibility for what he becomes. Usually, the oldest son of the family is pressured by this Korean cultural tradition, and thus feels heavily obligated and motivated to make accomplishments in his life. Taek-kyu was the oldest son in his family and thus he was very conscious about his position in his family. He felt that he has to "succeed" in order to keep his parents from losing face, and at the same time, in order to maintain the well-being of the whole family.

Min-yong Kim is the second son of the family, and he was less pressured by the "oldest-son-drive." He was also from an upper-middle class family. After the sudden death of his father about two years ago, the family had to made great adjustments in their standard of living. Min-yong Kim had been studying in America at the University of Wisconsin even before he joined the army. The reason he joined the army at that time might have been due to financial difficulty with paying the high tuition bill at the University of Wisconsin. Thus, it is not entirely accurate to generalize that all Korean students studying in the U.S. are from rich families. This is true in my own case as well. I started my studies through the support from my parents. I relied on their financial support for awhile. However, they could not keep up with the increasing expenditure and I had to find my own ways. For the past couple of years, I have had to finance my own studies, which is another reason to discredit the generalization that all Korean students are from affluent backgrounds.

The reason I asked Min-yong to participate in the interview was because, unlike Taek-kyu who came to the United States for the first time after his army duty, Min-yong had been in America learning English before the army service, and came back after military duty. He had finished his army service about six months prior to the time of the interview. He is 29 years old and had returned to school in Madison to finish his undergraduate degree.

Min-yong shared his ESL learning experiences of when he first came to the United States. The first two years of that time were the most critical for him when the issues of ESL learning took place. Even though Min-yong was not an ESL student at the time of the interview sessions and was in his senior year at the University of Wisconsin as an Economics major, I saw similar and relevant ESL issues arising in his daily and academic life.

This perspective also stems out of my own experiences in that I still view myself as an ESL student after living in America and American academia for nine years. Although I am not enrolled in any ESL courses, the struggles with the English language, living in American culture, and feeling incompetent to communicate in English as a second language are still urgent issues in my life. This was the same for Min-yong and we call ourselves "extended ESL students." I see Min-yong's situation and experiences in the American academic institution as relevant to the learning situations of students who are currently in ESL classrooms.

The Procedure

Taek-kyu and Min-yong willingly accepted my request to take part in the interview session. Both of them also agreed to be audiotaped. This was possible mostly due to the network I have with them in my Korean church community. As Koreans, they would not want to be rude by rejecting a favor asked by another member of our narrow community. Also, I had already been friends with Min-yong for 5 years, which naturally allowed me to have strong support from him from the beginning. It is possible that Taek-kyu decided to join the interview procedure because Min-yong had talked him into it, or Taek-kyu might have felt it was permissible since Min-yong was there, too.

The attempt to find the explanation of why Taek-kyu had joined the interview has a purpose. That being, to discuss the cultural appropriateness in the Korean socializing circle. There are relatively strict rules of appropriateness in Korean culture when it comes to inter-gender interaction and socializing. By Korean standards, as a 30- year-old woman I should already be married. Yet I am single, a fact which is supposed to make me more reserved and careful in establishing friendships with male students. If I am too outgoing or aggressive in making friends with male students, I run the risk of having my behavior perceived as indecent and inappropriate. At first I felt uncomfortable approaching Taek-kyu and asking him for a favor. Being a Korean woman was a barrier at this time. Asking for a favor I ran the chance of being misunderstood by Taek-kyu as making an overture for personal and emotional affection. As well, I feared that such a request could have initiated serious rumors in my Korean church community. Regardless of the risk, I had to initiate the talk with him, and fortunately, Min-yong acted as a "buffer," lessening the chance for people to misunderstand my intention. I am a Korean woman, and I wished to stay in my Korean church community without losing face. The dilemma of cultural appropriateness emerged again as I had to schedule interview sessions.

In the following section, in which I discuss the reciprocity of the researcher-participant relationship through my procedures in carrying out the interview sessions, I would like to draw upon three excerpts from my daily journals. The daily journals were written during the course of the interview sessions and served as field notes for the procedure. They are significant in representing the procedural aspect of the interview because I see the daily journal as reflecting the reciprocity of researcher-participant relationship. For the purpose of wanting to reveal what has happened in the field, and to prove the "believability" and a feeling of the organism, I am presenting three segments of the daily journal I wrote as field notes during and after the interview session.

Here, through my daily journal, my perspective and stance as a researcher is embodied to share how I have interacted with the participants. Although the journal is a product of my reflections and interpretations about the fieldwork, I see the journal writing as valuable to validate my position as a researcher. In terms of sharing how I went on with the procedure, the readers can see how I collaborated with the participants. Thus, it is my intention to make the research-participant relationship transparent by providing actual journal excerpts around different themes. The readers should be able to see what I have been doing and how I carried out the interview procedure in which reciprocity and mutual collaboration should be the central mode of interaction. I wish to present my journals which Marcus, called "messy text" and by which I aim "to be persuasive rather than demonstrative" (Clough, 1999, p. 428).

Thus, I will explore three themes related to the research procedure of narrative inquiry by presenting my journal as field notes. First, the cultural appropriateness and insider-outsider dilemma will be discussed. Second, the situations of interpersonal interaction, which enabled the interview sessions to be abundant in mutual relationship, will be described. Third, the relationship of trust and friendship, which had been building and developing in the course of the interview process, will be presented.

April 15, 2000 Saturday

4:20-pm-5:30pm (1 hour 10 minutes)

The first time for the three of us to meet, Min-yong, Taek-kyu, and I met in front of the Memorial Library at four. I was a little late. My concern for the fact that, this interview session would not turn out to be an efficient way to let them talk freely of their stories due to the group meeting instead of the individual, worried me. It was not appropriate to meet them individually, as a Korean female. In my Korean culture and my age of being old enough to have gotten married, yet being a single woman means many things, such as the implication of the risk of being mistaken as overly, overtly, and aggressively interested in the opposite sex. This would give me a bad name. Here I realized my "outsider" position as a researcher. Only being a Korean did not give me an "insider" position as a researcher.

So, I had to come up with this group interview session, which would release me from the suspicion of holding personal attraction for male peers. Actually, Min-yong has been my good male friend in my church community for about six years, and I have known him pretty well. It was relieving that, at least with him, there was no risk of being mistaken. Well, the other eyes in my church community can still make gossip out of it.

On the other hand, Taek-kyu had come to Madison about four months ago, and he is a new face to our church community and me. Before meeting him for this interview session, I have personally met him once for lunch, and it was the only and first time to talk to him in person. Otherwise, we would meet as a group at the weekly student fellowship meeting on Friday evening or on Sunday for service. Freshly off the boat, he could really get me wrong if I would ask him to meet me in a quiet sealed room, where it suits to tape the interview. Thus, it was a better idea to meet these guys in a group.

In this daily journal entry, the issue of cultural appropriateness came up again as a dilemma, similar to the case at the very beginning of initiating and establishing the interview sessions. This field note about my struggle and dilemma to remain as a culturally appropriate Korean women represents the crystallization of the two opposing researcher identities I held. As a researcher, it might have been more effective to meet with each participant individually. However, as a Korean woman, meeting them individually might separate me from the Korean community and make me an outcast. Therefore, the question occurred to me: Am I an insider or an outsider?

Of course being a Korean and former/extended ESL student allowed me to share a great deal in terms of common identity, emotion, experiences and understanding with the participants. However, the fact that I am female, indeed, made me an outsider and limited my interactions with the participants due to my gender identity. Because of this fact, I had to have different ways of behaving to be a culturally appropriate Korean woman. The gender distinction made me an outsider. Cultural appropriateness was what it was all about.

The outsider identity of the researcher, though, turned out to be an advantage for me in the research. Because I am a woman, I experienced time, space, and incidents that made me explicitly aware of my Korean femaleness. This became a tool for me to see the Korean maleness, which was the opposite or different from what I had personally lived. Thus, my outsider identity of being a woman became an advantage for interacting and observing the participants more insightfully.

The second excerpt from my daily journal has to do with the interactive, interpersonal aspect of the research procedure. Narayan (1997) showed how she used interpersonal skills to create a mutual relationship with the research participants. She started first to tell her own stories in order to open the hearts of the participants: "Trying to fill the difficult silences, I took the tack of disclosing myself rather than trying so hard to draw her out. I chattered bravely on about what I had been doing: the places I had gone, the people I had visited" (p. 8). Narayan shared her stories, and that was what I did with the participants in the midst of the interview session.

April 16, 2000 Sunday

3:30pm-3:50pm (20 minutes)

The session today was rather brief. We meet once again after the Sunday service at church. After church we went to the Memorial Union for the interview. However, they seemed to be not in the mood today to talk.

I went ahead and told my story of feeling shame and inferiority I experienced nine years ago. I told them my own story about what I had experienced when I first came to the states related to the English language problem. My story (presented in this paper as the "Prologue") of having to confront the football players, which made me feel small, weak, inferior, shameful, and not respected. Both of them listened quietly. They did not say anything back to me. I wondered what they might have been thinking. However, there was no way I could read their minds. I was just hoping that my story would make a positive impact on them.

I realized it was not a good style to squeeze out stories from them. I should not force them, which would make them feel uncomfortable and passive.

I had to explain to them in detail why I decided to dismiss the interview meeting early today. First of all, it would not be right as a researcher to force participation. Secondly, I told them the story telling should be always spontaneous. It could get going sometimes and often not. I had to make sure that it was not because of their lack of "performances."

After my explanation to them, giving specific reasons why we were finishing the session early, we went for dinner.

Last, I would like to describe the research procedure in terms of "a relationship that continues to the present," in which trust, mutuality, and friendship were to be central (Rasbridge, 1996, p. 205). This is represented through the help I attempted to give to Taek-kyu when he needed practical advice and assistance in his daily personal life. He needed to find a sublet, which was a very new task, and I helped him to find an apartment to live in during the summer.

April 23, Sunday

At church I met Taek-kyu, and he needed help.

Last time after the interview, he said he was finding the interview session very helpful to his own language learning. He said that the discussions we usually had were directly related to the current issues he had to deal with, and the talks gave him insights and knowledge about how to go about the conflicts and crises he was confronting. He felt encouraged that he was not the only one in the world with these kind of struggles. What we told him in a form of narration or feedback to his narration became advice. He came to realize more and more about what specific things he was facing. He said the level of his self-consciousness rose, so that he was able to hold a wider and embracing viewpoints about the process of language learning. I was glad to hear that the interview session was not only beneficial to me but also to one of my research participants.

"What do you need help for?" I asked.

"I am trying to find a summer sublet and... ."

Reciprocity, a true one...

I made up my mind to help him out with finding him a summer sublet.

Indeed, I was going to give him some situated language lessons. He could utilize the language for finding apartments, to speak to people and, to find out sublet information. I designed a one-time short lesson plan for him, so that he could learn how to catch a fish.

When Taek-kyu told me that the interview session was giving him helpful and positive feedback for his ESL learning I felt there was a true reciprocity between us — an indication that our friendship was growing as the interview session went on.

We met seven times, and each time we spent about one and a half to two hours. The testimonies from Take-kyu and Min-yong, which were told on the first meeting turned into the stories I have presented in this paper.

The Interpretation

Min-yong and Taek-kyu used the typical Korean-male-language which consists of less formal addresses and more swear words and male slang. I explained that it would be interesting to pick up the cultural and gender identity embedded in the typical Korean male vernacular. Also, some topics, which may appear to be irrelevant to the ESL issues or English learning were said to be acceptable to Min-yong and Take-kyu and to be included in their narration. I felt it was important for me not to reinforce my focus, but rather let them expand the storyboard by narrating freely without limited boundaries for topics. By doing so, I hoped that their Korean male identity would emerge more clearly in their speech and stories.

However, as I had to translate the interview data from Korean into English, I faced a challenge of losing the authenticity of the speech and style of the participants. This drawback became even more apparent as I attempted to write them into stories. Through a two-step process, I seemed to lose one of the important focuses of my research: the maleness of the language and speech. The loss of the authenticity was unavoidable for two reasons.

First, English language does not have the system of expressing differentiated status of the interlocutor, which demarcates seniority of age. For example, Min-yong and Taek-kyu were a couple of years younger than me, and thus, they had been using a language that reflected my seniority. In Korean language, for instance, they attached a suffix of "-yo" at the end of their sentences. This was a language form that was more formal than without the suffix. The more formal sounding expression implied placing a slight distance between the speakers to show politeness and appropriateness to each other in terms of age.

The age consciousness of Korean people, which has its roots in the Confucianist tradition of Korean culture, is explicit, and thus Korea is a society where people are hypersensitive about their own and other's ages. Almost without exception, people differentiate their speech to elders by means of formal address in order to reflect their elder's seniority.

It is not an exaggeration to say that it is almost impossible to open up a conversation between two strangers before making assumptions about each other's age. Once it is evident to each interlocutor how old the other is, they can think of the right form of address for one another. Thus, it is not a surprise to see that Koreans make sure we know each other's age.

As a result, talking less formally, placing less distance, disregarding the age consciousness, and being less polite could appear to be manlier. Thus, the switch from formal to less formal speech was an important marker in that it was an exhibition of their Korean male identities.

Second, the vernacular language, slang, swear words, and harsher expressions, which were used to highlight their Korean male identity were important for me to catch. They would use many swear words and slang expressions as they were describing certain situations and incidences. In the beginning of the interview, they used the less casual type of language because they might have taken my seniority and age into the consideration. However, at the same time, they naturally mixed informal expressions into their speech using more and more vernacular forms. There could be a couple of possible motivations for them to switch. Not only was our age gap not that great, but also the fact that among younger people we could be more casual rather than sticking strictly to formal address and expressions resulted in freer and more casual speech forms. It sounded more natural to talk without the "-yo" at the end of each sentence to de-formalize our relationship.

Furthermore, they used swear words and male slang more frequently as we proceeded with the interview sessions. The typical male language, swear words, such as "ship-pal/ssi-bal" or "tchot-na-kae", equivalent to "fucking" or "shit" were increasingly inserted in the midst of their speech. Later in the interview typical male slang was used more often. It was not possible for me to translate it into equivalent language forms in English. Eventually, as I wrote the stories in English, the stories sounded flat. This was more overt in the "Dialogue," the story about Taek-kyu's experience, where I was lost in how to demonstrate to the readers the way typical Korean men act, think, and speak. As I was paying attention to the culturally charged language I noticed at various points which, I initially thought to be typical Korean male identities being asserted, were more explicit and valuable in terms of what kinds of emotions they were exhibiting in their testimonies of ESL learning. I could relate this language of Korean maleness with emotional expressions. Through switches, they displayed ups and downs in their emotional state as they were talking about their ESL learning experiences.

It was important for me to catch the emotional moments in their speech in order to interpret the data. As they switched from more formal to more casual and freer speech forms, I could identify where they intentionally made the switch to more casual expressions in order to display drastic changes in their personal feelings. For such cases, I could mark their speech and stories as a signifier to investigate the given ESL issues.

The interview data seemed at first to be significant because it appeared to be loaded with the cultural perspective of ESL acquisition. However, I came to see the emotional attributes were as critical as the cultural factors in investigating the ESL issues. The interview data of the participants revealed the emotional difficulties of being a Korean male in the American society. Presented in the content of the data, negative emotional difficulties in language learning implied identity crises which were observed as barriers against effective language acquisition. Thus, I came to see that there were complex relationships present in the three ESL issues of culture, emotion, and identity.

These moments of exhibiting emotional challenges and identity problems were frequently occurring in both of the participants' speech. Again, I was unable to demonstrate the emotional aspect of the style and content of their speech as the translation into English cannot express parallel nuances and authenticity that were present in the original speech in Korean.

Nevertheless, this barrier of having to translate from Korean to English was extremely valuable. At first, as I was aware of the cultural aspects of language learning, I looked for culturally-charged data. I thought investigating the Korean cultural identities of the participants would bring me answers to identify the invisible factors of ESL learning processes. However, when I had to face the limitation of translating from one language to the other, this barrier allowed me to grapple with a critical aspect of Korean male language. I came to discover that the Korean male language was significant in terms of exhibiting the emotional challenges and identity crises of the participants in ESL experiences, and in showing that the cultural identities of the participants were interrelated to the emotional challenges.

The Stories

In this section of the paper I will tell the stories of the two research participants in which the emotions of the participants are explicit. The emotions displayed in the stories are salient examples of affective states of typical Korean males in the process of language acquisition. I will then analyze the two stories to make a connection to current ESL educational practices. Also, in this part, I will make a conclusion about how my perspective about the given topics changed. I will offer an alternative viewpoint to understand the issues in ESL education.

With 'Another Monologue,' which is part of my own narrative, I will conclude this paper. 'Another Monologue,' has the purpose of making the readers think about their own situations in their day-to-day learning and teaching situations. I hope this brings out the emotion of the readers, which will create a constant effect of echo in the readers' minds about the topics and issues discussed in this paper.

The Story of Min-Yong

Learn to swear and survive, or kill yourself.

After I stayed in New Jersey for a year, I realized that being with too many Koreans was not helpful for me to learn English. I had to move to a place where there would be no Koreans so that I would speak English all the time. Leaving all my Korean friends behind, I had to go somewhere else to learn English. "Hanging out with my Korean friends did not do any good to my English," my parents used to say, "There is an old Korean saying; 'Your friend or the friendship alone does not win you bread,'" So I left New Jersey.

I moved to Virginia without the slightest hint that I would come to such a difficult place. The trading off of leaving all my Korean friends and heading to an English-only town to pursue more English learning resulted in a harsh punishment.

I transferred to a military high school, which I was advised to attend for its absolute non-Korean environment. I had no idea what the school was like. Now I questioned who had given me the advice to attend that specific school. Why?

The logic for attending that military school was the following; there were no Korean students at all, I would be forced to speak only English all the time, and eventually I would learn English more and more and faster and faster.

On the first day of my arrival in that small town of Virginia, I became a monkey. I had my luggage in both of my hands, walking down a street of less than a mile in length which was called 'downtown.' There were a few people out on the street and they stopped walking and stared at me. I could instantly sense that they must have never seen an Asian person. Some people would come out from buildings to see me as I was walking down the street. They never saw an Asian man, and now they were looking at me as if they were looking at a monkey at a zoo.

This scene was also found at the school. As I entered the hallway, kids would come out to the hall to see the monkey. In the dorms, 'there goes a monkey' I heard in my mind. Everybody was truly speaking English only. I could not hear nor see any Koreans, which I must have had in mind already upon my arrival at this school. Yet, it still struck my mind. No Korean students, no Korean food, no Korean language.

It was a military school. It did not occur to me as bizarre at that time since an only-English-speaking setting was the only and very good reason for me to be there. Students had insignias on their shoulders to show the differentiated military order or rank by their seniority. Since I had just entered the school, my order was the lowest.

That was why I had to clean the bathroom every day. For about a month I kept doing the bathroom-cleaning job. Then, I found it unfair.

I could not speak English at that time. Almost none. I could not understand what the kids were saying and what they were laughing at. I had to be alert all the time to figure out what was going on. Each time I would face a situation in which I heard English and something had to be done or said by me, I took rough guesses on what I should have been doing. This was how I figured out about cleaning the bathroom.

The problem was that the kids seemed unfriendly to me. I had no clue why. I could see it through their violent facial expressions and body language. Also, the words they were saying were words I had never seen in my dictionary. Later, I learned that they were constantly saying was swear words. Many times they would say those harsh-sounding words to me as well.

I could understand some of their words ridiculing my poor English. They would say that I was dumb or stupid. They laughed at my broken English and I would feel a terrible shame. One thing is certain: they were not nice kids. And I did not know why. The only thing I could think of was that, my English was so bad. Every night before sleep I would swear to myself that I would learn it.

However, "I will learn it" did not make those kids stop the harassment. I came to sense that the kids were straightening out their hierarchical seniority through fights. I did not know what to do but to beat them up as hard as I could. I was engaged in frequent fights with the kids. I also learned that I had to prove my strength by saying swear words back to them. I started to write down all the swear words-like sounding words. I would look them up at night before I went to bed. However, the dictionary I brought from Korea did not have those words so I bought a new one, an American dictionary, in which I could find most of the meaning of the swear words. I learned them by heart and I would secretly practice saying them if I had time by myself.

The Story of Taek-kyu

I am so old, I am an outsider, stranger, and loser.

"Shit! I am 28 years old and now I am talking like a baby. Nobody understands me and it is painful to hear myself stuttering and mumbling. I do not understand much about what those English speaking bastards are saying." He says he wished he could forget who he was and how old he was now. He continued, "Today is the day of my fifth month in America. Exactly four months, and I still cannot speak English." According to his description of himself, he sounded as if he was mute, impotent, and deaf.

"The reason why I came to America is to learn English. This is the only and sole motivation for me to be here in the States. As soon as I finished my 26 months of mandatory army service in Korea, I went back to school to finish my bachelor degree in social work. I graduated last year, and I knew I had to study more English in order to get a job in Korea," he explained to me.

He continued. He said the reality in Korea for job-hunting dominantly entailed the ability to speak English. Many Koreans may be able to read some, but not many can actually speak the language and write in English. "English is everywhere, so it is in Korea. You have to have a high TOEFL score to get a job at a prestigious company, or to be employed at all. There is no choice whether you want to learn English or not. You simply have to or you remain an eternal loser." He sounded upset when he said it.

He did not look old or anything, but he looked like a typical Korean man who had finished college and army service. It is hard to describe why I felt so, but there were certain traits in him that made him an outsider. Was it due to his over-consciousness about how old he was? He looked more rigid in terms of interpersonal relationships. Or, perhaps it was too frustrating for him having to learn everything from the beginning. This status of novice ESL learner seemed to trouble him as no longer was Korean male chauvinism available.

"The fact that I am older than the others are at the English institute among Koreans and other foreign students makes me nervous and uneasy," he said. Why is he so self-conscious about his own age? He said it bothers him the most to see younger kids talking to him without differentiation in terms of seniority. "In English everybody is 'you.'" There is no system in the language to reflect the age order or seniority of the speech participant.

I was surprised at the fact that he was desperate to be respected for his seniority among his peers. I speculate that this tendency of stressing the importance of seniority in interpersonal relationships is one of the traits of Korean maleness which is a left-over from the experiences in the military service. The hierarchical order in the military continues to be present in the Korean men's interaction. The interpersonal skills based on hierarchical structure of the military order is added to age-conscious relationships and results in a hypersensitive awareness of seniority. Relationships are more rigid, less fluid, and fixed on whom you may and may not can call by name.

He may be suffering from the sudden loss of power that he possessed back in Korean society. He feels he is not respected, he cannot express himself, and he has to face so many limitations in his daily life. Every moment is a struggle with the language. This was not the way he is used to existing.

"Shit! I am 28 years old and now I am talking like a baby. Nobody understands me and it is painful to hear myself stuttering and mumbling. I do not understand much about what those English speaking bastards are saying."

Tae-kyu's outrage was following me as I left to go home.

Implication to ESL Education

Implication of this Paper and its Relevance to American Education

Earlier in this paper I attempted to define the invisible factor of language learning. Now I would like to continue to explore Schumann's topics of "affective component" and "social component" (Bialystock & Hakuta, 1994, p. 144) with a more narrow focus made possible by conducting research through the method of narrative inquiry. After the inquiry, I arrived at a slightly different focus and viewpoint on the two topics. I came to attend to the emotional difficulties in the process of second language acquisition with more emphasis which led me to understand why cultural factors are critical in SLA.

Then, I interpreted the emotional difficulties as identity crises in the ESL learning procedure. Why do emotional difficulties arise? My understanding about the cultural aspects of language learning had changed a little: Cultural aspects of second language learning entailed more than "living in a different culture and speaking in a different language." I had to incorporate "student-centeredness" and "power dynamics" into the two topics in order to reason out the causes for the emotional challenges the participants went through. By doing so, I guide the readers to "see" the invisible issues, and at the same time, understand the mechanism of employing narrative inquiry to give voice to the invisible, and once silenced factors in ESL education.

Through the narrative inquiry, I began to see the highlighted emotional perspective of the ESL experiences of the participants. The emotional aspects of language acquisition enable me to relate it to the issue of culture. How emotion and culture are interrelated seems to be my next step in grappling with ESL issues. The practical, actual, and authentic challenges were mainly emotional difficulties, which again, inhibited the SLA. Why do such emotional hardships occur? Why is diverse culture to be blamed for emotional hardships? What makes the culture be responsible for the identity issues and negative emotional outcomes that inhibit SLA?

Larsen-Freeman (1991) posed a useful question: "The question of differential success is one of the major conundrums of SLA: Why is it that all individuals with normal faculties successfully acquire their first language but meet with different degrees of success when they attempt to master L2?" (p. 328). Under this focus, various factors are supposed to determine the success of the individual learner, and these were discussed in terms of: age, aptitude, attitude, motivation, personality, cognitive style, and learning strategies. However, the emotional factor was not handled by itself. Rather some points related to the topic of emotion were briefly discussed randomly within the various sections. For example, in the personality section, Larsen-Freeman (1991) lists the following concepts related to the impact of emotion in SLA: self-esteem, extroversion, reaction to anxiety, risk-taking, sensitivity to rejection, empathy, inhibition, and tolerance of ambiguity.

Brown (1994) talks about the "affective factors" by which he insufficiently tells the reader about emotional needs of the language learners in terms of inhibition, anxiety, and risk-taking (pp. 93, 255). He mentions, though, a notable point for me: he relates the negative emotional reactions to the self-perception of the learner. I found it parallel to my own rationalization about the greater impact of emotional aspects in SLA. The association of emotion with "language ego" (p. 255) was important for me in order to discover why there were emotional challenges in the process of ESL learning.

Let me redefine what it means to refer to affective or emotional factors in SLA. Affective factors are those that deal with the emotional reactions and motivations of the learner.

The most intriguing work was done by Peirce (1995), which assisted me greatly in narrowing the definition for identifying the invisible factors of ESL learning with the participants in my research. She brings attention to the emotional difficulties of her research participant, Eva. While she gives socio-cultural explanation rather than an affective justification, her viewpoint still bears how affective factors are related to identity issues in language acquisition.

As Eva felt "humiliated" by the comment of a conversation partner on Eva's ignorance of who Bart Simpson is, the process of language exchange by Eva resulted in inhibition. In 1994, Peirce explains that the cause for Eva to feel offended was due to the identity problem. "A learner's social identity is ... 'multiple and contradictory.' " "Learning is successful when learners are able to summon up or construct an identity that enables them to impose their rights to be heard and thus become subject of the discourse" (Ellis, 1997, p. 42). By this, I understand that a sound social identity would allow language learners to be more apt in the process of language learning. By the same token, if there is a difficulty in drawing on a supporting or relevant social identity to the main discourse, it is likely that the language acquisition will be less effective. Peirce's distinguishing effort to relate emotional difficulties to the intricate nature of human identity, and again to the impact on the language learning, is remarkable.

If I apply Peirce's notion to the analysis of my research participants in searching for the invisible ESL issues in their language learning experiences, I arrive at the following understanding. Min-Yong and Taek-kyu have shared testimonies about their emotional difficulties in the process of ESL acquisition. That they had been struggling with negative emotional reactions can be traced back to identity problems. They could not find the sound, relevant, or supporting social identity in the American culture, and thus were going through the confusion and frustration of having lost the old Korean identity, and finding a new identity as ESL students. As a result, their ESL acquisition was inhibited by such identity crises.

My journey to search for definition of the invisible factors of ESL education is about to arrive at its destination. As I mentioned earlier, I began with the focus on the cultural aspect, which again made me attend to the emotional difficulties of the ESL learning. Then, I had to ask the question, why do ESL learners have to go through such emotional pain? To answer this, the concept of identity conflict was brought in by way of Peirce (1995). These comprehensively guided me to view the cultural aspects of SLA in a different way.

Peirce (1995) helps me even further for analyzing the data and coming to a conclusion. Ellis cites Peirce and gives me the answer: "Language learners have complex social identities that can only be understood in terms of the power relations that shape social structures" (Ellis, 1997, p. 42). Earlier I thought the cultural factor in SLA was significant because of the differences and diversity present across various culture. Now, I understand the definition to be tightly bound with the power dynamics. Culture and language are bound together and they are inseparable (Agar, 1994). How it is bound? Now, for me, cultural aspects of language learning accompany the issues of power dynamics.

This is it. Now, I am able to define the invisible factors. Emotional difficulties reflect identity conflicts, which overall are the results of the impact of cultural and power relational factors in SLA. Arriving at this point, I am expanding these issues even further to establish a correlation with my own research diagnoses.

What role has power dynamics played in Min-yong's and Taek-kyu's cases? First, participants' negative emotional reaction to the English language and American mainstream culture plays a large role.

> The long-term effect of coercive relations of power are evident in the educational performance of groups that have been subordinated in the wider society over generations. Several theorists have pointed to the fact that minority groups ... tend to be characterized by *a sense of ambivalence about the value of their cultural identity and powerlessness in relation to the dominant group.* [emphasis added] (Cummins, 1994, p. 369)

For example, English is often seen as the language of hegemony, imperialism, and superiority. Thus the participants, many times, struggled with the resentment of having to comply with the dominance of the English language in their reality. This means that their egos or identities became subordinated to the dominance of English. Then, under this dominance a sense of shame, inferiority, loss of power, subordination, and oppression arose. As such, the native cultural identity and mother tongue of subordination caused isolation and a desire not to follow the dominant discourse, which largely resulted in failure in second language acquisition.

The monkey scene of Min-yong's experience could be associated with this point of view. He had no choice but to learn and learn English in a place where the population was predominantly white. He felt emotional challenges for this reality and felt troubled. The monkey metaphor implies that Min-yong was feeling a negative emotional reaction, because he felt subordinated to the English language and the dominant white culture. This again reproduced a sense of shame and inferiority in his consciousness. I can suggest that this cultural aspect with the emphasis on power dynamics caused another set of bad emotions which hindered effective ESL learning. If he had not felt like a monkey, nor had any shame or feelings of inferiority, then he might have accelerated the process of ESL acquisition.

Second, due to the minority status of their native cultural identity and the mother tongue of the students, there are distances and opposing values. Since the ESL student's cultural heritage is more often of a nonmainstream background, there could be remoteness from the culture of the target language. Schuhmann explains this remoteness of the learner's identity from the culture of the target language as "sociological distance" and "psychological distance" (Ellis, 1997, p. 40).

We see that the participants were experiencing emotional tensions of feeling alien, a lack of self-esteem, and insecurity due to the opposing values and viewpoints. Taek-kyu's imploration about "everybody is *you* in English" reflects the fact that his cultural frame is no longer in power, but the norm of the dominant culture is subordinating him, forcing him to be someone with whom he does not identify. He does not want to be *you*. He wishes to be "a person of seniority, an elder person, who can expect politeness and formality from younger peers."

However, this Korean cultural frame is not acceptable and does not work any longer. And accordingly, the ESL student, Taek-kyu feels an enormous gap between himself and the rest of the society. He may turn reluctant, hesitant or hostile to the outside world, which results in a failure to interact effectively with the mainstream culture.

Such psychological distances can be reinforced by Peirce's notion again. The positioning of the (social/cultural) identity within the context of power dynamics intensifies the feeling of discrepancy. The learner is "distanced" either "socially" or "psychologically," for the outer world is ruled by the power dynamics.

Ogbu and Matute-Bianchi maintain that "caste-like minorities may tend to experience the conflict of two opposing cultural frames of reference—one appropriate for the dominant group and one appropriate for minorities" (Mckeon 1992, p. 22). These effects of the student's native cultural identity and mother tongue on ESL learning are marked by power dynamics in terms of the remoteness and irrelevance of the two opposing cultural identities.

It is often the case that the minority identity is subject to power dynamics in a wide range of everyday life activities. This idea is supported by Hutchby (1999), where he cites Foucault, contending that "power operates in the most mundane contexts of everyday life, not just at the macro-level of large process."

Hutchby (1999) continues, "Foucault (1977) suggests, that power is pervasive even at the smallest level of interpersonal relationships" (p. 587). If we recall the story of Min-yong, he had to live a difficult life at the military school. He had to clean the bathroom for months. He later turns furious about the fact, that the rest of the English-speaking American students victimized him for his lack of competency in cultural adjustment and English proficiency. As a result, he becomes increasingly aggressive, which hampered the SLA. Thus, these factors of the cultural non-mainstream identity of the ESL students actively play a role in hindering participant's ability to engage in the learning process of the new culture and language.

In order to sum up, I will restate the definition of the invisible factors in SLA. The interplay of power dynamics on ESL students' cultural identity constructs the non-mainstream identity as well as the minority identity. This non-mainstream/minority identity results in a troubled and disadvantageous state of the learner's identity, which comprehensively troubles the emotional well being of the ESL student. This again will force the ESL learners to fail to effectively engage in the process of language acquisition.

Cultural identity and affective factors create an extremely complex and non-separable conglomerate of critical and invisible ESL issues. The complexity of the factors and conglomerate issues which reflect students' inner states comprise the basis for individual students to sustain their personal identities in the dominant culture. The various aspects of each student's identity should be seen not only as complex but also as critical to ESL learning. After all, in language/ESL acquisition, emotion and personal identity play critical roles because they are culturally situated, and culture is ruled by power dynamics.

How does this logic apply to our participants? The emotional difficulty of Min-yong and Taek-kyu implies that there is a discrepancy of personal, social, and cultural identity as ESL learners. Identity crises are caused by the fact that both of them had to pick up a new ESL identity in America. This new minority identity, however, works in a way that they lose all status and power associated with native Korean identity. This loss of power due to the shift in the identity from mainstream Korean male identity to minority ESL identity result in identity crises and emotional troubles.

As I am able to imagine and relive the perspectives of the ESL students, I regard student-centeredness as one of the central interests in ESL education. By student-centeredness, I mean that the diverse aspects of the student's identity, that is the emotional suffering and troubled cultural identity from coming from a non-mainstream background, must be considered as the most significant variable of language acquisition. These are the entities of the invisible factors. Now made visible, they can be seen as the following: negative emotional state, problematic self-esteem, and subordinated non-mainstream identity that is consumed by the dominant English speaking culture.

Through presenting the narration of the two specific Korean males, Min-yong Kim, and Taek-kyu Park, I brought out practical emotional and identity difficulties that arise in the process of English acquisition due to their non-mainstream cultural identities of being ESL students in the U.S. Holding non-mainstream cultural and linguistic identity in the U.S. as, for instance, Hmong students do, implies multiple, complex, and critical issues in ESL acquisition. These issues have to do with determining the success of non-mainstream students in the American higher educational institutions.

However, it is my intention neither to construe the Korean male students' difficulties as "deficits," nor to simply sympathize with them for the sudden loss of their privileges and the cultural capital they are used to having back home in Korea. Rather, it is my proposal to suggest new ways of understanding critical factors in ESL acquisition. I hope that consideration of the distinct aspects of identities of culture, minority, and emotional challenges will be central to approaches to ESL education.

The following points are suggested as important to ESL education through this paper:

- allowing opportunities for students to acquire the competency of the discourse of interpersonal skills;

- attaining cultural norms for interaction in the mainstream culture of academia;
- making the role of the educational institution transparent in order to bring equity to marginalized students;
- giving voice to those invisible populations of students and making them visible.

As a last comment, before the "Another Monologue," I would like to add that it has been a great challenge to incorporate narrative inquiry as methodology for it is a non-conventional and new way of writing academically. The more traditional topics of ESL issues and the nontraditional method of narrative inquiry seemed to be resistant to integration, of the nature of blending oil into water or vice versa. Though, if the two had mixed well into each other, the strength of narrative inquiry to give voice to the previously silenced facts in ESL education could have been a great achievement. It is the emotional difficulties of the ESL learners that should be attended to as the most critical factors of SLA. The significance of paying attention to emotional challenges comes from the fact that they reflect identity clashes due to the non-mainstream backgrounds of the ESL learners. Thus educators in the field of ESL research and institutions must understand that language acquisition is determined by successful management of emotional difficulties and balancing one's own personal cultural identity as to nourish and nurture the mainstream cultural identity of power dynamics.

Another Monologue

Who are you?

A girl who came to America 9 years ago found what she was dreaming about. The ideas of "land of opportunity" awoke her. Opportunity, freedom, independence, self-determination, equality, and self-assertion as a woman seemed to allow her to breathe. Learning English was the way. "I will speak the Language!" She thought she could be happy. She thought she could be who she wanted to be. She thought she spoke English.

She thought she wrote in English.

She thought she was learning English very hard.

She thought she was going to live her life as she wished.

Then, a time came when she found herself floating in air. She belonged to nowhere. Being too Americanized as a Korean woman, she blamed her English. She was too outgoing and independent to be a Korean female.

But still, in the classrooms she was too Korean, passive, reserved, and less assertive. She was too quiet. She could not deny inside herself who she had been for all those years. She is Korean, a Korean woman, a girl who would always fear talking in front of people. She had to learn that there was a clear boundary that would not let her into America. It was not the U.S. Immigration offices. It was English. She could not speak and write it enough.

Opportunity, freedom, independence, self-determination, equality, and self-assertion! Those are the words that disappeared from her hope as she could write only Konglish, and not English. Opportunity, freedom, independence, self-determination, equality, and self-assertion! These are the words that did not mean anything to her any more as she could not express herself as much as she wants in English.

She started to look inside herself.

Who am I?

If there is anybody who would be curious to know what happened to her?

I am a Korean girl living in America and in American classrooms speaking and writing Konglish, instead of English.

Hail to the Email:
Tales about Foreign Language Education in a Globalized Age

Sabine Raizler and Gloria Carter

Introduction

Two women, both of them foreign language teachers, begin a conversation in the US about foreign language education in a globalized world and continue it through the exchange of emails. Coming from different countries, they examine the way in which their cultural experiences affect their perspectives on this issue. As they discuss the impact of globalization on foreign language learning and teaching, it becomes clear to the women that there are issues affecting foreign language teaching of which they were unaware. These issues, having been brought to the surface, encourage them to revisit their beliefs about the meaning of foreign language. Some of these questions include: Must a literate citizen of the global village know English? What is the interplay between the symbolic significance of language and one's standing in society? How does a foreign language affect one's identity? Finally, Gloria and Sabine consider how these questions may affect their practice.

Madison, Wisconsin, March 2001

Two women sit in a café on a blustery day caught somewhere between winter and spring. Cups of steaming liquid warm them. Sabine is drinking café latte; Gloria is a tea-drinker. The conversation has wandered in many directions and now turns to a topic of shared interest, foreign languages and teaching. What does it mean to speak and teach a foreign language in a globalized age? Sabine, a native speaker of Portuguese, teaches English as a foreign language and Portuguese as a second language in Brazil, her home country. Gloria, a native speaker of English, teaches German as a foreign language in the U.S. Both women have experienced the life of a non-native speaker in a foreign culture. As the flow of thoughts touch upon the impact of globalization on foreign language education, questions of the politics of language and of identity emerge as well. The way in which their individual cultural perspective colors their discussion intrigues them. They have only skimmed the surface when the coffee, tea, and time run out before the conversation does. Unwilling to let go of this conversation just begun, they agree to continue it at another time. There is one obstacle — Sabine returns to her home in Brazil the next day. The communication technology of the age of globalization provides the answer. They will continue their discussion by email. As they part, Gloria wishes Sabine a *"Gute Reise."* Sabine responds with *"Obrigada." "Tchau!"*

Monday, April 16, 2001 11:23:22 AM

Hello again, Gloria,

As we continue our discussion, maybe we should look back to the question that has been dancing in our heads since we started thinking about this project. Our question is: What does it mean to speak a foreign language? Well, I will talk about my experience with English as a foreign language in Brazil. One word that comes to my mind is globalization. Globalization, in its hegemonic manifestation, is a universalization of the values from some of the core countries. The "other" — be it the peripheral countries, be it the dominated classes of these countries — is degraded in this process or excluded entirely. In this process, not only the goods or the corporations are globalized but also the hegemonic ideology. However, this appears as a natural process toward progress, because it means more "civilization." If one speaks English in Brazil, (i.e. if one is given access to the "game") one is seen as a more "civilized" person. English brings progress, technology, knowledge, and status. It is the embodiment of the access to the dream. If one knows English, one has access to the "global" world. Let me hear from you on this idea.

Wednesday, April 18, 2001 10:02:43 PM

Hi, Sabine,

I hadn't thought of globalization in terms of a universalization of values. What are some of the values that you see as being exported and universalized along with the speaking of English? I could guess they may include materialism and consumerism (building blocks of the American Dream), but I have to confess my ignorance of Brazilian society. If Brazilian culture is the "other," what values are being degraded and excluded in the process of globalization?

If you were to ask someone living in the United States what globalization means, I doubt that "universalization of values" would be the first answer to enter most minds. Of course, if the values being spread throughout the world are those of one's own country, it does appear as a natural process, as you said. Rather than seeing a globalized ideology, many people in the U.S. would describe globalization primarily as an economic force in their lives. It is this economic view of globalization that has had an impact on foreign language education in the U.S. Because of globalization, I can lure students to foreign language classes by talking about the ways in which the peoples of the world have become more connected and the increased opportunities for intercultural contact that improved communications technology has afforded. But the most effective "sales pitch" to make to students, parents, and school boards for a foreign language program is to point to the competitive advantage in the global economy provided by the ability to speak a foreign language.

So, globalization provides an impetus for learning foreign languages in both Brazil and the U.S. The difference — and it is an important one — is the status of the language. The status of English as an international language, in fact, undermines the position of foreign languages in U.S. education. Some students see little reason to learn another language when everyone else in the world is learning English (or so it seems to them). Such an attitude reflects an arrogance on the part of those who hold it. In this view, the globalizing of values, language and ideology, as well as of the economy would not only be a natural process. It would be a desirable one.

Thursday, April 19, 2001   4:17:32 AM

Hi, Gloria,

You are right. It seems to me that when we see globalization described in the media, it is defined as an extremely positive and revolutionary process of internationalization of cultures, caused by the revolution of communications. It is also referred to as the universalization of goods and commodities and the interchange of people around the world. So, globalization is basically seen as a positive process by the capitalist conglomerates, the world financial institutes, and the media. According to Boaventura Santos (1997), every "globalized" situation presupposes a "localization" of something. If something is considered "global" it is because some other alternatives were banned and confined as "local." In every process of globalization some "voices" are silenced. Local languages and cultures are silenced. They are forced out of the circle, and often times seen as "exotic." Exotizing the other is at the same time a process of "normalizing" oneself, considering oneself "more universal," more ordinary, and maybe more "global." I often ask myself how "natural" the globalization process is. At the same time that it effaces "the other," by considering "the other" nearer and more similar, I have the impression that it works to otherize, too. The other is also the one who is construed as being outside of the global, as someone who failed to follow what has been dictated by the "norm." The myth of "no boundaries," then, creates a schism between what is validated as local and what is considered "universal." To use a metaphor, it creates more semiotic boundaries, and language is one of them. If you do not have the appropriate tool to engage in the process of globalization, you are out. One of the passports to a globalized world is, clearly, the ability to use English. The other day I was reading a study about critical pedagogy in Brazil by Cox and Assis-Peterson, (1999) and I was stunned by the assertion of one of the respondents of the study, who said that, "there's three kinds of illiterates: the one who does not know how to read or write, the one who does not know how to use the computer, and the one who does not know English" (p. 442). This commonsensical view seems to be one of the sad consequences of globalization, don't you think?

Thursday, April 19, 2001 9:33:04 PM

Gloria sits down at the computer, taking a break from grading papers. She clicks on the tiny blue telephone in the upper right corner of her screen and waits for the connection to the server. As she waits, snatches of school gossip surface in her mind...enrollments are declining...the budget is tight...teaching positions will have to be cut. The foreign language program had survived the cuts for next year. But foreign language courses were never considered part of the core curriculum, and shared the risk of all electives, that of being eliminated.

The computer informs Gloria she has new mail. She reads Sabine's latest message. "Ah, Sabine ... she worries about saving the world from the American hegemony while I worry about saving my job." Maybe, Gloria thinks to herself, I should start looking at other options. Globalization, as Sabine had pointed out, was making the ability to use English a sought after skill. One could always teach English overseas. Maybe join the Peace Corps. This was an interesting definition of illiterates Sabine brought up ... to think of someone who does not know English as illiterate. Interesting, and as Sabine wrote, sad. Gloria rereads Sabine's last sentence: "... one of the sad consequences of globalization, don't you think?"

Hello, Sabine,

Well, if that is true, what is sad about globalization is that I may be out of a job. From my viewpoint as a foreign language teacher in the United States, the definition of literacy should include speaking more than one language. Since nearly all of my students speak English as their native language, I would not consider knowing English adequate qualification for literacy in the global marketplace. So, while people in other countries, such as Brazil, may see the English language as the passport to the global village, in the U.S. we promote foreign languages as an essential tool for competition in the global economy. This thinking is apparent in the Wisconsin Model Academic Standards for Foreign Languages (Wisconsin Department of Public Instruction, 1997), which promote foreign language learning as critical for the U.S. to be "a front-runner in a global economy" (p. 1) and "to maintain international respect and economic competitiveness" (p. 10).

The most space and print in the standards, however, is allotted to discussions of communication and culture. There are two ways to look at the emphasis on students developing an ability to communicate in another language and an awareness of other cultures. One perspective is that we are preparing students to participate as productive members of a diverse global community. Learning a foreign language is supposed to foster respect and appreciation of other cultures. Thus, knowing a foreign language (and its cultural context) builds a bridge to intercultural understanding. It's interesting to me that this perspective sees the world as a multicultural community and sees diversity (and therefore, the "other"?) as something to be valued. This is a different image of the world created by globalization than the universalized one we spoke of earlier, isn't it?

Saturday, April 21, 2001 8:22:23 AM

Hi, Gloria,

I think that it's true that there is an attempt to see the world as a diverse community, but also, as I was saying earlier, there is the danger that globalization as universalization centers around what gets dictated by the core countries. In this process, we create "the exotic other," who gets construed as an outsider, because s/he is so genuinely different from the mainstream. So maybe the "bridge" is just an illusion, don't you think?

Saturday, April 21, 2001 11:07:12 PM

Hello Sabine,

Ah, let me see if I'm understanding your point better. I don't think I fully picked up on it earlier. Because the core countries determine what cultural values, ideology, language, and the like become universalized as the "norm," they also define what is "exotic." So, where I'm seeing a Coke-commercial-world of wonderfully different people holding hands, singing together, and appreciating each other's differences, those who have been labeled "the exotic other" may not feel that being considered "different" is justified ("different" by whose standard?) or desirable.

Sunday, April 22, 2001 9:23:10 AM

Dear Gloria,

This is exactly what I was thinking of. I like your Coke example. I think it's interesting how the different cultural assumptions and viewpoints construe the view of the globalized world, since it affects the image presented in FL classrooms. I am curious about what might be the image of the world in the economic perspective?

Before Sabine clicks send, she realizes how much she has been learning from this electronic conversation. It is so interesting to have the opportunity to get to know Gloria's perspective on these issues as a foreign language teacher in the U.S. Sabine has always wanted to know more about the standards for foreign language in Wisconsin, but never before had the opportunity. It makes her wonder whether there is such a thing as a model like the standards to guide the teaching of foreign languages in Brazil. She wants to take advantage of the fact that she's in Brazil right now to inform herself about it. While she waits for Gloria's response, she drinks one of her favorite local drinks, the mate, or chimarrão. The taste of chimarrão draws her into reflecting: Chimarrão is my passport to the local. Now I feel I'm back home. The local has languages other than the verbal. The smells of the herbs brewing make me feel I'm back. The local noises make me feel I'm back. Within all the familiarity, there is an inherent strangeness to my feeling. Have I become so "globalized" that the local has become almost exotic?

Sunday, April 22, 2001 3:33:02 PM

Hi Sabine,

I'm glad you asked about the economic perspective and the image of the world it presents. The economic perspective is actually somewhat in contradiction to the intercultural view. In this perspective, foreign language proficiency and cultural knowledge provide advantages in the global economic competition. We are arming the students with an "edge" in a world that is seen as a marketplace and one where other countries and cultures are our rivals. The importance of foreign language learning is not necessarily to build bridges, but rather to provide a weapon that will make the United States a winner in the global economy sweepstakes. By doing so, the United States can further globalize markets, recreating little bits and pieces of itself throughout the world. (Does the world really need a McDonald's in every major city?)

You may be able to tell from my tone that I prefer the intercultural model. Although I feel a need to play up the practical economic advantages of foreign language learning in order to win the support of students, parents, and the school board, my FL teacher's heart wants my students to leave my classroom with an appreciation for another culture and a greater awareness or understanding of the different ways in which people manage their lives. Maybe that seems naïve or unrealistic, but I think back to my own experiences. I was 22 years old, newly graduated from the university, when I experienced my first real engagement with another culture as a student in Germany. At that time, culture was not a major component of foreign language education. That year abroad filled in some of the gaps of my education. It gave me a glimpse into another culture ... and a glimpse, through other eyes, into my own. German students questioned me on U.S. policy and challenged me to rethink my beliefs about my country and culture. Many years later, when my husband and I had the opportunity to live abroad again (this time in France), I thought of it as a great experience for my grade-school-aged sons. They would learn, at a much younger age than I did, that there are many ways of being. Although I've been talking about living abroad as a means of expanding one's horizons, the point I'm trying to make is that foreign language education should function in the same way. Whether it's through the classroom interaction or through the use of language beyond the classroom, knowing a foreign language should open more windows on the world. And, yet, from what you have told me, I would say that English as a foreign language in Brazil opens a window onto the U.S. culture while closing others. Does it close more windows than it opens?

Monday, April 23, 2001 8:01:14 PM

Hello Gloria,

I wouldn't say so. I guess what I'm hinting at is that the teaching of English as a FL should be able to open up many different windows, not only to the U.S. culture, and not only to the mainstream U.S. culture. It should be able to open up windows to different voices, to different realities, to different accents, to different life stories and colors, so that it can challenge our taken-for-granted certainties of what these apparently monolithic cultures look and feel like. By challenging our assumptions about the foreign language culture(s), it seems to me that we can more easily engage in challenging our own, in rethinking our cultural models and regimes of truth, to use Foucault. This is the beauty of the foreign/second language learning process, I think: to promote a meta-understanding of our own inner language(s) and to challenge our perceptions of the world. The way different "languacultures" (Agar, 1994) both construe and express meaning seems to vary considerably, don't you think?

Monday, April 23, 2001   11:28:03 PM

Dear Sabine,

I really like the way you have described what you term "the beauty of the foreign/second language learning process." And you are right in saying that "languacultures" construe meaning differently. We have been talking about English as an international language, but I question how valid that is. Users of a language, whether native or non-native speakers, bring to the language their own cultural concepts and their own unique *Weltanschauung*. Claire Kramsch (1996) gives an example in her article, "Wem gehört die deutsche Sprache?" At a conference of foreign language teachers from France, Germany, and the U.S., a native speaker of French discussed the concept of *privilège* with an American and how it differed from the American concept of "privilege." According to the speakers in the article, the French *privilège* is something one expects, something that is one's due. When an American speaks of "privilege," the sense is more of something that has to be earned. Similarly, two people speaking English may use the same words, but when they come from different cultural backgrounds, how can we be sure that the meaning is the same? Language and culture are intertwined. If that's the case, then to think of language as culturally neutral, is indulging oneself in a myth, I'd say. Would you?

Tuesday, April 24, 2001   7:40:02 AM

Greetings, Gloria,

Languages certainly are not neutral. Recently I have read some writings by Bremer, Roberts, Vasseru, Simonot, & Broeder (1996), Norman Fairclough (1989), and James Gee (1996), who, drawing on the work of Foucault (1972), Bourdieu (1991), and critical theory, have studied the ways in which language is used to establish and reinforce ideological positions in society. For these scholars, the ways language is used are laden with sociopolitical connotations. In this 'critical' perspective, language, or discourse, is seen as social practice. Linguistic phenomena are regarded as socially implicated, because whatever use we make of language, we do it in ways which are "socially determined" and which have "social effects" (Fairclough, 1989, 23).

This is certainly the case with the role of English as a foreign language in Brazil — it is so laden with sociopolitical meaning. The apparent neutrality of English that is "sold" in Brazil is part of this hegemonic/globalizing process. English is "sold" as a beneficial, natural, and neutral language (Pennycook, 1994). According to Pennycook,

> The spread of English is considered to be natural because it is the inevitable result of global forces: neutral because it assumes that English has been stripped of its original cultural contexts and has been transformed into a transparent, universal medium of communication; and beneficial because it is a condition for cooperation and equality. (P. 9)

We can see here how apolitically English seems to be represented in the world. In Brazil, I see a total absence of a critical view in EFL, and maybe this is due in part to the submission to traditional applied linguistics and to teaching methods (Cox & Assis-Peterson, 1999), but I also think that textbooks, teaching materials and curricula are imported from either the U.S. and Britain without our questioning of the "hidden curriculum" (Auerbach & Burgess, 1985). I dare to say this happens not only in Brazil, but in most of Third World Countries that seem to digest anything that comes from the core countries as universal truths, failing to examine the local necessities and struggles.

Responding to your last comments about language and culture being intertwined, it seems to me that the cultural model (Gee, 1996) that the English language is identified with the American culture is also pervasive. Here enters the status of the English language. It's common sense that if one has access to (American) English, one can more easily mimic the access to the American dream. The myth of the American dream, i.e., of the access to material goods, good education and health care, symbolizes a can-do philosophy, a myth that through enough tenacity and commitment we will "get there," and that this depends solely on one's will and perseverance. One becomes a micro cosmos of one's self and everything seems to be generated from within.

Tuesday, April 24, 2001 4:47:32 PM

Sabine, could you explain this idea a little more?

Tuesday, April 24, 2001 5:27:21 PM

Sure, Gloria.

Well, I see the idea of the individual in the American dream as a decontextualized, disengaged perspective, one that is disassociated from the dynamics of the social and the political. The American dream is sold like an attainable goal as long as we put enough effort into it. In other words, if you fail, it's your own fault. It's marketed as an individual process.

Tuesday, April 24, 2001 6:51:39 PM

Hi Gloria,

And how would this affect what it means to speak English as a foreign language in Brazil, Sabine?

Wednesday, April 25, 2001 9:37:41 AM

Sabine,

Well, the way I see it is that if one has access to English, one is elevated to the category of "educated Brazilian." Following this line of thought, having access to the First World through the English language compensates us for our "deficiencies" and for the "cultural isolation" one may claim to feel as a member of the "periphery." Not having access to English (as a foreign language) in Brazil, though, equals being a foreigner of the American (and thus, of the global) discourse. The English language, then, becomes the symbolic passport through which one will gain the automaticity of the "game" (in the Bourdieunian sense). In this "game" of symbolisms and sociocultural representations, then, I see the role of English in developing countries as one of the important symbolic resources that enables one to enter the (symbolic) global community equipped with (symbolic) cultural capital (Bourdieu, 1991).

That's why I see access to English as a semiotic equivalent to access to the axis, to where the perceived action is. Admittedly, real access to the English language is for a privileged few. The periphery of the periphery remains outside of the game, bearing the brunt of an increasingly disrupted system where the "successful few" control the margins and dictate the rules of the game for their own good. For the less privileged, access to English (as a metaphor to the American dream), is constantly denied. I think English as a Second Language plays a similar role in the U.S., what do you think, Gloria?

Thursday, April 26, 2001 8:37:01 PM

The week almost over, Gloria sits in front of the computer with a glass of iced tea in hand, reading Sabine's latest thoughts. The symbolic role of language that Sabine described intrigues her. As she prepares to respond to Sabine's email, she places her glass on the desk next to two piles of papers. A scene of horse-drawn carriages and stately buildings fills most of the cover of a thin booklet on top of several sheets of explanations. Beside that pile sits a thick booklet, more sheets of explanations, and a brochure showing smiling faces of various hues in unfamiliar places. Gloria glances at the two application booklets and wonders why the Peace Corps wants so much information about her while the Graduate School wants so little.

Returning to Sabine's email, Gloria reflects on English as symbolic access to the American Dream. Does it play the same role in the U.S.?

Greetings, Sabine,

Yes, I think the role of ESL in the U.S. is not just about learning English, but also about gaining access to the "game." Without English one cannot achieve the American Dream. Like the "educated Brazilian," an "educated American" must speak English. In some sense, language ability comes to equal intelligence. Newcomers to the United States, even those who speak more than one language other than English, are not truly "educated" until they learn English.

The debate over bilingual education in the U.S. in recent decades makes it clear that the debate is not actually over language, but over the symbolic significance of language. It also poses some interesting questions about attitudes towards monolingualism and foreign language education. Donaldo Macedo (1994) quotes this bumper sticker: "Monolingualism is a curable disease" (p. 125). I think that's a perspective that would not be generally shared by mainstream Americans when viewing their own monolingualism. Though Americans may believe that monolingualism is curable — with much time and effort — the idea of monolingualism as a "disease" is problematic for many Americans. With the idea of disease come the notions of undesirable, unwanted, and abnormal. And yet, monolingualism is the norm in the mainstream culture of United States. To view the condition as "diseased" means we have to quarantine the entire nation.

And who would be the healthy members in such a diseased community? Those who are now looked upon as low status—the immigrants speaking a "foreign language" as their first language and working on English as their second. Or third or more. Newcomers to the U.S. whose English is imperfect have long been regarded as deficient in languages by monolingual English speakers. Speaking one language is perfectly acceptable—as long as that one language is English. In the United States monolingualism is a disease only when the language spoken is not English. That is the way it appears to me as one inside the U.S. culture. I'm wondering if it looks different to you, Sabine, seeing it from another viewpoint?

Saturday, April 28, 2001 2:12:34 PM

Hi, Gloria,

I agree with you that the linguistic minorities (as well as the racial, sexual, economic, and social minorities, for that matter) are seen as the diseased ones, the ones who are considered as outside of the mainstream, or outside of the "game," like I had said earlier. Macedo (1994) suggests that the diseased ones are the English-only proponents, the ones who "don't allow other cultural subjects ... to be present in history" (p. 125), those who point to a "xenophobic culture," and whose hidden curriculum is "to promote a monolithic ideology" (p. 129). What we can see from this perspective is that the society as a whole is diseased.

I have to admit that when I first arrived in the U.S. I was not too familiar with the socio-political and linguistic situation faced by many immigrants in this country. It was only after I was exposed to this issue that I started to understand the weight that language carries in society. As a non-native speaker living temporarily in the U.S., I think my situation differs completely from that of immigrants. For one thing, I carry the status attached to being in graduate school. This seems to confer to me the badge of "cultural capital holder." The fact, then, that I fail to master the practices of daily life and of grad school life like a native speaker gets somewhat excused. So this exemplifies the claim that language does not stand alone in this game — it is part of a set of props that one has to have in order to be "accepted" in it. Socio-economic and intellectual status seems to erase a bit of the linguistic deficit, although this may not be true in all instances of daily life. Going back to your question, your comment that the debate over Bilingual Ed. is not actually about language, but about how the semiotic significance of language seems to fit right into our discussion.

Sunday, April 29, 2001 6:17:47 PM

Hello Sabine,

Yes, we can see this semiotic significance in the emotional response — on both sides — to the question of bilingualism, which indicates that there is more going on here than appears on the surface. In the minds of the "English Only" proponents, English is under siege and must be preserved and protected by a fortress of laws decreeing English to be the official language. Without this protection the United States is in danger of becoming a Tower of Babel. The common language of English is the glue holding the diverse American society together.

Opponents of the move to make English the official language believe it is not language that binds us together, but our common beliefs in democratic principles. Among those principles is the freedom of speech and expression. Language, then, is the vehicle of freedom of expression, and speakers should not be restricted to a second, less-proficient tongue. Opponents also dispute the idea of English under siege with facts pointing to both the continued dominance of English in the U.S. and its growing influence as a world language.

If the facts give a different picture of the dominance of English, why do some feel that immigrants represent a threat to the English language? Perhaps it is not the English language that is threatened, but Americans' sense of who they are. Perhaps they see the recent influx of immigrants as a flood that threatens to wash away the American way of life, the American Dream.

Are the attitudes toward language that emerge in the debate over bilingualism tied to attitudes toward speaking and learning foreign languages? It is ironic that we spend so much time, effort, and money trying to teach native English speakers a second language in school at the same time that we spend so much time, effort, and money to insure that immigrants learn English without maintaining or supporting their inherent bilingualism.

What does it mean to speak a foreign language in the United States? It depends on who you are. A native English speaker struggling to learn a second language sees speaking a foreign language as a "laudable," though unnecessary, goal — one with which many Americans choose not to bother. But ... for a native speaker of a language other than English, the first language — a "foreign language" — can be represented as an obstacle holding the speaker back from learning the language of power, English. And those who don't learn English are not "good" Americans.

Monday, April 30, 2001 7:40:01 PM

Sabine remembers having read something from a book she brought along to her homeland on the issue of foreign language in the U.S....some interestingly critical comments ... she wonders where it may be. She shuffles her papers and books in search of it ... while she is looking for it, she comes across a note stuck in the pages of a book she is leafing through, which says: "At the end of an article, let it marinate for three or four months, in a drawer. Then, as visiting an old friend, go and visit it some night and see the journey you've taken in its absence" (Freire, 2000). She recognizes her own handwriting in the note. Interestingly, Freire's words are translated into English. She asks herself what the original in Portuguese might be like. Anyway, Freire's thought makes her draw the parallel with her personal history: being back home after so long, she sees her homeland as an old friend who she hasn't seen in a long time ... This makes her think about what might be inherently "local" in her identity. Being back home is like traveling back to this identity, which was seemingly forgotten, but which she realizes, is so entrenched into her ways of being ... She continues running her eyes over the book ... there! Yes, it is certainly related to what they have been talking about.

Hi, Gloria,

This is very true, and seems to resonate with something that I read in an article the other day in which John Ogbu (1988) writes:

> [T]he liberal rhetoric of language-as-resource for the 21st century perpetuates the entrenched myth of foreign language learning as an elite endeavor: mastery of a second language is presented as a desirable cultural capital (Bourdieu, 1982) to equip majority English speakers for the challenges of a competitive market, while the bilingualism of minority speakers is treated as a hindrance to academic and socioeconomic success, or as an unnecessary and unrealistic effort in a caste-regulated distribution of jobs in the corporate economy. (Ortega, 1999, p. 24)

This has a lot to do with what we've been talking about, don't you think? And it adds this perspective that foreign language learning is seen as an elite endeavor — this is very much so in Brazil, too.

Your thought that in the United States monolingualism is a disease only when the language spoken is not English is really thought-provoking. It is very true. English monolingual speakers are not usually considered as diseased. Non-English speakers are seen as lacking. I certainly feel this way in some instances of graduate-school life. I know that in some instances of grad school life I lack the cultural capital that comes along with being a native English speaker in academia. Like you said, it's like intelligence equals linguistic ability. It seems very easy to blend these two variables together. Moreover, my identity as a non-native speaker is revealed in my accented English. I remember we talked about accents earlier. Although I don't want to erase my accent (and can't do it, however hard I should try) because in it is my identity, it also represents my outsiderness. Maybe I am not an outsider of the hegemonic discourse, since I am a middle-class, white woman, who is a graduate student in the U.S. with mastery of the English language (not flawlessly, though), but still, my accent otherizes me. This example illustrates that accents are also semiotically interpreted — accents are laden with meaning. Any thoughts on this?

Tuesday, May 1, 2001 5:23:21 PM

Dear Sabine,

It seems you are saying that one can have the knowledge or understanding to gain access to a discourse, but an accent will still identify one as an outsider. That has certainly been my experience as well. When I speak German, it is obvious that I am not a native speaker. Most Germans can also identify my accent as that of an American. The native speaker's reaction to my identity as an American seems to be as much influenced by the images of Americans in the mind of the speaker as by anything I say or do. At the time I was a student in Germany, "Amis" (Americans) were not politically popular with many people, especially students. That first experience living in another culture gave me an awareness that my identity abroad was not just my own individual representation. I had a corporate identity as well — I was an American. As a speaker of American English, I symbolized the United States, the American culture, and American politics. All that was wrong with the U.S. and all that was right were embodied in me. Before I left for Germany with the group of students who would be spending the year abroad, the president of the university called us into his office. He wanted to impress upon us that we would be representing the United States during our study abroad. I thought it was a ridiculous notion. (I particularly disliked the idea of representing a U.S. president with whom I strongly disagreed.) Ridiculous or not, the notion was valid. In my later stay in France, in my travels throughout Europe, Israel, and Japan, and in my more recent visits to Germany with my students, I still feel that my identity extends beyond my personal identity as Gloria. I am viewed first as an American. The stereotyping of identity occurs with other nationalities as well, of course. We talk about the folly of seeing culture as monolithic, but it seems to be a human tendency to distill the essence of a culture into one person when that person is an outsider.

In my interactions with others while abroad, once the relationship moved beyond that superficial stereotyped identity and became an exchange between two individuals, the use of language became perhaps even more important. I think, in that respect, being a non-native speaker was more difficult for me in France than in Germany. I knew little French when I arrived and began attending French classes for foreigners. It had been so long since I had to start over learning a language that I had forgotten what hard work it was...and how stupid it could make me feel. It was also in France where I felt most inadequate in speaking a foreign language. More than once a native French speaker snickered at my clumsy pronunciation and struggles with vocabulary. For a foreign language teacher (though of another language), this identity created by my flawed language, an identity of an inarticulate, uncomprehending, bumbling foreigner, was certainly not the way I wanted to be viewed. I've recently read in Danesi (1999) that discourse "provides resources for presenting the self to a social audience" (p. 80). I wonder what kind of self is presented through speaking a foreign language. Are we always able to present the self we want to, or think we are? Or does speaking a foreign language, and the accent that usually goes with it, present an unintended self? How does that affect the interpretation/meaning which the listener takes away from the conversation?

Wednesday, May 2, 2001 12:02:43 AM

As Sabine reflects upon Gloria's message, her own experiences come to mind. Hmm...interesting remarks and questioning, she thinks to herself. The experience of living in the U.S. and speaking English on a daily basis often made her think how that may affect the way she presents herself to people...or what assumptions people make of her. Because she doesn't have the same range of vocabulary, the same automaticity with the language as native speakers do, she feels she is much more aware of herself in this foreign language environment. At the beginning, she used to pay attention to every word she said and to what kind of reaction it would produce. Would she be able to convey the message she wanted? As time went by, this concern became less apparent, but she still asks herself whether she presents herself differently when she speaks her native language. Sabine begins to write...

Hi Gloria,

I've also been thinking a lot about the issue of identity and communicating in a foreign language since I got to the U.S. two and a half years ago. I've always asked myself how my identity changes (or does it?) when I am communicating in English, or how I am perceived differently as a person when I speak English. In a way, I feel like I am wearing a different costume (to avoid the usual expression "wear a different mask"), because I think that not only our face changes, but the whole body seems to be entrenched in this mechanism of communicating in a language that is not as much a part of our "automatic" repertoire as our native language is (that's why the metaphor 'costume' comes to my mind).

Although I believe that intense and painstaking practice with the foreign language can give one this automaticity, I've wondered whether this can be achieved in the language class without immersion in the environment where the language is spoken or without long daily hours of practice with a native speaker of the language. The example of a bilingual marriage comes to my mind. In my personal example, the foreign language class certainly gave me the tools to be able to live in an English-speaking environment with ease. However, I've felt that, when it comes to having to express myself in a situation when the language is not controlled as it is in the language class, I've faltered. The language class is undoubtedly a safe environment for language practice. When it comes, though, to delving deeply into the universe of the speakers of that language in a full-fledged way, I've asked myself where all those years of foreign language instruction back home went...or to what extent language practice in the classroom can equip one with an understanding of the nuances of complexity that are inherent in human experience and that can sometimes be translated into language. Maybe a possible answer to this question is that there is only so much that instruction itself can do. After all, what else can it do for you than show you the way and give you the sense of how complex this process is, infusing one with the need to go further? Learning a foreign language is certainly more than just words; it involves one's identity, the whole body, the discourse code, and even one's "habitus" (Bourdieu, 1998) and world view. What might be the implications of this understanding for foreign language education, do you think?

Thursday, May 3, 2001 4:23:53 PM

Sabine,

While thinking about the implications of our discussion for foreign language education, I went back to Danesi and read again what he has to say about the "discourse code." You may remember he described it as enabling people to know what to say to whom and when and how to say it. Though this aspect of language learning, the "pragmatics" of languages, is important, I think our discussions about the inseparable intertwining of language and culture point us in the direction of a broader view. What is this bigger picture, and how do we teach it?

Friday, May 4, 2001 5:12:08 PM

Gloria,

You touched on very important points. Teaching the pragmatics of a foreign language is an important, though neglected, issue. However, lately I have been thinking a lot about the need to go further and to focus on wider societal issues, too, in the language class. The claim that "because language is never neutral, learning it cannot and should not be either" (Ibrahim, 1999, p. 349) seems very pertinent, and has been inhabiting my thoughts heavily. In my country (and I would dare to say, in most developing countries), the curricula adopted by most EFL programs and textbooks seem to place a big emphasis on the development of linguistic skills work, with the major goal being the learners' acquisition of 'communicative competence' (Hymes, 1974). Regrettably, no attempt is made at promoting reflection on a more sociopolitical domain vis-à-vis foreign language learning and teaching or on the sociocultural context of education. I think this may work at perpetuating elitist views of EFL education in Brazil and at reproducing common sensical views of what it means to speak English as a Foreign Language in my country. As I mentioned in an earlier email, according to Pennycook (1994) the English language is widely and passively seen as a vehicle for development, democracy, capitalism, and modernization, and this view ignores the need to question whether it embodies a discourse of domination. In referring to the teaching of English as a foreign language, Pierce (1989) rightfully claims that, "if we wish to be part of a discourse that opens up possibilities for students, we need a more powerful theory than that of communicative competence to inform our teaching" (p. 407). She goes on to say that if we, as educators, want students to be able to "explore what might be desirable" (p. 409), we need to go beyond language *per se* and consider how it is part of a complex tapestry of social, cultural, and political phenomena. I wonder how feasible you think it is to propose a more critical curriculum in the foreign language class. By "critical," I mean a curriculum that challenges students' certainties as to what the target language culture(s)/ speaker(s) may be like, and as to students' own roles in society.

Saturday, May 5, 2001 11:17:37 PM

It is late when Gloria reads the most recent conversation from Sabine, but she decides to respond. She will be driving to Minneapolis the following day and won't be back until Monday night. Gloria checks her calendar ... in the box for the 7th she sees in black ink "Peace Corps interview."

She turns her attention to Sabine's sentences on the screen in front of her ... a discussion of critical curriculum. It's an idea that Gloria wrestles to understand. In her own school experiences as a language learner and her training as a foreign language teacher, a critical view of the sociocultural and political implications of language was never a topic of discussion. More recent reading and discussions were nudging her to examine such ideas. Dialoging with Sabine about "a critical curriculum" would perhaps help Gloria to clarify her own thoughts. Could such lofty intentions be translated into the reality of high school foreign language teaching? Or is a critical curriculum only grist for academic debate?

Hello, Sabine,

There are two strands of thought related to the idea of a critical curriculum (I think) that seem to me contradictory. Perhaps they're not; I'm having trouble sorting them out. On the one hand, ESL and EFL curriculum materials have been criticized as promoting a "hidden agenda" of the dominant culture's values and ideology. I have the impression that those concerned about the "hidden curriculum" would like to strip the materials of all cultural content. At the same time, others (such as Norton) assert that language teaching must go beyond mere communicative competence and look at the sociocultural context. I strongly agree with your quote from Ibrahim. Both language and language learning are not neutral. How can one teach the bones of a foreign language and ignore the flesh of the culture? As a learner of foreign languages, I *want* to explore the values of the people who speak the language as revealed through the language and the materials of that culture. I don't want to learn German from a textbook that has either been scrubbed of its cultural context (if that were possible) or adapted to my values. What do I learn about the language in all its fullness from that? The danger comes from being unaware of all those cultural, social, and political factors that give language its meaning (or multiple meanings). This is where the critical approach fits in. I think it seeks to make the hidden agenda visible ... like showing us the wires making the marionette dance.

But is it feasible in the foreign language classroom? In a high school classroom, short on time and resources, with teachers who may lack the necessary training (I'm not confident that I have the necessary background), it wouldn't be easy. And then there's the question of what language to use — the students' native language (allowing more self-expression) or the target language (encouraging meaningful, but perhaps limited, use of the language). But shouldn't we try...at least to some extent? I'm curious to know how you would try to incorporate a critical approach in teaching foreign languages.

Monday, May 14, 2001 6:14 PM

Hi, Gloria.

Sorry it's taken so long for me to respond to your question. I was away in the mountains... winter is beginning to take hold here, so all those sweaters are back to the closet. I imagine you must be enjoying the beautiful Wisconsin spring now...

In responding, I wish to say that I, too, have been wrestling with the idea of implementing a more critical perspective in the EFL class. Sometimes I don't think I've been sufficiently trained to do it, and sometimes I am not sure myself about what I understand by a critical perspective, and on top of it I've been puzzled at how an understanding of it could be translated into the language class. Enough "what's" and "ifs," huh? It's not been long since I started thinking about these issues. I think a nice way of incorporating a "critical" approach is to start working with the materials we have (like textbooks, for example) but to look at them in a different way. Undoubtedly, it has to be started by the teacher. For example, we could look at a unit or a textbook and ask ourselves questions such as: Who is the activity designed for (a white, middle class, young audience? If so, why?) What signs help me decide (topic choice, characters displayed, vocabulary choice, for example)? Who is included, and who is excluded in this activity? How realistically is the topic being treated? What kinds of assumptions may the learner be led to develop unconsciously about the target "languaculture" through this activity? Of course these are just some examples of questions that come to my mind right now. Only after the teacher has engaged in reflection about the "underlying agenda" of the material can s/he invite the students to think critically about it (following a similar process to the one s/he went through) and to relate it to wider society issues.

A second suggestion would be the incorporation of "non-traditional" reading texts, such as readings by non-native speakers of the language in the target language (to deconstruct the myth of the native speaker's ownership of the language), or texts that deal with problematic aspects of the target "languaculture," such as immigration issues, discrimination issues, and so on. I think this approach may help learners understand that language learning does not stand in a social vacuum, and that the target "languaculture" should be seen in a more realistic, less idealized way.

Monday, May 14, 2001 11: 30: 49 PM

Hi, Sabine,

You have made some excellent suggestions, but I have to ask myself if my students would be able to approach the issues in the manner you described. How does the teacher prepare the students to think critically if they have had little practice? Also, such discussions require a fairly proficient language level if the discussions are to be conducted in the target language. I think that could present problems, don't you?

Tuesday, May 15, 2001 10:00:38 AM

Gloria,

Of course there is the concern about the learners' linguistic ability and their readiness to deal with such issues. However, if we start implementing this critical view early on, students' familiarity with these issues may be enhanced, as well as an appropriate lexicon to tackle them. I think it's important to fight the idea that the target language is a monolith and to confront stereotypical views about its speakers and practices. I see the language class as a good setting for the discussion of issues related to identity, ethnicity, race, gender, sexual orientation, minority, discrimination, and many other relevant topics for our "modern" and "globalized" societies. If not in the language class, where? If not now, when? Language, as we discussed earlier, functions as a carrier for our social representations and for our meaning-making processes, as much as all these topics do. I also think that the language class could be the appropriate place to encourage students to draw parallels between the target culture and their own "languaculture," not in order to establish which one is "better" or "worse," but because it seems to me that if students are given the opportunity to reflect upon their own situation, they may be better prepared to tackle the material in the foreign language at a deeper level. Kramsch supports this notion by maintaining that, "if they [the students] have not reflected on their own culture in a critical manner, they cannot appreciate the differences when presented only with the foreign cultural facts" (Schultz, 1990, p. 175). Does this make sense to you? Do you think these are feasible suggestions, or do you see any obstacles for their implementation?

Wednesday, May 16, 2001 10:24:17 PM

Greetings, Sabine,

We could talk about the obstacles to implementation of your suggestions ... there are always obstacles to change. But maybe it comes down to one question: What is the purpose of foreign language education? We've touched upon many possible answers. Learning a foreign language can be an endeavor for the elite ... a badge of status. For the non-elite, does it promise the key to a better life, maybe even to the American Dream? For the economic warriors competing globally, do we sell foreign languages as a weapon? Can knowing a foreign language open windows to other points of view and challenge the myth of monolithic culture? Is it a bridge for intercultural understanding? Or does it represent the imposition of one dominant culture on another culture?

For me, knowing a foreign language (even imperfectly) connects me to other people in a way that I wouldn't have otherwise. It gives me a tool to communicate with others, to experience another culture, and maybe to increase my understanding of the global community. I agree with you that the foreign language classroom should be a place where students reflect on their own culture as well as on the target culture. If the purpose of foreign language education is to create connections between people, then we should foster students who think critically about the globalized world and their place in it. I'd say we have our work cut out for us.

In closing, I just want to share some exciting personal news with you. I'm taking some time off from my teaching position to return to school. I start graduate school in the fall. Maybe our paths will cross.

Ate mais (I hope),

Gloria

Madison, Wisconsin, May 2001

Two women sit at a table on the sidewalk outside a café, delighting in the unexpectedly warm weather, the soothingly cool drinks and the chance to once again enjoy one another's company face-to-face. The conversation wanders over many topics, then turns to an assignment for a class they share. They talk about writing a paper together...maybe as an email conversation.

Acknowledgments

We would like to express our gratitude to François Tochon, who challenged us to explore other avenues of educational research and guided us through the process of writing this chapter. We would also like to thank the members of the seminar for their valuable feedback on our paper and for the sense of community that they helped to build, both of which were essential to the completion of this project.

Minority Languages in the Classroom: Promise becomes Possibility

Elizabeth R. Miller

Introduction

Research on bilingual education indicates that when linguistic minority students receive classroom instruction in their own languages, they usually learn English better as well (Genesee, 1987; Cummins, 1989; Faltis & Hudelson, 1998). Cummins' (Genesee, 1987) pithy statement that "less equals more" points to findings showing that linguistic minority students who early on receive less academic instruction in English, but more in their own languages, tend to learn more English in the long run because they have been allowed to participate meaningfully in academic activities throughout their school experiences. However, Cummins (2000) does not advocate withholding instruction in English from linguistic minority students. Rather, he insists that instruction in both languages is essential. While adopting a similar perspective on bilingual instruction, Macedo (1994b) warns that education for linguistic minority students dare not be reduced to teaching them to speak English. Advocating a radical pedagogical approach that he claims is consistent with the ideals of a democratic education, Macedo argues students must be allowed to draw on their own realities, including using their own languages, in the classroom.

In the multilingual microcosm of Mr. Agnew's classroom, I noted that much of its interactional life seemed to align with the notions presented by Cummins (2000) and Macedo (1994b). Mr. Agnew provided American civics instruction in English which was then translated into students' own languages, and students were allowed to speak their languages freely in the classroom, both for social and academic purposes. But I also sensed a growing ambivalence towards the dynamics of this sheltered classroom as I began to notice that use of students' native languages did not necessarily translate into recognition of or respect for their cultures and linguistic identities. Although students' minority languages were heard, it seemed to me that they themselves were rarely heard. This was not because Mr. Agnew is a mean-spirited person. Students like him and colleagues respect him. However, despite the use of minority languages in the classroom, it seemed that English language skills remained the most valued and a mainstream American cultural model prevailed. The apparent inferiority that was assigned to alternative languages and cultures is particularly troubling given Macedo's (1994b) and Cummins' (1989, 2000) insistence that power relations in the broader society, reproduced in the local classroom environment, may be the most significant factor in leading to linguistic minority students' underachievement. Not only were these broader power relations not interrogated in Mr. Agnew's class, but it seemed they were reproduced there.

Even so, I observed incipient signs of how the active presence of students' native languages can lead to challenging "the discourse of superiority...[of] the wider society" (Cummins 2000, p. 10). Macedo (1994b) argues that "educators have failed to recognize the 'positive' promise and antagonistic nature of the minority language" (p. 133) when it is spoken in the classroom. Thus, while one can readily find fault with an education system that seems stalled in reproducing status quo power relations rather than creating emancipatory interactions, I find hope in discovering that even a minimal bid toward accommodating minority languages in a classroom holds "'positive' promise" for its students. I do not want to suggest that we should settle for such minimal accommodations and ignore the need for radical pedagogical interactions which can facilitate changing existing social structures more directly. Rather, I will attempt to explore how it is possible for this "'positive' promise and antagonistic nature" to exist in a classroom environment where it seems unlikely to prosper. Pennycook (2001) argues that resorting to broad critical analysis often results in overwhelming pessimism concerning possibilities for social transformation. However, by focusing on a microanalysis of interactions in Mr. Agnew's sheltered civics classroom, we can uncover not only the reproduction of macro power relations at the local level but also the potential and active power of the micro relations for resisting and transforming these larger systems.

The classroom data collection was part of a five-year longitudinal study[1] in which the research team visited Jefferson High School[2] twice a week, videotaping and recording field notes. In addition to collecting classroom data, they conducted informal and occasional formal interviews with the teachers as well as focus group interviews with the students and collected written responses to questionnaires from students. Since I was not a member of the on-site research team, my access to Mr. Agnew's classroom comes from my close viewing of the classroom video recordings as well as immersion in the extensive documentation provided by members of the on-site team.

Students Use their Own Languages

Most mornings, students streamed into their third-period American civics classroom chatting in Hmong and Lao and some English. Since Mr. Agnew regularly participated in the school-wide morning announcements, he was not in the room for the first few minutes of class. However, Mr. Tong and Ms. Li, the adult translators, were there taking attendance and answering individual students' questions. As the students settled into their desks, arranged in rows facing the front of the room, those students who were the most recent arrivals to the United States found their assigned seats in the two rows by the windows. Mr. Agnew had seated these students together allowing Mr. Tong and Ms. Li to direct their translation talk to that side of the room.

The class was populated predominantly by Hmong students, but there were also several Lao students, a few Thai students, and several Spanish-English bilingual students. The Spanish-English bilingual students were in Mr. Agnew's class at the request of adult family members who taught at Jefferson High School and who liked Mr. Agnew's teaching style. Although the school had a large bilingual program for the majority Hispanic student population, the much smaller Asian population (about 5 percent) had fewer options: they could attend ESL classes or they could attend "mainstream" classes taught solely in English. The year Mr. Agnew taught the civics class, he was the only teacher providing sheltered classes for the school's Hmong and Lao students, and he claimed the only reason the program still existed was because he "went down and fought for it" with the school's administration (Interview).

I was delighted to find that students' minority languages had a strong presence in this class community. I saw students freely using their first languages when chatting with friends. If they felt uncomfortable asking questions in English, they could direct their questions to Mr. Tong or Ms. Li. Students smiled and sometimes laughed when they heard Mr. Agnew draw from his limited repertoire of Hmong phrases. For example, he frequently checked for understanding after ending a topic or definition by using the Hmong word *totau* meaning "understand" in his English instructional talk. He claimed one reason he used Hmong words and phrases in his lessons was so that students would hear him "butcher" the Hmong language, laugh about it, and realize that it is okay to be an imperfect speaker of a language (Interview).

The most striking characteristic of this civics class, and the feature that earned it the label "sheltered," was the translation talk provided by Mr. Tong and Ms. Li. In the brief example of translation talk shown in Excerpt 1 below, Mr. Agnew had just finished a review of the three branches of American government, ending with the judicial branch. As a way of providing an example of a crime over which the judicial branch has power, he produced a participant example (Wortham, 1994) in which he described Ms. Li as making counterfeit money in her basement. After soliciting and confirming students' responses in identifying the kind of crime Ms. Li, as counterfeiter, was guilty of (lines 1-4), Mr. Agnew glanced down at his textbook. Ms. Li took the brief one-second pause as a signal that it was her turn to begin translating, and the classroom talk smoothly transitioned from English to Hmong (lines 5 ff.). I observed that students treated this change in linguistic code matter-of- factly; most did not even bother to look up from their books as Ms. Li began speaking. What seemed novel to me was an everyday feature of classroom life for them. (Italics signal that the talk was originally produced in Hmong.)

Excerpt 1

1 Agnew: Now what kind of crime did we say that was?
2 Ivon: Federal.
3 Fernando: Federal.
4 Agnew: Federal, right? That's a federal crime.

Brief pause during which Mr. Agnew looks down at his textbook.

Li moves towards the front of the room and immediately begins translating into Hmong.

5 Li: *He is reviewing the things we covered yesterday about*
6   *the tree that is divided into three branches.* The legis-
7   *lative comes from the congress...*

I noticed a second translation routine commence during Ms. Li's Hmong instruction when Phancha nudged her desk towards Anong's and began translating in Lao. (A third Lao student, Khammay, joined the class and the Lao translation group in the second semester.) Phancha was a senior and had been at the school since junior high, longer than any of the other Asian students in the room. Although she too was a student, because of her strong oral English proficiency, she had been recruited by Mr. Agnew to provide Lao translations to Anong. Phancha seemed to have favored status with Mr. Agnew and the adult translators because of her role as student translator. I noticed several occasions when Mr. Tong or Ms. Li completed their Hmong translation talk before Phancha finished translating for Anong, and Mr. Agnew waited for her to end before re-launching into his English instruction.

Seamless as Ms. Li's transition into Hmong translation talk appears in Excerpt 1, the translation talk was not without its complications. Not surprisingly, there were times when there were no available words in Hmong or Lao that would precisely correlate with American civics terms. For example, in the interaction shown in Excerpt 2 below, Mr. Tong was explaining the economic concepts of supply and demand in Hmong. He had just finished demonstrating this economic system by using the example of the low prices for papaya "over there" (in Thailand or Laos) where the supply is plentiful compared to the high prices for papaya in the Midwest where the fruit must be imported. One student, Choua, questioned the Hmong words on their vocabulary list which did not match the English terms exactly (line 5) and then asked if the words should be translated together (line 9). Mr. Tong confirmed that that is what they must do and went on to explain that they (Hmong speakers) do not have words like supply and demand (lines 10 ff.) and that they must understand the concepts through the examples he and Mr. Agnew provided. Again, the words in italics indicate they were spoken in Hmong.

Excerpt 2

1 Tong: *These are important things, supply and demand.*
2 Mai: (unintelligible question)
3 Tong: *They are the same.*

4	Tong:	*It's the demand, the usage.*
5	Choua:	*This word here translates as "not enough."*
6	Tong:	*That demand here?*
7	Choua:	Uh huh.
8	Tong:	*This demand is like having-*
9	Choua:	*Do you translate it together?*
10	Tong:	Translate it together. *We don't have words like that.*
11		*You should remember that we give examples be-*
12		*cause we want you guys to understand what he*
13		*meant. Sometimes there are words that we don't*
14		*have to translate into, but we give examples so that*
15		*you understand. For example, if the price of rice*
16		*rises, you buy it anyway right?*

In addition to the instructional talk in students' first languages, I observed that Mr. Agnew's classroom provided a space for students to receive help for their other classes. At the beginning of class and often during the morning announcements, I frequently noticed Mr. Tong and Ms. Li kneeling beside a student's desk, offering homework assistance for one of the student's other mainstream classes. Mr. Tong noted that they came to him and Ms. Li for help in all their classes. He added, "And if I can't help them, then I say, well, then you have to go talk to the teacher. And then they say, 'Mr. Tong, I can't ask her (with emphasis) because she won't understand,' and I say, 'You try.' That's all we can say, 'You try'" (Interview).

Thus, initial observations of the linguistic activity in Mr. Agnew's classroom suggest that students' languages were granted space and time, and that students could feel linguistically at ease in this environment. Indeed, students in Mr. Agnew's class seemed to appreciate the linguistic accommodations made for them. Responding to a questionnaire asking them why they chose to attend Jefferson High School, several of them indicated it was because the school had special programs that helped them. A few mentioned the school's ESL classes and access to a Hmong aide. One student added that because "lots of Asians go there, you don't have to feel bad about yourself." Furthermore, in an interview, Mr. Tong commented that in his years of working at Jefferson High, he found Mr. Agnew to be one of the best teachers in the school to work with Asian students.

Distorted Legitimation of English

While students were free to use their own languages, they regularly heard Mr. Agnew's English instruction and read English texts (along with written vocabulary translations for them to study in conjunction with their English texts). The goal, after all, was to transition students into mainstream English classrooms (Genesee, 1987; Faltis & Hudelson, 1998). In an interview, Mr. Agnew showed his alignment to this well-accepted goal:

I don't believe students should be in ESL or bilingual classes from cradle to the grave. That's detrimental to them. My goal is actually to get them mainstreamed as soon as possible. Some of the kids can handle mainstreaming faster than others due to the nature of their personalities. Other kids may be more ready with the English language, but socially they haven't internalized it; the socialization process hasn't given them enough self confidence, and what else have you, to go into a regular class yet.

Mr. Tong, the Hmong and Lao translator added his support to this view in a separate interview. He remarked:

We try to help them use more English in the classroom. Even with the bathroom, they always ask me when they have to go to the bathroom. At the beginning, they would come to me and say, 'Mr. Tong, can you write me the pass to go to the bathroom?' And then I would talk to Mr. Agnew and say, 'You know, they have to ask you and you should tell them that too.' And that's what we've been doing. And it's helped a little bit and in time it will help.

While Macedo (1994b) supports the teaching of standard English to linguistic minority students in order for them to be "linguistically empowered" (p. 128), he warns that students' own languages should never be silenced by a "distorted legitimation of the standard English language" (p. 128). In observing Mr. Agnew's classroom, I began to notice subtle ways in which English, the default mode of instructional talk, was positioned as holding greater cultural capital (Bourdieu, 1991) than the other frequently heard minority languages. For example, during Mr. Agnew's English instruction, everyone listened (or at least there was no other authorized talk). By contrast, during Mr. Tong's or Ms. Li's Hmong translation talk, other simultaneous talk was common and ratified. Phancha's Lao translation talk could be heard, and students frequently used these interactional spaces as opportunities to ask Mr. Agnew questions in English, usually by motioning him to their desks but sometime by voicing their questions loudly across the room. Just as frequently, students used these times to engage in social interactions. I could regularly observe a group of Hmong girls near the door giggling with each other, sometimes passing candy among themselves, and nearly always chatting together in Hmong. Even though their social talk was usually conducted in Hmong, the fact that they could use the translation spaces to indulge in social talk allowed them to display themselves as participants in the classroom English talk and not as dependent on the translations.

I observed a more transparent case of the "distorted legitimation" of English in Mr. Agnew's classroom on a test review day. Fragments from this extended seven-minute interaction are presented in Excerpts 3 and 4. In this interaction, Mr. Agnew demanded that May voice a request to him in English. May was one of the Hmong students seated by the windows whose English proficiency was quite low, and I had never seen her participate verbally in the English classroom talk before. She asked Ms. Li a question about their upcoming test and Ms. Li redirected the question to Mr. Agnew although she refrained from uttering the request herself, choosing instead to frame it as a question from several of the students (lines 1-2). Mr. Agnew expressed willingness to entertain the question (lines 3-4) and hearing May utter her question in Hmong (line 5), he seized the moment as an opportunity for May to speak some English (lines 6-7). However, he did so playfully, uttering his demands in Hmong, perhaps to exhibit his own willingness to take the risk of speaking in another language. Students responded with laughter to Mr. Agnew's Hmong usage and urged May to make her request in English. However, she resisted and begged to say it in Hmong (lines 8-9). She finally voiced her request (lines 12-14) to have Mr. Agnew write their essay question on the board in advance of the test so that the students could prepare for it—however, she did so in Hmong and not English. Finally, Mr. Agnew shrugged his shoulders and commented to Ms. Li that the students do not want to talk (line 17) even though talking was occurring at full volume all around him. He must have meant that they did not want to talk in English. Again, the italicized words indicate Hmong speech that has been translated into English.

Excerpt 3

1 Li:	I don't know about the whole class, but I guess part of
2	the class wants to say something.
3 Agnew:	Well sure, you want to talk to me? We can take time.
4	What do you want to ask?
5 May:	(unintelligible)
6 Agnew:	(With a smile and looking directly at May.) *Speak English only. Don't understand.*

Students laugh at Mr. Agnew's use of Hmong. There is a lot of simultaneous chatter among students in Hmong.

| 7 Agnew: | *Don't understand. Speak English only. Right now.* |

More laughter and chatter among students.

8 May:	(To other Hmong students.) *Stop that. Just let me*
9	*say it in Hmong.*
10 Li:	*You guys just mention it and I will help you.*
11 Agnew:	Well, who wants to talk?
12 May:	*Later...tell him that if we are going to be tested, then*
13	*he should write out the essay question, so when to-*
14	*morrow comes, we know what to write.*
15 Agnew:	(To May) What do you want to say?
16 ?Female:	*Just tell him to write it out on the board.*

Volume of classroom chatter rises.

| 17 Agnew: | (Looks at Ms. Li and shrugs.) They don't want to talk. |

The classroom chatter, mostly in Hmong, continued for several minutes. Even though other students relayed May's request to Mr. Agnew, he refused to accept it from them and focused good-naturedly but adamantly on the need for May to produce the request herself and in English (lines 18-19). In fact, he recruited other students to help her and to convince her to do so (lines 21-22, 31). Another student, Mao, whose English proficiency was more advanced than May's, provided a simplified version of May's request (line 27) and enunciated the words slowly and clearly for May to repeat. Finally, after much peer urging, and Mr. Agnew's refusal to give up, May, very quietly, uttered "No essay" (line 34) to which Mr. Agnew responded with "Very good" (line 35) and the class clapped at May's accomplishment.

Excerpt 4

18	Agnew:	Soon as my sweetheart here talks to me in English, I'll
19		make a decision. If she can't talk to me in English—
20	Fernando:	We're screwed.
21	Agnew:	(To the other Hmong students) Okay, so now start
22		talking to her. Convince her.

More chatter, in the middle of which:

23	May:	*You guys tell me to say it but I don't know how to*
24		*say it.*
25	Agnew:	(To May) Mao wants to talk to you.
65	Mao:	(Looking at May and enunciating words slowly
27		and clearly.) Please don't give us essay.
28	Li:	*May, if you say it, say that.*
29	May:	*Say it, how do I say it?*
30	Li:	*Just say what Mao just said.*
31	Agnew:	Listen. Shh, please tell her again.
32	Mao:	Please don't give us essay (again slowly and clearly).
33		*Just say no essay, only like that.*

Finally, after continued urging and prompting, with all eyes focused on her:

34	May:	No essay. (Very quietly)
35	Agnew:	Very good.
36	Ivon:	Yeah.

Whole class claps.

In the lighthearted, noisy classroom incident displayed above, I observed May receiving a lot of encouragement in Hmong and direct English dictations from her peers for uttering her request. Much laughter was heard, especially at Mr. Agnew's own inept use of Hmong. And yet, in this seemingly lighthearted talk, May's inability to speak English became the focus of all eyes in the classroom. Her very quiet two-word English utterance "No essay" bore little resemblance to her earlier Hmong request to have Mr. Agnew write their essay question on the board. In fact, the propositional content of her request was rendered inconsequential. What did become all important was that she say something, anything, in English. As mentioned previously, this was the only time I observed May participating in the English classroom talk. Thus, her most public identity in the class was marked by her language deficit. That it was this English-deficit identity which was salient seemed to be confirmed when I noted that Mr. Agnew walked from

May's desk, following her vocalization of "no essay" to Anong's desk and said, "Your turn." Like May, Anong never participated in the English classroom talk and appeared to have by far the lowest English proficiency of the three Lao students in the class. Mr. Agnew seemed to suggest by choosing Anong to repeat May's performance that it was high time these students produced some English. Anong offered a whispered "No essay" while looking down at her desk. Phancha, who was sitting beside her, said to Mr. Agnew, "Yeah, I heard her too," and Mr. Agnew walked away, undoubtedly pleased that he had "encouraged" these two young women, with the help of their classmates, to display that they could speak a little English.

But this was hardly an empowering moment for either of the female students. In fact, much later in the class session, I observed Ms. Li interrupting Mr. Agnew's English instruction, a very unusual move for her, and she requested that he allow Mr. Tong to clarify the decision the class came to concerning the format of their essay exam, brought on by May's request concerning the essay question (see Excerpt 5, lines 1-7). Both she and Mr. Tong explained to May the agreement several of the most vocal of the students came to with Mr. Agnew to have only one essay question on the exam instead of two (although not written on the board in preparation for the exam as May requested). Ms. Li then appeared to try to ameliorate May's embarrassment by reassuring her, in Hmong, that Mr. Agnew was only joking with her (lines 12-13).

Excerpt 5

1	Li:	Mr. Agnew, I'm just going to have Mr. Tong explain
2		what you just explained about the test (although it has
3		been some minutes since Mr. Agnew finished explain-
4		ing that he would compromise on the exam by includ-
5		ing only one essay question on the test). Because you
6		asked her to speak, and she spoke, and you're still
7		giving her her essay, so just so that she understands.
8	Agnew:	Explain the compromise, okay? Rather than get two
9		essays, now she only has one, and that's because I love
10		her.

Students laugh. Mr. Tong and Ms. Li both take turns in explaining the test to May in Hmong.

11	Tong:	Okay, she's fine with it Mr. Agnew.
12	Li:	*Hey, May, you know that he's like that, that is why*
13		he likes to joke with you.
14	Agnew:	Okay, you all set now? All right, next word.

Although it is hard to deny that May's life in the United States will undoubtedly be better if she learns English, I am bothered by Mr. Agnew's public demand that she utter her request in English and his refusal to accept it when voiced in Hmong in the local microcosm of the classroom. Mr. Agnew's own imperfect use of Hmong in no way endangered his status in the classroom. Indeed, one can argue that Mr. Agnew's use of Hmong is a "strategy of condescension," described by Bourdieu (1991) as a means of accruing greater social capital even as one appears to close the gap between higher and lower rankings in the social hierarchy by adopting the language of those with a lower social ranking. Mr. Agnew's dominant position in the classroom microcosm was secure, mostly because of his position as teacher but also because of his native proficiency in English. For him, risking poorly spoken Hmong in the classroom had no negative consequences since the Hmong language carried no real cultural capital—not even in a classroom where minority languages ostensibly were valued.

In considering May's situation the day Mr. Agnew insisted that she speak English, I find it interesting to read Cummins' (1989) words on students' "internalization of shame" with respect to their languages and cultures (p. 58). He insists that covert shaming may be more devastating than the overt punishment that was doled out by early American public school educators any time students spoke their own languages in school. Cummins suggests that "institutionalized racism...hidden behind the genuine efforts of well-intentioned educators" contributes to the disempowerment of students (p. 59). More significant, perhaps, is his insistence that linguistic minority students will succeed in school only to the degree that the patterns of interaction they encounter in schools are the reverse of those found in society outside of school. Although the students in Mr. Agnew's civics classroom have freedom to speak in their own languages—most of the time—and have access to the course content via their first languages, purportedly granting them equal educational opportunities, the classroom interactions I observed seemed to reinforce in subtle and not-so-subtle ways the larger society's devaluing of their language and its disproportionate legitimating of English.

Cultural Reproduction Not Production

Cummins (2000) notes that educational structures tend to "reflect the priorities of the society," reproducing the relations of power found there (46). Macedo (1994) asserts the same idea, noting that the "status quo functions as a cultural reproduction mechanism that does not allow other cultural subjects, who are considered outside of the mainstream, to be present in history" (p. 125). One way to combat this in educational settings, he argues, is by transforming and producing new meanings, drawing upon the histories, cultures, and languages of linguistic-minority students. Here Macedo and Cummins part ways with many bilingual teachers and theorists. Assimilationist ideologies justify the cultural reproduction model by suggesting that when minorities adapt themselves to the dominant culture, they will be empowered to participate freely and equally in that culture. Assimilationists, therefore, insist that educators must assist linguistic-minority students in gaining access to the dominant culture, largely through learning standard English. However, Macedo and Cummins suggest that this concern for granting minority students access to the dominant culture masks a deep fear by dominant-culture members that their way of life will be threatened if minority-culture members are empowered to bring about social change. Cummins (1989) argues that until linguistic-minority students are encouraged to use their own language and culture to generate their own knowledge, they will continue to fail in disproportionately large numbers in the American academic context.

In my ongoing observations of the classroom interactions in Mr. Agnew's American civics class, I found it disturbingly easy to spot status quo maintenance. For example, in the interaction presented in Excerpt 6, Mr. Agnew introduced a new unit on civil rights and had students repeat the phrase after him (line 3), a vocabulary recitation routine regularly practiced in his class. While admitting to past inequities in American history concerning the right to vote (lines 7-8), Mr. Agnew voiced the commonly accepted textbook description of American democracy, one in which all citizens now share equal power through their shared right to vote (lines 10-19). Implicit in this message of equal voting rights for all citizens is the notion that protesting a lack of social power can be turned back on the protesters: lack of a voice in the American democratic system results when citizens fail to actively participate in it. Mr. Agnew's implicit and explicit message about the constitutionally protected right to vote glossed over the pervasive inequality endemic to American social and political culture. Indeed, the voting irregularities uncovered in Florida (and other states) in the recent 2000 presidential election which are alleged to have prevented a large number of African Americans from casting votes suggest that the right to vote is not always equally shared, not even now.

Excerpt 6

1	Agnew:	We're going to talk about civil rights. Come on, civil
2		rights.
3	Students:	(chorally) Civil rights.
4	Agnew:	A right is something that you are able to do. When we
5		talk about civil rights, it's the right guaranteed to all
6		Americans.

Several minutes later, after describing the meaning of "suffrage" and the fact that early in American history only white males who owned property could vote, Mr. Agnew continues:

7	Agnew:	We said that today anybody—you have to be 18 to vote
8		now— but you can be white, you can be black, you can
9		be Asian, you can be rich, you can be poor, you can be
10		male, you can be female, alright?...So, today, we've
11		made the United States, shall we say, more demo-
12		cratic. It's more equal because in the beginning obvi-
13		ously it wasn't. A few people had that power and that
14		right, but today we all have it. ...The key thing again is
15		to go vote. That's where your power is. Your power is
16		in you going to the polls and voting for who you want
17		to.

Perhaps as unsettling as Mr. Agnew's silence about inequities that persist in American society despite constitutionally protected rights such as suffrage were his appropriations of Asian cultural features into his discussions of American civic life. At first glance, it seemed his frequent lecture examples using artifacts or practices from Asian culture were laudatory in that he attempted to make the classroom talk as relevant to the students' daily lives as possible. However, I began to wonder how benign it was to interpolate an Asian commodity such as egg rolls into a lesson about the American market processes of supply and demand as displayed in Excerpt 7 below. When Mr. Agnew unquestioningly treated artifacts like egg rolls (line 8)—and, by extension, members of the culture—as functioning according to his American understanding of the way the world works (line 1), there was no opportunity granted for an alternative voice to suggest a different understanding of the world. He seemed to assume that like any person the world over, Mai would "pay 50 bucks for an egg roll" if he were desperate enough (lines 25-27), thus allowing Mr. Agnew to establish the universality of the "law of supply and demand" (line 2).

Excerpt 7

1	Agnew:	Alright? This is the entire thing that generates our
2		economic process. The law of supply and demand.
3		Now we're going to take a look at this. There are two
4		parts to this: one is how many you have, and the other
5		is who wants it. Now, let me give you an example. If all
6		of us are in this room and we're going to be here for
7		the next week, and our supply for the week is going to
8		be 10,000 egg rolls to eat.
9	Fernando:	Mmm
10	Agnew:	Is that a lot of egg rolls?
11	Fernando:	No.
12	?Female:	Yeah.
13	Agnew:	I think that's even more than I can eat. So, if we have
14		10,000 egg rolls, I'm going to sell egg rolls for 20 cents
15		a piece, right? Any problem with that?
16	Fernando:	No.
17	Agnew:	No. Will you pay 20 cents a piece for an egg roll to live
18		on? Yes. Now, let's reverse this. We're going to have
19		the same week except now we only have ten egg rolls
20		instead of 10,000. Am I going to sell egg rolls for 20
21		cents a piece?
22	Students:	No.
23	Fernando:	You're going to sell them for a hundred dollars.
24	Agnew:	Because when Mai gets really hungry back there, and
25		he's starving to death, I'm going to say, "Mai, I want 50
26		dollars for an egg roll." Is he going to pay 50 bucks
27		for an egg roll?
28	Fernando:	Sure.
29	Agnew:	Rather than starve? Yeah. Why? That's all there is.
30		The demand is so great and the supply is so low, I can
31		charge a higher price.

By positioning features of these students' Asian cultures within American cultural norms, Mr. Agnew was able to legitimate and *reproduce* the dominant culture's norms and values, in this case a sanitized and simplistic rendering of the capitalistic processes of supply and demand. Furthermore, there was no opportunity provided for critiquing these processes by drawing on students' potentially different perspectives (recall Excerpt 3 in which it became clear that Hmong has no exact translation for supply and demand) or allowing for the possibility of *producing* new meanings. When students' histories and experiences go untapped, potential sources for making new meanings, Cummins (2000) suggests students are "being prepared to accept the societal status quo and their own inferior status therein" (p. 257). He adds that when the curriculum is "sanitized with respect to issues of historical and current power relations, and students are expected to emerge from schooling as 'good citizens' who will comply with the expectations of the societal power structure...[this] makes coercive power structures invisible, thereby reinforcing their discriminatory effect" (p. 256).

Challenging Linguistic Dominance

Despite the concerns one might have at finding yet another example of bilingual education "whose basic assumptions [seem to be] at odds with the democratic spirit that launched [it]" (Macedo, 1994b, p. 134), I find evidence that even here the potential for challenging the dominance of English and dominant social structures is active by virtue of the active presence of minority languages. Although English interactions in Mr. Agnew's classroom continued to dominate the classroom talk throughout the year, and students were afforded few opportunities to challenge the dominance of American culture, by spring semester, I began to notice that several of the Hmong students seated by the windows, Mai and Choua in particular, were participating much more actively in the Hmong translation talk. As a result of their and others' questions and expanded verbal participation, the Hmong talk occasionally took up larger quantities of classroom instructional time than did the English talk.

On one of these, admittedly rare, occasions, as Mr. Tong fielded questions and heard examples from several students about cases of free competition among local Hmong grocery stores, I noticed Mr. Agnew shifting positions while leaning against his desk and then pacing behind his desk. It appears that he had—if only briefly—lost his position as chief arbiter of the classroom culture and language, and he was rendered silent in the face of the noisy Hmong interactions transpiring around him. When Mr. Tong finally signaled the end of the Hmong translation talk, Mr. Agnew quickly uttered, "All right, next word. Let's move along" and announced the students' next vocabulary word. He seemed impatient to continue with his lesson and even slightly ill at ease that the class discussion had continued for an extended period of time without any input from him. It appears that as some of the Hmong students became increasingly comfortable and willing to contribute to the classroom talk in their minority language, Mr. Agnew showed signs of increasing discomfort. Perhaps, the Hmong interactions in this class period as well as on several other occasions in which students and the adult translators extend their interactional space beyond perfunctory translations of Mr. Agnew's English talk signal their potentially "antagonistic nature" to "challenge the privileged standard linguistic dominance" in this local sheltered classroom community (Macedo, 1994b, p. 133).

In fact, in the same class period described above, I was intrigued to find that Mai showed evidence of resisting Mr. Tong's descriptions of the American economic system. As displayed in Excerpt 8, Mr. Agnew provided a description of the terms "economic system" and "economy" (line 1) as "how we buy and sell goods, and how we distribute them in America. In other words, how business is run, how you earn a living" (lines 3-5). By describing an economic system as how things get bought, sold, and distributed, the role of power in the distribution of economic resources is rendered opaque. He did comment that while mangos may be imported from Laos to the United States that did not "mean our stuff is being imported over to Laos for you to have" (not included in the printed excerpt in the interest of saving space). However, Mr. Agnew did not probe that difference in the importing of goods and merely repeated his earlier neutral rendering of an economic system as "how business is run, how you earn a living." Interestingly, Mr. Tong was the one to expand on the differences in economic systems between the United States and Laos in his Hmong translation talk, and noted that American "money is more valuable compared to other nations on the earth" (lines 6-7). He did not divulge explanations for why this might be true other than to note that the U.S. has "more material [resources]" and "people have jobs" (lines 10-14). At that point, Mai appeared to challenge Mr. Tong's explanation for the high value of American money (lines 15-16). Unfortunately, his full comment is indecipherable on the video tape, but we can see that Mr. Tong admitted immediately after Mai's comment that there are other things beside the economy that are important in contributing to this high valuation (lines 17-18).

More interesting and more clearly expressed, however, is Mai's later comment. Following the Hmong interactions focusing on defining "economy," Mr. Tong briefly updated Mr. Agnew that he and the students had also discussed the high value of American currency in comparison to other countries (lines 19-24). To this, Mr. Agnew added that "keef" (Lao currency) is "no good" in the U.S. although the dollar can be used in Laos (lines 25-27). As both Mr. Agnew and Mr. Tong displayed agreement on the dominance of the American economy and currency and no need to interrogate factors contributing to this dominance, Mai interjected, in Hmong, that if Japan had won World War II, Japanese money would be more valuable (lines 28-30). Mai's comment seemed to suggest his recognition of the role political power plays in economic power, a relationship that was ignored by both Mr. Agnew and Mr. Tong. While Mr. Agnew displayed agreement with Mai's comment and conceded that Japan would control the economy if they had won the war (line 34), he chose to focus on the fact that Mai and other Asians would now speak Japanese and would be ruled by a military government had Japan won (lines 34-39-33). There is no uptake to the seeming subtext of Mai's comment: the American economy is strong because of its political might. This subtext emerged more overtly when Mai laughingly responded to Mr. Tong's questioning of why Soviet money has no value (lines 40-41) by claiming it was because they "lost to America" (line 42).

Excerpt 8

1	Agnew:	Okay, our economic system or economy—basically
2		they're the same thing—now what does that mean? It's
3		how we buy and sell goods and how we distribute
4		them in America. In other words, how business is
5		run, how you earn a living.
6	Tong:	*So that's why American money is valuable. I'll men-*
7		*tion the economy. It's better and the money is more*
8		*valuable compared to other nations on the earth be-*
9		*cause of the material you have to make things...So if*
10		*you have more material, right, then you have a more*
11		*valuable economy... They have the material, they*
12		*have factories, so that is why their economy grows.*
13		*People have jobs so the standard of living is higher*
14		*than in other countries.*
15	Mai:	*Mr. Tong, American money is valuable because*
16		*America (xxx).*
17	Tong:	*No. It's not because of the economy only; there are*
18		*other things too.*
19	Tong:	((To Mr. Agnew)) We went a step further. I was talking
20		about currency and why American currency is more
21		valuable than in other countries, and I explained to
22		them it's because of the economy, because America
23		has a better economy than other countries in the
24		world so that's why.
25	Agnew:	That's why "keef" (Lao currency) is no good here. You
26		can't spend your keef here, but I can take my dollar
27		there. In Laos, will they take my dollar? ((nods))
28	Mai:	*Mr. Tong, I think that in World War II, if Japan had*
29		*won the war, would Japanese money be more valu-*
30		*able?*
31	Tong:	((To Mr. Agnew)) He's saying that, basically, if Japan
32		had won World War II, the economy wouldn't be so
33		valuable.
34	Agnew:	No. Mai, if Japan would have won World War II, today
35		you would be speaking Japanese. All right? Japan
36		was not a democratic country. They ruled through a
37		military, so the military would still be controlling all
38		of you. . . and Japan would have control of the econ-
39		omy.
40	Tong:	*Okay, look, why does Russian money not have any*
41		*value at all? Why? Can they do anything?*
42	Mai:	*They lost to America. ((laughs))*

While Mai's understanding of economic theory is undeveloped, he shows an awareness of the incomplete picture presented by Mr. Agnew and Mr. Tong of economics as merely the processes of buying, selling and distributing goods; running businesses; and making a living. Because he can and chooses to participate in the classroom talk in Hmong, Mai can contest that picture. Although neither Mr. Agnew nor Mr. Tong allow space for a fuller discussion of the political dynamics inherent in economic superiority, Mai's questions and comments force them to concede that American money is valuable for more reasons than the economy (Mr. Tong, lines 17-18) and that military power is correlated with economic power (Mr. Agnew, lines 34-39). Mai's actions seem to demonstrate, on a small scale, ways in which the minority language can be "brandished as a weapon of resistance to the dominance of the dominant standard language of the curriculum" (Macedo, 1994b, p. 133).

In considering the interactional events I observed in Mr. Agnew's classroom, I find Pennycook's (2001) words useful. He asserts that one of the key challenges facing critical researchers today is to discover "ways of mapping micro and macro relations" (p. 114), adding that "micro actions on one level may be part of macro forces on another, [but] within the macro forces of society we still are able to change, resist, act with some degree of autonomy" (p. 139). While the predominance of the English language and American culture in Mr. Agnew's sheltered classroom indicates one way in which the micro relations reproduce the macro relations of the broader social order, still the presence of minority languages, even if assigned no real cultural capital, allows them to resist being ignored and discounted. For this reason, I take heart that the "promise" Macedo speaks of when repressed languages are spoken could be observed as a real and active possibility in Mr. Agnew's sheltered civics classroom.

Acknowledgments

I am grateful to Jane Zuengler, Principle Investigator of the Project on Academic Language Socialization (PALS), for allowing me access to the extensive video and written documentation data from Mr. Agnew's civics class. PALS was funded by the Center on English Learning and Achievement, headquartered at the University of Albany, SUNY, which has a center at the University of Wisconsin-Madison. Although a member of PALS, I was not part of the field team who visited Jefferson High School twice a week. I am indebted to Jane Zuengler, Diana Molina, and Xang Vang for their careful video recording, field note documentation, interview transcripts, and student questionnaire results, data which allowed me to join Mr. Agnew's classroom vicariously. Although they do not know me, I want to thank Mr. Agnew, Mr. Tong, Ms. Li and all the students in the sheltered American civics class for the rich experiences and hope they granted me through my observations of their daily classroom life. In addition, I would like to express appreciation to Xang Vang for his Hmong translations, Suban Keo for his Lao translations, and Cathlin Davis for her English transcriptions of the classroom interactions. Finally, I want to thank Kim Marie Cole, PALS field team member and project manager, for her invaluable suggestions and input.

Notes:

[1] I am very grateful to have been granted access to the extensive data set collected by researchers from the Project on Academic Language Socialization (PALS) funded by the Center on English Learning and Achievement (CELA). Jane Zuengler was the Principle Investigator for PALS.

[2] All names and place names have been changed.

Practicum Students' Confessions on Truth-telling in Reflections: Kurosawa's *Dreams*

Mary K. Thompson-Cooper

In this chapter I will examine reflection through practicum student interviews in a Research I University. In the interviews pre-service teachers discuss how they utilize reflection in their education coursework. I conducted fourteen interviews over the course of the fall semester in order to critically examine reflection from the student perspective. The interviews appear in this chapter in the form of case study excerpts which I frame conceptually with the film *Dreams* by the famous director Akira Kurosawa. Each theme on reflection corresponds to one of the eight vignettes in the film. I utilize the film as my conceptual framework to present each student in relation to a visual dream image from the film. This creates a spun metaphor that runs parallel to the reflection discourse throughout the paper. It is the imagery of the film and the pictures from the film that create a unique pictorial discourse in this discussion regarding reflection.

Introduction

I have divided the chapter into four main sections. The first is the literature I believe best focuses the discussion regarding reflection from a historical aspect, the barriers to reflection and last the larger socio-cultural and political aspects that impact reflective discourse. Second, I present my journey in utilizing film as a conceptual framework in my methodology section. Third, I interpret and analyze the student interviews in relation to the eight themes in Kurosawa's film. Last, I include an interpretive discussion in which highlight the important themes that emerged in the analysis and provide recommendations for further discussion regarding reflective discourse. My desire is to create a new lens in which to revisit the discourse regarding reflection.

The Literature on Educational Reflection

Reflection is one of the goals of many teacher education programs. However, what reflection means and how reflection is implemented varies widely from program to program. It is clear reflection is a popular practice, but how it became so widely circulated in so many divergent areas remains unclear. Reflection as a term may have become trite in some respects because it is used in many ways for a variety of different fields. It becomes difficult to imagine anyone being against the idea of reflection in its most basic sense. Reflection has taken no sides in the paradigm wars in education because so many researchers in various levels utilize it. Yet, to interpret reflection is a difficult task. It is everywhere: as a descriptive, as an implementation tool, critical theory, methodology, explanatory term, and project outcome, depending on where you search and who you read. It is clear that reflection is here to stay. What form or forms it will carry-on into our new century remains uncertain. This chapter neither tries to define the "best" reflective practice nor will it focus on theorizing what methods to employ when using reflective practice. My goals are threefold: one, to create a foundation in which to understand the historical underpinnings of reflection; two, discuss the possible barriers which hinder the reflective method or process in teacher education; and three, understand the larger issues which impact and problematize reflective practices.

Historical Perspective on Reflection

In this section, I will briefly discuss some of the historical conceptions that have dramatically altered or impacted the study of reflection in education. It is not my aim to discuss all of the notable researchers who have added to the debates. The purpose of reviewing some of the highlights of reflection, is to create a shared foundation to the discourse of reflection. This will enhance our later discussion and create a common thread to interpret the data from the student interviews. I highlight the works of Dewey, Schon, and Zeichner because I believe they represent some of the most influential work in the area of reflective study as applied to teacher education. Each adds insight and influence to the study of reflection that impacts the field of research today.

Reflective practice has its roots in the Enlightenment idea that we can stand outside of ourselves, and come to a clearer understanding of what we do and who we are, by freeing ourselves of distorted ways of reasoning and acting. Descartes, as the father of modern philosophy, regards the reflective process as the ability to take an objective view of one self. This Cartesian methodology appeals to the humanistic perspective that states we must no longer rely upon a "higher authority" for expertise and/or revelation regarding our experiences. Researchers today refer to Descartes in reference to the sense of self known as the *cogito*. Moreover, reflective practices in some teacher education programs continue to promote an Enlightenment ideal in which to further understand the scope of human reason as an essentialist foundation for knowledge (Hatton, 1995).

John Dewey (1933) who drew upon the ideas of early educators such as Confucius, Aristotle, and Plato, is acknowledged as a key originator in the twentieth century regarding the concept of reflection. He believes reflection is a special form of problem solving or thought process designed to resolve issues that involve a careful ordering of ideas. Dewey writes: "quality of educators and education cannot be derived from the imitation of techniques that have worked in the past, but rather teachers should be trained in analyzing and defining principles behind the techniques. In short, it is theorized that the more teacher reflectivity occurs, the better quality of teaching" (Dewey, 1933). Dewey criticized education as "fad-driven" because teachers were learning only "how to do things" but were not learning "why they did things," or how to think about how to improve things based on their experience. Dewey, as a strong proponent of scientific reasoning, believed teachers should incorporate the "why" and "how" into their teaching to be thoughtful and inquisitive, rather than habitual in their actions. Dewey states this about unreflective teachers: "Unreflective teachers tend to accept everyday reality, working only to find the means to carry out the most effectively the ends demanded by their culture, which leads to further enslavement for it leaves the person at the mercy of appetite, sense, and circumstance" (Dewey, 1933).

In his famous book, *How We Think: a Restatement of Reflective Thinking to the Educative Process* (1933)," Dewey specifically addresses three prerequisites for reflective action: open mindedness, responsibility, and whole heartedness. Dewey believes open-mindedness is imperative to seek-out and consider alternate possibilities, and be open to the possibility that anything we believe in may be false. Further, he contends that responsibility considers the consequences of an action, as well as where that action may lead. This responsibility requires extended concern rather than just immediate reaction to an event. Last, whole-heartedness considers the combination of open-mindedness and responsibility and needs to be consistently applied to each situation, not just when it is convenient to do so (Dewey, 1933). Four key issues with regards to reflection emerge from Dewey's original work. The first is whether reflection is limited to thought processes about action, or if is it more bound up in action. The second relates to the time frames when reflection takes place, and whether it is relatively immediate and short term, or systematic and extended as Dewey implies and suggests in his writings. The third aspect questions whether reflection is problem centered or not. The last key issue regarding reflection concerns how consciously the person reflecting takes into account the wider societal issues including: historical, cultural, and societal values and beliefs (Dewey, 1933).

Later, Donald Schon's (1983, 1987) work, is referred by some educational theorists as more important than the earlier works of Dewey. In his body of work, Schon clearly writes about reflection that is intimately bound up with action. Rather than attempting to apply scientific theory to reflection such as Dewey, Schon suggests that professionals learn to frame and reframe the complex and ambiguous problems they are facing, test out various interpretations, and then modify their actions as a result. He discusses two forms of reflection: one, 'reflection-on-action;' and two, 'reflection-in-action.' The first form refers to conscious thinking and modification while performing a task or while on a job. The second form of reflection involves simultaneously reflecting and doing. Reflection-in-action implies that professional competency occurs where the person can both perform and modify, while consciously thinking about the task at hand. Both of Schon's reflective forms incorporate rational and moral processes in making reasoned judgments about a preferable manner in which to act.

The educational community embraces Schon's work because it is able to incorporate all levels or types of reflection, including critical reflection. His "reflection-in-action" and "reflection-on-action" involve an epistemology of professional practice based upon knowledge-in-action and knowing–in-action (Altricher & Posch, 1989; Munby & Russell, 1989). This knowledge is a construction and reconstruction of professional experience rather than an application of scientific or technical rationality. Reflection-in-action as well as knowing-in-action are characterized as part of the craft-based and intuitive knowledge one builds upon from professional experience. As an example, Tabachnick and Zeichner (1991) state that the enormously popular work of Schon has challenged the dominant technical rationality in professional education and argued for more attention to promoting artistry in teaching by encouraging 'reflection-in-action' and 'reflection-on-action' among teachers. Schon provides a means to uplift the educational community by raising the status of professionalism in reflective practice. Schon's definition promotes a practice in teaching that is artistic and action-based. In contrast, Dewey believes reflection is both scientific and positivistic. Calgren (1999) compares Dewey and Schon's work on reflection:

> Although Schon has been seen as belonging to the Dewey tradition, the way in which he differs from Dewey is more interesting ... While Dewey was preoccupied by 'seeing' and the theoretical, Schon has been preoccupied with 'doing' and the practical.
>
> However, these differences between Dewey and Schon's concept of reflection partly disappear since the kind of practice Schon refers to is, to a large extent, a virtual practice. His prototype is "the architect who designs buildings but does not build them." (pp. 51-52)

This implies that Schon misunderstands the complexities of teaching. One who teaches realizes the duty of teaching, and the implications derived of this practice. An architect who designs homes, but never builds them can erase his work without hurting anyone. This implies only a shallow interpretation of the implications of reflection-in-action and all that is encompasses for teachers in practice. Further, Zeichner (1994) provides a historical perspective on four of the main approaches that have guided reflection in teacher education (Valli, 1992). First, there is the academic tradition where teachers grasp the essentials of how to transform discipline knowledge in order that students might learn from it. Second, the social efficiency tradition attempts to develop 'best' practice, based on research findings. Third, the developmentalist tradition emphasizes teachers understanding and application. Further, it claims that through time, students grow and change in their behavior and thought patterns. Last, the social reconstructivist tradition recommends that teachers work at changing their practices, because schools continue to reproduce a society based upon unjust race, class, and gender relationships. The first three traditions are identified as existing in the dominant social and political order, while the last tradition expects teachers to work towards a better social system based on equality and justice (Zeichner, 1994b; Valli, 1992). In addition, Zeichner states that beyond the four traditions of reflective practice discussed, there is also a great deal of advocacy for reflection in general. He refers to this as generic reflection. He states, "the implication here is that teachers actions are necessarily better just because they are more deliberate or intentional." In Harvard & Hodkinson, Zeichner writes: "How to get students to reflect can take on a life of its own, and can become the programmatic goal. What they reflect on can become immaterial. For example, racial tension as a school issue can become no more or less worthy of reflection than field trips or homework assignments" (as quoted in Zeichner, 1994b; Valli, 1990).

In closing, our historical foundations are based on overlapping and conflicting ideals of reflective practices. Each definition must be analyzed within the context of a specific historical period. We must carefully consider each historical figure within the socio-cultural, political, and economic context that each work is produced. Dewey is an educational theorist, who at the turn of the century, promoted self-discipline as a means to social control and order among individuals. Further, Schon regarded reflection as an artistic endeavor, which is in contrast to Dewey's scientific reasoning in relation to reflection. Finally, Zeichner strongly advocates for a social reconstructivist ideal in reflection, where the teacher works towards an improved society based upon unjust practices regarding race, class, and gender. Each historical definition and transformation involving reflection demonstrates the changing tides, movements, and transitions in our educational and historical trajectories.

Barriers for Reflection in Teacher Education

It is difficult to discuss the historical perspectives of reflection without entering an uncertain place where the historical meanings of reflection, and the current discourse merge together. In this section, it is my goal to discuss specific issues regarding the practice of reflection for students in the teacher education program. Students in the teacher education program are an integral part of this discussion because it is from their interviews that I am able to highlight their feelings toward reflection. Many students are required to use reflection as a part of their coursework in the education certification program.

In the following section, I will discuss the different types of barriers that exist with regards to reflection. The barriers that arise with reflection are often due to the confessional nature and insecurity of sharing what is considered to be of a private nature. As well, students believe that reflection is somewhat esoteric or removed from the technical work they are asked to learn. In addition, the obstacle of changing students' original beliefs about schooling and education is difficult to adhere to in a short amount of time.

Further, the time to include reflective growth is in direct conflict with the need student teachers have to learn technical skills first. Another barrier is students are apt to feel vulnerable when sharing their private feelings and thoughts on paper. Moreover, students feel their voices are over looked in the process of assigned reflections where the structure and ideologies of the program design may be in direct conflict with their own beliefs. Finally, reflection appears to be a "catch-all" term that embraces conflicting ideologies. My goal for this second section is to highlight the student perspective of reflection, and present how the program goals are often in conflict with their own.

To begin, student journals, portfolios, formal reflective writings and learning logs, are all the rage among teachers who advocate experiential methods. Teachers believe that encouraging students to speak personally and directly about their experience, honors and encourages authentic voices. That this often happens is undeniable. However, journals, portfolios, formal reflections, and logs also have the potential to become ritualistic and mandated confessionals (Usher & Edwards, 1995). According to Brookfield (1995), "This becomes the educational equivalent of the tabloid-like, sensationalistic outpourings of game shows and daytime television." In addition, students who sense that their teacher is a strong advocate of experiential methods, may pick-up the implicit message that good students reveal dramatic private episodes in their lives that lead to transformative insights. Students who do not have anything painful, traumatic, or exciting to confess may begin to feel that their reflective writing falls short. Not being able to produce revelations of sufficient intensity, they may decide to invent some, or they may start to paint quite ordinary experiences with added significance (Brookfield, 1995).

Another barrier for practicum and student teachers, is that reflection is not generally associated with working as a teacher. Teaching is seen as an active immediate response on the job, a technical pragmatic skill learned with practice. In contrast, reflection is considered more of an academic pursuit that emphasizes critical thinking (McNamara, 1990; Elbaz, 1988). Further, an emphasis on reflection too early in a preparatory teacher education program can have the effect of alienating new teachers before giving them the opportunity to master this new skill. It can also be difficult to sustain the use of reflection because student teachers may see the practice of reflection as rather esoteric, and a meaningless pursuit when they are working to master the technical skills they feel are more important to their training (Zeichner, 1990; Hall, 1985). Further, in a study of American programs in education designed to encourage reflective thinking, Valli (1992) identified a number of obstacles in creating reflective teachers. Specifically, the persistence and strength of participants' own conceptualization of teaching proved to be an enormous barrier. For instance, many students in the Florida PROTEACH program were seen to comply on the surface with strategies that encourage reflective thinking, but their deep reflective positions depicted a fixed view of teaching that they developed prior to entering the program (Valli, 1992). Moreover, in order to foster reflective thinking, time and opportunity for reflective growth is a necessary requirement. This enables students learning the process to acquire meta-teaching and meta-cognitive skills (McNamara, 1990). It appears to work best when students' early survival skills are fostered and addressed through technical education before attempting to develop the skills necessary to become a reflective practitioner. After progressing from the technical skills, students can begin learning the process of reflective writing in order to encourage their development sequentially to include other forms of reflection. These forms of reflection may include broader socio-political and economic contexts (Hall, 1985). Another difficult concern related to this issue is the identification of a suitable knowledge base as a starting point for encouraging student teachers and practicum students to begin to comprehend the concepts related to reflection. After which, they can begin to apply the more demanding forms to their teaching practice. As well, students may feel vulnerable when asked to expose their beliefs and perceptions on paper for others. Students may believe that reflection uncovers weaknesses, and may blame themselves or others for a loss of control within the program (Wildman & Niles, 1987). Such possibilities support collaborative rather than individualistic approaches to reflection. In this structure, students can support each other as 'critical friends' (Smith, 1991; McNamara, 1990; Smyth, 1989).

According to Valli, the voice of student teachers is often over-looked in the critique of programs. She stresses the need for teacher education to encourage student teachers to dialogue with themselves and with others, as they seek to describe, question, explain, explore, and challenge their fundamental beliefs and ideas about teaching. In the process of encouraging reflective dialogue, two aspects are identified. The first refers to speaking the truth as one sees it in order to articulate and clarify ideas and beliefs on a given topic. This provides a useful basis for entering reflective thinking and understanding of one's self. Second refers to giving voice to ones ideas to be heard. This is valuable in learning the art of listening and understanding what others are saying. The need to listen is de-emphasized in our culture, and is uncharacteristic of teacher educators and teachers in general. This supportive listening environment leads to greater opportunities for verbal reflection. Dialogue with others or with oneself can lead to powerful insights and potential solutions for teaching and learning (Valli, 1992).

Another related barrier is the structure and ideology of the educational program. This encompasses not only in its component parts, but also the development of how reflection may be utilized and encouraged (Zeichner, 1990; Valli 1992). A critically reflective approach demands an ideology that differs from traditional 'best practice' emphasis and competencies. In the critically reflective method, there needs to be changes in emphasis and created opportunities that establish appropriate and supportive conditions for fostering in students producing different forms of reflection (Calderhead, 1989). Staff ideologies over which methodologies are the best way to encourage reflective practice also surfaced as a concern. For example, many teachers in the Maryland program had difficulty conceptualizing alternate views of what teaching and learning are all about. This leads to programmatic concerns for what types of reflection are 'best' suited for educational programs (Valli, 1992).

A final problem with reflective practice is that it has become a "catch-all" term embracing ideologies and orientations that are often contradictory. As Zeichner (1994) points out, there are several quite separate and distinct interpretations of reflective practice, only some of which would be considered critical. The terms reflection and reflective practice are becoming so overused that they are in danger of becoming buzzwords without any real meaning (Brookfield, 1995). Smyth (1992) warns that reflection, "runs the risk of being totally evacuated of all meaning" as it becomes attached to any teaching that we happen to favor at the moment. Consequently, reflection practices become overused and misunderstood in the process of creating paradigms and classification systems. It is difficult to exclude reflection from the political agendas of schooling and schooling practices. Reflection is intimately connected to our political ideals. We simultaneously engage in reflective discourses that are tied to our essentialist notions of oppression or political correctness. Either way we are surrounding ourselves in the system we are trying to overcome in the process of critical pedagogy.

In short, the barriers students face in utilizing reflective practices are well cited in the literature. Students' fears regarding reflection undermine and perhaps deter from the original goals and objectives regarding reflection practices. The obstacles students face range from feeling they are mandated to confess their feelings on paper, to not even associating reflection as a practice that teachers in the field undertake. This is due to many students' preconceived notions that teaching is technical, not esoteric in nature. Moreover, it has proven difficult to change student teachers preconceived beliefs about the discourse of teaching with reflective tools. Further, teachers are more concerned with learning survival skills for teaching rather than the abstract ideals associated with critical reflective practices. In addition, in the process of reflecting student teachers discern high levels of anxiety due to the vulnerable feelings associated with reflection. As well, the structure and ideology of the education program and how it promotes student teachers to voice their opinions about their reflections, appears to be a barrier for some teachers. Finally, reflection has become so widely utilized, its meaning has become difficult to interpret. Reflection is widely accepted as a method to improve teacher education practices despite some of the controversies surrounding its practice. The barriers discussed above highlight some of the practical concerns students encounter with reflections. We now turn to some of the more institutional issues that impact reflective practices.

Issues Impacting Reflective Discourse

In this final section, I have loosely defined the issues problematizing reflection to include the individual and societal aspects that impact reflection practices. These concepts emerge out of discourses regarding our conceptions of hegemony, pastoral power, and governmentality. It is my aim to shed light on how these issues frame and impact the private nature of reflection. The figures that partake in this discussion include philosophers and educators who have had a role in defining and encouraging how reflection is an act of power and control in our society. The concepts of shame, self-deception, and 'other' surface in this discussion from the student's interviews. It becomes apparent in this last section, that reflection is a complicated and often contradictory process, involving many opposing and parallel discourses. I have tried to highlight a few of these oppositional forces in order to frame our reflection discussion about the broader issues surrounding it as well.

The term hegemonic is often discussed as an issue that is problematic for critical reflective thinking. In this type of thinking, hegemonic describes the process where ideas, structures, and actions come to be seen by the majority of people as wholly natural, and working for their own good. Yet in fact, it can be constructed by powerful interests to protect the status quo that serves those interests. The subtle strength and tenacity of hegemony is that over time it becomes embedded and part of the cultural air we breath. It becomes difficult to even realize that we may be oppressed or even disenfranchised. The hegemonic beliefs become part of our everyday life, a type of common sense that we take for granted. It is the belief that student teachers are often unaware of the assumptions they have about teaching, and may become embraced by beliefs that in effect are untrue to their best interests and ideas. The irony of hegemony is that teachers take pride in acting on some of the very assumptions that enslave them to be "true" to their profession. It is not a coincidence that teachers still tend to be female, underpaid, and blamed for the social ills of our society. It is not happenstance that in this years political arena, many seemed to think they knew more about teaching than teachers (Brookfield, 1994).

Moreover, this relates to the reflective process in two distinct ways. One, student teachers are part of a society that believes in many of these hegemonic assumptions. They are also part of the system that creates and builds upon the oppressive identity of their trained profession. Because they are within the system, reflective thinking, writing and dialogue may encourage further oppression. It is difficult to change something that on the surface appears so normal. It is difficult to become a critical reflective thinker when the ideas one has about "good teaching" are hegemonic assumptions related what may be harmful or even destructive (Brookfield, 1994). Second, if they become aware of the hegemonic assumptions, student teachers may have difficulty distinguishing between what is a true reflection and what is perceived to be a true reflection. This inability to draw a clear distinction between what one believes to be true, and what one has been told is true, can be extremely frustrating and unnerving when confronted with the nature and essence of ones beliefs.

In addition, Foucault describes this hegemonic assumption as the role of pastoral power as a form of power that does not just look after an entire community, but each individual during his entire life. Most importantly this type of power cannot be exercised without "knowing the inside of people's minds, without exploring their souls, without making them reveal their innermost secrets" (Foucault, 1997b). This power of the conscience implies an ability to direct an individual from inside out. In terms of reflection, this is an enormous issue of control and power. The reflective process uncovers ones secret feelings, thoughts, and ideas about the self. In relation to the pastoral confession, it appears institutions such as the University or even our larger political process, take on the role of what is possible to even think or feel.

"Govermentality of the self by oneself in its articulation with relations with others (such as one finds in pedagogy, behavior counseling, spiritual direction, the prescription of models for living and so on)" (Foucault 1997a, p. 88). In this sense, others use reflection as a means of control and regulation of the self. One of the main purposes of our political system has been to advocate self-discipline. In Foucault's words, "This encounter between the technologies of domination and those of the self I call 'governmentality.'" (1997b, p. 225). The notion of governmentality becomes important because it promotes self-discipline, which is a key component to the nature of our democracy. This expectation of self-regulation and self-discipline is set according to our expectations of social 'norms.' What is considered normal is part of the larger matrix of power within our notions of modern democratic governance or governmentality. It becomes impossible to distinguish self-discipline from modern forms of democratic governance. This invisible line is based on what our possible 'authentic' reflective thinking has been socialized and disciplined to become. Reflection becomes what we are socialized to believe is true and normal to believe. Our act of self- regulation becomes a regulation of the greater democracy in which we have been socialized to behave and act in accordance with social norms that are created and exercised all around us. The reflection act is undistinguished from other acts of self-discipline because its purpose becomes obscured in the technology of the self-regulatory cog in the wheel of governmentality (Foucault, 1997).

Shame in reflective thinking is another issue problematizing 'true' reflection. Sartre and de Beauvoir (1967) refer to shame as a relation to oneself in the presence of another, whereby one evaluates oneself negatively through the look or gaze of the other, or internal monitoring of the self. The experience of shame with being 'caught' deceiving oneself in reflection involves not only seeing oneself as the object the 'other' sees, but seeing oneself as others will judge one as possibly reprehensible, faulty, and/or inferior. Therefore, one does not just feel shame in the act itself, but of the self. "Suddenly the 'I' is seen as shame, and shame of self is the recognition that one is both the object and the subject that is looked at and judged" (Kruks, 1999). Students involved in reflection can often feel this type of shame described, because of the scrutiny they feel towards not only deceiving the self, but also deceiving the 'other.' According to Foucault, shame as any another emotive state is not possible without the action of power. This act of power is defined as a relationship of power, "that is a mode of action which does not act directly and immediately on others. Instead it acts upon actions: an action upon an action, on existing actions or on those which may arise in the present or the future" (Foucault, 1987, p. 220). This concept of power, which arises from actions, embodies a relationship of power of the 'other.' The subject and the object in reflection become undistinguishable from one another due to the notion that reflection is a type of power pro-moted as self-discipline, which in turn creates a power struggle within the individual that has been socialized within the hierarchy of power upon ac-tion. Foucault also locates the problem of reflection as a task of fiction. He argues that the task for both is to make the invisible visible, but within the limits provided by our thoughts and language. This becomes problematic when one tries to bring the invisible into the processes involved in the cre-ation of visible. In this scenario, the "Other" becomes assimilated onto fa-miliar ground and loses the 'power' and character that distinguishes it as the "Other."

Any purely reflexive discourse runs the risk of leading the experience of the outside back into the dimension of interiority; reflection tends irre-sistibly to repatriate it to the side of consciousness and to develop it into a descriptive of living that depicts the 'outside' as the experience of the body, space, the limits of the will, and the effaceable presence of the other (As seen in Fendler 2000, Foucault, 1998, p. 151-152). Thus, reflection can or may not become an obstacle onto itself when there is nothing more than what is already known. It is not separate from the regulated conscious understand-ing that is already controlled by ones already "regulated" self-discipline. Ev-ery thought, feeling, gesture, and written word has the risk of becoming the "Other" by repatriating it to the side of consciousness. The idea that reflec-tion can be used as a means to critique the systems outside of the self be-comes nearly impossible when the reflective act is nothing more than the social institution guarding against the "Other" (Fendler, 2000).

Further, both Foucault and de Beauvoir contend that the term "au-thenticity" as the search for inner meaning or quest to become familiar with one's real self, is false. Both believe there is no real notion of self "there" to be discovered. Rather, what is at issue here is the choice of an ethical stance in the face of one's situation and its "facticities." As with in-authenticity, a person affirms ones selfhood to be constituted by exterior conditions and forces even when this is not wholly the case. Therefore, the "bad faith," or self-deception in reflection lies in the fact that one is still making choices and exercising a degree of freedom, while perhaps by the power of govermentality claims to be unable to do so. De Beauvoir insists, contrary to Foucault, we must accept responsibility for our choices and values (Kruks, 1999, p. 11). Likewise, self-deception is defined as purposeful or intentional evasion of fully acknowledging something to oneself. It is distin-guished into five distinct aspects: one, willful ignorance where one proposes they had no prior knowledge that anything was wrong; two, systematic ig-noring where one refuses to think about what the implications of the act may be; three, emotional detachment whereby one detaches emotionally from the action and content of deception; four, self-pretense where one pre-tends that nothing "really" serious was involved and their action was harm-less to themselves and others; and last, rationalization where one convinces oneself that the action is/was technically reasonable and or permissible (Martin, 1986, p. 8).

Furthermore, reflection subsumes a type of recognition of ones feel-ings thoughts and ideas about various topics. This discussion is related to teaching and learning. When the possibility of self-deception arises, it conflicts with the very notion of what reflection ought to be and do for the student being asked to do reflections. Students who deceive themselves in reflection, are presumably doing this to hide or falsify what they believe to be uncomplimentary to their notion of what reflection should mirror of themselves. It is human to want to show ones best face to one's superior. In terms of reflection, being self-deceptive becomes problematic when the student believes that what they are doing is aiding their teaching by presenting a "better" self than their "authentic" self. This creates a wall and prevents them from seriously considering their actions. Some may utilize this as a way to get out of deeply thinking about their actions. In the rationalization distinction, students may talk themselves into believing their deception, and in turn, become victims to thinking this is a part of who they are. This can become a habitual activity of the consciousness (Martin, 1986).

The paradox of self-deception exists in the possibility that in the self-deceptive act, one simultaneously is able to persuade oneself intentionally into believe something, while also knowing that it is false. This assumption presupposes that the self-deceiver could presumably be both the deceiver and the deceived victim. As an epistemological paradox, this centers on our belief of what it is to know and believe to know. This contradiction or paradox can live either in the philosophical or literary sense. As an illustration, in George Orwell's book *1984,* 'doublethink' is defined in the story as the power to hold two contradictory beliefs in one's mind simultaneously, and also accept both of them. Orwell contends that in the real world of politics, as in his imaginary world of *1984,* "language and concepts were being systematically abused in order to form contradictory ideas about freedom, government coercion, and war. He identified the use of conscious fabrication and more-unconscious self-deception." To use against logic, to repudiate morality while laying claim to it, to believe that democracy was impossible and that the Party was the guardian of democracy, to forget, whatever it was necessary to forget, then to draw it back into memory again at the moment when it was needed and then to promptly to forget it again, and above all, to apply the same process to the process itself (Martin, 1986). In relation to reflective dilemmas, self-deception in the Orwellian sense can create reflections whereby students can hold mutually exclusive and contradictory beliefs about themselves. This can become extremely problematic if the student believes that the perception of their false reflection is the only "true" reflection.

The act of reflection becomes muddled when larger issues of politics, power, and oppression take center stage. The act of reflecting for oneself is compounded by the powers of govermentality and confessional pastoral power. We begin to question our most basic assumptions about whom and what our basic concerns are, and if they even belong to ourselves. The shame and feelings of self-deception transform who we are in our reflections based upon how or in what form we believe we should present ourselves to others. The issues problematizing reflection are many. I have chosen the ones I thought most appropriate to the student discussion and case studies. It is their discourse, which I find most fascinating because it is built on assumptions of hegemonic oppression and power that they appear to act within their particular discourse. Finally, I think it is important to remind ourselves that we teach to change the world. The hope is to help out pre-service teachers with reflective practices. This will assist them to act toward each other and their future students, with understanding, compassion, and fairness. We attempt to teach, thinking we are democratic and respectful of people's diversity, when they may experience our methods as repressive and constraining. The complexity of teaching within the socio-cultural, political, and psychological milieu is compounded when we believe our attentions are sincere and pure. Unfortunately, teaching is a complex undertaking and it is difficult to comprehend the motivations that our students perceive when methods are undertaken. We are never fully aware of our motives and intentions when we apply a specific teaching strategy such as reflection, and how this will affect our pre-service teachers. In the ensuing themes, I will provide the student perspective on reflection. My aim is to provide a lens on their experiences to discover how we can improve reflection to make it a worthwhile endeavor for all of our pre-service teachers.

Methods

The process was intended to be simple, but with any journey, the process is never simple or without "ruts" and new discoveries. My adventure begins in the usual sense. I was curious with the idea of putting my ideas regarding reflection into a hypothetical question. The study begins with the question of asking students about what they do, think, and feel when asked to reflect. The goal is to demonstrate what is transpiring with reflection in the University. My research expedition began as a small sample from my supervision group, and ended with the participation of fourteen undergraduate students from many supervision groups.

The group of undergraduate students participating in this study are all in their literacy practicum semester. The undergraduates range in age from twenty-one to thirty-eight. Of the 14 participants, five are male, and nine are female. The students come from various ethnic backgrounds. All of the students chose to participate and were not given any incentive to join the study. All three elementary education cohorts are represented: first, the preschool to third grade certification cohort; second, the first through sixth grade certification cohort; and last, the first through ninth grade certification cohort. The mixture adds not only a unique perspective, but also, provides students within small cohort groups the anonymity to participate without identifying themselves in the process. The students', who volunteered to participate, share a variety of reasons for doing so. Many students describe what they believe is wrong with reflection, while others describe their desire to improve the program. Further, some students thought it would be a good experience to take part in a study. All participants were given a copy of their interviews to look over for content and ideas before writing this paper. As a result of student individuality, variations occur in their responses. All names, places, and identifying characteristics are changed in order to protect the confidentiality of the participants. Finally, as an additional measure of protection, individual personalities and interests of the participants will be withheld.

Interview Process

It is important to note, the students who participated are not sharing their theories about reflection, but rather, they share the practices and experiences they have had in their studies with reflection. Each student presents his or her own preconceived ideas about reflection in a one to two hour semi-structured interview. Each student volunteered to participate in the reflection interview, and signed a consent form. To preserve the flavor and authenticity of the student interviews, I will utilize and rely upon student excerpts in the form of case studies in my analysis. The students revealed an aspect of reflection that I had not anticipated. In the interviews, rather than discussing their pragmatic uses of reflection, the students reveal problematic issues surrounding reflection. They share in a manner I did not think possible or expect with a tape recorder running. As I was listening closely to the students, I was stunned by what I heard. I knew this would make for an intense experience, but I didn't know how to make sense out of all these hours of transcription.

Analysis Process

Thus, what began as a small study became much larger, as I counted many hours of transcription time. Research may sometimes appear as a chaotic process with few clear-cut answers, methods, or theories. As I read and reviewed the returned transcripts, I began to see thematic elements emerge. As the themes began to transpire, Francois Tochon had informed me that a leading metaphor or myth often sheds light on a corpus of data (Tochon, 1994, 1999a). I was looking for such a metaphor or story that would emerge from the corpus or match it's meaning. My husband rented one of my favorite director's films in order to persuade me to take a break from my ever changing and evolving project. He successfully convinced me to revisit Akira Kurosawa's *Dreams*. It is a strange film in which eight separate dreams are interwoven on life's journey. I had watched it last in 1990 when it was first released. *Dreams* caught me off guard, and I couldn't stop thinking about what I had viewed. It provided a mirror effect with my data. Indeed, it became more than I had expected not only as a film, but also as a method to integrate into my reflection project. After revisiting Kurosawa's *Dreams* that Friday, I watched it again on Sunday in order to transcribe it, and discern if its contents could enlighten or decipher my data, and thus lead me into a revealing process.

While I pride myself on being able to integrate a variety of perspectives and think in divergent ways about a variety of possibilities, I had not expected to add film to my existing project. After transcribing *Dreams* though, I read through the transcripts as I had done with the interviews, and the similarities manifested in exciting ways. I know the uncharacteristic combination of film and educational theory may be viewed critically, yet the parallels between film and interview data are unmistakable. Notwithstanding, I decided to track new territory in my research expedition, and utilize film and theory as part of the discourse on reflection. As part of my discourse, I include Kurosawa's journey of life through dreams in order to discuss reflection. The vignettes of the film became the framework where themes from my data could be discussed and interpreted. It adds depth to a conceptual framework. The film provides meaningful pictures and creativity to the data, something I was afraid would be lost in the research process. The transformation provided a research project with new methods using a post-structural methodology with film to frame my data. The eight film vignettes construct and provide the framework to the eight themes of reflection. Each vignette carries a story synopsis narrating the motifs within the film. Interpretive excerpts from the movie are then added to provide greater insight. Next, one or two pictures per vignette are inlaid into the paper in order to supply greater substance to each section. Following this, I draw parallels between the film and the student interviews to demonstrate how the two pieces merge together to form a perspective regarding reflection. Based upon the student interviews, themes from the film are illustrated by case studies featuring two to seven students who best exemplify the issues presented. Each vignette and theme presents a different aspect of reflection. Each student is featured at least once in the eight themes.

Each dream in Kurosawa's film has a title, and I have chosen to keep Kurosawa's titles in order to maintain the integrity of the film. The synopsis of each dream is to help the uninitiated reader understand the context and the images within the dream vignettes. It is important to remind ourselves of the open literary analysis within each dream as they are used to discuss reflection. The range of interpretations can vary depending on the reading of the dreams. The art of Kurosawa is in the variations of interpretations. It is used in this discussion to provide another lens with which to examine the act of reflection. The utility of Kurosawa's dreams naturally is to provide a visual and conceptual integration for reflection. It is useful to the analysis of this discussion, because it allows the reader to create an image of reflection through a portrait that is newly developed. However, once the portrait is clearly formed the tool no longer becomes useful to include. I have integrated Kurosawa's imagery in the analysis for this purpose. In the interpretive discussion to follow, I intentionally left Kurosawa's imagery aside, in order to allow the reflection motifs an opportunity to be disentangled and interpreted on their own merits. Moreover, the utility of grounded theory became a categorization process once again in my interpretive discussion. I began to re-interpret the data through the lens of Discourse as defined by Gee.

Discourse are ways of being in the world, or forms of life which integrate words, acts, values, beliefs, attitudes, and social identities, as well as gestures, glances, body positions, and clothes. A Discourse is a sort of identity kit, which comes complete with the appropriate costumes, and instructions on how to act, talk, and often write, so as to take on a particular social role that others will recognize (Gee, 1996, p. 127). Utilizing the above definition of Discourse, I re-grouped the eight themes into two main categories: institutive-Reflective Discourse (IRD) and Student-Reflective Discourse (SRD) as defined by the corpus data from the student interviews. Thus, through the use of grounded theory in the interpretive section, I integrate the data to build yet another perspective in which to discern reflection from the pre-service teacher point of view. According to Glaser (Charmaz, 2000) grounded theorization enables the researcher to discover a schema that relates to a particular situation. A grounded theory must work; it must provide a useful conceptual rendering and ordering of the data that explains the studies phenomena. The relevance of grounded theory derives from its offering analytic explanations of actual problems and basic processes in the natural research setting. A grounded theory is durable because it accounts for variation; it is flexible because researchers can modify their emerging or established analyses as conditions change or further data are gathered (Charmaz, 2000).

Finally, my methods merged to create an exciting journey thus far. I did not know what I stepped into as I confronted this research expedition. Kurosawa's imagery both fascinates and bewilders me. The student interviews still surprise me with their depth and perceptions. I have learned that abstraction is difficult to articulate. Above all, I have learned the importance of taking my time to revisit, review, and rethink how each aspect of my research adventure is a discovery. My intent is to create a new way to think about our reflections and improve upon the practice and process of reflective thinking with our pre-service teachers. "At the end of an article, let it marinate for three four months, in a drawer. Then, as if visiting an old friend go and visit it some night and see the journey you have taken in its absence" (Freire, 2000).

Analysis

Theme 1: Sunshine through the Rain

Film Synopsis

The first dream finds young Kurosawa being told not to go into the forest on a rainy day because this is when the foxes hold their wedding processions, and he must not look at them. Young Kurosawa does indeed go into the forest to see the forbidden procession. When he returns home, his mother tells him the foxes have come in his absence to deliver a dagger with which he is to kill himself. If this does not occur, he is to find them and apologize for seeing their forbidden procession. The dream ends with Kurosawa searching for the foxes under the rainbow, where they supposedly live.

Interpretive Film Excerpts

The following quotes are said to Kurosawa by his mother, after he returns from the forbidden procession:

You saw something that you were not supposed to see. I cannot let you in now.

They don't usually forgive–you must really be willing to forgive.

In this theme, the idea that reflection is not what it seems is brought to the forefront. Each student is asked to discuss what they do with reflections, rather than what they are told to do with reflections. The focus of this discourse is the process of reflection, and how the reflective process is accomplished by each student. In this forum, students speak openly about what reflection homework means to them. In relationship to this theme, we will look closely at three case studies: Stacy, Val and Erin. As I discuss each interview in light of Kurosawa's dream, I will shed light on how the fox procession is intimately connected with Stacy, Erin's, and Val's experiences regarding reflection (all names in text are pseudonyms). Stacy's conversation regarding reflection addresses the issue of reflection as a method of checking-up on students to see if they are completing work that is assigned. In addition, Stacy claims that while reflection is something she adamantly dislikes, it is useful for thinking about how to be the type of teacher she has set out to become. In Val's interview, a different form of discourse is disclosed. She discusses reflection in terms of a formulaic process that is part of the assigned work that must be accomplished in order for her to become a teacher. In this process, she reveals what she will and will not discuss in her reflection work. Last, Erin speaks of reflection in abstract terms. She asks how truthful can reflection be to our perceptions. It is in this pretext, Erin appears to filter what she reflects on in terms of the personal nature surrounding the material. Finally, in conducting the interviews, I felt like young Kurosawa. Kurosawa saw the forbidden fox procession, and I felt as though I was hearing the forbidden reflection experiences. In the following case studies by Stacy, Val, and Erin, I will demonstrate how reflection has a forbidden element in it. This discovery leads me to demonstrate the parallels between reflection and the forbidden.

Case Study Stacy

In the first case study, Stacy expresses her feelings about being asked to do reflections. She states, "Yeah, we reflect all the time. To the point where I get sick of it." In this excerpt, Stacy is referring to her current semester where she is writing reflections in all five of her educational classes. She continues to explain, "I want to say assign us busy work, but that probably is not right. I don't know except to make sure we did it, you know, check-up on us." The checking-up aspect becomes a common phrase to many of the students' feelings and reactions related to reflection. Stacy is certain in her statement that reflection is used as a way to see if assignments are completed. Consequently, Stacy appears to think it is more important to finish her reflections than to critically think in her reflections. Thus, completed work becomes more important than the quality of the work. In comparison, the fox in the *Sunshine through the Rain*, checks-up on young Kurosawa after he has seen the wedding procession to see if he will use the dagger to kill himself. In Japanese folklore, the fox often represents deception. Generally, it appears when something forbidden or untruthful is taking place in a story. Obviously, deception is defined as a trick, some sort of ruse, or the use of deceit. In addition, deception may take on three distinct forms: one, self-deception; two, overt deception of another; or three, some combination of the two.

Stacy appears to be checked-on to see if she is in fact doing her assigned work or not. Since the potential exists for deception to occur, among a host of other reasons, students are checked-upon to determine if they are completing their reflection assignments. The concept of checking to see if assignments are completed, seems logical. However, as a result of the private nature of reflective assignments, many students such as Stacy have the potential to deceive either themselves or others in their reflective work. The possible full benefits students can derive from authentic reflective assignments may be reduced if one of the aforementioned forms of deception is utilized. While it is evident that Stacy completes her reflections and likely discloses some portion of truth in her reflection assignments, it is unclear whether Stacy presents a shallow picture of her thoughts or if she is "truthful" to her thinking. In the theme, the dagger is symbolic of the forbidden wedding Kurosawa has viewed. In the beginning, Kurosawa knowingly deceives his mother, and tells her that he did not see the fox procession. He is checked-on in his own "truth-telling," when his deception is discovered. While Stacy's assignments will be checked-upon, her deceptions likely will remain undiscovered.

In her next quote, Stacy provides another facet regarding her reflections, and seems fearful of the consequences this may bring to her. She relates the following story to describe her feelings:

> I was in class listening to my teacher, when we start talking about this teacher during share time. One of the girls is an African American, and the other is white; and the teacher is white too. When the white girl was sharing her story, the teacher asked all the right questions, and was really facilitative and there was this flow. The teacher didn't throw her off at all, and the teacher was really pleased. But when the African American girl got up to share, the teacher got all frustrated with her, and when she asked questions to the African American girl, it didn't help at all. It distracted her and threw her off, cause she told the story, and it was like a cultural thing, and the white teacher thought this girl had no point, and was just going off on tangents. The white teacher thought she was telling tales, and none of her story was true. To make a long story short, it was the first time I realized how little I really think about stuff. It makes me see the stuff I don't know about; like all the ways that I damage kids that I would never think about, like this white teacher. I don't think she was like racist, she's not like, "I don't like African Americans or whatever." But she didn't understand where this girl was coming from, and that is me...

Stacy realizes in her retrospection, she could be that white teacher. When asked how this makes her feel she responds, "Scared. Absolutely terrified. It makes me see all the things that I don't know about." Stacy's realization is beneficial in this stage of her learning because she is developing increased awareness that teaching is a complicated process. While reflection is a type of thinking she dislikes, she realizes reflection facilitates a process of resolving these complex issues. In contrast, young Kurosawa sees things that he is not supposed to see, and obtains knowledge he is not supposed to have. However, Stacy lacks knowledge and Kurosawa obtains knowledge. Stacy seems to believe or has discovered her realization that she may be another white teacher who doesn't "see" cultural differences. This frightens Stacy into seeing another facet of reflection about herself that may be beneficial. However, in relating to her own experiences, Stacy demonstrates she has yet to connect the act of reflection to her practicum experiences. She states (*pseudonym): "I didn't really think there's something I could do differently, although now that I saw it I probably should have…I kind of thought this is Danny's* problem, like Dan was acting up. Dan was being obnoxious; I couldn't be a part of that, or done anything differently. I just thought "no," he's the one with the problem. So no, I wasn't really reflective on how I could have dealt with the situation better yesterday." In the aforementioned, Stacy readily admits she should have thought about Danny. Her honesty and behavior towards reflection, appears to demonstrate that whereas she is not doing it without reservation, reflection is becoming a process that she believes is beneficial to her teaching career. In closing Stacy responds, "Even though it is a pain in the butt, like this constant reflect on this, reflect on that, even if I'm not reflecting all the time the way I am supposed to, it makes me realize that we need to be reflective."

In *Sunshine through the Rain*, young Kurosawa learns he must listen to his mother, the authority in the dream, because her experience and wisdom are crucial in his moment of crisis. He learns that if he apologizes, he won't have to use the dagger the foxes have given him. Stacy's experience, while not as "artfully severe" as the fox offering the dagger, corresponds to her fear of not becoming the white teacher in her commentary. She knows she needs to be reflective to be the teacher she sets out to be. Unfortunately, the process of becoming the teacher she desires to become is more difficult than she anticipates. Stacy sees that reflection is necessary, but cumbersome to her thinking. As Kurosawa must journey to the end of the rainbow to find the foxes and be forgiven, Stacy must forgive herself so she can improve her teaching. Albeit, not as severe as Kurosawa's dream, I hear and bear witness to the struggles of the students who are learning how to become teachers. They share as if asking for forgiveness for not liking, doing, or thinking in the "right" way. They reflect on not being reflective, and what that means. However strange this has become, in this process, the act of reflection becomes a reflection on reflection in its "truest sense." I am the messenger of their truth telling. It is in this frame, Kurosawa's film emerges as an essence of reflection within the confessional self.

Case Study Val

In the next case study, Val speaks of her own experience in relation to reflection. She explains, "I honestly don't spend that much time really thinking about them or thinking up questions. I'm doing it to get it done, mark it off my to-do list." This response corresponds to every interview I conducted, except one. The process of writing formal reflections seems to be a chore to finish. Val continues, "I feel it is hard to disagree with my instructors on a reflection. They know more about education than I do, so maybe I should agree with them."

The ability to present one's own thoughts and feelings in reflection assignments, permeates a large portion of the discussion. Val states, "I feel like I have to be polite in my reflections and water-down my true feelings." Val believes the process has nothing to do with her feelings or thinking, but rather is a formulaic process. She continues, "We have a format to follow in our reflections, so I can't say what I want because it prevents me." This is interesting to the act of reflection; a formula is the preventative force for Val. Finally she states, "Well, my professors and instructors don't really know me, and I don't want them to get a bad impression of me." Therefore, it appears Val considers herself either inhibited or unable to portray her thoughts and feelings accurately as a result of the structured nature and vulnerability involved in the reflective process.

Much like the foxes who need to protect the secrecy of their wedding procession in Kurosawa's dream, Val does not want to be seen as she really feels. She seems to believe reflective homework is nothing more than an assignment to complete. The homework does not serve self-analytical purposes. Whereas Val has not found a place to include reflections in her learning, Stacy is beginning to understand the connection between reflection and increased competency in her practice. Notwithstanding, neither Stacy nor Val have incorporated reflection into a self-evaluative and critical thought process. Hence, Val is reluctant to present an authentic or true representation of her thoughts, feelings, and self in her reflective writing.

Case Study Erin

In the final case study, Erin begins with an intriguing statement about her reflections: "I don't think reflection is that honest. How truthful can I be to myself? I don't know if what I am perceiving, is actually what is happening." This corresponds with Kurosawa's questionable perception of reality in *Sunshine through the Rain*. When he sees, of all things, a wedding procession for foxes, his preconceived notions of reality are called into question. Due to the strange nature of Kurosawa's dream, the viewer can empathize with his confusion as a result of our own experiences with dreams. Similar to Kurosawa's perceptions, Erin is uncertain of the accuracy of her self-perceptions in reflection. Many frequently attempt to interpret dreams or make them "fit" into one's conscious experiences. Often times, we try to find rational explanations for what seems to be inherently irrational or non-rational. Thus, considering the potential flawed nature of our external and internal perceptions, Erin questions the validity of using reflection as a tool or means of improved teaching through enhanced self-knowledge.

In the previous excerpt, Erin sees self-perception as something she may have little control over. Erin uses a filter for her self-reflections to decide what is in her best interest to disclose. Her filter comes to play in her next excerpt when she tells us: "I don't talk about the touchier issues like race, or something like that. It's too hard to do in a reflection." Erin makes it clear that she filters many of her true feelings in reflections. She goes further by saying, "I would never write down something personal to me. I don't want to share my real feelings in a reflection!" Erin becomes quite emotional when referring to reflection with such distaste: "I hate it, I think reflection is dumb in this program, it is pushed too hard. All we do is reflect, reflect, reflect, and it's never ending." Erin emphasizes her strong disdain for reflection, and admits to this in the interview. How does Erin go beyond her own distaste for reflection? During the conclusion of the interview, Erin responds, "I think a lot of my negativeness has to do with being nervous of actually realizing I am a future educator of American children, and that is scary! That is a scary thing. How many parents want their kids in my classroom?" It seems as though Erin may not want to confront her fear and anger towards reflective assignments, the reflective process, and becoming a future educator. The program appears to facilitate this lack of self-examination regarding sensitive issues. In the dream, Kurosawa's mother hands him a dagger with which to kill himself. Erin appears to be fearful of what may happen if she discloses the more personal issues in her reflections. The fear she describes likely causes her to filter the "touchier" topics in her reflections. As a consequence, Erin does not write for herself. She writes for her audience who perceive her through the filter she provides. In the last three case studies with Stacy, Val, and Erin each disclosed their feelings toward reflection assignments. It is apparent that each of them deals with reflection assignments in unique ways. For Stacy, reflection is a cumbersome yet necessary process for her to work through her discovery that she may not be reflective enough to improve her practice. In contrast, it appears Val finds the reflective process inhibits her authentic feelings. Last, Erin is fearful of sharing personal material in her reflections, and prefers to filter thoughts and feelings for her audience. In each case study, the reflection becomes an inaccurate representation of their authentic or true thoughts and feelings.

In *Sunshine through the Rain*, Kurosawa must decide whether to see the forbidden fox procession or to obey his mother. When he disobeys his mother, he must deal with the consequences of this action. The dagger is the last opportunity Kurosawa is given to apologize to the foxes and be forgiven. In this same sense, Stacy, Val, and Erin must each confront their fears and mistakes in order to forgive themselves for their imperfections. In each of these case studies, reflective assignments appear to mask their fears of knowing themselves, as well as their fears of others knowing them.

Theme 2: The Peach Orchard

Film Synopsis

In the next dream, young Kurosawa is a bit older and is celebrating Hina Matsuri (a festival usually associated with the cherry blossoms in the spring). However, in this dream it is associated with the peach blossoms. Kurosawa sees a strange girl in his home, yet no one else can see her. We discover she is the spirit of the last peach tree in the orchard that once stood near the family home. It turns out the peach orchard was cut down, and the spirits of the trees come alive in front of Kurosawa in full Heian period costumes to dance their last dance in the orchard. In the end, they disappear leaving nothing but their peach blossoms to blow in the wind.

Interpretive Film Excerpts

The following quotes are said by the peach trees to Kurosawa:

Hey little boy, we have something to tell you. Listen carefully you'll never go to your house again.

We the dolls personify the peach trees. We are the spirits of the trees, the life of the blossoms.

Don't blame him—this child cried when they cut down the trees; he even tried to stop them.

In the *Peach Orchard* theme, Kurosawa is blamed for having had a part in the peach trees demise. The trees blame Kurosawa for not taking enough measures to have them saved. It is Kurosawa's guilt for not having done more to save the beloved trees and their loss for this years' festival, that becomes part of our next theme regarding reflections. Here, reflection is portrayed as the guilt of feeling, thinking, or believing in things that are out of ones hands. This sense of inadequacy plays on our next two case studies: Tony and Pam. Both students share feelings about reflection that mirror the guilt and loss evident in Kurosawa's dream. For Tony, his guilt stems from believing he is not good enough. He is lectured on the importance of receiving a 4.0 in his education classes and feels that this pressure is "guilting" him to present a falsified representation of himself in his reflections. Further, Tony discusses his anger at hearing people spout their feelings in lecture, when time could be spent on other more worthwhile topics. In classroom discussion, Tony experiences a dilemma between admiration and disgust about hearing others discuss and share their emotive reflections. In addition, Tony feels that reflection is too invasive. In the end of the interview, Tony adds sarcasm to the discussion, perhaps to mask his discomfort over the issues. In a similar conversation, Pam shares a story that leaves her feeling inadequate for a variety of reasons. She confides the topic will never make it into a reflection because she only reserves positive thoughts for discussing her reflective experiences. Last, Pam indicates discomfort for not knowing the full purpose of the interview. She insinuates her feelings regarding this topic, because she is unable to echo what it is she thinks I want to hear.

Case Study Tony

In his interview, Tony exposes a side of his experiences in reflection. He discusses his feelings in the following excerpts:

A: As a student, I think it is something we get lulled into because we're in a system that we're supposed to come out of this program with a 4.0. And we hear stories from certain professors —well you know—what if the school district calls me and asks me why you didn't get an A. You might have trouble getting a job.

B: In some ways it feels a bit invasive to reflect in the way I'm told to reflect. It almost forces me to be invasive in a way that I probably wouldn't want to be invasive to somebody [else]. So in that sense, the pure aspect of reflection, I feel a loss of control to my thinking and feeling of what is right.

C: Some people really piss me off about how open they are with their real feelings, and I'm torn because I am simultaneously respecting them and very upset with them. I feel guilty when I feel upset, because I know this person actually is saying how they feel. They're actually saying how this aspect of the program affects them.

These three quotes reflect a sense of loss of control and guilt regarding the act of reflection. In excerpt A, Tony presents a common concern many students in the teacher education program discuss. Tony believes if he does not reflect in the structure provided or requested (among other assignments), it may threaten his chances of getting the teaching job he desires at the end of the program. This rumor is likely to be only among the students themselves, and it is heard repeated in some of the education courses where large assignments are due. Similar to quotes A and B where Tony's states concerns regarding loss in reflections, the trees experience a sense of loss, and ask Kurosawa why they were cut down. The trees bemoan a sense of loss by not sharing their blossoms at this year's matsuri (festival). Tony's loss is that he has to conform a part of himself when following the standards and expectations of the program. He defines this loss in excerpt B, when he explains the invasive measures he feels he is undergoing during his focal child assignment (which he calls an "extended reflection"). Tony equates his loss of control to the invasive regulations involved in reflective writing. In quotes A and B, Tony discusses the program and the limitations it places on the freedom to be true to oneself in writing. In excerpt C, a very different kind of guilt is insinuated. Tony feels guilty, not because he disapproves of his cohort's commentary, but rather he experiences a dilemma in his feelings. In his guilt, he knows that some students use the discussions to espouse their own feelings, and is part of their reflecting process. Yet, this is upsetting for Tony. In a contradictory fashion, he simultaneously respects and disrespects his peers for sharing their feelings in an open forum. It is in this guilty dilemma, Tony realizes some experience reflection as a venting process. This is a form of processing reflections that he dislikes for himself, but understands its benefit for others. A contradiction lives within the peach trees as well. They perform their last rights for a boy who is blamed for and has no part in their painful destruction. However, they bring back their spirit specifically for him at a special time when they know they will be mourned. The trees remind Kurosawa of the guilt he should feel for not having them at this years' festival. They play out this loss, by performing a dance reminding Kurosawa of all that is lost in their death.

Tony ends his interview with the comment, "You're making me do this now, so is this reflection that you're asking me to do; and then, I am supposed to use my "real" feelings. What if I don't want to?" He continues, "I just know reflection is tedious, tedious memory building. I'm sure forced reflection plays into that tediousness in some ways, but I am having trouble. Clearly, I need to go home and reflect on this." In an added comment after reading over his reflection interview, Tony writes, "I don't think I even know what is meant by reflection. I think I've only been ruminating all this time. Memory is a strange thing." Tony's humor and sarcasm play into these quotes. As a result of Tony's feelings toward reflection, he loses the opportunity and benefit of gaining appropriate feedback regarding his reflections, as well as the growth and development that this can provide. As a consequence of his perceived powerlessness, he seems to feel unable to present himself in an authentic or truthful manner. In the commentary above, it is unclear how Tony relates memory to reflection. Perhaps Tony is referring to the fact that occasionally reflection relies on the details of memory and perception (internal and external) for its potential accuracy. As well, he appears uncomfortable with the discussion, and begins to question the definitions of reflection. For him, reflection may be taking on distinct levels of hierarchical significance: in the lowest level, reflection is merely a recollection or memory of past experiences; in the next level, reflection is a careful consideration of previous experience; and in the last level, we can infer that reflection results in an opinion derived from careful consideration. Tony's questions demonstrate his insecurity with his answers. We are uncertain whether he feels inadequate to discuss issues of reflection in the interview, or if he is uncomfortable sharing. It is unclear from his discussion where his "true" discomfort lies.

In the *Peach Tree Orchard*, it is the trees memory of what they once were, that they perform for Kurosawa in grand Heian costumes on the day of the festival. Kurosawa cherishes their memory as he watches their dance and full blossoming with wonderment. The memory of the peach trees is all that Kurosawa has after their dance. He must remember their beauty and grace. In a similar way, Tony must redefine what reflection means to him as he changes perspectives throughout his interview and later reading. During his interview about reflection, Tony not only reflects about his reflective interview and the reflective process, but also reflects upon his reflections in the interview. Therefore, Tony shares his belief that questions regarding reflection are constructions of reflection. This unique aspect of Tony's realization of what reflection entails, remains undefined. In addition, Tony attempts to blame the program for forcing him to think and write in the subscribed style. In contrast, the trees blame Kurosawa for their death. Yet, they realize it is not his fault because he is only a child. Finally, Tony adds his commentary on reflection after reflecting on his reflective memory. This confusion for Tony is expressed in his comment on needing to reflect further on what reflection means.

Case Study Pam

In her interview, Pam takes a different perspective regarding her feelings about reflection. She explains in the following story: "My focal child; he's having severe home issues right now. Last week he was talking to another girl, and he was like, "I'm going to rape you." And I was,"what did you say?" And said something like, "Do you know how inappropriate that was? And do you know what that means?" He's like, "I have no idea what that means." It was something that happened to my mom and she's mad. I don't think I want to share this. It's a bad memory. I feel guilty in one sense because I don't know how to deal with stuff like that. What would I say if I wrote about it in a reflection, it's a lot you know…" In the above discussion, Pam shares a difficult conversation with her focal child. She knows that her guilt stems from her inexperience and lack of knowing what to do when difficult situations like this arise. She appears to feel this lack of ability, confidence, and powerlessness during her interview. This recent experience is a memory she does not want to share or deal with. Pam knows that the severity of her focal child's home life is not a reflection of her. Yet her sense of guilt and loss for not being able to "save" this child, is not something she feels can be part of a reflection in her education program. This conflict between what is, and is not right for written reflections is complicated for her.

Pam continues to explain, "I don't know, but there is this need in me for all my reflections to come out positive, even if it wasn't a good experience. I feel bad about myself if I don't find a way." In this response, Pam discloses the discussion of rape does not fit into formal reflections in a way Pam feels comfortable with as it likely exposes her vulnerabilities as a teacher. She explains this again in another response she makes towards the end of our reflection interview saying, "I first hate to say this, because I don't know what you want to hear or something. I feel bad because I feel torn about it. It's so hard, I wish I knew what you wanted, so I could support you and all my assignments better." In the aforementioned statement, Pam discloses her insecurities and uncertainties of what to say in the interview. Without a focus to our discussion, she appears to feel somehow wrong in her own feelings. This truth telling is similar to a "pastoral confession." Pam cannot share her feelings, without creating a story in her reflection that ends positively. She feels a sense of guilt and remorse without this "recipe" of what she believes reflection is supposed to center around. From the start, her discomfort is apparent when she is asked to speak without knowing the purpose of the assignment. For Pam, what she wants to hear is more important than what she thinks or feels. Consequently for Pam, the act of thinking freely may be corrupted by doing reflections.

Pam feels inadequate in her interview. She hears a child talking about rape, and knows it is not her fault that this is happening. However, she feels her response and decisions regarding the topic are poorly executed. Unfortunately, Pam is unable to see a reflection unless it is caste in a positive light. This inadequacy corresponds to the peach trees. They are inadequate to produce beautiful blossoms as they once could, and blame Kurosawa for this. They want to be brought back to life, but know that this will never happen unless someone believes in their power and nourishes them back to life. Pam is unable to see that her voice is important to reflection. She feels inadequate and guilty for not being able to better serve the child in the interview. Pam blames herself because she cannot see a positive outcome to reflect upon in the rape story. The trees mirror both Tony and Pam's feelings when they bemoan their loss in their dance. They can no longer participate in the festival. Tony feels a sense of loss for being unable to perform to the standards of reflection in the program, and Pam's feels a sense of loss and guilt for inadequately portraying herself in her rape story.

In closing, the trees perform a ritual dance as their last appearance for Kurosawa to remind him of their beauty and splendor. He feels guilt for being unable to save them, and this guilt ruminates in reflection as well. The reflections for Tony and Pam are torn between what are their true feelings, and what is the correct method of displaying them. For Tony, reflection is an invasive process. It is a game to play for the 4.0. Tony cannot play the game and be true to himself at the same time. For Pam, her loss is not being able to "fix" her focal child. She feels guilty for his behavior towards a little girl, but knows this is something she is not responsible for.

Theme 3: The Blizzard

Film Synopsis

In Kurosawa's third dream, a known figure of Japanese folklore comes to life. She is known as yuki-onna, or snow woman. She brings the possibility of fear and death to an adolescent Kurosawa, who is lost on a climbing expedition in the mountains during a horrible blizzard. She appears when the members in the expedition lay down for a nap. The snow woman appears as death, and her dream-like appearance turns the filming into slow motion as Kurosawa wakes to see her. Kurosawa lives to wake up the rest of his climbing party before cold death becomes their slumber.

Interpretive Film Excerpts

These excerpts are said by the snow woman to Kurosawa when he lays down in the snow for a nap.

It's just an illusion. The snow is nice and warm. The ice is hot.

The theme of *The Blizzard* represents our false perceptions of reality. When Kurosawa and his hiking party lay down for a nap, they are erroneously led to believe that the blizzard snow is warm and the ice is hot. This mistaken error based upon deception, almost leads them to their death. In their dreams, the snow woman helps build this false perception around them. In Japanese folklore, the snow woman is evil. She creates illusions to trick us into believing that all is safe. In our false perception of reality, everything is the opposite of what we are led to believe. It is in this sense that reflection plays on our notions of reality. In the next two case studies, both Will and Erin discover that their reflective experiences do not necessarily match their mistaken perceptions of reality at the University. In Will's quote, the unexpected becomes the truth. Will realizes he has stereotypical views of race, class, and ethnicity. He displays cognitive dissonance regarding his preconceived notions of reality. Will displays anger and mistrust toward the University, and blames the institution for being unprepared to cope with multicultural issues. In addition, Erin contends there is a contradiction in the University between what it proposes and believes it teaches, and what Erin believes it teaches. Both students must face their respective dilemma's in order to transcend the superficial nature of their reflections.

Case Study Will

Will begins with a story: "Just knowing this, I didn't think I had any vision in my head of what I was expecting when the mother walked into the room. But then I started thinking of what I was expecting when the mother walked into the room, I was actually surprised. And looking back, I know I was surprised because I had an image in my head of what I was expecting from hearing the background story [of mother and child]. I know that they are poor, and just really struggling to get by, and so I had this subconscious image of what this person should look like." Will continues to describe what he saw: "The mom was dressed real properly, and she carried herself in a real proud manner; and I didn't think of it right away, but she was also white. That was a shock. A white woman with a black child. But I realized after some internal reflection, that I did have a stereotype in my head somewhere, and I expected to see a woman in ragged clothes or not real nice clothes, and it was terribly frustrating that I had this preconceived notion."

Will states in response to this story, "It was upsetting because I don't have any negative prejudices, but then this happens. I didn't know I had a stereotype of what a poor person is." In this story, Will shares what happens when he is confronted with his stereotype. He is confused and frustrated by the inaccurate nature of his system of classifying others based on ethnicity and socio-economic status (SES). Will realizes what he has done, and attempts to sort this confusion. Will continues: "I want to work with urban kids. The University prides itself on preparing educators for teaching diverse populations and multi-educationalism, and other stuff. Well, I don't see it. We get a little bit of it, but the stuff we get is superficial. It's a major issue the University is not preparing us to really deal with these issues. We read a story with a minority character in it, and they call that bicultural education. That doesn't give you anything to confront the issues I am talking about. And then you get into the harder stuff about race, racism, differences between the African American dialect of English as opposed to formal English. I want to talk about this stuff, and figure it out, before I have to deal with these issues on my own. I want the University to give me what it promised." In the above excerpt, Will is angry with himself and the institution. He believes he is seeing an incongruity between what he wants to learn, and what he is learning. His unconscious stereotype towards the struggling white mother, is only the beginning of his cognitive dissonance with that stereotype. Further, Will believes he is seeing a paradox that the University is creating. Will says, "How can I reflect deeply when the University is giving us nothing but superficial stuff. It is a real paradox for me."

The "illusion" for Will becomes the University creating a program that touts multicultural education; but in Will's experience, the opposite is occurring. According to Will, instead of receiving training in the issues of race, homelessness, poverty and so on, the University superficially touches on these issues without confronting what they entail when teaching children. This illusion corresponds to the blizzard. In the blizzard, the fear of dying in the mountains becomes masked by the illusion of warmth in the snow and ice. In our politically correct language, Will contends we mask our fears of discussing the "real" issues of race and multiculturalism. The snow woman creates an illusion by hiding the truth about the cold. In his experiences, Will seems to feel angry with the University for promising an education filled with diverse experiences, but delivers the opposite of this. Will says the following about his reflections: "Reflection is an open flood, a stream of consciousness; so when someone tells me specifically to reflect on this, in this way, it automatically gives me a negative connotation. I can't do it like that." This contradiction exists between how Will reflects for himself, and how he reflects for reflective assignments within the University. The illusion of reflection as a truth-telling confessional is perpetuated when one is told when and how to reflect. Will frames it this way: "I don't like reflection in homework, but I like doing my own reflective writing when it is shared. If a professor is telling me you have to do this reflective stuff, then I don't nearly put in as much time into it, because it doesn't matter what I say. They can't go into my head and check to see if I am really thinking deeply. It's so bogus." Will sees that he can keep what is personal inside of him. This is a tool in the power relationship with the institution. Will knows that he can pretend to act in a reflective manner without revealing true reflective experiences. It is a form of reflection that he utilizes, because others cannot recognize, accurately evaluate, or judge the quality and content of his thoughts as he portrays them in his reflective assignments. Will creates distorted views of truth about himself in his reflection assignments, whereas the snow woman attempts to distort or conceal Kurosawa's perception of reality with an illusion. The blizzard is not warm and ice is not hot, but in the snow woman's hands, it becomes a distortion of truth. Will knows that he can "create" reflective assignments without holding true to what is real in his experiences.

Case Study Erin

Erin begins by commenting on the superficial nature of her reflections. "Yeah, it's all pretty superficial for me, I do it to get it done; jump through the hoop and prove to them that I can play the game. I don't believe in it [reflection] at all. Why should I, when they don't really want to know what I am thinking. And even if they do, shame on them for wanting a piece of me. I am not willing to go there." Erin casts a shadow over reflection in her next excerpt, when she shares a story about her educational experiences at the University. "I used to think that reflection would be useful, you know, helpful to me when I wanted to think things through. Then, it comes down to me reflecting because I have to in my ed. classes. It becomes a band-aid on a big problem. How am I supposed to sort out the complexities I am thinking all by myself? It is not enough. I don't just want to read about African Americans, like that is going to solve the reading problems in third grade. I want to know how to confront this stuff. Yesterday, my focal child was picked up by the cops for setting fires on the neighborhood with his brother. How does a reflection solve that? It doesn't. The University is somehow afraid to talk about this kind of stuff with us. Has anybody noticed that all the people in my program are white? I think that says a lot. So… it's a mess…and I don't know …"

Erin discusses the superficial quality of reflection work. Erin appears unable to share her real feelings and discusses this at length. She seems to find comfort in the fact that no one can tell her if her feelings and thoughts are true in her reflections. In addition, Erin believes that her thoughts do not belong in a writing assignment for the University, and does not want the University to know how she really feels and thinks. In Erin's last commentary, she describes reflection as a "band-aid" for larger social problems. Similar to Will, Erin describes learning about other cultures in a paradigm that is superficial. Erin believes her story about her focal child who sets fire on houses in the neighborhoods is a "taboo" topic for the discourse of reflection in her educational classes. She does not see the connection between reflection, and its relationship to her experiences. Erin appears to want someone who can explain the unexplainable complexities around her. Like many of us, Erin craves solutions when the issues are far too complex to easily be solved. This is Erin's paradox. She wants the University to set foot in a place she has already set off limits. Erin appears to think the University is both incapable and unwilling to analyze some of these deeper fears. Yet, Erin still wants answers to the questions she is unwilling to bring to the discussion. Her anger may be preventing her from her learning on a deeper level.

In the blizzard theme, Kurosawa is torn as well. The storm is increasingly getting worse as the party of climbers trudge toward base camp somewhere in the distance. Each climber is worn and tired, and afraid they will never make it to camp safely. As the blizzard increases, their hope of reaching their destination decreases. They stop to rest and fall asleep in the midst of the snow woman. Kurosawa is torn between the mirage of warmth, and his fear to find the base camp. The illusion of warmth created by the snow-woman is similar to the illusion of safety created by the University for Will and Erin. Both Will and Erin contend that the University is shielding them from understanding anything but superficial knowledge about multi-cultural education. However, both students appear to be afraid to share their true thoughts and feelings. They talk about the superficiality of the University, yet they internalize their reflections and only share a superficial amount in their reflective assignments in order to camouflage their deepest fears and regrets.

To conclude, Will and Erin are dealing with the paradox between what is promised and what in reality occurs. In Will's experiences, the University falls short in its goals to educate its students on diverse issues in education. Yet, he is placed in a situation where this reflection develops genuinely. Will believes he is unable to resolve or confront his stereotype of poverty and homelessness due to the nature of his feelings towards the University and reflection. Will's University reflections seem to be places of forced confessions, rather than authentic places to share his concerns on a deeper level. In a similar fashion, Erin must deal with complex issues surrounding her focal child. She sees reflection as a superficial enterprise where it is easy to hide or distort the truth. This illusion of how Erin and Will feel, and how they write is not only personal but public as well. In their experiences in the education program, the University takes a superficial grasp of the issues. This shallow attempt of creating a multicultural environment dissuades Erin and Will to put forth the effort themselves to be authentic to the larger issues of society in their personal reflections. In light of the blizzard, the illusion of warm snow and ice creates a contradiction of what the climbing party is in reality facing. They must contend with their fears of death in order to deal with the snow woman and all she represents. The snow woman's attempt at hiding the truth is a reminder that we must face our deeper fears in order to contend with the issues facing each of us.

Theme 4: The Tunnel

Film Synopsis

In this dream, the dead soldiers of Officer Kurosawa's wartime regiment return to our world, not knowing they are dead. Kurosawa must convince them they are dead in order to wake. The tunnel from which the soldiers appear, echoes the footsteps of the platoon as they approach him. Kurosawa is torn in this dream, and cries that he is unable to save them while they are in his command.

Interpretive Film Excerpts

Kurosawa speaks to the dead soldiers in the following excerpts:

...but it is a fact you died. I am sorry, but you died, you really died, you died in my arms.

I could place all the responsibility - in the stupidity of war - but I can't blame that, I can't deny my thoughtlessness, my misconduct.

In this theme, the "rules" for reflection are compared to the rules in life. In this bizarre dream, Kurosawa must convince his platoon that they have died in battle. In life, we know that in the end we must all die. However, this rule is not "fixed" in Kurosawa's dream world. Respectively, the rules of reflection in the education program seem to produce forms of inhibitive reflective thinking and lying for our next two case studies: Sam and Anna. Sam describes reflection as a prescribed form of thinking that must be adhered to for her reflections to be considered sound. In a parallel fashion, Anna describes her fabricated reflections as her method of following the guidelines set forth in reflection. Both students counter the rules created for reflections, with their own set of rules to follow.

Case Study Sam

In her interview, Sam talks freely about her inability to reflect her way. She talks about this in the following three quotes:

Okay, um. Yeah, I've been prevented from thinking my way in all my reflections. ...

That's one way to kill free responses by putting me down for how I feel, and then judging me and critiquing me for it. ...

I might say in one of my reflection assignments, there's this bossy kid in my class I can't stand. And then, when I sit down to write my reflection paper, I can't say that I can't stand this kid. No, because my TA [teaching assistant] will write back it's not that you can't stand him, it's that you haven't found the right tool in which to relate to him yet. I can't say it. Do you see what I mean? Now I have to write that I am looking at how I relate to this kid differently, now that they have given me this profound advice. It's not a free reflect at all. There are rules and they are different for every person I write for. I wait for feedback so I can tailor it to their liking. It is the only way to get by in the end.

In the next excerpt, Sam states she has learned to reflect the method the University prescribes: "I've learned the hard way to just do it their way. You have to do it their way. They hold my future; I just want to move on. It's just easier, you know." Like many of her peers, Sam feels she is prevented from thinking and writing in a manner that is unconstrained. She states this by giving an example of writing about a bossy child. When she sat down to write, Sam's voice is silenced when she attempts to share her true feelings about the situation. Instead of support for her feelings, Sam receives commentary that she perceives as unsupportive and judgmental, informing her she has not acquired the appropriate educational strategy. This proves to become a disincentive to telling the truth in her reflective assignments. She believes she is implicitly told through comments on her free writes to follow the guidelines for thinking in a free response. This occurs after she has provided a truthful reflection. Sam appears angry for being forced to reflect within the boundaries of what is considered "good" reflective practice. In Sam's words, the freedom of a free response is destroyed. She wants support for her thinking, and instead she is judged by authority figures within the University who tell her how to think and feel about a child.

The above is similar to Kurosawa telling the walking dead they are no longer living. It is an *a priori* fact or rule that the dead do not share life in the world. In the dream, the soldiers feel, talk, and move freely. In Kurosawa's dream, life and death are indistinguishable. Sam believes she cannot describe what she feels, because everything must be tied to methods, strategies, and deep meta-cognitive analysis. It appears Sam is not given permission to reflect upon her frustrations with teaching in her first practicum. Rather, Sam is thrown into a world where she must convince her supervisors and instructors of how and why she is feeling to create a valid prescribed reflection. In this sense, Sam is forced to follow rules that she believes prevent her from reflecting on her feelings. Yet in Kurosawa's dream, the soldiers break naturalistic rules of life in order to ask him the reasons for their death. Kurosawa must convince the dead soldiers they are truly dead. It seems absurd that ones' death must be convinced of when it is the final chapter of life. However absurd, this nonsense is similar to Sam's feelings. She feels it is ridiculous to have to back up ones' feelings with analysis and methods when sometimes it is valid to vent on the frustrations we experience without explanations about why it is that one feels, thinks or experiences something in the fashion that they do. It feels illogical to Sam that she must think within these boundaries to discuss feelings that are neither right nor wrong. Kurosawa in his world where death must be proven to the dead is in a similar circumstance. The dream is evidence of the absurdity by taking us to a place where reality is suspended in order to grapple with the issue of rules within the bounds of a system. Whether it be rules of life and death, or rules about how we think and reflect, it comes down to the guidelines that we must each struggle with, in order to find a method that makes sense to the people within it. While Sam's thought process may be methodologically unsound, in order for her to improve on her practice as a new teacher, she must have a non-judgmental place to share what is happening to her.

Case Study Anna

Anna also shares similar feelings in her responses:

"I've been conditioned to reflect, so it is easy now to whip them out. We've been conditioned to say, "Well, I think this went well. I think I could improve this,…" and on it goes. There is this unspoken formality of it all, and that is very easy once you've mastered it. I think they are expecting me to say the positive aspects of whatever I did, to relate it to what we've learned or heard in our educational classes and that you also know different ways to improve yourself, and honestly I repeat that a lot in my reflections. I just, once I've established something I need to work on, I typically refer to that in every reflection I have to do. … If I have trouble thinking of something to say…um, I have to make it up. That's the way it is. It's all part of the formality we play.… If I don't have the grounds to back up my feelings about why so and so is doing this or that, I am tempted to lie about it and say this is exactly what is happening. You know, even though it has nothing to do with what is actually happening. That's what's frustrating. They seem to prefer it when we lie. It resolves the issue, and it makes for a "valid" reflection. … I think it is ridiculous to be asked to reflect all the time. Some things don't require a reflection. Something that takes a lot of time and effort you want to reflect on it to see if it met the goals you set out to meet. It is something like making a sandwich. You just need to do to get by and you don't need to sit there and decide on whether you made the best sandwich or not.

In her honesty about lying, Anna believes that lying is a necessary condition or component to the rules that are set out by the University. According to Anna, she follows the University prescribed guidelines regarding reflection. Unfortunately, she appears to believe these guidelines prefer her to lie, and "create" her truth telling in a way that "fits" the guidelines. She claims, the rules promote this type of thinking and lying. Anna speaks of the issue in detail:

Well, we're doing these focal child assignments, and we don't know a lot about the child… We're prone to lie about it, because we are supposed to have a thorough explanation of why we feel the students are the way they are in the classroom. ... I lie when I know the instructor quite honestly likes the made-up version better. You get a feel for this. I say it the way they prefer. I don't think these reflections mean a lot, I know when I am being true to myself and whether I am truly reflecting, versus doing what I do when I make it up at times. I do it to get by to meet what is necessary for school.

Anna believes school reflections have nothing to do with her feelings on a topic. She reflects the way she is told, and if that includes fabricating the assignment, she is willing to do it. In Anna's mind, lying is relative to the task of reflection. Anna believes she can be true to herself, without being true to her reflections. She claims to know the difference between lying to herself and lying to others. The guidelines of reflection are more important than telling the truth in reflection. Anna's confessions are particularly informative, because she is not the only participant to talk openly of lying in her reflections. However, she does so in a manner that creates a strong stance to the act of lying to others while reportedly being true to herself. When Anna begins her soliloquy about lying in reflection, she does so as if to tell me this is the way she keeps her sanity with rules that are enforced in reflection. The University creates reflection guidelines, yet students such as Anna modify the rules to protect themselves from telling the truth. Anna contends the truth is not what the University is looking for. The guidelines seem to be a systematic method of thinking within the University. Yet, the moment she veers from utilizing the University's suggested method, Anna believes she is given feedback to re-program her thinking into a format the University prefers to substantiate as a valid reflection. The cycle of reflection assignments, guidelines, and instructor feedback, continues until Anna believes the truth no longer matters in her reflective coursework. Anna contends she is aware of the differences between her lies and the truth. She feels that assigned reflection has little to do with sharing the truth, only the University's creation of the truth. She thinks reflections are a place to make up experiences in order to fit the guidelines of the assignment. In this fashion, the dead in Kurosawa's dream become a form of the living. Kurosawa must convince them of their death, and face his own fears of death in his conviction. The strange notion between what is true and what is false or fabricated, blurs the distinction between fact and fiction. Consequently, if the University supports, endorses, and believes her fabrications, the fabricated versions of truth may begin to take on a certain form of validity for Anna.

The theme of the tunnel creates a topsy-turvy world. Both Sam and Anna create systems for themselves which are altered versions of what the University is asking for in reflections. In Sam's reflections, she is forced to write about her experiences in a form that is not true to her feelings. This prevents Sam from seeing reflection as a helpful tool. For Anna, the system becomes even more complicated because she feels it is necessary to lie in order to make valid reflections. The reflections are unrelated to Anna's thinking and feelings. She creates a false portrayal of herself, and defines this as separate from her authentic and truthful reflections. Sam and

Anna's reflections are buried in rules and guidelines that they feel are wanted by the University. In the same guise, the tunnel blurs who and what is real in our world. We believe that there are rules to life in which we follow, knowing that we must eventually all pass on. In this theme, that rule is broken, and we are left with a new set of rules to explain death to the dead. Sam and Anna have created modified rules for reflections that have undermined the reflective purpose of reflections. They believe they have done this, in order to create acceptable reflective assignments as set out by the guidelines of reflecting. In contrast, they fabricate a new lens of and for themselves that appears to be less true to authentic or honest reflection.

Theme 5: Crows

Film Synopsis

In this dream, Kurosawa enters the paintings of Van Gogh. We see Kurosawa talking to Van Gogh inside his painting of crows with his ear bandaged. Kurosawa walks within the paintings, and slips on brush strokes. Van Gogh is seen painting with his ear freshly bandaged. The sounds and picture of a locomotive racing by is cut into the painting when Van Gogh observes, "I drive myself like a locomotive." In the end of this dream, Kurosawa must leave art behind to live in our world.

Interpretive Film Excerpts

While he is inside his painting, Van Gogh says the following to Kurosawa:

> Why aren't you painting? To me this seems beyond belief? A scene that looks like a painting does not make a painting. If you take the time and look closely...all of nature has it's own beauty.

> When the natural beauty is there, I just lose myself in it. And then as if in a dream, the scene just paints itself for me.

In this theme, Kurosawa walks into the paintings of Van Gogh to discover the beauty of art in its creation. While in the painting, Kurosawa confuses art with reality. He finds difficulty distinguishing between what is real, and what is fabricated. In this dilemma, our next theme of reflection becomes realized for Marty and Olin. In Marty's discussion of reflection, he reveals his dilemma of exploring the creation of myth, rather than lies. Marty explains this fabricated method of reflection, and the guilt he experiences when he writes. Olin, on the other hand, tells one story with two separate versions: the first, is the true, accurate, and authentic version; and the second, is the untrue, inaccurate, and inauthentic version. He explains the differences between the two, to highlight his reasons for the modifications in his reflections. For Marty and Olin, reflective writing is altered to meet the needs of the assignment rather than their personal and professional goals of improvement. The theme of Crows is similar to the previous theme The Tunnel, in that both display altered versions or aspects of the truth within reflections. In *The Tunnel*, the truth is altered despite the rules of the assignment, and in the *Crows* the truth is distorted and faded. While both themes are similar, the distinct perspectives each draw upon to highlight various levels of falsehood, makes them unique. The concept of entering a painting to create a new version or altered reality is important to the theme of *Crows*, because it draws on our versions of what is real and "unreal." Marty and Olin uncover their own renderings of truth as they write reflections.

Case Study Marty

Marty observes what happens when he fabricates a reflection assignment: "I don't necessarily get into it, I just kind of like B.S. my way through it. And then I have to reflect on it, and I don't want to say, "Oh, I just B.S'd. that whole assignment," because I did it, and I handed it in. So then, I want to kind of add on that, and you kind of dig yourself a hole here. And the farther you get with the reflection, the more you have to B.S., to cover all the other stuff you already made-up." Marty continues to describe this process: "So I'm going to reflect on what I did, which I made up. Now I'm reflecting. And see what I mean, it just gets to be a deeper and deeper pile I dig myself into. And then you feel guilty. You're like, I can't believe I'm writing this, but you do it anyways, because it's like you are going through the motions, sometimes, when it's like that. I feel programmed to find a reflection. It's an artificial process, but it becomes a habit." In the aforementioned excerpts, Marty discusses his dilemma of lying repeatedly in his reflective writing in order to "cover-up" his original lies. He displays guilt or pleasure and art for this action, but appears to see himself stuck in this predicament. Marty believes he is without recourse or the ability to change this situation when he creates one lie after another. In fact, Marty presents his action as a habit that cannot be broken. In Kurosawa's dream, he enters paintings of Van Gogh's from a gallery. It is unclear as Kurosawa enters the painting, whether he creates a "reality" around him or if the painting alters his "reality" when he enters its canvas. The uncertainty of reality and truth in the painting resembles the fabrication of truth in Marty's reflective writing. In his lies, Marty creates a new yet untrue reality of himself that only exists within his fabrications. Therefore, Marty's lies in essence create an altered perspective or view of himself. He lies knowing that with each continued lie, he is further and further from the truth. When Kurosawa enters the canvas, he is in a different form of reality that he has created in his dream. The painting represents another world for Kurosawa. Both Marty and Kurosawa create their worlds presenting an altered version of truth. Reflection assignments change how Marty presents himself because he feels compelled to be something he is not in his formal reflective work. The reasons behind Marty's changes are unclear, but it appears Marty feels inhibited by the reflective process.

Case Study Olin

In Olin's interview, he tells a story of his experience in two different versions; one for himself, and the other for his reflection. "I'm in my practicum, and we were reading this book about words for things, and the word [for pants] comes up. I ask my group what that means, and one of the students shouts out "underwear" over and over again. I couldn't help but to start laughing. The bad thing is, I had trouble stopping which just eggs him on, you know. It made me look like a real screw-up as the teacher in charge. I kept laughing, and just couldn't stop once I started. I would never talk about this in a reflection the way I just told you the story. I don't want my professor to think, what is wrong with this guy." In Olin's re-telling of the story for reflection, he shares:

> The word [for pants] comes up, and the student says underwear instead of pants. I remark that it is close, but not quite right. I give hints by pointing to the student next to me. He correctly responds, and we move on to the next page of words. I don't go in to the laughing part for writing. It's not necessary. It just makes me look stupid, and I'm not going to share that. I think I tell the jist, which is important; but I don't want to share the laughing part because, because it isn't what I want them to know about me. I think it is too personal, I guess...I don't want them to think I am too much of a "screw-off" to be a good teacher.

In Olin's telling and retelling of an event in his practicum, he shares his fear of looking unprofessional if he admits to his bout of laughing. He appears to be apprehensive to display this insight of himself to his instructors, due to the repercussions he believes it may cause. Olin's suspicions that reflections ought to exhibit positive images of one self, prevents him from sharing the event as it actually occurs. This self-censorship in Olin's reflections, disguises his true feelings about his teaching. In retelling the story, Olin purposefully leaves out evidence that the experience is anything but ordinary, to protect himself from portraying an accurate and incriminating version of himself. Olin claims that the truthful experience is personal, and therefore unnecessary for his reflections. Olin's learning appears to be stagnant in his reflections, because he seems to be afraid to learn about the true nature of his feelings as it relates to his teaching.

In the theme of *Crows*, Van Gogh appears with his ear bandaged after having chopped it off because his self-portrait appears distorted with his ear in place. In his statement about why it is bandaged, Van Gogh replies, "I just couldn't get the ear right, so I cut it off and threw it away." In this dream, Van Gogh is portrayed as the historically accurate figure; and the story of Van Gogh chopping off his ear for his portrait is well known. In writing reflections, Olin fears that he cannot share his entire true self with his flaws and mistakes. When Olin shares his retelling of the event, he removes the perspective that constructs him as unique, inexperienced, and perhaps vulnerable. Likewise, when Van Gogh removes his ear for his portrait, he tries to remove his own vulnerability in his painting. Both Olin and Van Gogh fail in their attempts to be something they are not. Olin fails to share his insecurities in his re-telling, thus making the story nothing more than an account of an event with little significance. In a similar fashion, Van Gogh removes his ear instead of altering the painting. Once the ear is chopped off, it cannot be replaced. In this impulsive act, Van Gogh proves he is incapable of sharing his mistakes on the canvas with his true form.

In their reflections, both Marty and Olin remain unable to disclose their fears and mistakes without distorting the truth. In Marty's interview, he examines his lying to disguise his prior fabrications in his reflective writing. He displays guilt, but appears unable or unwilling to change his reflective persona in his writing to match or be in accordance with his true or actual self. He seems to claim his fabrications are habits that grow with each reflection. In contrast, Olin presents a story with two variations: one, the event as it occurs; and the other, the retelling it for his reflection assignments. Olin conceals his mistake in his re-telling to obscure his methodological error. Both students seem to falsify their true feelings to appear more competent than they are in their teaching. In their creations (reflection assignments), Marty and Olin produce false versions of truth. When Kurosawa enters the paintings of Van Gogh, he creates a false sense of reality inside the canvas. Kurosawa desires to live in this fabricated world inside the painting, but is forced back into reality; and realizes the painting is only part of his dream. The dream of living and speaking to the painter inside his painting is far from real, and Kurosawa must contend with this in our world.

Theme 6: Mt. Fuji in Red

Film Synopsis

Kurosawa's sixth dream begins with Mount Fuji blazing in flames due to a number of nuclear reactors that are exploding nearby. The sky is flaming red and people below are fleeing to safety as rolls of smoke whirl in the air from the disaster above. Among the fleeing crowd, is a mother and her gasping children. The mother exclaims in disgust that nuclear power was supposed to be safe. The scene changes to the next day when all who remain are the scientist who created the reactors, Kurosawa, and his family. At the end of the dream, Kurosawa, his wife and young children are trying to flee from a menacing cloud of red radioactivity after the scientist jumps from the cliff in an act of suicide.

Interpretive Film Analysis

The following quote is said by one of the scientists who helped create the color-coded system for radioactivity inside the nuclear reactors. He is speaking to Kurosawa and his family.

> *Man's stupidity is unbelievable. Radioactivity was invisible and because of its danger, they colored it; but that only let's you know which kind kills you.*

This dream examines the possibility of nuclear reactors exploding, and what occurs when the safety system breaks down. It is this fear that brings attention to our next theme. The scientist in the dream commits suicide because his system of identifying the radioactivity becomes meaningless in the midst of the disaster. The color-coded radioactivity is a form of classification. However, in the aftermath of the explosion, its use becomes significant only to identify what types of radioactivity are associated with what types of diseases. In the next two case studies, both Tony and Zack experience a form of classification within reflection. They describe how the definitions within reflection vary, and how the system confuses them. Tony describes his own system of classifying reflections, and how he discerns the different types of reflection within the program. Zack also describes the forms of reflection within the program, as well as how he distinguishes between the types for his classes. Finally, Tony and Zack discuss their frustration with the system, and its lack of consistency with the concept of reflection.

Case Study Tony

Tony observes the following about the various ways reflection is classified:

> Reflection is the most used term I run into in the Department, but it is also the least defined. So many people use it [reflection], and it's clear that at any one moment they probably mean different things. Read this and reflect on it. Some people mean read it and think about it for 15 minutes. Where someone else saying that might mean, read this chapter and spend two or three hours going over this-and-that reference material in your head and on paper, and write this analysis. So, for some people it's like almost an analytical skill, and then for other people it's almost used as a tool for synthesis. So people use it as an analytic tool and a synthesis tool, but they're using the same word and not distinguishing. So, it's a question of when, you ask the question about how do you feel about reflecting as a homework assignment I have to..., it depends on which instructor or professor it is, and what their definition of reflection is when they are saying it.

In the above excerpt, Tony appears to feel frustrated with the apparent variety of definitions of reflection within the education program. He describes reflection in two distinct ways: first, as an analytic form of reflection; and second, as a form of synthesis. Tony displays confusion over the lack of specificity and distinction between the two forms of reflection he describes. He appears to use both types of reflection, depending on the instructor and the class he is attending. Tony demonstrates an inability to answer the question without distinguishing between variances in the definition of reflection. Reflection becomes a word without a coherent, stable, and unchanging classification or definition. The boundaries become distinguished only by the person using them, and are subjective in nature. Hence, reflection lacks a sufficient degree of objective criteria students can utilize in an organized fashion. The University seems to lack a consistent definition for reflection, thereby leaving students such as Tony perplexed as to what is meant when the term reflection is used within an assignment.

Tony continues to describe the types of reflection he encounters within the education program: "Another kind of reflection is the "touchy-feely" kind. I don't know how to describe this one in any other way, but: "Tell me about how it felt, and share your thoughts as you process the experience." This is by far the one that I hate the most. Give me a break on this kind!" In this proceeding dialogue, Tony describes another form of reflection that he believes is neither analytic nor synthetic. Tony refers to this type as "touchy-feely." He appears to dislike this form of reflection the most of the three types of reflection that he describes. Tony believes reflection is a tool for logical formal thinking, rather than a method of sharing ones feelings regarding a particular topic. Tony designs the classifications for reflecting, to determine how to write the reflective assignment for each particular instructor. His classification system is only meaningful to him, and does not appear to influence how others view reflection assignments. Within the University classification system, Tony demonstrates the term "reflection" has multiple definitions that seem to be defined and dependant upon individual interpretation. It stands as a word with so many expectations and connotations, that as a student interpreting this, at times Tony is at a loss for what to do. In the following two excerpts, Tony explains how he approaches reflection when it is assigned: "So, I guess the first component of reflection, is taking reflection as homework, is being clear on what somebody actually means by reflection. And sometimes it takes a bombed assignment to figure out what they are looking for. ... So in a sense, there's an unwritten probe. It's reflect on this particular aspect in your classroom, or reading, or whatever, and write what you think I want to hear. I become focused in my reflections on trying to provide what it is people are asking of me in these reflections, particularly in reflection homework, as opposed to being purely intellectual and thinking as broadly and deeply as I can about things." In the above remarks, Tony demonstrates how he maneuvers within the system of reflection assignments. He explains that he often must guess on what is wanted in an assignment to understand what each individual instructor is asking, when they assign reflection work. Tony believes it is unimportant to discuss his views on the topics in class, because his instructors are more interested in hearing their own. In this sense, Tony believes reflection is not a tool for either analytic thinking, synthetic thinking, or "touchy-feely" processing. The reflection becomes a place to prove that one understands what is taught in class by repeating it in a reflection assignment. Nevertheless, Tony appears to desire reflection homework where he can be purely intellectual in his thinking. Tony is baffled by not knowing what is being asked for when the word reflection is part of the assignment. He deals with this, by creating his own system of classifications within reflection based on what each individual instructor demands.

In relating Tony's experience to *Mt. Fuji in Red*, it is important to re-examine what is meant by reflection. Reflection, in its most basic sense, is the act of thinking carefully with consideration about a particular event or occurrence. Tony classifies reflection into three basic forms in order to understand what his instructors ask for when they use the term reflection. In Kurosawa's dream, the types of radioactivity are classified by colors so that each form of radioactivity can be seen to inform its creators of the types of hazardous materials it carries. This becomes a horrible waste, when the nuclear reactors explode and colorful radioactivity is everywhere. Now, the survivors can determine what type of radioactivity will kill them first as they wait to die. In a similar fashion the reflective assignments are utilized as aggressions to the self. The irony of the color-coded radioactivity is similar to Tony's experience with the various forms of reflection. Tony determines the variations of reflection in the program. However, it is not the three classifications that are important, but rather, what the instructors want to hear that influences Tony's writing. Thus, systematic truth-telling leads to lying, that is the death of truth. He admits that he tries to fit what it is they want to hear into his reflective work, because obtaining a favorable evaluation is more important than thinking deeply in a purely intellectual manner. *Mt. Fuji in Red* produces an ironic twist for the system of classifications in radioactivity. The classifications in reflection approach "unusability" when one must rely on individual instructor opinion of what is required in each reflection. Tony constructs classifications in order to help him decipher his reflection assignments, but it appears to be more useful for Tony to use trial and error with each instructor. In the end of the dream, the classifications are meaningless for the survivors of the nuclear fallout. For Tony, his classifications appear to be only applicable up to a certain point and then they are useless as well. Tony categorizes reflection into analytic, synthetic and "touchy-feely" classifications. These are categories of his own, and are mechanisms to attempt to make clear distinctions with the term reflection. Tony also discusses its over-use, a reaction many of his classmates share. A system of over-classification occurs in Kurosawa's dream. In contrast, the University system becomes one with distorted classifications in reflection. Without a coherent and agreed-upon foundation of meaning, reflection becomes difficult to classify. Each student must flounder through attempting to distinguish one person's personal definition from the next. Instead of a systematic perspective of reflection, reflection is blurred by subjectivity and the (lack of a) classification system itself. The result seems to be confusion and distrust in the students, and the death of the educational sense of purpose.

Case Study Zack

Zack shares his experiences with reflection homework in the following excerpts:

> I do reflections in my journal, but that is not school. School reflection is a formal, 'tell us what you did', 'what you learned', and then we'll tell you if it is good. It bothers me that's what reflection is, you know. ...What is it? The reflections, right? I think reflection is something you think about that you are doing. In the readings, we aren't doing it; we're reading about it, that's a response, or a did you REALLY read it assignment. I don't think of it as reflection. They call it that, but it's totally different than what's going on in my head.

Zack describes reflection homework as separate from the type of reflection he does when he writes in his personal journal. Further, Zack differentiates between actual (self) reflection and completing reflection assignments. Zack believes that reflections about readings are a misuse of the term reflection, and are used to determine whether or not students complete assigned work. Zack refers to these types of reflections as response assignments. Thus, Zack discusses reflections in three distinct forms: one, personal reflections in his journal; two, formal reflections in writing about himself; and three, responses to readings. According to Zack, each reflection appears to have a distinct function. Zack believes reflection is a process of thinking about what one is doing, but it varies according to whom one is writing for, and what one is writing about. In his response to reflection, Zack differentiates between completing reflection assignments, and doing actual (self) reflection. "Reading reflections" are less useful for him. He believes it is a tool to determine if reading assignments are completed. This appears to function as a mechanism or form of socio-cultural control. Zack continues to explain how he understands reflection in his reflective homework: "You all use the same word [reflection]; that's not how I differentiate. I look at the person giving the assignment to figure out what they mean when they say, 'Write a reflection.' It is something I think we all do. We have to write it for the person, not ourselves. Every semester it has been different. Me and my friends, we get together and talk about it too. What do you think so and so wants in the reflection, and we try and figure each personality out. It's all part of it. We all do it, you know. This 'reflect and write' jargon is completely meaningless." In the above remark, as a consequence of the inconsistently applied definitions and classifications the university makes regarding reflection, Zack believes these definitions and classifications are lack coherent meaning. He uses the word reflection, but describes it as meaningless jargon. In addition, Zack explains that his system of reflection is dependent on the personality of the instructor assigning the reflection. He discloses that he and his friends discuss this to understand what each instructor is expecting when they ask for a reflection assignment.

In *Mt. Fuji in Red*, the classifications of the radioactivity become meaningless after the explosion. In his explanation of reflection, Zack demonstrates that the definitions of reflection hold less significance in his education classes than they are intended to hold. He determines what to write, not by what is said, but by what he believes the instructor wants. He discusses this process with friends in the program, to decide what is the best method to approach a reflection for each instructor. It is ironic for both Tony and Zack, that the University systems of definitions and classifications become irrelevant to their reflections. As a result of the information gathered from the interviews, it appears that reflection has no common understanding or definition within the education program. Tony and Zack describe their frustrations at figuring out how to approach each assignment to best fit the instructor, rather than relying upon what they believe reflection should signify, what it means to them, and/or any objective criteria or considerations of the definition of reflection. It appears from Tony and Zack's comments, that reflection is a term without an agreed upon and understood classification. The "un-classification" of reflection creates a program with elements that lack cohesion. The word is classified not within the institution, but within the subjective power of the individual instructor. Each semester, Zack has to start again with reflection assignments to decide what is intended by the person assigning the assignment. Coherent and consistent classification becomes lost in individual struggles, and the system continuously reinvents new uses and purposes based on the individuals coming and going within the University. While this strategy works for Zack, it is complicated by abuses of the reflective tool itself. If one instructor uses it to see if readings are read and understood, and yet another is using it to discover students inner-most thoughts and feelings related to their practice (and grades are earned within this individual power), a student can become confused and misguided by the uncodified and inconsistent differences in each definition of reflection. The students seem to be rightfully confused under the current system. The power of assessment spreads a reflective fear which leads us to the next dream

Theme 7: The Weeping Demon

Film Synopsis

In his seventh dream, Kurosawa finds himself wandering in a ruined landscape. He hears footsteps in the distance, and finds that he is being followed by a hungry demon. In this world everything is mutated, and the dandelions are as large as humans. The demon takes Kurosawa to the pool of blood to observe the misery of the moaning demons. It is here that Kurosawa discovers he will be the next meal. We end the dream, watching Kurosawa running away with the demon close on his heels.

Interpretive Film Excerpts

In the following quotes, the demon is talking to Kurosawa in the strange world:

> This is a rose. The stem grows from the flower, and a strange bud at the top. The flowers are crippled.

> We feed on ourselves, the weak ones go first. It's about my time now; even here we have grades.

In this dream, Kurosawa brings us to a world where humans are transformed to live as demons. Each demon must fend for himself in order to survive the plight of other demons. It becomes clear, the system of who eats whom is based on grades (of who is dominant and who is non-dominant in the system). Each demon must find their place within this hierarchy to outlive others beneath him. Here, the topic of grades within reflection standout. In this theme, I have provided six case studies on the theme of grades in order to display the variety of perspectives, in what may appear to be a "cut and dry" topic. Not surprising, the topic of grades seems to claim the most disagreement among students in the interviews. Each of the six voices provides a unique perspective that is distinct from its counterparts.

First, we revisit Val who is certain that all her reflections are graded. She provides evidence to her claim from two of her education classes. Next, Zack believes he is not graded, but judged on the quality of his work. He discuses how this judgment factors into the style he expresses in his written reflections. Following Zack, Rachel observes her confusion over what occurs when a reflective assignment is handed in. Further, Pat argues that reflections should demonstrate quality of thinking and effort. However, Pat believes he can do this without actually putting forth the effort, and believes he has out-witted the system in his reflections. In contrast to Val, Anna explains that she has never been graded on her reflective work, and desires to be graded in order to motivate herself into putting more into her reflective work. Finally, Erin discusses her confusion in how the grades and/or points are decided upon. In her perplexity, Erin discloses her resentment towards the grading system altogether. It is important to note, all the voices in this section are in the same semester in the elementary education program. In fact, variances in student responses occur within the same program of certification.

Case Study Val

Val begins by describing an incident with a graded reflection:

Yes, absolutely, I have been graded on my reflections. An example... well, for my music class I turned in my personal reflection and I lost points on it, because it was like you didn't make enough connections to the text. And I was like okay, so for the next reflection I was making sure that I put in little quotes from the text to show that I was connecting what I was saying to the text. I feel so strongly about being graded on my reflections. It's my reflection, so how can they say it's not this, or that; it's me.

Val continues to present evidence from her educational classes that reflections are graded:

We have to write reflections in children's lit. I did a read aloud for the assignment, and then you have to reflect on how you know it went well, and tell about what you did and how the kids interacted with you. But, for this grade I didn't feel like I could tell what my feelings were during the read aloud. I feel like I have to pretend that they were great and I chose these books and I'm so happy those were the books I chose, and I have to advocate for why I chose them because I know I am being graded for having the right answers to these questions. I have to say everything was wonderful, even if it wasn't in order to get the points for my grade.

In the first quote, Val states that if she does not connect the text to her personal reflections she will lose points in her analysis. This realization bothers Val. She believes that she should have a voice in her reflections, and should not be penalized if her voice is different from the text in class. Val appears to frame it as a form of repression because she is unable to say what she believes, in fear she will lose points. In the second excerpt, Val discusses her experience in writing reflections for her children's literature class. Here, she feels she must frame her experiences in a positive light, regardless of the actual experience in order to receive the appropriate grade. From Val's interview, it is clear she feels reflections are graded. As a result, she cannot share her experiences without conforming her thoughts to correspond with the graders perspective. In comparison to the *Weeping Demon*, by being graded Val is subjected to hold an oppressed role within the un-codified and informal rules of the program, instead of abiding by her own beliefs and experiences in her teaching. She seems to feel strongly about receiving high marks. This creates a system where Val feels she must subordinate her own thoughts to the thoughts of others, leaving her thoughts excluded and potentially unexamined.

In the dream, the demon is also forced into obedience. As a former human, the demon shares his previous life with Kurosawa to explain the system of survival in this strange world. In order to survive, the demon must eat demons below his grade, level, or station within the hierarchical system. He lives within a hierarchy of demons, and in this world he must abide by certain rules in order to live. In the dream, it is apparent the demon dislikes this grading system, and is ashamed of the choices he has made in order to survive. With his survival, the demon perpetuates his existence in an oppressive world. Likewise, in her reflective writing, Val is oppressed by a program that she believes forces her to behave in certain prescribed yet inconsistently applied ways.

Case Study Zack

Zack voices his opinion regarding grades in the following:

I don't think we're graded, but we're judged. I think it is just part of it. If you see someone that doesn't seem to reflect too much it looks bad, and it ties in with motivation, and that sort of thing. If someone doesn't think of their own learning, and where they are going with their learning, that's not good.

Zack alters his reflective style based on this judgment, and explains:

I alter my reflection style because I know I am judged. It makes me motivated though. I have to accommodate the University style. My word choice and style are more formal and thoughtful to the reader. I think it makes me look better when I do this. The few times I have just slapped a reflection out without doing the formal thing, I have been given negative feedback about my thinking. It happens every time.

In the above comments, Zack differs from Val in his opinions regarding the grading of reflection. Zack differentiates grades from judgments. In his excerpts, Zack appears to believe that reflections are not formally graded with a letter grade or point value as in Val's experience, but are judged by their content and writing style. Zack explains that he writes differently for his formal reflections, because he knowingly expresses accommodations for the reader in order to understand his thinking and feelings on a particular topic. In addition, Zack believes when he does not take the time to write in this formal manner, he receives criticism for not thinking in a logical precise format.

Zack claims he is judged rather than graded on his reflective writing. Some people would ask, what is the difference? I speculate that Zack refers to "grades," as a letter grade given on some of his assignments, and "judgments," as a critical process designed to assess, evaluate, and improve student performance and/or practice. If we take this definition as Zack's, it is clear that students are judged by the individuals reading their reflections. Zack shares that the readers of his reflections prefer formal thinking in reflections, and display negative feedback towards his writing when this not provided. In light of the dream, Zack believes that within the system all participants are judged in their reflective writing. The demons are also judged by the system to see who is weak and who is strong. Zack voices a common sentiment that formal reflections are judged favorably (by instructors) when compared with informal reflections. However, to build a program on one type, model, or paradigm of reflection, becomes an indoctrination that lacks variety and indoctrination that prevents a diversity of individual voices.

Case Study Rachel

Rachel takes a reticent approach towards reflection in her comments:

Graded? Hmmm I don't know what really happens. There is never a grade on top of the page or anything, but things I say are underlined and stuff. I always had the impression they are more for us. But I don't know that for sure. I don't know if they even care. Well, care is probably not the right word... but it doesn't seem to make a big difference for me. I do think we are judged by them. I don't think they're really passionate about the judgments that they form of us, and well, we all have our own opinions...I don't think they invest a lot of time judging them, the reflection assignments that is, unless they are really bad or "out there" somehow... I guess I try not to think about these things too much.

In her comments above, Rachel displays her confusion over the system of grades. She feels she is not graded in a formal sense, but believes it is inevitable that she will be judged by the people reading her reflections. Similar to Zack, Rachel thinks judgments are "part and parcel" of the way people view others work. Yet unlike Zack, Rachel is perplexed by the system and appears willing to entertain the notion that her reflections may be graded. Her uncertainty and ambiguity is fascinating, considering that Rachel is finishing up her second semester in the program. This ambiguity is part of the system itself. Reflection work is part of each semester, and Rachel discloses her doubt over this issue. Her closing comment on the topic, strikes me as most interesting of all. Rachel does not want to examine the possibility of being graded or judged. She appears uncomfortable with the conversation about her reflections being viewed in this matter. It seems from her comments, Rachel is afraid of the consequences of being judged and graded in her reflections, and is nervous what her writing may signify to those who read it.

In the *Weeping Demon*, the demon shares why he is in this horrible world. He explains that in the other world he discarded acres of food from his farm, knowing others were starving in order to drive up the prices of his produce. As he divulges this information to Kurosawa, he cries knowing he committed evil acts. In a similar fashion, Rachel appears to share her authentic feelings in her reflections without thinking closely about how they are either graded or judged. She appears uncomfortable with the possible consequences of divulging her personal feelings in her reflective writings. While Rachel is not committing evil acts, she appears unwilling to consider how her lack of consideration on the matter of grading may affect her relationship to the reader or she may be fearful of the possible criticism encountered through the interview process. The demon in his evil actions, does not consider how this will affect him later in life or in death.

Case Study Pat

Pat discloses his feelings on reflection grades in the following conversation: "

> Umm, I bet the people who read them probably think about it, um whether this is worth it for me or whether this is a half-assed attempt to get it done. I think I can pretty much hide whether or not I'm actually giving a lot of effort, and so yeah, I think I have been graded but probably erroneously.

In the aforementioned comment, Pat demonstrates his belief that he is able to use the system of grades in his favor. Pat explains he accomplishes this by appearing to produce high levels of effort (yet this is not the case). Pat is able to disguise his lack of effort and continues to receive good grades (even though he is aware he is not putting forth the effort). The system rewards Pat for his actions and is deceived in the process. In his comments, Pat demonstrates the flaw of grading reflections on ones effort. Pat thinks that grading reflections is a process where it is difficult to untangle the truth from a fabrication. In comparison, the *Weeping Demon* must also hide the truth. The demon discusses his survival dilemma with Kurosawa as he prepares to make him his next meal. The one-horned demon is aware that in order to survive in the hierarchy of a system dominated by multiple-horned demons, he must deceive others. Pat deceives his graders about the effort he puts forth in his reflection homework. While Pat divulges he receives good grades, he comments that he likely does not deserve them based upon his low effort. It also appears Pat will not modify his behavior because it works in his favor not to divulge this information to his grader. Pat will probably continue to deceive in this manner as long as he is capable of the deception. Likewise, the one- horned demon will continue to deceive travelers and fellow demons of his dominance in order to survive.

Case Study Anna

Anna discusses what she believes she would deserve if she were going to be graded in her reflection homework:

I think if I was graded on my reflections, I would not be graded high. If they looked at what I was doing, and how consistent I was doing that throughout the years, I don't think I'd get a very high grade at all [laughs], because I'm just doing the same pattern over and over again; saying the same things with every reflection.

In the above response, Anna believes she has not received grades on any of her reflections. She appears relieved; likely due to the fact that she believes her grades on reflection would be poor (based on her formula of following a similar format in each response). She appears to disclose her reflection format as evidence that she is not reflecting in any or of her reflective work. In the next excerpt, Anna discusses how grading her reflections would be a motivation for her to discontinue her patterned reflections: "I would actually start using reflection homework to think about my teaching more, if I knew it was going to count. Knowing it doesn't count makes it hard for me to do. If I knew it was worth points, I think it would make a difference. Yeah..., I think it would; definitely." In the previous remark, Anna shares her desire to be externally motivated in her reflection homework. She believes that if her reflections were graded, she would be more apt to think thoroughly about her work. In contrast, Val's comments that having assignments graded would distract her from being authentic in her reflections. For Val, the grading system appears to restrict or inhibit her thinking in a formatted manner. Without an external system to motivate her in her reflection homework, Anna is willing to commit neither the time nor effort to being truly reflective. The difference of opinion within the system of whether to grade or not to grade assignments, is problematic to decipher. Both students bring "valid" argumentation to the discussion regarding grades in reflection work. Val does not require the external motivation of a grade in order to create a reflection that is meaningful, but Anna cannot motivate herself to write one without it. The system motivates students in different ways.

While I tend to agree with Val's argumentation, I realize students such as Anna have been academically rewarded through a graded system for as long as they have been pupils. Unfortunately, grades are what will motivate both Val and Anna to perform in their reflections. Grading academic work is not a new concept, but grading a reflection becomes difficult when one contemplates the standards with which an evaluator will assess a reflective assignment. The personal nature of student thoughts and feelings within reflection assignments are what makes this a decisive issue in the education program. Anna believes that grades are a driving force in her motivation to do well in her educational classes. Without grading, Anna feels reflective assignments are insignificant. She discloses how her reflections have not changed since she entered the program. The demon is motivated by grades as well. In this system of grades, the demon has remained alive and successful in his ability to deceive other demons. While the motivation for the demon is survival, it can be argued or postulated that the same is true for Anna in her survival as a student. She puts forth effort when she knows it counts towards her grade point. While reflections are intended to influence students on their daily practices and provide them with a "safe" place in which to share their feelings and thoughts, if it does not "count" for a grade, Anna is not motivated to add it to her daily work. She realizes this will not change unless reflection assignments are graded, in the same way her others assignments are "counted."

Case Study Erin

In her interview, Erin examines her difficulty understanding the criteria whereby a reflection is graded, she responds: "How do you say my reflection is better than your reflection? I hope they don't say, "I agree with that student more, so that is an "A," and this reflection is just totally off, so let's give it a "B." I don't think that happens, but how are these things graded? I get points, and I don't know how I get them and how I lose them. It's all a bunch of B.S.ing. Yeah, there's definitely a lot of that going around." Erin responds to her lack of understanding regarding how points are earned in a reflection assignment. Erin appears to describe it as an arbitrary process that lacks measures to ensure students are treated fairly in the process. She seems to believe that her reflections are graded without careful consideration. In this sense, Erin feels her reflections are possibly graded based on agreements with her instructors on the issues regarding reflective assignments. In Erin's comment, it appears that grades can become meaningless to students if they are not informed about how one earns and loses points. Whereas many other students feel they are graded and judged based on the quality of their thinking, Erin believes it does not matter what she thinks or feels because the method of grading reflections is a haphazard enterprise she has no control over. As in the *Weeping Demon*, Erin believes her grades are out of her hands. She has little control on how she will be judged in her reflection, and how the grader will interpret her thoughts and feelings about a topic. In some respects and in a similar fashion, the demon is also powerless. He can maneuver and deceive within the system, but he does not take part in the systems creation. The grades and hierarchy existed before he became demon. Erin also is not part of the creation of the grading system in which she is judged. She must perform within it in order to survive, but she is not privy to the inner workings of it. To survive the judgments and grading, each must contend with the system using their idiosyncratic methods.

In closing, from this discussion on grades it appears that opinions vary across the spectrum. Val strongly believes she is graded in her reflections, and feels this causes her to comment superficially in her assignments because she is afraid to lose the points in her reflections. Zack describes his reflections as "un-graded," but judged. He shares his formal writing style for reflections that appear to benefit him. On the other hand, Rachel is unclear how or if she is graded or judged. She appears uncomfortable with the topic and avoids thinking about how this effects her work. In addition, Pat discovers a "loophole" in the grading process where he can hide his "true" feelings, but still appear adequately reflective and thoughtful in his assignments. Anna believes she is not graded in her reflective work, but unlike Val, discloses her need for them to be graded in order for them to be worthwhile. Finally, Erin believes she is graded but is uncertain to how these grades are evaluated. She fears that grades may be based on subjective value judgments, rather than formal evaluation measures. Similarly the demon discovers his own mortality is related to the hierarchy of cannibalism. He fears for his own life, and develops a system where he appears dominant despite the truth.

Theme 8: Village of Watermills

Film Synopsis

In this last dream, Kurosawa is taken to a place of earlier times. In this sleepy village, waterwheels creak in reassuring rhythms, adults live to old age, and children are polite. Kurosawa meets an old man who describes the modern world where things are made to look simplistic and convenient, but in reality he believes everything is more complicated. In his hundred years of experience, the old man convincingly argues that a life which is natural, is most satisfying. At the end of the dream, we are left to watch a joyous funeral procession of his friend through the village. We view him joining the parade as the lead marcher. It is the joy of living fully that is celebrated in this village, not the mourning of an unfulfilled existence.

Interpretive Film Excerpts

The old man who is working at his watermill talks to Kurosawa in the following quotes:

...but nothing is so dark. Yes, that is what night is supposed to be. Why should night be as bright as day.

Perhaps people get used to convenience. They think convenience is better. They throw out what is truly good.

Unlike all the other dreams, this theme does not examine blame, guilt, loss, deception, or fear. In the *Village of Watermills*, Kurosawa takes us to place where life is lived basically and time is taken to enjoy living in a simplified form. The village does not have the modern conveniences of running water, electricity, or even heat. Kurosawa is lectured on the important virtues of life by one of the elder members of the village. He shares his wisdom and insight on a life well-lived. The old man explains why he believes modern conveniences take us away from nature, and how to relish the beauty surrounding us. Kurosawa and the old man discuss their opposing views of life, and Kurosawa learns to stop and listen to himself for the first time. In the *Village of Watermills*, time is valued because the villagers make it a priority. It is in reference to time, we examine our last two case studies on reflection. Both students examine their experiences and needs in order to improve the reflective process. Allan discusses his desire to improve reflections by the creation of a reflection discussion group during the semester to share his thoughts and feelings regarding teaching with a small number of individuals. He also examines the need to discuss his experiences one-on-one with his supervisor over the course of material, rather than relying on the written form. Pat informs us that personal connections with his supervisor are necessary for the reflective process to be fruitful. Further, he shares his need to for the reflection experience to be based on mutual trust in order for him to gain the benefits he has observed in others. Allan and Pat believe they are describing an improved method of reflection in their comments and recommendations. They believe in the power of reflection on many levels, but do not feel the University is providing the appropriate conditions to make it possible.

Case Study Allan

Allan discusses his need to share his reflections one-to-one. While others also expressed the concern for time to reflect, Allan describes this eloquently in the following remark:

> The program requires a lot out of us all the time. It also requires a lot of reflections. For me it is a time issue. I want to do a good job, and I'm finding it difficult because there are so many things pulling at us; I want to give my 100% to all of them. Reflections are really important to me, but when I don't have time to process; it's all in the processing that I think is what is lacking for me. I need to have time to do the real thinking to make it worthwhile in my reflective writing. That takes a lot of time, and the University is forgetting that.

Allan describes the need to process his thinking for all of his assignments (including his reflective assignments). He believes that if more time to process his work were allotted, he would have more time to reflect upon his teaching. Allan believes the reflective process is important to become a good practitioner, but views reflection as a process that takes time in order to gain valuable meaning from experiences. In the next two comments, Allan prescribes recommendations for an improved system for reflective thinking. He states:

> It's an issue of quality over quantity. If I were to change something, I think it's good for us to think about what we're doing. But why every single class? If we do it for every class it loses something for me. I would love it if I only had to do one for a small meeting group throughout the entire program. We could build a community, and that would be ideal. ... I want to talk to my supervisor more one-to-one too. She is so busy with us, I know, but it would be much more meaningful to sit with us individually during the semester, instead of just writing us. That would give us time to talk to someone with more knowledge and experience on topics that are particular to us in a safe way. I think that would add a lot. Well, ideally we would have only five or six people to a supervisor, and that person would follow us for a year. Our small group would last for the entire professional program. We would become a family in the program, and would support each other as teachers. We would be required to invite people to our meetings at least 6 times or so in order to get professional feedback or something. I think we would need to think of a system, so the university knows we are meeting. I don't know how we would do that exactly, but the idea is to make it more informal and natural.

In the aforementioned excerpts, Allan recommends a variety of changes for the education program. He believes strongly in reflection, but in order for it to be a positive experience for students, he suggests quality over quantity with reflections. Further, Allan recommends small groups with a supervisor all year, so an informal family can be created within each program to share experiences around teaching. Last, Allan advocates for more time to discuss issues with one's supervisor during the course of the practicum and student teaching. He believes conversations regarding one's thoughts and feelings should be more informal, in order to create an environment that is more comfortable to discuss one's true feelings. In comparison to *Village of Watermills*, Allan demonstrates the power of reflection if the necessary conditions are rendered. In the dream, time is valued as a priority for living well. In addition, Allan mentions time as a necessary condition to make reflections useful to his teaching. He argues for quality of reflections over quantity of reflections, and believes less reflective writing is not synonymous with less reflective thinking. In his recommendation for a small group over the course of the entire program, Allan describes a place like the village of watermills where family takes precedence over everything else. By creating the feel of family in small reflection groups, Allan desires a place where students can go beyond the formalities and ritual pleasantries to discuss the problematical issues they are facing as beginning practitioners in the field. This type of social space takes time and trust to build. In Kurosawa's dream, the village is built on the community belief of trust and care for each other. This is demonstrated in the final scenes when the old man joins the funeral procession of an old friend who he describes as a first love. Their lives intersected because the village believes everyone must be a part of its creation to make it successful. Allan believes the program can be successful if a place is created where reflective discourse is valued, and made a priority in the University.

Case Study Pat

Pat describes what he believes would make the education program become a better place for reflection in the next two excerpts:

> I love my computer, and I don't know what I would do without it now. But I hate writing reflections on it. I can't describe how strange it feels to write down my feelings and stuff, when it would be much more helpful to talk to someone and get feedback at the same time. I can't do that with a reflection I write down. It doesn't say anything to me. I can't hear other perspectives and think about that while I am all by myself. It doesn't work. I thought emailing my reflections to my supervisor would help, but it doesn't. I need to see her face and expressions when she tells me her thinking. It is totally different when we meet than when I write. ...
> I feel like I am talking about a restaurant or something. Good food, good people, and time to share with each other— that should be our motto for reflection. It is kind of hokey [laughs], but I think it would work better than what we do now. I think food makes a big difference. I would put it first, because it warms you

up to talking and sharing your feelings with someone else. It is really trust that makes reflection work though. Our program is too stale and formal with it, to make it really useful for me. It needs to feel real, to talk real, you know what I mean?

In the above conversation, Pat describes how he would change reflections at the University to produce an environment that brings reflections to an informal discussion over a formal paper. Pat explains his discomfort with email reflections because he is unable to have a dialogue with his supervisor face-to face. He appears to acknowledge the benefits of reflection when he can have more than a one-sided and self-generated perspective on his thoughts and feelings. He jokingly describes a restaurant where everyone is able to eat, share, and express themselves in a casual environment away from staleness of the classroom. Similarly, Allan describes his small reflection groups throughout the year. Pat and Allan desire a way to make reflections more informal in order to create trust among the participants sharing. In a sense, they are both claiming that the nature of reflections (as they are currently administered) is without elements of trust, family, or dialogue. According to Pat and Allan, reflection is lacking in these aspects because reflection is seen as something that should occur by oneself. Both dispute the notion of a "private" reflection, to the creation of a small group conception of sharing ones personal thoughts and feelings. In order to create such a place, they believe trust and long-term commitment must be valued in order to make it worthwhile for the participants. In the *Village of the Watermills*, this community exits within Kurosawa's dreams. It is built on the same elements discussed by Allan and Pat. The people of the village value time and trust in order to build community support for their lifestyle. The village relies upon the simple ways of life to bring people together for common purposes. Allan and Pat believe in support from their peers to discuss what they believe is important and relevant to their teaching. They feel this is not supported as the University hoped in the form of written reflections. They propose reflection dialogue groups that have the same purpose as written reflections, but strive to accomplish their goals through other means. In their attempt to creatively use their reflective style, they prioritize three basic concepts: trust, open dialogue, and community. They feel this will be embraced by both instructors and students, and will create a new form of reflection for the University.

Interpretive Discussion

The eight themes provide the imagery in which to fully comprehend students' perceptions, feelings, and understandings regarding reflection. In this interpretive discussion, the conceptual frame of Kurosawa is set aside in order to re-interpret the themes from their case studies with a new light through which a broader categorization process emerges. I believe it is crucial to revisit the student beliefs regarding reflection in order to view the larger perspectives that integrate their thoughts and feelings into a complete portrait through grounded theorization. I realize this is not entirely possible due to the biases and preconceived framework that I apply to the research process. It is in my interest to discuss what I believe has become apparent from the analysis of each case study, theme, and open dialogue about how the students view reflective practice from their experiences and perspective. I hope to add insight and dialogue to the discussions regarding reflection such that it will improve as we discover how students feel about the process of self-inquiry. The goal of the interpretive discussion is to look deeply at how the students view reflection and provide a synthesis from the corpus data. Through the use of grounded theory, I divided this discussion into five aspects. First, I present the idea that students view reflection as a confessional act. Second, I discuss how reflective practices for the students are based on their firm beliefs of fear and power. Third, relates to how students discuss the system of judgments and grades within reflections. Fourth, the students' regard reflective thinking as integral to self-improvement but feel this process is jaded by the formality insisted upon by the University. Last, I utilize Secondary Discourse as defined in the methods section (Gee, 1996) as a tool of analysis to re-interpret student perceptions on reflection.

The confessional nature of the reflective practice is based primarily on the definitions surrounding the act of reflection. Students' are assigned reflective homework that specifically frames the reflective process in a self-disclosing manner. Each student is asked to expose themselves and their hidden feelings regarding sensitive topics such as race, gender, and class in hopes of uncovering something of a "confessional" nature. The act of writing a reflection becomes a discovery into the secrets behind the students, and a form of disempowerment for the individual confessing. In conducting the interviews over the course of the semester, I felt like I was hearing things from the students in this same confessional manner. Information was disclosed to me, because it would be confidential. I did not expect reflection to have such a secretive and hidden agenda attached to it. In the interviews, the students disclose their apprehension towards revealing the true nature of their feelings towards teaching and other sensitive topics. They feel vulnerable sharing their true feelings in a formal reflection, and believe the task creates anger and resentment since they are asked to reflect in such an open forum. This resentment creates a belief that reflection is a place to either transform their daily experiences into something more significant and transformative, or fabricate their thoughts and feelings altogether to avoid the vulnerability attached to the reflective process. Fabrication diminishes the utility of the reflective methodology by utilizing it in a manner that is completely meaningless to self-awareness and understanding. Moreover, the confessional nature of reflection directly relates to the fear and power many of the students discuss in their interviews. The fear of telling the truth in a reflective assignment, and to have their revelations turned against them because of how they think, feel, or act in a certain manner creates great divides in the basic trust students divulge. In comparison, Dewey believed that unreflective teachers work to find a means to an end without reflecting on the deeper issues that shape their profession. Thus, Dewey contends that unreflective teachers are enslaved by what he refers to as "appetite, sense, and circumstance" to their culture and in a sense enslave themselves by accepting their everyday realities (Dewey,

1933). Many of them learn to discontinue revealing the true nature of their feelings due to the criticism and frustration this brings. Further, many of the students fear the discovery of their lies in reflections, yet realize this is nearly impossible due the private nature of the assignment. However, still anxiously feared is a day when an instructor or supervisor discovers that their reflections are fabrications.

The power struggle between what and how to share ones feelings on paper, causes many of the students I interviewed great grief. They disclose a need to shallowly interpret their feelings on paper, because they are never sure who will read their reflections and how they will be treated. This fear, that the University holds tremendous power, greatly influences how students react when writing reflections. They confer being able to openly discuss their fears and concerns with one another without fear of being judged. The fear of being judged out of context and being misrepresented, figures largely in how comfortable most students are in reflecting about the private experiences that shape their educational practices and beliefs. Furthermore, the idea that grades and reflection are intertwined is apparent in the interviews. The students strongly believe that reflections are graded, and this informs their decisions about how and what to write about in their reflections. The confusion over what to write when assigned a reflective assignment, is another aspect of grades. As well, the students do not feel that the University provides a systematic and clear definition of reflection. In fact, in many of the discussions, students express their need to confer with one another and define what is entails each reflection assignment by the personality of the instructor (over any other principle). Due to the fact many of the students express concern over being graded in their reflections, they tend to be less open about expressing their authentic concerns because of fear that they will be graded. Pre-service teachers feel that their reflections should be in accord with University teaching policy. Many student interviews articulate their concern for the rubric or criteria used to distinguish a "good" reflection from a "bad" reflection. Many believe it is a discretionary act based on the opinions and beliefs of the grader, over any other formula of what makes an excellent self-inquiry.

In addition, the students believe in the power of reflection for self-improvement, despite some of their complaints about the process of reflecting as part of their University coursework. Most students feel the process of "formalized" reflection defeats the purpose of assigning reflection. They prefer reflecting utilizing open dialogue, a process that most seem to enjoy and benefit from. Many of the practicum students discuss using reflection more informally as a method of sharing their teaching experiences. They enjoy listening to others share similar issues, and this camaraderie creates an atmosphere surrounding reflection that encourages students to be more open to thinking critically about their teaching experiences. Overall, the students I interviewed liked the idea of using reflection when it is not assigned as a formal piece of writing to turn in. Furthermore, many enjoy writing reflections in the beginning of class when a question is assigned by an instructor as way to begin open dialogue. I am surprised that the students do not feel as judged by their instructors and classmates when they reflect in discussions. It is the writing that seems to disturb them the most in the reflecting process. I can sympathize with the difficulty of putting thoughts into coherent sentences, but I am distracted by this apparent contradiction in their understanding of the reflective process.

In this final section regarding reflection, I will present Gee's notion of secondary discourse (as previously defined in the methods section). A secondary Discourse refers to anything that one is socialized into after one's primary Discourse, which are our first experiences with our primary caregivers. In any Discourse, one can presume from the definition, there are certain traits, actions, and activities one adheres to in order to belong to a particular identity group. In the case of reflection, I believe there are two possible Discourses occurring simultaneously and separately from one another. The first reflective Discourse I will refer to as the Institutive-Reflective Discourse (IRD), and the latter I will refer to as the Student-Reflective Discourse (SRD). The former requires its participants to uphold the policies and procedures considered to be "best practice reflection" by the certifying institution. The participants in IRD may include graduate students, faculty members, students, as well as the political bureaucracy surrounding the University. The SRD includes the practicum and student teachers who are required to utilize reflection in the course of becoming a certified practitioner. The aforementioned forms of reflective Discourse are defined as such by the criteria of a discourse as categorized and defined by Gee (Gee, 1996. p. 132). I will now systematically define and argue each point for the two simultaneous and opposing forms of reflective Discourse (IRD and SRD).

There are five distinctions made in what defines a discourse activity from another action we partake in on a daily basis (as defined by Gee, 1996). First, IRD is valued by the University as a congruent and logical method to teach and require students to use. Second, IRD is fairly resistant to internal criticism that it is un-useful and/or disrespected as a method of teaching and learning about oneself (Some in the educational program may dispute this second notion, but their voices are not changing the Discourse policy, which still encourages reflective writing and discussion.). Third, IRD is defined in relation to SRD. As oppositional dichotomies, they are in relation to one another and are defined partially by what the other is not. For example, IRD can be both respected and disrespected as a method of teaching about the self, but it still remains the accepted discourse for most educational coursework. Fourth, IRD puts forth a notion that may at times be incongruent with other concepts and values. It can marginalize SRD and consider it an incongruent, but marginalized notion, that helps create IRD as a Discourse. Last, IRD is related to the distribution of social knowledge and control over goods. In this case, the goods that IRD controls include: grades, career, and reputation. IRD is the dominant Discourse in the reflection pair because it is associated with the University.

In comparison, SRD is valued primarily by the students who are required to perform under the standards demanded by the University (Note: SRD seems to be subsumed within IRD and is defined by the corpus data). In this sense, students are both required to act in accordance within one discourse activity, while maintaining their own beliefs and deceptions that do not follow the mandates given within IRD. First, SRD is valued by the students as the means to survive the "required" reflections and still maintain a sense of self that is not privy to the institution. In this sense, all the students in SRD value a type of privacy that they feel is being invaded with reflective thinking. Second, students who partake in this Discourse may value self-deception and fabricating reflection as a means to keep the "true" self-hidden from others. They internally defend their deception as a means to work within a mandated system of thinking and acting. Third, in order for this Discourse to hold credence for its members, the dominant Discourse must appear threatening or somehow oppressive in order for students to feel justified and rationalize their perceived feelings towards reflective practice. Fourth, SRD encourages students to act as though they are in full support of IRD policy towards reflection, while simultaneously opposing IRD policy by creating and possibly fabricating reflections, which are "in-authentic" to the self and others. This in turn leads to further distortions of the truth, while maintaining a perception that reflection is a worthwhile endeavor to pursue. Last, due to the nature of reflection students in IRD are holding back their true and authentic reflections. This practice creates a conflict between what the University perceives it is accomplishing, and what is actually being accomplished. Thus, the students are holding onto the social goods that the University perceives it already has (authentic reflections from educational students), when the discourse of IRD defends and protects their deceptive practices of reflection from the University, while maintaining a façade that student reflections are authentic and valid in nature. However, I believe it is difficult to draw upon such a drastic interpretation from a limited number of students. It is difficult to make my findings generalizable to a wider audience when there are distinctions between age groups, programs, and other University settings. What is important to take from the case studies is the notion that reflection within the SRD is conflicting with the IRD because it builds upon a competing taxonomy. Perhaps, our culture of "nice-ness" plays a part in our students' feelings toward reflective coursework because they are afraid to offend and be themselves. This is fodder for a further study on reflection.

To sum up, Discourse as a social "identity kit" carries with it a social "membership card" for particular groups about how to eat, dress, act, and think as a member of that Discourse. In IRD, the policy of reflection is the outwardly endorsed methodology of thinking and behaving towards reflective work in the University. In contrast, the SRD outwardly performs and is congruent with the policy of IRD but secretly distinguished itself as an altered social identity group as a reaction to the invasive quality of reflection. The SRD identity does not want to outwardly go against the imposed reflective practices, rather it seems to prefer the individual deceptive means of fabricating and deceiving the IRD policy by holding their "real and "truthful" reflections hostage from the University. The barrier to reflection is clear when the practices of the SRD are uncovered. They are not only deceiving the institution, but the notion of reflection itself.

In closing, I believe this discussion regarding students' beliefs surrounding reflection sheds light on many of the factors we overlook when discussing the pedagogical concerns regarding reflection as a methodology for pre-service teachers. It is crucial we do not dismiss their concerns as mere indiscretions. First, it is important to give students the freedom to express themselves in a variety of ways. I do not think the University should do away with formal reflection assignments, but should offer a variety of venues in student discussions, and formal and informal writing to discuss their concerns about teaching and becoming practitioners. Second, the fear and powerlessness derived from the student interviews can only be diminished with open dialogue concerning the purpose and reasons behind reflection as a method of improved practice.

Many students fear they will be reprimanded or judged poorly if they divulge their true feelings in reflection. This needs to be addressed directly with supervisors and instructors who are in direct contact with students to discuss their fears and concerns of feeling vulnerable with the reflective process. If this is not given priority, students will continue to fabricate their reflections in order to protect themselves from sharing what they believe will lead to poor evaluations. Finally, students need clear definitions of what is meant by reflection, and how and if they will be graded, and by what standards. This confusion in the education program provides evidence that we need to include more dialogue with new supervisors and instructors as to what our mission is when including reflection as a method of instruction. It is necessary to be in agreement as to what we are accomplishing and teaching with this method of instruction, so students moving across courses can see a continuum of learning that builds upon a common framework. I believe these steps will lead the University program towards unifying their goals and creating teachers who are concerned and reflective practitioners.

In regards to this method, there are both merits and limits to Kurosawa's *Dreams*. I believe the strengths on the films interpretation adds more than they lose. However, I realize the pessimistic view may be seen as a bias to some in the analysis of my corpus data in themes one through seven. Yet, the film themes portray the case studies in a manner that allows for a multi-sensory image to aid in the comprehension of the abstract-ness of reflection itself. I feel the Kurosawa lens creates a deeper understanding of the individual students portrayed in each theme. Further, the re-interpretation of the broader themes adds another dimension to the data, and brings the larger issues regarding reflection out of the Kurosawa's *Dreams* to complement the insights gained from my analysis. Thus, to summarize in order to improve IRD I return to Dewey (1933) who addresses three main prerequisites for reflective action: open minded-ness, responsibility, and whole-heartedness. I believe all three items should be considered in the on-going improvement for reflective practice at The University. I propose the following improvements for "truer" SRD:

- Create dialogue opportunities for instructors to create similar standards for reflective practice in their coursework.
- Give students' time and opportunity to meet with their instructors' in a non-invasive manner.
- Stress that reflections are personal and confidential.

- Emphasis that reflections are un-graded assignments where personal growth and responsibility are emphasized.
- Remind students that they are responsible for their learning and growth.
- Require students learning the rigors of reflection that it must be applied consistently to their teaching, not just when it is convenient to do so.

Last, I believe my reflective study brought a new manner in which to understand the pre-service teacher perspective toward reflection. The eight themes provide a unique lens to the study of reflection by highlighting the complexities within the students' experience, and demonstrate this through visual imagery and myth. Further, the utilization of grounded theory in both theme analysis and interpretive discussion allowed the reader to distinguish the individual student cases from the broader themes that unite them. Most importantly, the findings present hope that reflection is a useful tool when it is given the time and energy needed to be true to oneself.

Acknowledgment

I would like to take this opportunity to thank François Tochon for his support and guidance throughout this chapter.

Finding the Truth in Our Inclusive Community

Amy Krauthamer-Maloney

The stuffy classroom filled with proud 5th grade students and parents exploded with applause as each individual came up to receive their 5th Grade Diploma. As I stood and presented each of my unique students with the piece of paper, that to them was a symbol of what lied ahead in Middle School, I reflected on what we had all accomplished as Room 135. We had come a long way. I thought back to that hot day in August, much like this one in June, when these same students also stood before me. Yet, I only knew them as my new class, not as the individual learners I know so well now. The image of a vegetable soup came to my mind. Our classroom, filled with all types of children, those with obvious abilities and disabilities, all blended together to create a flavorful taste.

A classroom poster caught my eye, "Classmates By Chance — Friends by Choice." Did this happen in our classroom? Research, as well as my own experience, has proven to me the power that community can have in learning as well as in simply living. Did our classroom truly create a community this year? Were the indicators of community researched by Jeanne Gibbs (2000), Alfie Kohn (1996), Mara Sapon-Shevin (1999), and Patricia Calderwood (2000) present?

I snapped out of my daze and saw Nate striding up with two skinned knees, to receive his diploma. His eyes were smiling as he reached me and I shook his hand. My mind wandered again to the time I was sitting across a table from him a few weeks ago asking him what he thought our of classroom. A tiny smile spread across his face, but he tried to contain it. "Well, I like to be with my friends," he replied shyly as if he did not want me to know his TRUE reason for liking school. In other interviews with my students, it was clear to me that connections between kids were important and that there were connections present in our classroom. What other aspects of community did our classroom demonstrate? Did everyone consider this classroom to be a community? How did student differences play a role in this? What areas did we needed more focus more for community building? How did all of these questions help to flavor our vegetable soup?

The Cast Iron Pot

I began my career in a Madison Public Middle School as a Special Education Teacher. The philosophy of education with which I arrived — from my previous formal and informal experiences — was one of inclusion of all learners regardless of ability, into a community of learners. As a novice teacher I had identified many key elements of inclusion. The most important of these elements being relationship building. As teaching developed and I received my regular education license, I began to fully explore what I meant by "community." I used four major authors, Jeanne Gibbs (2000), Mara Sapon-Shevin (1999), Alfie Kohn (1996), and Patricia Calderwood (2000) to help create a framework and inform my conclusions about classroom community and holding together our classroom "soup."

The semantic definition of community, according to Websters dictionary, ranges from all the people living in a particular area, to a group of nations loosely or closely associated because of common traditions or for political or economic advantages, to similarity; likeness. Historically, the root community is derived from the Latin word *communis* meaning; under obligation, with, together (Calderwood, 2000, p. 6). According to Calderwood (2000), logically this community, which is under obligation to be together, must know how to "communicate," or in other words, talk together and construct shared meanings. This definition of community has been seen throughout history when people have been dependent on each other for survival.

Jeanne Gibbs (2000), developer and author of *Tribes Learning Community* — states, "Tribes is not a curriculum, not a program or list of activities. It is a 'process' — a way to establish a positive culture for learning and human development throughout a school community" (p. 11). This new pattern of interaction and way of learning together is based on a synthesis of studies on children's development, cooperative learning, cognition, systems theory, multiple intelligences, human resilience and the skills needed for the 21st century.

The Tribes process is a sequence of events that leads to developing a positive environment and in turn promotes human growth and learning. It requires building a community through three stages of group development, Inclusion, Influence, and Community. The three stages of community on the Tribes Trail are traveled by the teaching and building of collaborative skills. These skills include:

- Participating Fully
- Listening Attentively
- Expressing Appreciation
- Reflecting on Experience
- Valuing Diversity of Culture/Ideas
- Thinking Constructively
- Making Responsible Decisions
- Resolving Conflict
- Solving Problems Creatively
- Working Together on Tasks
- Assessing Improvement

- Celebrating Achievement

The new way of being depends on agreements that are made and monitored by all group members. These include:

- Attentive Listening
- Appreciation/ No Put-Downs
- Right to Pass
- Mutual Respect

The role of the teacher or facilitator is to gradually transfer responsibility to the group as they travel the Tribes Trail.

The first stage in the Tribes process is Inclusion. In a new classroom, both teachers and students can feel fears and anxieties of the unknown. Inclusion is a basic and human need. It is the stage of trust, kindness, and a sense of belonging. At this stage, it is the teacher's responsibility to create an environment that allows for initial inclusion. This includes getting adequate recognition as well as being able to present oneself before tasks are required. It requires intentional use of small temporary groups that will make it easier for all to feel included before relating to a larger group of people. Inclusion- the sense of belonging involves:

- Presenting Self
- Stating Needs and Expectations
- Being Acknowledged

The second stage of building community is the stage of Influence. This occurs when members feel of value, that they are of worth, have power within the group, and feel needed. It is a time when members struggle for ways to have influence. A natural "restlessness" occurs in the community. People are not always being as polite or patient with each other and conflicts begin to arise. By ignoring the issues, the energy of the group deflects away from the potential it can have when they accomplish tasks together. The stage of Influence is a time to teach the skills it takes to value diversity. Influence- valuing differences involves:

- Setting Goals
- Managing Conflict
- Making Decisions
- Solving Problems
- Celebrating Diversity

The third stage is Community. The one intentionally developed through creating inclusion and working through influence. Members feel confident that they can handle whatever comes their way. They are dedicated to resolving rather than avoiding problems or conflicts that could separate members, they learn and practice skills that enable collaboration, they have agreements about how each member is treated, and time to reflect on how the group is doing. The stage of Community-working together creatively includes:

- Group Challenge and Support

- Constructive Thinking
- Social Skills
- Shared Responsibility
- Calling Forth Personal Gifts
- Celebrating Achievements

The Tribes process is not one that moves from beginning to end. It is not a straight path where members must accomplish one section before moving to the next. Gibbs (2000) describes a helpful way of visualizing the continual growth of a group as an ascending spiral that moves up through the levels of inclusion, influence, and community as it rises. The spiral is a continuous and never-ending process of developing. While each loop is a completion of all three stages, the loop begins again throughout time and the stages repeat. This is how communities gain strength.

The reason for community, according to Sapon-Shevin (1999) in her book *Because We Can Change the World; A Practical Guide to Building Cooperative, Inclusive Classroom Communities*, is so that students learn new skills. Learning is difficult in an environment that is fearful, anxious, or uncomfortable. Sapon-Shevin does not prescribe a "quick-fix", but rather activities that build on the principles of community building. She provides characteristics of school communities.

- *Security:* The idea of security goes beyond physical safeness. It is the sense of security that students feel safe to show others who they truly are. A classroom with security provides students with opportunities to ask questions with dignity, show talents without judgment, and take risks to expose the true person they are becoming.

- *Open Communication:* The open communication in a classroom community is one of freedom. It means freedom to discuss what is happening, worries, needs, and differences between group members. It means that conflicts will be dealt with and not ignored. Students and teachers feel free to talk about anything that is of concern.

- *Mutual Liking*: In a classroom community, while students are not forced to be friends, they are given plenty of opportunities to appreciate, work with, and connect with a variety of students. Fluid groupings are used for students including partner work, peer reading, and group projects. Students are given a framework and encouraged to appreciate their classmates.

- *Shared Goals or Objectives:* Students work with each other rather than against each other on common goals. Other students are not seen as competitors or enemies, but rather friends or partners. A shared sense of responsibility is seen and spoken. Children are encouraged to help each other solve problems and complete tasks. Whole class projects, such as a group mural or class play, encourage all students to work towards a shared accomplishment.

- *Connectedness and Trust:* Students in a classroom community know they are of value and are a needed part of the group. They know that others are depending on them and their contributions will be missed if they were gone. The trust aspect of a community means that students feel free to ask and share without the risk of being ridiculed. It means that students trust other classmates to help them with problems.

The rest of Sapon-Shevin's (1999) book provides examples of classrooms in which particular aspects of community were either present or missing. Following the vignettes, she identifies a brief vision statement of what a potential community can provide. Sapon-Shevin continues each chapter with challenges to the vision. Following the challenges, a majority of each chapter is dedicated to suggestions and examples of activities for classroom practice related to the vision statement. Finally, each chapter is concluded with questions for self-evaluation that encourage reflective practice. The following visions are included:

- Schools as Communities
- Sharing Ourselves with Others
- Knowing Others Well
- Places Where We all Belong
- Setting Goals and Giving and Getting Support
- Working Together to Learn
- Speaking the Truth and Acting Powerfully

Sapon-Shevin (1999) sees the vision of communities only beginning in the classroom. The skills and attitudes that students gain within a strong classroom community have strong implications for the broader community. She states, "We teach, we change our students, the world, and ourselves" (p. xi).

Alfie Kohn (1996) begins his book *Beyond Discipline; From Compliance to Community* with a critical question when looking at classrooms. His first question is "What do children need? — followed immediately by "How can we meet those needs" (p. xv)? This is very different from the question, "How do I get children to do what I want?" He looks critically at classroom management systems that rarely have long-term results, which he posits is the reason for teachers constantly looking for new techniques. His purpose is not just to criticize, interpret, and analyze current classroom management systems and how to guides, but rather to offer a framework that can help schools change what they do.

Kohn (1996) advocates for teachers to look beyond the methods of discipline and look at the goals. The central question to our classroom development should be "What are we trying to do here?" Are teachers trying to reward or threaten students into compliance, or do we want students to become ethical people, as opposed to people who merely do what they are told? He is a strong believer in the process being the point, not the product. The process is one that students are involved in to become the ethical people that will be leaving the classrooms and entering the world. Students should be encouraged to make classroom rules, wrestle with dilemmas, clash ideas with others, and consider others' needs. He states, " It means shifting from eliciting conformity and ending conflict to helping students become active participants in their own social and ethical development" (p. 77).

The process, Kohn (1996) goes on to explain, is grounded in the idea of community. The grounding force being that if you want students to achieve academic excellence, schools and teachers must attend to how children feel about school and their peers. Kohn makes the distinction between a collective or a pseudocommunity and a true community. In a collective, all members simply give in and give up private needs or feelings in order to serve the group. Compliance rather than learning, stopping the behavior rather than identifying the underlying motives and needs, are the goals in a collective. A community is one in which all the individuals which make up the community are not only preserved, they are nourished and the relationships between the individuals are deemed vital.

Kohn (1996) identifies three prerequisites to helping students build an authentic community. First, students need time. Time to be and work together. Not just a 45-minute community time is required, but extended hours, weeks, and years. Second, groups need to be limited in number. The larger the number of students, the more problematic it will be to building community. The last prerequisite relates to the teacher. The teacher must be in a community of adults within the school. Teachers themselves must be a part of a collaborative team with their colleagues and feel safe enough to look to their peers for support, help, and celebration.

Once the prerequisites are met, Kohn suggests four levels of building that need to happen to create the community. The four levels build simultaneously.

- *Relationship with the Adults*: Kohn calls for teachers to be real people in front of their students. To show that they are vulnerable, that they make mistakes, and that they have feelings. It requires teachers to develop genuine, warm relationships with their students. They should know more about their students than their names, know the details of their lives, what is important to them, and how they think. To build the relationships that Kohn is suggesting would mean to cross over the traditional line of the student and teacher relationship to one of true caring.

- *Connections between Students*: This level acknowledges the base of the community- the relationships between its members. In a classroom community, students have opportunities throughout the year to connect with all the students in the room. Playing, working, and reflecting together are everyday occurrences. Working with a group or partner is considered the norm for the classroom, individual work happening less frequently. These are activities that allow students to gain an understanding of how someone else's perspective might feel or sound are fostered.

- *Classwide and Schoolwide Activities*: The individual relationships are the base of a group, but to develop into a community the group must have plenty of opportunities to work towards common goals. Creating a class mural, quilt, performing a class play, doing a class service project are all ways to help create a common force. Class meetings, Kohn states are, "the single most significant and multifaceted activity for the whole class," (p. 114). It gives students an opportunity to come together as a group to share honest feelings, problems, and attitudes. Extensions of the classwide activities are the suggestions given for schoolwide activities.

- *Using Academic Instruction*: Community building should not be separate from what students are learning in other subject areas. Integrating the focus of community into academic issues must be a priority. Using community issues to guide the academic focus was also suggested. Providing opportunities for cooperative academic learning, rather than competitive grade races is another way to use the academic instruction to build community. Finally, themes of units can be selected or centered on community construction.

Kohn calls on teachers to look at the big picture. Teachers must reflect on the social learning of the students as well as the academic. The job of the teacher is to create a classroom where students can be autonomous as well as a valued member of a community. He calls the result democracy.

Patricia Calderwood (2000), in her book *Learning Community; Finding Common Ground In Difference*, examined at four different sites, a Catholic Elementary School, an all-girls private Catholic high school, a remedial writing class at an urban college, and a restructured public middle school. She spoke with participants to uncover what was important about community at each of the sites and then looked at the practices that were actually occurring in each of the environments. She found that while community did emerge as important for participants at each of the sites, the meanings and practices of community were quite different. Each community's vulnerability, fragility, and resilience were different as well. She looked at what emerged as consistently important for all of the sites, what was only of local importance, and how it relates with the previous notions of community that she was using to compare them.

While each community is different and operates with varied practices, beliefs, social relations, and values, Calderwood (2000) identified common conditions that a group must operate under in order to create community. These conditions do not operate separately, rather one influences the other and they work in conjunction:

- *Creating Group Identity*: For a social group to be in community, there must be a belief that they in fact share identity, beliefs, values, norms, practice, history and goals specific and unique to the group and distinguishable from those of other social groups.

- *Celebrating Community*: There need to be actual times and events which celebrate a sense of being in community, including celebrations which mark the ingress and egress of a community member or changing status within the community.
- *Learning How to Be in Community*: Competent membership within community must be learned.
- *Accounting for Internal Difference and Diversity*: Existing or potential differences between competing values, beliefs and practices within the group must be recognized, reconciled, or tolerated.

Calderwood continues, "The basic task of community is not to make common but rather to differentiate, that is, to account for the differentiation of insiders from outsiders and of insiders from each other" (p.3). In order to build a resilient community that will continue to grow, groups must attend to the vulnerabilities that come from differences. Vulnerabilities give the community the opportunity to develop habits and practices that will protect and deepen relationships between members, which will in turn strengthen it's resiliency.

Three of the sites investigated were able to continue to maintain the balanced relationship between vulnerability, fragility, and resilience of community. They all had unique vulnerabilities and avoided or dealt with them differently.

In comparing the four sites, the ability of a group to be resilient is found in its vulnerability. It could be measured by the groups ability to tolerate fractures while maintaining the overall group strength. The actual vulnerabilities were different between all groups and dynamic within each group. Because of this element, a set of rules or practices cannot be created to instantly create a resilient community. Calderwood found that while commonality between group members was important in all sites, the maintenance and celebration of differences was equally as important. Finding and nourishing the balance between commonality and difference takes consistency, time, energy, common practices and common activities (more than one). Critically looking at everyday activities and practices also helps to support the community. This questioning together as to what is important to the group, while it can become a potential fracture among group members, can be another way to build the resiliency. Calderwood completed her study proposing questions that groups could use to examine or prepare for community. Some of the suggested questions were:

- Why do we desire to be in community? What functions might it serve for the group?
- How will we account for identity or diversity?
- How will we learn and teach each other to be in community?
- How will we celebrate ourselves in community?
- How will we respond to our vulnerabilities?
- How much fragility can we bear?
- How will we know when we are in or out of community?

At the beginning of the school year I had bits and pieces of all of these indicators/definitions of community that I was using to form the cast iron pot. While I had not defined them as eloquently as the above researchers, I had purposefully made community an important part in our day-to-day functioning as a class. Throughout my career as a teacher (and before) I knew how important community was in a classroom. Creating an environment with students where they felt safe enough not only to learn, but take risks in their learning was what my teammate and I agreed was important. I had taken some classes on strategies, but most recently I had taken a class about the TRIBES process that is described in Gibbs (2000). In this class we not only learned about the process, but my teammate and I actually experienced a "taste" of what it is like.

Curriculum and class activities had been implemented with TRIBES in mind. Each school day ended with a Community Circle in which all students came together to share with each other. This sharing was structured around a sentence that the students completed, such as "Something good that happened to me today was ... ."

Along with Community Circle, each morning, as they arrived the kids would "check in" by placing a mood stick (happy face, sad face, or straight face) in their name pocket. They chose the stick based on how they are feeling about the day ahead. The mood sticks served two purposes, one to let us (community) know which students were absent, and second to let us know how students were feeling. If we saw that a student had a sad face in his/her pocket, we assumed that it might be a hard morning for that student and we would check in privately with that student sometime during the day. It also allowed students to check in with each other. It gave some of the responsibility back to the students to help each other when needed. When we introduced the mood sticks, we had a class discussion about how to support friends when they are having a bad day. Periodically we also took a few minutes at the beginning of the day to check in with the mood sticks and have kids share with the class or with their table why they chose the stick they did. From there, sometimes we would have a "mood wash", where a student who was having a rough morning would walk between two lines of students (like a car wash) and classmates would shower the student with positive statements such as, "You are a good friend, You tell great jokes, etc."

One morning a usually very easygoing student came into the classroom and placed a sad mood stick in his pocket. We had class mood stick sharing that morning and the student explained that he woke up late, forgot his homework at his mom's house last night, it was raining, and he just realized he forgot his lunch too. We decided to do a mood wash for the student and statements that came from the class that day included, "I will share my lunch with you." and "I will save you a swing at lunch recess since you will miss morning recess to make up your homework." Students really understood how this particular student was feeling and took the responsibility to help. By morning recess that day the student had changed his mood stick from a sad face to a straight face.

The format of Literature Circles was also used and was based on the work of Daniels (1994). As a part of the language arts and reading curriculum, students chose from a teacher-reviewed selection of theme chapter books. I placed students into book groups based on individual student book choices. Students were then assigned "roles" to complete after reading an assigned section of the book. Twice a week, students met as a group to share what they had read and participated in the group with their assigned "role." Students rotated roles for each meeting. The roles included:

- *Illustrator*: Drew a picture of an important part from the section read to share with the group.

- *Discussion Director*: Developed questions (and answers) based on the section read. Was responsible for leading the discussion of the book, involving all group members, and "making the group think".

- *Connector:* From the section read, was responsible for finding connections between the book and the individual, the book and another book, and the book and the world around them to share with the group.

- *Passage Picker:* Was responsible for selecting passages to share with the group from the section read that were interesting, had excellent word choice or were very descriptive, were confusing, important, etc.

- *Summarizer:* Created a summary for the section read and then shared with the group.

The concept of Literature Circles was chosen as a framework for reading for a variety of reasons. First, all students in the community were able to participate in circles. I met all student abilities by using: a) adapted role sheets, b) a wide variety of book levels, c) books on tape, or d) creating a different role based on individual needs. For example, a student who was non-verbal could use sign language to teach his/her group a word important to the section read. Second, Literature Circles provided a set structure for students to interact with each other around their learning and understanding of the book. I participated in each of the circle meetings to both model and assist the groups when needed.

During one meeting while reading *The Winter of Red Snow, A Diary of a Young Patriot Girl During the Revolutionary War*, students had a wonderful discussion about how the book would be different if it was a Loyalist girl writing the diary. The Discussion Director started the discussion and students were fully engaged with each other discussing what would be different from an alternate perspective. Students also helped repair meaning for each other. While reading *In the Year of the Boar and Jackie Robinson* the connector cleared up another student's confusion about a dream the character was having by relating it to his or her own experience. It was incredible to watch the confused student say to the connector, "I had no idea that was what happened! That has also happened to me." The confused student now understood the meaning of the dream due to a peer's anchoring of the experience for him.

Writing workshop also occurred in our classroom weekly. In Writing Workshop, students wrote pieces and were required to share their pieces during as well as after they completed the writing process. Like Literature Circles, students were not always working individually. They depended on their community to help them succeed. Energizers, or quick refocusing activities, gave the students a chance to play and have fun with each other. Each of the energizers were made to be cooperative so that students would again need to rely on each other to have fun. The science/social studies curriculum was also viewed with a community lens. We looked at units and put into place activities that allowed students to work together cooperatively to learn from each other. As conflicts or problems arose within groups or the community we did address them with a few lessons involving direct social skills or community building instruction. We took some time to help students talk about, role play, and evaluate what was happening with our classroom. It was a deliberate process occurring over the entire school year. With this pot in place, how did it truly affect the soup inside?

The Broth

The broth that surrounded the students, the day-to-day classroom functioning that we all swam in was intended to be warm and comforting as soup on a snowy day. However I did learn that it also got so hot that it stung the top of the mouths of the tasters as well. Following is an example of how one student described his feeling on our classroom atmosphere during student interview with me.

Teacher: Describe a time in our classroom when you felt really safe and like you were a needed part of our classroom.

Student: When we do a tornado drill or a fire drill, because when they go out and count, or if they count and someone is not there then everyone freaks out.

T: Okay. Is there a time when you felt safe?

S: Well, what do you mean? When something has happened?

T: I'll say the questions one more time. Describe a time in our classroom when you felt really safe and like you were needed in our classroom. So, safe meaning really comfortable.

S: Okay. I don't know. Like during community circle.

T: Why do you feel safe and needed during community circle?

S: Because it's a time when everyone has to say something that they did. Or they can pass if they want. Because then you have an option to say something or pass.

T: What do you think of community circle?

S: I like it.

T: Why?

S: Because you can hear things other people have done in the week or the day, or going to do. And you can sometimes see how they feel.

T: Describe the easiest time for you to learn.

S: Well, I like when it's nice out... the feeling in here or just the subject?

T: Both.

S: Well I like it when I wake up and it's hot and partly cloudy, cause, and there's not a lot of humidity and you can just breathe good. And when I don't go to bed too late so I'm not that cranky, I feel better. And usually when I have taken a shower the night before I feel clean and ready to learn.

T: What about in the classroom? When is the easiest time for you to learn?

S: I like, when it's the easiest for me to learn, probably in science because I really like it so I listen more and stuff. And when I feel group members are really nice.

T: What do you mean by really nice?

S: Well, they don't yell or fight or anything.

T: What else is going on in the room when it's easiest for you to learn?

S: When everyone else is happy. Because when everyone else is happy it makes me happy. And when people are getting along good. And everyone is just good.

This student started with the concrete and moved to the more abstract with probes. His tornado and weather account can fall under Sapon-Shevin (1999) "security" category of community, however this is only in its most concrete form. While security from the wrath of nature (this student later goes on to describe our classroom as safe because it is made of brick in case there is a tornado), is important to establishing the community, he did touch on the feeling in the room. He has had some experiences of "connectedness to students," as Kohn (1996) describes, that now affect his mood and his learning. He did not accurately articulate the feeling of "happy" as the feeling of community that he felt with the other students. He could however, define his mood and easiest time for learning in comparison with others. This same student later goes on to state, " When I'm in a good mood then I work better, I go faster, and when I am in a bad mood I usually go slower and just want to get out of school and go home". The broth that this student floated in did affect his mood. He made some realization that the broth was not just him; it was all of us together.

Another student described part of the broth like this:

T: If you had to describe our classroom to someone coming in next year, how would you describe it?

S: It has good teachers, we do energizers every day, usually every day, but on Mondays we don't do them. We have computer time, and that is really fun. After lunch you get to read, we always read good books. We do lit. (literature) circles, and that is really fun. Unless you have to write a summary or discussion director.

T: Those aren't good?

S: No. (laugh)

T: What makes literature circles good?

S: Well, usually it's a book that I like. Sometimes people might not like the book. But usually you can have fun, because it is a group, you don't have to work lots, well you do all your homework alone, but you get to share it and it's kind of fun to share it .

T: Why is that good to share it?

S: Because then people can know from your point of view sometimes of what it was like. But, if you didn't read it then you are like.... You could go in the group and you learn from other people that what happened, but you would still have to do it, the thing (role sheet) over.

This student captured the part of the broth that Gibbs (2000) describes as the Inclusion — a sense of belonging — on the trail of becoming a community. The student identified that while he did not particularly enjoy doing all of the role sheets required, he did appreciate and feel like he belonged in his group. Over time, as Kohn (1996) describes, I found that the literature circle groups really did become more and more dependent on each other to truly understand the book they were reading. It was wonderful to watch kids respond to each other, "Wow. I never really thought of it that way." It is a powerful thing to watch as kids teach each other.

Another example of the broth, or day-to-day activities that bound us together as a community, were the classroom energizers. These happened during the day, especially during long blocks of time. They are short activities that students "play" to help them redirect their energy to the upcoming activity. Similar to traditional class games, they focus on first giving students a break to then refocus their attention afterwards, and second to help build the community. All three of the students interviewed mentioned doing energizers in a positive way.

T: Describe when you feel most connected with other kids and give an example from yesterday, or today, or last week when you felt this. When you feel connected with other kids.

S: When we play energizers. And yesterday when we played the fish ....

T: Fish Gobbler?

S: Fish Gobbler. It was fun.

T: Why did you feel connected to other kids?

S: Because everyone was having fun and we were not just worrying about anything else.

T: Having fun together?

S: Yeah.

The final example of the broth flowing around the students in a comforting fashion was told by a student in regards to a science lesson. Similar to the above examples of the classroom atmosphere, literature circles, and the class energizers, this student identified a time when he felt valued in the classroom. The concept of using academic instruction to facilitate a community as Kohn (1996) describes, can be illustrated nicely with this section of the interview.

T: Describe a time in our classroom when you felt really safe and like you were needed, a needed part of our classroom.

S: Everyday I haven't been bullied.

T: Like what?

S: Like from this week or the past week.

T: Can you give me an example?

S: Well, Motion and Design.

T: Tell me about that.

S: In Motion and Design, me and my group, T, me, and M, had to build a vehicle that would carry the moon rocks, represented by blocks. And it had to make it in between 4-6 seconds. And it had 11 blocks when it hit 5 seconds and 6/100 of a second.

T: And that's when you felt needed?

S: Yeah. I had to help design the vehicle.

This student did experience the concept of Inclusion in one sense; he did feel like he was needed for his entire group to succeed. He was obviously proud of that fact. His group had what Sapon-Shevin (1999) describes as a mutual goal or objective that is a characteristic of community. They had a shared goal of making the vehicle. He does however, also touch on the true stinging that the broth can also have.

The same broth that can be so warm and comforting can also burn the taste buds. In the above example, while this student did feel some inclusion at that particular activity, he mentioned throughout his interview the idea of being bullied or teased by others. As an observer and participant in the community, I could identify times that I indeed witnessed it happening and as the teacher did intervene. This student was also one who happens to have a labeled disability. Earlier in the interview, it was clear that this student did not always feel the mutual liking that Sapon-Shevin (1999) talks about in her characteristics of a community.

T: Think about our classroom now, this years classroom. Do you think that most kids like to come to school?

S: Um.. I think so, but sometimes I don't feel like coming to school.

T: Why?

S: Some days they just tease me a lot.

T: They do? What kind of things?

S: Like when T called me booger nose.

T: How did that make you feel?

S: Stupid.

T: So bullying makes you not want to come to school. What do you think about other kids, do you think they like coming to school?

S: Yeah.

T: How do you know?

S: Well, they act like they really want to learn. And get good grades. And I want to get good grades, but not when there's bullying around.

T: Can you give me an example from last week when you didn't want to come to school?

S: Last week?

T: Uh uh.

S: I felt like I wanted to come to school the whole week.

T: Well, when was the last time you didn't want to come to school Can you think about that time?

S: I'll try.

T: But last week, the whole week you wanted to come to school. What about this week?

S: Same thing.

The interventions that I had been doing throughout the year may have helped the broth become better at times for this student; it did not however make him feel like he was a part of the community consistently. The connectedness and trust that needed to be present in the community at all times did not happen for this student. Again, while I did know it existed to some degree, I did not realize the true power of this rift for this student within our classroom community. I do not think it was obvious to the other students interviewed as well, because according to their interviews, they felt as if everyone was included. The strategies that I had used were obviously not enough. In retrospect, this problem for the community should have been solved by the community. Calderwood (2000) would describe this situation as one of vulnerability, which is fundamental to the workings of a community. She states:

> Groups and their members might act precipitously to eradicate the perceived dangers without a full understanding of the opportunities they present to build resilience. Perhaps vulnerabilities are perceived as trivial or inconsequential, and thus ignored or tolerated. Even vulnerabilities viewed as extremely threatening may be ignored or tolerated, perhaps because the community is in denial or because it lacks any other method to attend to them. Even when vulnerabilities are noticed, examined, and attended to with the intention of building resilience, resilience is not always achieved. Sometimes the vulnerabilities prove fatal to the health of community despite all efforts. (p. 4)

The truly cohesive community that I was striving for did not exist for this student, nor did we as a community use it as an opportunity to build resilience. While it did not prove to be fatal to our community, it in truth made our broth taste rancid at times.

The Peas and Carrots

In each of the definitions or indicators of community, individual difference and diversity should make the taste of the soup come alive. As Kohn (1996) explains, "A community not only preserves and nourishes the individuals who compose it, but also underscores the relationships among these individuals" (p. 107). In the soup metaphor, the students are able to retain their shape of individual peas and carrots (or any other vegetable that you like in soup!) and the differences between them are respected and celebrated within the community. This aspect of community can be described under Sapon-Shevin's community characteristic of Open Communication. She states:

> In safe, accepting communities, people's individual differences and different needs are openly acknowledged: 'Caitlin's eyes are that shape because she is from Korea,' 'Aryah doesn't share other children's lunches because he keeps Kosher and eats only certain foods,' 'Daniel uses a communication board to 'talk' because that's the easier way for him to tell us what he's thinking.' (Sapon-Shevin, 1999, p.16)

The truths behind what the student really felt about this aspect of our community was quite enlightening to me.

At the beginning of the year I had done, what I felt was a good introduction about individual differences, mostly in regards to abilities. We started our year with a discussion about what the word FAIR really meant. As a class, with facilitation, we decided, that fair was not each person getting the same thing, but rather, fair was each person getting what he or she need. Our discussion started with the example of eyeglasses. Should Samantha take off her glasses because it would not be fair to everyone else in the class, since we did not ALL have glasses? Students understood, with that and other examples, that each of them did indeed need different things. Our poster, with the definition of fair, hung in the front of our room. I do think that on a surface level the kids did have a true understanding of what that meant. What I found however was that while the initial conversation was important, it needed to be continued through out the year and as our community took more of its shape.

One student in our classroom with a significant disability had his day highly structured with a behavior reinforcement system to help him be successful. He earned points for keeping control of his behavior that could buy items. This student worked particularly hard to buy Silly Puddy®. One of the interviews highlighted that students did have some understanding of individual differences and our class definition of fair.

T: What do you think about him getting all that Silly Puddy®?

S: I don't mind it really at all. I think it is kind of cool.

T: Why is it cool?

S: It would be cool to have him have so much Silly Puddy® that he would be in the World Record Book.

T: It doesn't really make you feel anything?

S: I don't care.

T: Do you know why he gets it?

S: The point system.

T: Why does he have a point system?

S: Because he has learning disabilities? Or something? I don't know.

T: So what do you think he needs it for?

S: Maybe to help him learn he might, when he concentrates he gets points he can get Silly Puddy® and it might help him concentrate more and not .....

T: What about you? Could you use something like that?

S: No. I don't really need it.

T: Why?

S: I, myself I don't think I need it. I just feel I don't need it.

From this conversation, this student did understand on the surface level the reason for the points; however, I do not think he had a true understanding of why this student relied on it so heavily. More opportunities for conversations about how we are all different needed to happen. This became especially clear to me when I overheard one student ask another, "Why is she getting candy?" The student pointed to our classroom poster of the definition of fair and replied sarcastically, "She needs it. She NEEDS the candy." The conversation between the kids stopped, both understood; yet I think they had much more to say about what they were feeling than that. The students were only seeing this student getting something they weren't. They acknowledged the reason with the poster, but it was clear that they did not truly understand why this student was getting the reward. Again, more opportunities to discuss how they were feeling, and how they as a community could help nourish the individuals within the community, could have been provided. These opportunities relate again to Calderwood's (2000) idea of building the resiliency, which is essential to community as well as Gibbs (2000) idea that a dedication to resolving rather than avoiding uncomfortable problems that can separate members is an aspect of a community.

The Curly Pasta

When individuals truly feel safe and that they can give their true opinion or feelings, conflict will naturally arise. The curly pasta or conflict that occurred in our soup community did happen quite frequently in our classroom. Since we have conflict, then "voila!" we have created a community! Unfortunately, simply the presence of our pasta in our day-to-day broth, isn't for us sufficient. Jeanne Gibbs (2000) states:

> Conflict is a natural part of life because as individuals we differ in what we want, need, and think. Conflicts occur over these differences. But the conflict itself isn't the problem — it's how we deal with it. Within each conflict there is an opportunity to gain new knowledge. If our intent is to learn, we will seek to understand why the conflict happened. (p. 118)

This blends beautifully with Calderwood's (2000) theory that conflict can also be seen as the vulnerability that the community can choose to use as part of it's resilience or it's fragility. What was the truth about our conflicts? A student explained ways it happened in our classroom.

T: Think about a time when you were having a problem with someone in our class.

S: Well today, T.. (student).. I had a big heavy waterbottle that I had in my back pack and it was kind of heavy, it was kind of big. And whenever, they (the rest of the class) were getting Fun Friday, she would knock it down, she would get her hands away and it make this big "BUMP" sound. I forgot what she is called, the person who helps out in here...

T: Mrs.F?

S: Yeah, she yelled at me because of it and I wasn't doing anything.

T: How did you handle it?

S: I moved away and started reading over there (pointed to chair on rug).

T: How did you feel about that?

S: I was kind of mad, ticked off, and mad at her. So I just moved.

T: How did T respond?

S: Um. She did it once more while I was gone and then she just sat there and then I came back and picked it up.

T: And just ignored it?

S: Yeah.

T: Do you think you stopped it?

S: Well, yeah and before I put down, like by my chair, then I put it back up when she wouldn't do it anymore.

T: How do you think most kids solve problems with other kids in our classroom?

S: They might get a teacher and help them work it out or they might just work it out by themselves, or they just might keep fighting and then later they forget about it and just become friends again.

T: Do you think that happens a lot?

S: Um hm.

T: Which one happens the most? Getting an adult, working it out themselves, or just forgetting about it?

S: Working it out themselves.

T: How do kids work it out themselves?

S: They might say like, "I'm sorry for doing this. And if you say sorry I'll say sorry.

T: Does that usually work?

S: Yeah.

T: Did that work with you and T today?

S: Well, I think she just kind of forgot about it and stopped.

T: And did you forget about it?

S: Yeah. Or I didn't really mind anymore.

In this example, this student was obviously annoyed by the water bottle bouncer. He did have in his repertoire some skills to help him understand the conflict. He knew that he needed to move away from her so she would stop. He noticed her need for his attention and he handled it by not giving it to her — or moving away. He understood that if he ignored her and waited until she was done, she would forget about it and get back to work. In this specific situation, and with the personality of these two particular students involved, this resolution did work. Simply ignoring the behavior however, is not the only skill that people need to resolve conflicts.

The next example was from a student in our class who attended a daily math class in another classroom. While he tried to solve this conflict similar to how the above student handled his, the resolution, I believe still made this student feel helpless.

T:	Was there a particular subject that you had last week that was hard for you to learn? Time of day?
S:	Well, in math there was this kid named J, and he was, he always talks in class and it's kind of hard for me to learn then.
T:	What kinds of things does he say?
S:	Well he says, he says like sick things. And he says, like, like I'm gonna cut your mom's head off or something. He doesn't mean it, but he's just, I don't like him very much.
T:	He's saying it out loud?
S:	Well, no, he's saying it just within the desk group.
T:	Hmm. So just you kids could hear it.
S:	Yeah.
T:	How do you think that makes the other kids in the group feel?
S:	Well, probably not very good. Usually we just can't really ignore it. So you have to listen, and you can't write your math problem or whatever. So...
T:	Why do you think you can't write your math problem?
S:	Because it is harder for you to think when someone else is saying something. Cause then, like sometimes when I'm writing a math problem and the teacher is saying some numbers and I actually write some number or whatever. So the same with other kids when they're talking.
T:	When you are in math with J.. does it make you not like math or not necessarily?
S:	No. I still like math a lot, but I just wish I were to sit somewhere else, cause then it would be easier for me to work.
T:	What do you do when he is saying those things?
S:	I usually just ignore it. And just try to keep focused.
T:	Does that usually stop what he is doing?

S: Yeah. He usually, after a while he usually just doesn't do it anymore. Or someone else close to us hears and then they just tell on him.

T: They tell ...?

S: They tell the teacher and she gets really mad.

T: Does he stop then?

S: Yeah. But then the next day he does it again.

T: It's hard...

S: Yeah.

T: It's a hard situation.

S: Yeah, but I usually deal with things pretty good.

T: Why do you think that is?

S: Well, I just don't want to get into it, cause then if he gets in trouble then just because I was talking to him I might get in trouble to. I just try to stay out of things unless they are good.

T: Do you think you could do anything to help him stop that?

S: Yeah. I think just saying "stop" and kind of helping him with his work. Well, he does good, but just kind of showing him stuff, that would make him get off track of his head and do his math and stuff.

T: Why do you think he does it?

S: I have no clue.

Only after having time to reflect and talk about the situation with me, did this student begin to come up with some ideas of what he could do, instead of just ignoring, in this situation. Unfortunately, this student was not provided with the opportunity to reflect on this with others before the interview. Having the opportunity to talk about what was happening with his classroom community may have given him, what Sapon- Shevin (1999) calls speaking the truth and acting powerfully. This student needed to find strength in his community to help him navigate his outside world. This student did learn however, what Kohn(1996) calls the "compliance game". He learned to not make waves that will get him in trouble. Is this a true community?

Now do these two examples mean that every time a conflict pasta bubbled to the surface we just ignored it? There were many times that student conflict arose that I met with students, we went through a specific conflict resolution plan, the conflict was resolved, and I felt that students did grow from the conflict. Plenty of conflicts I did not know of also arose that students handled themselves. In looking back for the truth about how conflict flavored our soup, I feel we needed more practice and group reflection. The time that was devoted to teaching kids how to resolve conflict was well worth it, however it only scratched the surface. Within a strong community, students can learn the skills to resolve the conflict throughout their lives.

BUZZ ... The Timer Goes Off

Kohn (1996), in his book *Beyond Discipline: From Compliance to Community*, refers back to workshops he has conducted. He starts the session with the question, "What are your long term goals for the students you work with? What would you like them to be — to be like — long after they've left you?" In almost all of the sessions he has done, in different parts of the country, no educator says that their long-term goal is for their students to be able to solve an equation with two variables, or remember the names of the explorers of the New World. Instead, psychological and social characteristics emerge. Examples he gives of what came up were caring, happy, responsible, curious, creative, lifelong learners. In doing the exercise myself, I came up with a similar list.

When the year was up, and the timer went off on our classroom soup, what was the truth about the community we shared? As Patricia Calderwood (2000) stated, "Community isn't always as lovely in practice as it may be in our dreams" (p. 1). She went on to say, "Community, however, is a slippery state of social relations. It is not a commodity easily obtained. There is no storehouse stocking tempting varieties and flavors of ready-made community, nor is there a warehouse filled with the ingredients that, when properly arranged, transform into community" (p.2). The truth that I learned about our community was that it was still in progress. As the teacher, I learned so much from my students about what our community had and what it was missing. In my development as a teacher, I now have the incredible opportunity and responsibility to use this in my future classrooms.

With the final hugs after 5th grade graduation, kids skipped out of the classroom, onto bigger and better things in their minds. Our year together was over. What was the truth about our community? I realized that what we had in place did fulfill part of what we hoped to accomplish, however, it was only part. Teasing and bullying were still happening in our classroom. Creating more opportunities for students to really understand and celebrate each others differences and similarities were needed. Conflict, the idea of growing from conflict, was the final area that needed more emphasis. Allowing students to have more opportunities to practice and gain and understanding of how to deal with conflict should be available. I switched off the lights and locked the door. One community was dissolved, yet as I walked down the hallway I took with me the powerful truths about that community that will help me construct the bridge to the next one.

Between Black-and-White and Blue-White-Red: Pictorial Illustrations and Color in the Foreign Language Textbook

Hyo-Kyung Ahn

The following short stories are drawn from my previous experience that focused on illustrations and color.

From a Blue Fantasyland

My story begins with some bland adjectives: non-figurative, non-colored, and therefore non-nuanced prosaic textbooks designed to deliver grammatical knowledge of a foreign language. This is how my first acquaintance with a French textbook began at my high school. Even though I didn't know the theories of didactic methods for foreign language teaching/acquisition at that time, I could feel my French classes were conducted in the grammar-translation method[1] based on textbooks with no illustrations. (As my subject in this chapter is not the problem of foreign language teaching/acquisition in its entirety, I will focus only on my experience with pictorial illustrations and color). So, translation was used to check comprehension of the rules and readings, and the proper answers to some "structural exercises" (Réquédat, 1966) tested whether or not new grammar and expressions in the chapter had been learned. The two pages of discourse in the dialogue sections stood on their own, playing a supporting role to the grammar's lead. THAT WAS IT! Without the presence of other actors and actresses, the curtain of each chapter had fallen.

But I knew there was *something* intriguing in other French textbooks that I happened to find on my parents' bookshelves. Even though I couldn't understand much of what I saw on the pages due to the difference in the level, I was infatuated with the illustrations and color that these books had and my schoolbooks didn't. The blue covers with dreamy and meaningful illustrations — flying over the clouds and the frontiers of L1 (first language) for the acquisition of a new foreign language[2] — led me to a fantasyland. Also, the colored pictorial illustrations on the first two pages of each chapter were certainly saying and doing their words and acts. I still remember how I used to "read" those illustrations as if they were picture books for children beginning to learn a language, wishing that my foreign language textbooks also had such nice illustrations. This is when my passion or, at least, preference for textbooks with illustrations and color began.

There is another story concerning pictorial illustrations and color which exemplifies the power of visual tools. This is an experience I had in some French classes at a high school in Seoul as a student teacher for my practicum course (Karak High School, Seoul, Korea, April 1994). This story will help you understand another motivation for my studying the role of pictorial illustrations and color.

There had not been many changes in the foreign language teaching/acquisition environment including the form and the use of textbooks since my high school days. I know we can't expect much change in just four or five years. So, the high school students of the newer generation had not had any pictorial illustrations or color in their French textbooks either. From my experience, I know that many of the foreign language teachers in my country "deliver" their knowledge to the target students with only the grammar-translation method rigidly based on the textbook, which makes use of only verbal language. So, it was one of the tasks of student teachers to procure or produce some necessary illustrations for teaching in the audio-visual method, to introduce so-called "desirable teaching" into our education environment. I made some illustrations in crayon for my class with 48 different colors, but had no idea how to use them in a wonderful way for better class management. Regrettably, I used them just as visual supporting tools and for some grammar practice. But I got at least one positive effect from my hand-drawn illustrations: my students paid more attention to class when visual aids were used. Those illustrations and colors appealed to the students because they had not commonly had classes utilizing visual tools. They could also receive some additional messages and visual impressions from the illustrations and color, even though those messages weren't enough to achieve the desired effect: an increase in interest in their lessons and an improvement in their retention of grammatical rules were considered the only positive results. I had well experienced the difference in students' reactions when using visual illustrations and color and when not using them. One day, almost at the end of my practicum course, I was assigned to give a class out of schedule, and as I didn't have time to prepare other supporting illustrations, I conducted the class in the traditional way with only the textbook that had no visual images and color. Result: I couldn't get as much attention from the students in comparison with previous classes, who, in general, didn't have much interest in a second foreign language (such as French, German, Spanish, Japanese, Chinese, etc.) which is ultimately not a required subject for their entrance examination at the university. I cannot hastily conclude that I could not achieve a positive result with my last class only due to the lack of some tools, but I could feel the power of visual illustrations and color from experience — they certainly inspired more interest and participation from the students.

My Color of the Frame

I have presented you with two narratives related to my experience with illustrations and color in the textbook. At first, it was difficult for me to be in the frame that requires a frank voice, and I learned how difficult it is to start a personal story, to offer my own voice and to be a subject in writing. But I wanted to try, because I learned through reading other narrative stories that personal history-telling is attractive and powerful. So, I decided to be frank but also reasonable: "Even those who tell all find strong obligation to winnow and consolidate" (Stake, 2000, p. 441).

In this section, I would like to share with the reader the charm and the power of this personal story-telling approach. When I first got the chance to read something written in this frame, I felt that I was flowing with the story and couldn't stop reading. I hoped I could achieve this in my story, too.

As the narrative story is from "a lived, identity-producing experience" (Tochon, 1999b, p. 110), I think it is like reading a personal journal or watching an autobiographical movie which makes the reader or audience curious and infatuated. In this way, it allows the reader, and also the author, to see the issues in the story better and lead them to better comprehension and interpretation:

Life history is any retrospective account by the individual of his life in whole or part, in written or oral form that has been elicited or prompted by another person (Tierney, 2000, p. 539).

Another reason for choosing this frame: I thought that this life story-telling frame would help me clarify the motives and direction of the writing, and also allow the reader to discover the correlation between the stories about illustrations and color and the universe of education. Also, I hoped the narrative frame would play the role of catalyst in relating my motivations and objectives for writing this study. And I hoped that it would be a mediator, unraveling the words and acts of illustrations and color on the stage of the textbooks, textbooks of different levels from the same series: "Nouveau Sans Frontières 1" (Dominique, Verdelhan, & Verdelhan, 1998) (NSF 1) and "Nouveau Sans Frontières 2" (Dominique, Verdelhan, & Verdelhan, 1989) (NSF 2).

My story telling continues with a section on illustrations and color in NSF 1 and NSF 2. The narratives on the textbooks and my educational background will be implicitly or explicitly interwoven with the above-presented stories. And if you have had an experience similar to mine, then "we" are all together on the stage in the narrative framework.

What am I Going to Talk About?: The Process of Making the Invisible Visible

Let's begin by thinking about what's said and done with illustrations and color in the textbooks. My aims are as follows. First, I will discuss the status and the function of pictorial illustrations in the textbook in view of the affective-motivational functions, and in the second part, discuss their possible use/practice in order to further my investigation into the what's said and done with color in the chosen contexts.

As color could have different meanings in different domains, I decided to set the bounds of my story of color to that of the clothes worn by characters, based on the psychological and sociological aspects of the color of clothing in the context of the target textbooks. With this language of color, the goal of this study is to reflect on the hidden meanings of color, found especially in the textbook dialogues, but also in my mind, with examples from NSF 1 and NSF 2 for French as a foreign language teaching/acquisition for the intermediate level. In this way, I hope to give a voice to the illustrations and color of the textbook, which play their explicit and sometimes implicit roles, but remain easily silent behind the veil of our minds. This is also a process of making the invisible visible, in that illustrations and color come to us with their own language interwoven with our untold stories.

In the second part of my story, to make more concrete the ideas on the color of illustrations, I use the two textbooks as examples. This is because NSF 1 and NSF 2 are my treasures, which helped me to learn French in a different environment and with different methods, thanks to their illustrations and color. I am going to tell this story in the main part of my paper. These books provided opportunities to compare the use of color in various modes of presentation: full-colored comic strips in NSF 1, and movie-like photographs in NSF 2. I'll examine Unit 3 in NSF 1, and Unit 2 in NSF 2, since I found that these units have a diverse cast of characters from various generations, occupations, etc. From this diversity of the casts, I think, we can have a chance to consider more about the language of color.

Through the study of nonverbal signs such as illustrations and color, I hope, we will have the opportunity to reconsider what we know, and to use or develop it in educational settings. Actually, the teacher's guidebook of "NSF" (Girardet, 1988) suggests that the teachers offer some activities to the students using the given pictorial illustrations in the textbooks:

> Analyze and comment on the pictorial illustrations, make hypotheses about the characters and the dialogue situations, and give information regarding the contexts and the cultural elements before listening to or reading the verbal communication sections (dialogues) in the textbook; imagine the dialogues among the characters. (p. 5)

What I propose here is to give more weight to the nonverbal sign: make it "alive" and "visible" in teaching/learning a foreign language to make the learning more meaningful and to think about how the illustrations and color can affect the learner. Even though this paper presents only a part of the magic that the color of pictorial illustrations have, I hope acquaintance with it will let us discover different ways of thinking about illustrations and color in the educational setting.

Greeting the Textbook with the Illustrations and Color

As a high school student and later as a student teacher, I had French textbooks with no illustrations and color. But fortunately when I came to be a college student, I was able to study with a French language textbook featuring illustrations and color, NSF 1 and NSF 2, at a foreign language institute[3]. I still remember how happy I was to have colored and illustrated books. And, as I said earlier, these books were so precious to me because I could finally learn a foreign language with a different method, which was not based on grammar and translation study, but with illustrations and color that allowed the learner to see more than just verbal discourses. As guided by the teacher's manual, the instructors paid attention to the illustrations in the beginning of the lesson and I could finally "see" the pictures in the textbook. It was an exciting and different experience for the student who had not had an education like this before. Only the fact that I had a textbook with French feeling and images in a small French land[4] made me say a different "That's it!"

Here, I would like to describe briefly the type of illustrations found in the textbooks. They can be categorized into seven types: rather realistic illustrations such as pictures, photographs, cartoons, and more schematic illustrations like graphs, diagrams, maps, and illustrated charts (Evans, Watson, Willows, 1987, p. 98). First, I am going to discuss the status and the function of the realistic illustrations in view of their affective-motivational functions and practical uses. For this, I am going to present some theoretical background within my stories. I think, in this way, the reader and I, together, will have the opportunity to verify our implicit thinking on the pictorial illustrations against concrete facts and opinions, which will ultimately help to understand the expectations I have of the illustrations in the textbook. Then, in the following part, I will address the next questions: what is *in* the cartoon-like full-colored-pictures (in NSF 1) and the full-colored photographs (in NSF 2)? What made me so attracted to them?

First, I would like to invite you to take a look at any (foreign) language textbook. There on the cover and inside of the book you will find, in general (except for my cases with bland-looking books), largely two types of meaning-conveying methods: text (verbal-code) and illustrations (non-verbal code). In other simpler words, we have the letters and the pictures in the textbook. The illustrations are here with us.

What do the illustrations in the textbook do? Selander (1991) classifies the function of the illustrations into the following three categories: "to give information, to illustrate [a certain situation and] to make the page more attractive" (p. 68). I don't think the function of any illustrations presented in a textbook is limited to only one of the above functions. This is because when I first saw the blue covered books I presented in the first page of this story, I was so charmed that I tried to understand the illustrated dialogues in the book. My writing is, as has been and will be shown, based on the assumption that illustrations effect learning positively: Dwyer (Levie,1987, pp. 15-16)[5], based on his copious research on the effects of pictures on teaching/learning of factual knowledge, found that pictures are most helpful in achieving objectives that entail visual discriminations.

I found, in my case, that the illustrations influenced my attitudes toward the text more than the non-illustrated textbook I had in my high school days. They were attractive enough to allow me to give myself over to the nonverbal messages leading me. I tried to imagine the play depicted in the book and relate my knowledge and experience to the staged acts, because they allowed me to see another world with purer eyes and mind, as if I were a child who couldn't yet read the text. The illustrations certainly had a powerful affective-motivational function, as defined in Peeck's (1987) remarkable studies. She suggests that, among other things, pictures invoke interests, create emotion, vitalize learning, and invoke the curiosity of the students (pp. 116-128).

Yes, what I had missed from the textbook with no illustrations and color were those affective-emotional aspects. I didn't want to learn the so-called non-authentic dialogues created for the acquisition of the grammar without even any taste of living life. What I expected from the class and the textbook of a foreign language was a balance of cultural and language aspects. I remember that many of my classmates at the high school showed interest in French class in the beginning of the year. But soon, failing to find any affective-motivational props, they put this subject aside until the examination, and the language became no more a language for discovering another life.

The situation was the same or worse when I did the practicum at a high school: students need some form of motivation for learning, even if it is for a good score on their school examination. It is not an exaggeration to say that, in my country, the stressful preparation for university entrance examinations influences the entire education period. Therefore, when foreign languages other than English are removed from the list of entrance exams, high school students who have no personal interest in foreign languages could easily lose their appetite for learning them. Then, I think, it is the teacher and the tool for teaching such as the textbook that could motivate the student to make the learning interesting, meaningful, and useful in some way. I would like to suggest the use of (real) colored illustrations because, I think, the teaching of a foreign language through illustrations can propose something beyond the text.

What are the pragmatic aspects of the illustrations in foreign language learning? Galisson (1980) has commented on the illustrations in the language textbook in detail. There are two dimensions: one is the referential (semantic) dimension of the illustration, which mediates and facilitates the transfer of meaning of the written text. The other is the stimulating dimension, which provokes verbal production from the students in a creative, non-repetitive way, asking them to be "engaged" in the scene through the illustrations. This dimension asks the illustrations to provide the students richer connotative meanings of the context and to be authentic by providing a cultural function, i.e. presenting authentic customs, time, place, space, etc. (pp. 97–101).

Because there were no illustrations in the high school French books for me and other Korean students, the above suggestions for the use of the textbook could be of no use. But in that case, I hope the teachers would devise ways to apply illustrations from other sources to give their students some chance to enjoy learning. Thus, an increase in interest and curiosity brought about by them could lead students to invest more cognitive effort in studying the illustrated text, to lengthen the time in reading word-materials, and to enhance and elaborate their semantic process of learning. These aspects are what I lacked with my schoolbooks for French (also for other subjects) in my high school days and in my practicum experience. As proposed by Galisson (1980), the illustrated textbook should be used from many angles to help the student to have more fun and to think in a creative way. We should not merely ask them to accept the facts and the thoughts of others through verbally written texts, but attempt to make the learning process more meaningful by introducing aspects of other lives and cultures through nonverbal messages implied in the illustrations.

Another Story on Illustrations, Color and Meanings with the Examples of NSF 1 (Unit 3) and NSF 2 (Unit 2)

My story began with some bland adjectives: non-figurative, non-colored, therefore non-nuanced textbooks at high schools. And when I did have my first full-color-illustrated French textbook, I was so excited that I thought I could learn more about everything with that book, because that book meant a lot more to me besides the fact that it had color illustrations: it was a French language book published in France, and it could introduce me to France through illustrations and color.

I have another story here that I usually avoid telling others. But I decided to be frank in telling my story on color, otherwise my story itself could lose its color and make the reader fail to understand why the colored illustrations had such significance for me. I lived in Paris with my parents for two years when I was five or six years old. I remember some scenes of this time in my childhood only vaguely, and I also barely remember some of the French expressions I used to know. Because I learned French for a short time when I was too young and I didn't have the opportunity to continue to learn and speak French, I lost most of it. But, sometimes I heard my parents speaking in French to each other, in the very language I couldn't understand, and that made me feel almost jealous and sore because I thought I also should be able to speak that foreign language. Most likely my parents didn't teach me French because they thought this language would not be useful for me at that time, and I could learn it again when I needed it: at high school when students have to take the second foreign language class for the exam.

More information about my country's educational and social situation might help you better understand what I mean. Education prior to university seems to have only one aim: to provide access to a prestigious university for a successful life. That is still our reality, even though educators say other things. This fact strongly influences the curriculum of most subjects in and before high school. Maybe foreign language education, in this case French, is also conducted to deliver some grammatical knowledge needed for the entrance exam. I tentatively assume that this could be one of the reasons why my French schoolbook didn't have and didn't need illustrations and color. That is probably okay for students who don't have much interest in learning about French and France. But that couldn't satisfy a person like me who had longed to see France and learn French.

This is the primary reason why I hold my first French language textbook with the colored illustrations so precious. I wished to see what I had longed for through the book. But tracing back in my memory, even though I had the colored illustrations in that book, the teaching and acquisition of a foreign language and culture through the language of color remained in another corner. Our instructors did structure some activities around the illustrations, but color was rarely put on the stage — it was usually regarded as an undoubted fact, which fills the interior of the illustrations. Therefore, in this part of my writing, I will try to uncover the meanings that color can give in the context of the two chosen books, hoping to hear and see beyond the dialogues.

Before getting started on our main stories on color, let's take a look at, with a different view this time, any language textbook you can find somewhere on your bookshelf. Now, you will probably notice how easy it is not to take color into deep consideration even though the illustrations are printed with charming full color. But when the book is printed in black and white, we notice there is no color and begin to wonder about the reason for this: whether it is an old book before the development of the art of printing, a book printed in black and white with intention for some special reasons, or a book made with less elaboration ... but we have illustrations as well as color in the two target textbooks. My writing on color is based on the premise that color could also have positive effects on education as with the case of illustrations. The use of illustrations and color came with the growth of printing and color technology, and with the increase of the illustration's aesthetic value, color lends additional significance to the realism/truism in the textbook by appealing to the reader (not only young but also mature readers) and by functioning as comprehension aids (Mulcahy & Samuels, 1987, pp. 43-44). And as shown by many researchers (see MacLean, 1930; Ibison, 1952; Rudisill, 1952; Dwyer, 1971, etc.), the effectiveness of color as an instructional variable in visual illustrations is that students prefer to view colored instructional material rather that black and white (Dwyer, 1972, pp. 28-33), as was case with me.

Figures 1 and 2 present the characters, the color of their clothes, and the messages of color in the dialogue parts of NSF 1 (unit 3) and of NSF 2 (unit 2) in the form of a concept map. By the form of the concept map, I intended to present color and meaning in an organized semantic network to place color in the center of the discussion. A concept map can help us look at concepts in a clearer and more efficient way without the real objects, if it presents the content with a reasonable number of boxes and ovals for a good overview (Nguyen, 1999, p. 133) and "relationships among the concepts are immediately apparent from their proximity to each other" (Tochon, 1990, p. 185). Furthermore, according to Aho (Ahlberg, 1991, p. 100), concept mapping has the power to make the implicit explicit by linking concepts in boxes and ovals of the text . This is a nice aspect of the concept map for my study on the language of color, in this rubric, because with the help of the concept map we can structure different implicit aspects of color to build a whole explicit edifice. But here, I prefer not to give any numbers[6] or hierarchical importance in my concept maps — that could be given by the form of the concept map — in the meanings of color and in color itself, because any details can give us some untapped stories.

By putting color in the center of our discussion with the concept maps, I hope to help you to follow the stream of my stories on color with the exam-

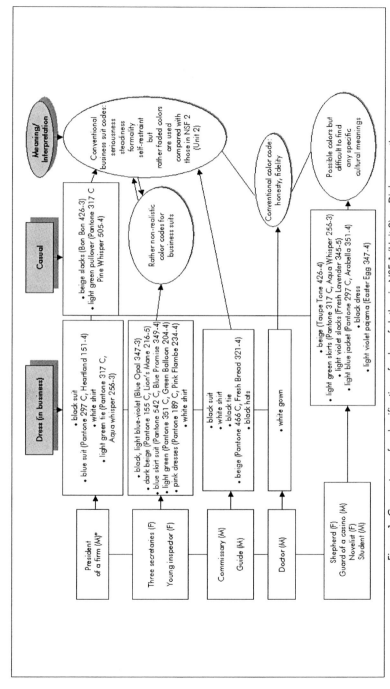

Figure 1: Concept map for classification of color of clothes in NSF 1 (Unit 3) — Dialogue sections

Legend: *(M): Male, (F): Female

All colors from Pantone solid start guide (1998) and PPG Architectural Finishes, Inc.
Black: Pantone Black C, Black Magic 518-7, White: Delicate White 518-1, C: Coated color

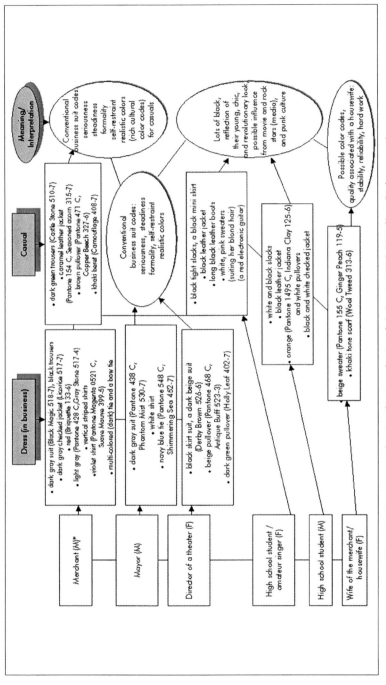

Figure 2: Concept map for classification of color of clothes in NSF 2 (Unit 2) — Dialogue sections

Legend: *(M): Male, (F): Female

All colors from Pantone solid start guide (1998) and PPG Architectural Finishes, Inc.

Black: Pantone Black C, Black Magic 518-7, White: Delicate White 518-1, C: Coated color ples in NSF 1 (unit 3) and in NSF 2 (Unit 2), even though you are not familiar with these two books. Characters are placed in the leftmost part. Then arrows guide you to the other boxes to show the color of the clothes, dress (in business) and/or the casuals, through which the authors of the books probably intended to tell more about the characters and stories. Color references are based on the Pantone matching system and the color tables from PPG Architectural Finishes Inc. With this aid I intend to show you how color is used in the books in a more precise way; please note that these are not the references used by the authors or the publishing house of the chosen books. The rightmost part of the maps are filled with ovals that give brief and rather objective comments on color language, primarily from Chambers (1945), Lurie (1981), and Fehrman & Fehrman (2000). These spaces don't contain any interpretations from my own personal experience, as this will be presented in the following pages. From those color codes, my images and stories on color begin.

In this part, I focus especially on the language of the color of clothes in spite of other intriguing elements (such as style, pattern, fabric, decoration, such as trinkets and jewelry, make-up, hairstyle, etc.) which also can influence the meanings of the nonverbal signs expressed by characters in the textbooks. This is because I think color itself is one of the primary nonverbal signs, which can say something more and which has more immediate powerful impact on the meanings that the textbooks have intended to convey. But many parts of the stories on color of clothes could be something that we have already tacitly known, because we live with color, everywhere in our system of everyday life, and because it is us, human beings, who continuously assign meanings to objects with color made by light and nature in a social context. But the concept is well imbedded in our minds and we have taken for granted that "color just exists." Through a closer look at color here, I hope we can hear the hidden voice of color through the stories and plays staged in textbooks.

But, wait a minute! Something's missing: the color of my stories. When I had discussions with my professor and peer-advisor for this chapter, I found they were curious about my own story on color, which I suppose means that they were curious about the color interpretations of a person from a different cultural and educational background. So, very suddenly, I found some conflicts, in that, my interpretations of color might be shadowed by my own different cultural identity, a problem that I couldn't have conceived of when I began to write this paper. At the beginning, I wanted to see those colors in the French textbook with rather westernized eyes, with the help of books written from a western point of view. Therefore, it will be another challenge for me to consider the meanings of color presented in the textbooks reconciling two different points of view — a rather westernized view and an eastern-centered one, reflecting my culture and my identity which are standing somewhere between the two points. So, I have to say that the following interpretation of color is, on the one hand, based on books about the language of the color of clothes written from a western viewpoint (Chambers, 1945.; Lurie, 1981.; Fehrman & Fehrman, 2000.), which reflect the psychological and sociological aspects of color of clothing, and on the other hand, or sometimes, the stories of color are also inevitably based on my colored personal view.

From Blue-White-Red

When I decided to write about illustrations and color in textbooks, I had to think a lot, and I am still thinking about how I can make use of my thoughts, dormant for so long. It is now time to take them out… My stories on color will follow some streams of images I have kept toward the colored illustrations in the books. I think it will be difficult to consider all colors found in NSF 1 (Unit 3) and in NSF 2 (Unit2). Therefore, I will present only some stories worth sharing. For a detailed account of the use of colors in the context of NSF 1 (Unit 3) and of NSF 2 (Unit 2), refer to the concept maps presented in the previous pages, and for the general language of color of clothes, the table in the appendix.

When I wanted to see France and its language through color, what color did I expect to see? This thought suddenly came to me. Maybe blue. White and red come next. The colors in the national flag, therefore the symbol of France. And I think that particular blue comes probably from the image of the blue-covered French language book which led me to a fantasyland. Here is a story of Freud with color impressions associated with his early experience:

> a dream in which he saw water of a deep blue, against which brown smoke rose from a ship's funnels by the red and dark brown building onshore. The colors were those of his children's toy blocks, shown to him the day before. The children's play buildings were linked with the recollection of a recent trip to Italy: "This was associated with color impressions from my last travel in Italy: the beautiful blue of the Isonzo and the lagoons and the brown of the Carso." For Freud the colors of the unconscious have a direct mimetic link to actual experience. (Riley II, 1995, p. 303)

Blue

What a surprise! Blue is rarely found in NSF 2 (Unit 2): a navy blue tie worn by the mayor is the only blue article of clothing. But this color was not that which I expected. Because it speaks rather a global language of clothes: color code, for business suits which are black[7], dark gray, or navy blue for suits and ties, and white for shirts (Lurie, 1981, p184-195). But I found blue on the partly dyed hair of the main actress, who is a high school student and at the same time an amateur singer. Blue first, her non-dyed blond hair color next, then red. This is a representation of the national flag of France: White, the color representing the king, and blue and red, the colors of Paris, symbols of the union of the royalty and the people (Le Petit Larousse Compact, 1996, see the word "Tricolore"). This could be a small but scrupulous detail in the use of color to show France. If so, and the book were an Italian language textbook, the actress would probably have dyed her hair green-white (blond)-red! I found more blue in NSF 1 (Unit 3), but in this case, blue seems to be chosen for a business-suit-code even though the representations were not dark enough to be realistic business suit codes. We can say then that blue in NSF 1 (Unit 3), carries both the connotations of business suits, i.e. seriousness, steadiness, formality and self-restraint, and those of blue in general, i.e. harmony, honesty, and faith (Lurie, 1981; Fehrman & Fehrman, 2000, p. 146). Is the blue in my mind that blue in the suits? Rather not. My blue is closer to that on the dyed hair of the main character of NSF 2 (Unit 2) or exists in my fantasyland.

White

I do think that color could have different meanings from culture to culture. Here is an example: in France, as we saw earlier, the king is historically symbolized by the color white, while in my culture white is the color of the clothes of the people. I think the former white could have the meaning of high status and delicacy, and the latter white — purity and innocence (Chambers, 1945, pp. 318-319; Lurie, 1981, pp. 184-187). But I found that white in the textbooks reflects another aspect of this color, the color of the shirts as a part of the business suit. This means that another interpretation is needed for this case: the so-called standard color of shirts representing honesty and fidelity. This is the almost required shirt color, especially for people who are in finance-related jobs. A white doctor's gown found in NSF 1(Unit 3) also speaks an international color language, representing a godlike authority figure that heals life (Lurie, 1981, p. 186).

There should have been something different in the shirt code: blue vertical stripes in the white shirts. It could not only be French but western. But unfortunately, NSF 1 (Unit 3) and NSF 2 (Unit 2) showed in most parts white shirt codes, except for two light gray and one red vertical striped shirt for the merchant in NSF 2 (Unit 3). As I said earlier, through illustrations and color, I would like to see something invisible from the text: French culture pattern or life, something which is different from mine. As I learned far later from my work experience with French friends and colleagues, many French men enjoy wearing blue striped shirts and I thought it very exotic and French. But even in NSF 2 (Unit 2), which represents visual images through photographs — considered to be desirable because they are, in general, more truthful and realistic than drawings (Galisson, 1980, p. 100) — I couldn't find this detail. While satisfied when I first had the language books with the fully colored illustrations, I see now insufficiency of the color codes. This may stem from the limited nature of the examples. I suddenly fall into an abyss of disappointment because I have to admit that I cannot see all that I wanted to see through the colored illustrations.

Red

This is a color I have never successfully digested in clothes. I tried in vain to like and wear this color — it just didn't go well with me. As you probably noticed from my writing style or from the content, I really am a shy and kind of timid person. But this is what I don't like to be, and to make some changes, I tried to borrow the power of red by wearing that color clothing, representative of energy: life, strength, vitality, passion, affection, and love (Lurie, 1981, pp. 195-197; Fehrman & Fehrman, 2000). Because I thought my mood and attitude could vary with the color of clothes I wore on a particular day, and if I wore some clothes of a color that can give a pleasant and active emotion like red, I thought that I, in red, could be like red. According to Fehrman & Fehrman (2000) relations between emotions and color come from a learned behavior. The following are about a myth of color they explain:

> Colors have been stereotyped by the public when it comes to emotions. In spite of physical evidence to the contrary, most people continue to equate red tones with excitement and activity and blue tones with passivity and tranquility in color-mood association research.... Further, the red, orange, and yellow tones in fire further cause association between those colors and heat and kinetic energy. We have seen how cultural biases that are a part of our language further support the red-equals-excitement myth. These subconscious messages clearly affect the response to red. (p. 82)

I presume the way I was educated could have influenced, at least partly, my character and attitudes. Foreign language education based on the grammar-translation methods could easily be a passive education without class activities. I think passive attitudes created in an educational environment could leave a mark on one's entire life. This is what I regret, therefore, I think the education should be an active one that helps students to build a positive and progressive attitude. The illustrations and color in the textbook, I think, can be one means of making invisible activities visible, uncolored education colorful in the classroom environment.

Getting back to the textbook: In NSF 1 (Unit 3) and in NSF 2 (Unit 2), I found red or red tone colors as rare as blue: red was used in NSF 2 (Unit 2) for the striped shirt of the merchant, as I already mentioned above, and for the electric guitar of the high school student/amateur singer. In the latter case, it seems to express other possible languages such as sexuality and desire, including the above-presented meanings. Pink, a tint of red, on the other hand, is not considered to be a flattering color for daytime wear except for some persons with pale blond or gray-hair (Chambers, 1945, p. 324), as was the case in NSF 2 (Unit 2). (See Figure 2.) Pink represents the affections and emotional life, popular mostly for girls' clothes (Lurie, 1981, p. 214).

An overview of black, white and gray[8]

These are colors frequently found in the two books. I think this is because of the setting of the stories in some offices that demand wearing (dark business) suits and white shirts, suggesting seriousness, steadiness, formality and self-restraint. Also NSF 2 (Unit 2) presents high school students who enjoy wearing those black and white colors reflecting their young, chic, and revolutionary look, possibly influenced by movie and rock stars (media) and punk culture (Danesi, 1999, p. 189; Fehrman & Fehrman, 2000, p. 161, p. 168). But it is quite surprising to have so much black in the two

French language books, because as I said earlier, I expected more blue. It is even more a surprising phenomenon considering of the survey presented by Pastoureau (1989): most of the surveys conducted in Western Europe, U.S.A. and Canada since World War II showed that the color preference for blue reached nearly 50%. The preference for green comes next with a little less than 20% of the responses, then white and red, each of which is around 10% (pp. 10-11). The preference for blue didn't seem to be reflected in our two books.

Black, white, and gray were representative colors of my schoolbooks and much of my life. My school textbooks were mostly colored in black and white except the art books, the atlas, and the first several special pages of science and history books, for the presentation of some photographs or pictures of some representative facts, but which remained in silence. I was so accustomed to the black-and-white-printing of language textbooks that I hardly posed a question on the problem of colored illustrations until I found my blue-covered fantasyland. Since then I have been eager to hear the speech of silence and hoped to see the roles of the illustrations and color on the stage of the textbook, when they play. But the control of the verbal texts were so powerful, that for the students, including myself, it was usually easier to see black and white verbal texts.

Before closing, there are still some brief thoughts to discuss about my impressions of color in the two books. I can say that NSF 1 reflects, for the most part, the research in terms of how the overall colors presented for our protagonists are based on the realism/truism of color in the textbook, for the color of clothes used for the president of a firm, the commissary, the guide, the secretaries, and the inspector in NSF 1 (Unit 3). But the female-protagonists sometimes show exceptions: colors like light violet and pink one-piece dresses don't match our conventional preconceptions about the dress code in the business world. We usually don't expect a pink dress for an inspector in her (in this story) travel-demanding work. I found that the drawings in the dialogue parts of NSF 1 (Unit 3) did not reflect much target cultural perfume as we discussed above with colors.

On the other hand, I found that NSF 2 (Unit 2) is more realistic and uses better-chosen colors than NSF 1 (Unit 3). This is probably because NSF 2 (Unit 2) uses photographs which show real clothes that are suitable to the situations considering social and cultural aspects, as is stated by Galisson (1980). NSF 1 (Unit 3) with its drawings, seems to have less sense of the real, even though many colors and elements are deliberately chosen to properly convey the contextual behavior of the characters. But we cannot hastily judge on the basis of color alone that photographs are always better tools than drawings for the descriptions of dialogue situations in foreign language learning/teaching[9]. For the case of NSF 2 (Unit 2), an example of the negative effect of the use of photographs could be: even though NSF 2 (Unit 2) has more realistically vivid color, the reader could receive negative impressions. The verbal texts of the dialogue sections possibly may not be clear since the whole view of the photographs can be distracting.

There is one basic or primary color[10], which can easily be found in our surroundings, but which did not appear in the two books: yellow[11]. On the other hand, there are brown tone colors including beige used for suits as well as casual clothes which represent neutral images and give impressions of stability, reliability, and hard work (Lurie, 1981, p. xi in Introduction, p. 204). For further color codes, refer to the concept maps and appendix.

I am a black-haired Asian woman. I, finally and definitely, give you my color identity. But it is only very recently that I found my color identity. I was in my country with people with black hair and rather yellow skin who are just like me and there were few with different hair and skin color. That made me see only the people with different coloring and kept me from seeing my own color that I was so familiar with. When I was with foreign friends and foreign people at my work place in my country, I wasn't aware that I was quite different from them, because I was a person who believed the world is globalized with faint frontiers. I just couldn't see. I belonged to the many. Now and here, I see different colors, cultures and thoughts in a multi-colored society. There are blue, black, red, yellow, and green[12] and I see that each its own splendid "color."

My stories on color end here. We took a journey together from the absence of color to blue, and from full color to black and white. In this part of my writing, I tried to see the meanings of color in the two textbooks with reflections on the colored experiences I have had but which up to now remained unarranged and untold. By writing and sharing them with the reader, I gave them a voice and made them visible. I feel happy to have discovered the once invisible actors, illustrations, and color, and to acknowledge the truth of myself.

Ending this Chapter

This was a story about making the invisible illustrations and colors of the textbook visible within my experience. As I began to write, even though many thoughts came across my mind, it seemed difficult to give them proper action and visibility and to stage them in front of unknown audiences. And it seemed impossible or inappropriate to blend two different situations into one story: the language of color and my own image of color. But collecting my stories in a written form allowed me to see better my missing color with the illustrated clothes and know better my once hidden self.

On the other hand, I found some limitations to my research. First, there were set bounds in describing the status and the functions of the illustrations for my second stories on color. Broader studies beyond the affective-motivational functions of the illustrations would give the reader deeper insight into the illustrations in the textbook. And by limiting the sphere of color to that of clothes in the dialogue sections, I had a limitation in interpreting the language of color, which differs from domain to domain. Therefore I cannot say I explored the total effects of color found in the two books. This requires deeper studies in broader domains such as semiotics, art, literature, psychology, philosophy, etc. and it leaves me much room for further study. However, I had a nice time reconsidering the color images I have kept in my mind for a long time and confessing what I have held down in a closed casket.

My work on illustrations and color with a truth-telling approach allowed me to have a different attitude about education: efforts to notice the implicit things would help avoid missing the invisible, and the efforts would yield a precious pearl. My educational environment was especially one, which requires more effort to make efficient and active use of the textbook with rich supporting materials to augment the interests of students who might otherwise remain passive due to persistent educational and social problems. The educational and environmental problems need more explications but I will put aside this question for the moment because it is beyond the scope of this paper. What I propose here, ending this chapter, is the full use of the textbook, which is the most basic tool for teaching and learning. Allowing the non-verbal sign to play a greater role by studying its variable areas, such as typology, would be one way to make education more meaningful and interesting. More research —Tin the domain of verbal and non-verbal signs — is needed from various angles to make better use of the textbook and to properly evaluate the textbook in different educational settings.

I am still in the early stages of my educational studies and I hope I can keep my passion for exploring the meanings of educational signs, treasuring in my heart the recollection of my blue fantasyland...

Notes

[1] The foreign language textbooks in my country were probably not made for the Grammar-Translation method but the teaching is certainly dominated by this method.

[2] The book covers of the series "Sans Frontières" (Verdelhan-Bourgade, Verdelhan, Dominique, 1982).

[3] In my country, at most universities just like at high schools, acquisition of "speaking" skills is not emphasized, and this skill is to be acquired at other foreign language institutions, like Alliance Française in the case of French, for volunteer-students only.

[4] The classroom or furthermore the whole space of the foreign language institute was for me a small French land with a different educational setting.

[5] He seems rather an earlier researcher, but I cited his name and studies because he is considered to be one of the renowned and prolific scholars in this domain. As Peeck (1987) declared educational research has not come up with much evidence in support of the claims that illustrations may result in positive attitudes, such as affective-motivational effects, toward the illustrated text — perhaps because researchers considered this too obvious for serious investigation (p. 117).

[6] There are some scholars like Ahlberg (1991) who suggested that arrows between concept boxes or ovals and numbers are useful in showing the order to best read the map (p. 97).

[7] Black, white, and gray are technically not considered colors, because black and white are respectively representations of the absence and pres-

ence of light, and gray is the one between the two (Lurie, ibid., p. 184), but I am going to present these in the story of color because they are considered as popular "colors" in our everyday lives.

[8]In this part of the color interpretation, I would rather present the meanings found in the chosen textbooks, but there are other meanings for black, white (please refer to the story of white presented above) and gray: black for all dark and negative sides except for some fashionable sophistication and gray for modesty, mystery, etc. (Lurie, 1981, pp. 184-195).

[9]There is a speculation that drawings that exaggerate the critical features of an object and de-emphasize irrelevant features might be more effective than photographs or accurate detailed drawings (Levie, 1987, p. 17).

[1] Primary colors are those, which cannot be mixed from any other colors such as red, yellow, and blue. And secondary colors are those obtained by mixing two primary colors together resulting in orange, green, and violet (Color Wheel, 2000).

[11]The cover color of the last version of the "NSF" series (1998) changed to a mixture of yellow and white. I think this change reflects a marketing strategy of yellow color code which is classified as the most visible and the most luminous color, therefore the first noticed and the loudest color for the success of the product (Fehrman & Fehrman, 2000, pp.143-147).

[12]Those are colors of the five rings in the Olympic flag, which represent the union of the five continents and the meeting of the athletes of the world at the Olympic Games. Though colorful explanations about the symbolism of the colored rings exist, the only connection between the rings and the continents is that the number five refers to the number of continents. Any other relation must be a post-facto interpretation (International Olympic Committee), therefore I don't specify further about each of the five colors.

Acknowledgments

I thank most of all François V. Tochon, who helped me expand my thoughts in the educational universe and freely gave me sensible advice and guidance during the writing of this paper. I also thank Gloria Carter, who kindly advised me to let my own voice and color shine. Finally I would like to thank all my classmates for sharing valuable thoughts in discussion.

Appendix

Color and the meanings based on Lurie (1981) and Fehrman & Fehrman (2000) which reflect the psychological and sociological aspects of the color of clothing.

White		• color of fair-weather clouds and the snow-topped mountains where the gods (Zeus) dwelt
		• purity, innocence, status
		• delicacy, physical infirmity/weakness
Black		• color of night, darkness
		• gloom, guilt, sophistication
		• sorrow, mourning, unhappiness, sin, evil, diabolic, death/ supernatural with the power of darkness
		• religious, secular asceticism (symbolic denial of the sensual life of monks, misers, priests, scholars)
		• sexual villainy, financial and political villainy
Gray		• color which suggests fog, mist, smoke, and twilight
		• modesty, mystery
		• ambiguous, indefinite color (combination of white, black)
		• modest, retiring individual, not to be noticed, puzzling
	(darken)	• conventionality, more stronger, dominant
	(whiten)	• more innocent, charming refinement, subtlety, sensitivity, sadness, regret
Red		• color of blood
		• love, anger, life, beauty
		• strength, vitality, heat, sudden danger (red light), sexuality, desire, aggression, passion
	(darken)	• related to sex, affection, (sexual, emotional) romantic love
	(whiten)	• physical energy, a lively interest in life, political radicalism, affection
Yellow		• color of the sun, light
		• youth, hope, cheer
		• energy, hopefulness
	(darken)	• wealth, material prosperity, naïve enthusiasm
	(whiten)	• optimist, extrovert

Blue	• color of the sky, of faraway mountain (distance)
	• harmony, honesty, faith (humility, devotion in the religious sense)
	• serenity, rest, peace, politically conservative opinions, a loyal acceptance of the status quo
(darken)	• black without its darker implications of death and sin
	• solemn importance, sophistication, well-balanced, hard working, trustworthy/resignation, melancholy, depression
(whiten)	• reverence, ease, reliable effort
Green	• hue of grass, trees and all growing things
	• outlaws, fairies, Irishmen
	• release into the freedom of the wilderness (forest — Robin Hood)
	• fertility, growth, magic, supernatural, power of nature, the life force, alternative energy source
	• ecological action, backpacking, love of outdoors, interest in gardening, natural foods
	• independence — Ireland (St. Patrick's Day)
Purple	• originally the most expensive color (dye from a rare shellfish)
	• royalty, vulgarity, pretentiousness
	• plum, heather tones — wealth, elegance
(darken)	• increased and ambiguous sensitivity, dreams, visions, illusions, enchantment
(whiten)	• aristocracy of the mind and soul, special refinement, artistic or emotional sensitivity
Brown	• color associated with the earth, nature (of dormant state - autumn, winter)
	• stability, economy, fraternity, security, strength, piety, poverty, economy (as a dye stuff), modest ambiguous
(darken)	• quiet, reassuring, solid, reliability, hard work, lack of social pretension
	• olive, khaki — practical, aggressive action (military look)
(whiten)	• tan, beige — most neutral of all colors, least communicative, neither cheerful nor sad, neither active nor passive

The Truth about Grooms
(or, How to Tell Those Tuxedoed Men Apart)

Marcus B. Weaver-Hightower

> Remember, you're only the groom.
> — *Advice passed from a father*
> *to a man getting married, then to me*

It was a late July morning, before the sun had even come up in the south-eastern United States, yet it was already hot and humid, with one set of bugs winding down for the night and another about to start their shift for the day. My grandmother shook me awake; I knew it was her even though I only barely saw her outline from the faint light filtering through the window. She whispered though everyone else was already up (maybe it was to keep from startling me awake). "The wedding is on," she said. I struggled out of the race car-shaped bed and shuffled, probably in footed pajamas — blue, maybe green — into the living room of the old farmhouse to sit in front of the flickering television that was just brighter than the two lamps that lit it. My grandfather was already up and dressed, eyes glued to the TV. My grand-mother, torn between feeding us kids and watching the wedding, kept one eye on the eggs she was scrambling and one on the tube.

July 29, 1981. It was 5:30 am and the Prince of Wales, Charles Wind-sor, was marrying a "commoner," Diana Spencer, in a lavish ceremony in St. Paul's Cathedral. It has been described as "The Wedding of the Century," a "fairy-tale wedding." I remember where I was, so some truth, to my imagi-nation at least, resides in that claim. And there were coins minted, stamps made, which my grandmother and grandfather brought back from their one and only trip to the island of their ancestry just after the wedding. So I know it was important.

I can remember just a little — I was only eight, after all. I remember pomp and a little circumstance. I remember the huge train on Diana's white, white dress, carried down the aisle behind her by a number of maid-ens. I remember the magnificent horse-drawn carriage, like something out of *Cinderella*. Flowers, dignitaries, and music filled the hall. I do not re-member much about Charles, though. What did he wear? Did he blush? Did he look scared? I suppose it hardly matters. I remember her, though.

* * *

This essay is a story about learning. Not the kind that goes on in school (though some of it surely does). This is a story of learning how to become a groom, to invest meaning in one's body, one's clothes, one's gender; this story is about how such meanings come about, how they are reenacted, and how they might change to make the world a more just and equitable place to live and love.

This is also a story about silences and absences and what those mean after all. This is a story about making the invisible visible and why we should.

Training the Groom

> Women are taught from early childhood to plan for 'the happiest day of their lives.' Men are taught, by the absence of these social-izing mechanisms, that their work is 'other' than that. (Ingraham, 1999, p. 81)

I do not remember being coerced into or trained for marriage as some women are (see Ingraham, 1999; Mayerson, 1996). I never had a Barbie that I dressed in a wedding gown — nor a Ken in a tuxedo, for that matter. My parents and friends gave me a great deal of latitude in putting off marriage. But I do not think I can remember a time when I did not assume that one day I would be standing in a church next to a bride in a white dress repeating vows to do all the things responsible heterosexuals would do for one another. No Barbies, but I must have learned it somewhere. I must have been taught the desire and its attendant denial. Weddings were something that girls *wanted* and boys simply *did*.

It cannot be that simple, though. Where are all the images? My parents' wedding pictures. TV shows with the inevitable wedding as the happy ending and the movies with the same. *Cinderella*. *Robin Hood*. Toothpaste ads. Various cousins getting married in small town churches with cookie and punch receptions in the basement. Colleagues excitedly gathering around a woman whose hand had the new addition of a large engagement ring. Flipping impatiently past the wedding announcements on the way to real news. So many beautiful brides. So many non-descript grooms.

And so it goes for many years. I had, by the age of twenty-five, a vast store-house of images — cultural models (Gee, 1996) — of what "wedding," "bride," and "groom" meant.

> *Seen on the Internet:* A paper doll of a woman wearing a slip and surrounded by wedding-themed accessories. The set includes a hat to put on her, as well as a bouquet, a full-length mirror with a little girl staring into it (the doll's face shows through in the mirror to convey the little girl's seeing her future self in the mirror), and a wedding gown of white with a groom standing behind its left shoulder. The groom is as much an accessory as the dress. (http://www.karenprincestudio.com/page11.htm; last accessed May 1, 2001)

* * *

I first met my wife at a New Year's Eve costume party dressed up as Star Trek characters. I was the dashing Commander Riker, second in command of the Starship Enterprise. She was the android, Data, with her hair slicked flat to her head and white makeup caked on her face.

The next time I saw her, on our first "semi-blind" date, I knew by the time I saw the bottom hem of her dress coming down the stairwell of her sister's apartment that I would marry her. And I did.

* * *

Amazon.com, at the time I'm writing this essay, lists at least ten books in print that focus on fear of commitment. It lists seven about the role and responsibilities of a groom.

I used the fear of commitment "conversation" (Gee, 1999) to my advantage. To conceal that I was going to propose to my (then) girlfriend on New Year's Eve Y2K, I spent months deflecting, ignoring, and criticizing her constant questions about where our futures lay. That way my whipping out the ring I had surreptitiously bought for her would be a surprise.

What are the politics of this deception, this cloak and dagger routine that uses the pain and suffering of millions of afflicted "commitment-phobics" (Carter & Sokol, 2000) for a cheap thrill? If weddings and marriage provide a possible route to privilege as Ingraham (1999) argues, then why would there be a fear of commitment at all? Perhaps we have not accounted for one privilege, one lost in marriage, one that makes the decision to marry somewhat more difficult. Perhaps a sense of loss must be struggled with before a man can "take the plunge." Just what is being lost, though?

> The mining, manufacturing, and marketing of diamonds has involved colonial wars, apartheid, racist violence, massive labor abuses, struggles between superpowers, the stability of nations, and the hiring of mercenary armies. (Ingraham, 1999, p. 54)

Two months salary will last forever, they tell me. I could hardly afford to live up to this expectation and could hardly afford *not* to follow it. The size of the ring holds significance, whether we want to admit it or not. Maybe like the size of one's car, the diamond's size says something about the size of other things.

The clock shows ten minutes to midnight on New Year's Eve of 1999. This year, I am Sam Spade, and she wears a Nancy Drew outfit. We are wondering if the lights are going to go out and whether computers will still work after the Y2K bug, though, in reality, by the time the midnight hour gets to the United States, we already know that nothing of consequence will go wrong (Asia is not on fire, and they reached midnight hours ago). She and I are in the driveway, going through the pretense of looking for something in the trunk of my car. I'm nervous, palms sweaty and knees shaking. By now she senses something out of kilter, and her nervousness begins to show, too. I drop to one knee, pull the ring from under my fedora, and ask her to be my wife. She says "I guess so," and, as the midnight fireworks explode in the sky above us, we seal the deal with a kiss. I know she wants this kind of romance, and, on my more honest days, I know that *I* want this romance, too.

I wore an engagement ring, partly because I wanted the attention and partly to subvert the gender domination inherent in only the woman having to wear an engagement ring, to show that she "belongs" to someone else. Truthfully, I also wanted the social kudos. Watch next time someone shows off *her* new engagement ring. Note the joy and acceptance, laughter, oohing and ahhing, the pleased cooing, the blushing new fiancée, the way the big news spreads and how absolutely everyone must congratulate her. I wanted that, too, to feel like what I was getting myself into was important and worthy of mass celebration. So my fiancée agreed to buy *me* an engagement ring which I wore every day on my left ring finger. Only a couple of people ever noticed and asked. Others probably just assumed I was already married.

Would I recommend wearing a ring to other men? Yes. I felt more connected and like there was a change going on in my life, like I was forming a more equitable partnership with my mate. But then again, do I want DeBeers to get the idea, to make millions more off of women getting married and off of the backs and blood of black and brown South Africans?

Hiding the Groom

Flip through a magazine or website or etiquette book on the subject of weddings and you'd hardly see the roughly 1.225 million males that get married every year (U. S. Bureau of the Census, 1996). They are, within those pages — perhaps even within our cultural models (Gee, 1996) — invisible, missing in discourse. While in some ways invisibility has always served to increase male privilege (you cannot criticize or change what you cannot see) (e.g., Kimmel, 1996a), this is a double-edged sword. Whose interests are served, really?

One almost immediately realizes, when faced with "getting married" (at least when planning a wedding), that the task involves complex practices, depends upon a vast network of cooperation (Becker, 1982), and extends far in advance of the actual wedding. While concerned with the ceremony and the reception and often the honeymoon, "getting married" also involves a vast array of literacy practices that must occur prior to the wedding event. Most of these literacy practices involve planning the various events of the wedding (such as reading bridal magazines, corresponding with service providers, writing invitations, reciting prescriptive vows, giving toasts, and filling out various forms and licenses), and most involve materials that position the reader in relation to a set of prescribed models of how weddings are done. More simply, weddings are done *one* way (with room for individual variation — one can elope or have informal clothing, but it still involves vows, a relation with the state, and so on), and literacy practices both shape and fulfill those patterns. Erving Goffman presents a persuasive argument that following preset patterns in social rituals functions to show ourselves we belong within a society and to show others we "fit"

(1976). What is more, the performative scripts for the social ritual of "getting married" are readily available, distributed as they are amongst many people and medias in the culture. To contradict the culturally agreed-upon patterns proves difficult and can be socially costly.

Literacy forms a significant method of disseminating the cultural norms about getting married, especially brides' magazines. Millions of copies of bride's magazines are purchased each year, and often old copies are shared among brides. Books, too, like *Emily Post's Weddings* (1999), now in its third edition, or a crossover effort like Bride's Magazine's *Bride's Book of Etiquette* (1999), offer advice and rules to guide the socially acceptable wedding plan. Not to be left out, the Internet hosts a number of sites, most notably The Knot (http://www.theknot.com), from which brides (and sometimes grooms) can plan, budget, and announce the wedding on their own personal web pages; and of course the site includes a gift registry service and an online store for purchasing wedding paraphernalia. The line between information site and capitalist venture, just as in the magazines, constantly blurs. Other ways of disseminating these cultural models exist, of course — like advice, solicited or otherwise — but literacy constitutes one of the most prevalent methods.

Our increasing dependence upon literacy practices in transmitting social norms such as those of "getting married" (possibly due to such forces as advances in technology, higher mobility creating more distant family units, and depersonalization and alienation within communities) creates both opportunities and challenges for representation and voice. The proliferation of literacy materials (like the explosion in magazine publishing and the rise of the Internet) means that there are many more opportunities to open up Discourses (in Gee's [1996] sense of the term) for more participation. The commercial potential of these new outlets, however, can endanger attempts at true reform and fuller participation for those who do not already have voice by reinforcing marketable stereotypes, images of what one can be or should be if they only spend enough money. Such a notion of spending one's way into identity, though, leaves out a considerable number of those who get married, namely those without the economic capital — the working class — and those without the symbolic capital to make economic capital matter (Bourdieu, 1977), such as men of color and gay men.

Some recent attention has been paid to grooms. Most predominantly, a magazine, *For the Groom* (hereafter, *FTG*), dedicated to men getting married (though marketed to women as well, for it was sold next to bridal magazines), appeared briefly (for two quarterly issues only) in January 2000. While on its surface an expansion of men's ability to get into the Discourse of getting married, there are a number of troubling contradictions. What kind of groom, what meanings and desires, are on offer to the men and women who read it?

One of the more significant contradictions lies in *FTG*'s attempts to capitalize on the relatively untapped market of males as consumers of wedding goods and services. The magazine clearly has economic reasons to want to bring males into the Discourse of "getting married." Their purpose might best be described as more profit-oriented than altruistic. The two are not mutually exclusive, but this does raise a serious issue. Tim Edwards (1997) puts this contradictory nature of the magazines quite aptly, saying:

> [I]t is perhaps ... accurate to see men's style magazines primarily as vehicles for a new 'all-consuming' form of masculinity, encouraging men to spend time and money on developing consumer-oriented attitudes and practices from shopping to leisure activities and to enjoy their own masculinity: in short, a narcissistic and particularly introspective set of primarily auto-erotic pleasures. Men's style magazines have very little to do with sexual politics and a lot more to do with new markets for the constant reconstruction of masculinity through consumption: buy this to be that; own a double-breasted suit, portable CD player or BMW and be a man! (p. 82)

A number of structural and rhetorical maneuvers help accomplish the marketing of masculinity as consumption. For example, the magazine's producers constantly blur the line between advertisement and information (see also Edwards, 1997; Finders, 1997), for the editors index every spread in the back according to the manufacturer of the products and always include addresses and phone numbers. Too, the fashion articles consistently complicate clothing, make it more confusing, in order to create a dependence upon the magazine's and manufacturers' advice. You can see this in the article on shirts from *For The Groom*, "Sit Down and Shirt Up" (Mayes, 2000), where collars and cufflinks take on a new level of complexity depending upon the jacket one wears and the color of the wedding rings.

Beyond attempts to turn men into "good" consumers, *FTG* — retrogrades to their purposes — limits the possible participation of men in the planning and carrying out of the wedding. If indeed grooms need the "support and advice" to "pull their weight," as the publisher's letter claims, then men (and of course the women they are marrying) will have to look to other sources for ways to expand their participation. *FTG* confines its advice to traditional groom responsibilities such as buying engagement rings, honeymoon planning, and groom fashion. In no way does the magazine attempt to advise men in areas of planning outside of those traditional responsibilities. For example, should the groom want a say-so in the flowers at the ceremony or the menu at the reception, he will not find education within the pages of *FTG*. While saying that picking out flowers counts as a social privilege to be sought out by men would be a stretch, I do contend that having the *choice* to do so if one wants to *does* represent a privilege. Most brides' magazines, in fact, give women many choices about their participation, information enough, in fact, to plan and execute the entire wedding alone, including picking out the clothes the groom will wear.

The presentation of who gets married, who has voice *amongst* grooms, and what kind of man proves worthy of desire makes a third contradiction to an expansive interpretation of the magazine. Certainly, a number of men do find representation, so if we look only at the category "man," then no lack of representation of grooms in *FTG* can be claimed. If we think of men, however, as residing within a vast array of social positions based on class, race, sexuality, and even nationality, then we can break down the notion that *all* men have voice because *some* men are represented. Actually, *FTG* presents a tightly defined masculinity which includes only white, heterosexual, Christian, young, thin, urban, hip, clean-shaven, upper-class men. Only this narrowly defined man has voice and has valid desire within the magazine.

African American men, for instance, are markedly absent, only appearing in illustrations or advertisements, rarely in features, and often then as servants or entertainers. Depiction in illustrations allows for a great deal of exoticization that may not be possible within a photograph (that is, one can more easily draw the Western image of the exotic Other than one can find a real person with those traits to photograph), and such Othering through illustration happens a number of times in *FTG*. The numerous depictions of people of color in servile positions reproduces racist notions of the "proper place" of certain marginalized masculinities (Connell, 1995) within a predominantly white, upper-class masculine milieu.

One inevitably asks about *FTG*, why did it fail? After only two issues, it folded its tent (and its website) and disappeared into memory. Even my attempts to contact the publisher turned up empty. Could it be that men were not ready to invest in the process of getting married? Could it be that they did not want to be seen caring enough to read a magazine? Or, could it be that they did not see it in the bride's section of the magazine rack from way over where the hot rod magazines are?

I contributed $8 to this cause (I bought the only two issues they produced). In return I felt represented, empowered, and informed. I convinced myself, though, that it was for research, for the purpose of critiquing the magazine. Can I have it both ways?

* * *

It was a sweltering Charleston day, the kind with humidity you could cut with a knife, made worse by our wearing clothing that we thought would make us look more middle-class and respectable to the vendors we were asking to provide our wedding services. We had not been treading the sidewalk long, but I was already a little tired and a lot overheated.

We had already picked the church; by the time we walked out of the chapel doors I think we knew it was the perfect place for us. The reception site, we knew, was going to be a little more difficult. We started with venues near the church, hoping that issues of transportation would then be moot. So, one of the first sites we visited, just across the street from the church, seemed like a perfect place. My fiancée thought we might even be able to have a New Orleans-style procession with a site that close.

We walked up the narrow steps of this historic-looking white and black-trimmed house, then past the heavy door and into a spectacular foyer with ante-bellum mystique and elegance. We nosed around while the director of the house, a thin, blonde, middle-aged white woman in a tailored, peach-colored suit was busy talking with a young woman and two people we took to be her parents. What a perfect house, we thought, as we ambled amongst the chandeliers, oil paintings of proprietors long since dead, and the fine oak furniture. Very Charleston, indeed. The director soon joined us and began explaining services that the house provided for receptions.

Why won't she look at me?

Explaining the various catering options, she flipped through a book of photographs from other receptions, and talked a little about the history of the house and its new ownership.

How come she won't look at me?

After a quick tour of the house, explanations of the disabled persons' accessibility, and an overview of the contract ("just in case"), she asked if we had any questions. *Now* she's looking at me. My fiancée had a few questions about having a band, about the decorations others typically use, and about some prices. My fiancée asks me if I have an opinion on something or other — flowers, maybe — and while I do, I just shrug my shoulders, shake my head, and play like I could care less about such frilly concerns. This is the masculine equivalent of giggling and coquettishly turning my eyes to the floor. For this display of appropriate manly indifference, I am greeted with a knowing smile from the director, one that says 'My husband wouldn't care either,' and maybe a playfully exasperated 'Men!' I have since played this scene many times, and if I ever want a cheap "fix" of social kudos, I just play the part of the disinterested man who only cares about his tux and about the honeymoon sex.

* * *

The FOX Broadcasting company has produced two insightful shows which have their fingers on the pulse of American marriage ideologies. *Surprise Wedding* (aired November 2, 2000) and the ill-fated *Who Wants to Marry a Multi-Millionaire?* (aired February 16, 2000) are both loosely based on the "reality TV" craze of the *fin de millennium* and the mania over prime-time game shows, the latter show obviously playing on the name and concept of *Who Wants to Be a Millionaire?* Both wildly popular marriage shows give intimate glimpses into what we as a culture believe about marriage. If this were not true, how would we make sense of these two phenomena; how could we encounter these texts as understandable? The roles men play in these games/dramas rest on our understanding of their roles in the "real world" institution of marriage.

Who Wants to Marry a Multi-Millionaire? drew from beauty pageants for its intertextual references (see Fairclough, 1995) as a frame through which the audience could make a sensible text of it. It started with fifty women who introduced themselves and what they do for a living. Short clips of the women's activities during the week in Las Vegas were shown, as each picked out jewelry and a bridal gown. There were several stages in the competition, ranging from a couple of brief interviews to a swim suit parade, not to mention a similar parading of their bridal gowns. The field was periodically narrowed from fifty to ten to three and then finally to one, Darva Conger, a former Gulf War-era veteran and a registered nurse. As for the groom, where was he? He was hiding behind a screen of course, watching the whole spectacle while we got only shots of the back of his silhouetted head, the avatar of the male gaze. He holds a position of power and not-power. There were a couple of obligatory clips shown with people talking about his sense of humor and giving a little vague background, but his most important characteristic (above any other) was that he had multi-millions of dollars. What else does one need to see or know? And for her part, the bride-to-be helps support the notion that women's value lies in what you can see in a swimsuit and that all women want to "marry rich" at all costs. Now who could have predicted that such a match would go awry?! Can we find connections here to the high divorce rate in the United States?

Surprise Wedding, for its part, also played off of the game show genre for dramatic effect. On the show, five women brought their boyfriends, under false pretenses, to take part in a show (the men thought their girlfriends were getting makeovers). The women came out first and were interviewed first, telling the story of their meetings and relationships, all ending with the pitiable story of how and why their mates would not make the ultimate commitment (i.e., marriage). Each also echoed the sentiment that this show was an ultimatum: marry me or we're through. Like *Who Wants to Marry a Multi-Millionaire?*, the women came out dressed in white wedding gowns that they had selected for the big surprise. Also like its predecessor, the groom in *Surprise Wedding* need only be silent (and here even be the deceived dupe). We see him being tricked, and the host insists that the men not say anything while the bride delivers the ultimatum in front of hundreds of people in the audience and millions at home. We do not in fact, get to see the men talk until they are offered a thirty-second phone call (in the style of *Who Wants to Be a Millionaire's* "lifelines") to discuss with a friend or relative of their choosing whether or not they should marry the woman who has just lied to them and put them on the spot. Not much time to chew on such a big decision, but all eventually do decide, and all concede to marry. The only other times we hear them talk they say either "yes" or "no" and then (maybe) say "I do." I am intrigued by the structuring of talk in *Surprise Wedding*. The women have primary voice; they tell the story and frame the problem; they take action and — in a reversal of gender roles — do the proposing. The men are the ones structured out of the discourse, who are left only to assent or deny. It is carnivalesque (Bakhtin, 1968), and yet it is not. In this context, this text makes sense to the viewer. The world does not turn upside down as in the carnival; the world of weddings as we already know it simply gets reinscribed.

* * *

I decided to change my name, to add my wife's maiden name hyphenated with mine. I suppose I did it partly to see what it was like, this business of changing your identity. I don't remember ever practicing, as a kid or as a love-sick teenager, signing my name as someone else's last name. Still, a certain mystique resides in changing who you are, for what is more core to one's identity than one's name? What better expression of patriarchal control of women than to insist they change that identity?

The other part of changing my name was, I suppose, a sincere desire to form a union, an equal combining, with my wife. Maybe it's vanity, or dread at having to explain to teachers and telemarketers why "Mrs. Hightower" isn't around and — actually — doesn't even exist. My wife and I wanted to have the same last name, but it would be unfair to ask her to carry the sole burden of losing her previous identity. So we both changed our names.

The experience has shown me, again, the deep structure — the institutional structure — that supports gender relations as they are. The etiquette books (e.g., Editors of Bride's, 1999) warn that men will have to get their names legally changed (with a lawyer, court fees, and all of that) should they want to take on a different name. Women must simply show the marriage certificate. (In truth, despite the etiquette books' insistences, I simply showed up with my wife at the local social security office and they changed it without question. I cannot say if this is a typical experience.)

My name has been changed, but the challenge has not ended there. Other structural hurdles have been set up that must be overcome to challenge the system of gender in our culture through resisting naming practices. One minor frustration shows up when trying to register oneself on-line, for many web-based forms (Yahoo! E-mail is a prime example; my account at the local grocery store is another) will not accept a hyphen within the last name slot. Though I'm sure this has been less than problematic for the majority of men who use these services, I can't help but wonder at the frustration of the many women I know with hyphenated last names. How is it that these retailers and service providers have been able to get away with making it impossible for these women to record the true spelling of their last names? Is it indifference, ignorance, or hostility to those who would buck the patriarchal system?

A second, more important hurdle also comes in the form of bureaucratic record keeping. Forms and applications often provide space to list one's maiden name. But what is the equivalent for men? Is there an English word that approximates "maiden" for men? Do I just use the space for maiden? Or maybe I use the space that is sometimes provided for "aliases" (which sounds decidedly criminal, like someone with a wallet full of fake identification cards and a rap sheet full of "AKA's")? But then, why should I have to use these alternatives? Isn't it entirely possible to imagine that if we provided the space for a man who has changed his name in marriage, more men would do it, more would realize that changing their names is possible? This is how structure, even the mundane forms we fill out, keeps gender relations in place.

Forms, institutions, and systems, however, are not the only culprits. Beyond such abstract, nebulous, impersonal sites of gender reproduction, there are specific, individual people deeply invested in keeping the state of gender relations as is. The reactions of family, friends, and interested strangers have helped define the boundaries of gender and tradition, boundaries which my wife and I have crossed by both changing our names. The expectation was that she would change her name (maybe Southern tradition plays a part in this expectation), an expectation that was reified in the form of gifts monogrammed with the name "The Hightowers" on them and the well-wishing cards addressed to "Mr. and Mrs. Hightower." I do not mean to impugn the motives and good intentions of these nice people, only it shows the sheer weight of expectation. The reactions of our families adds yet more weight. Her family seemed genuinely excited. They got to add another member (in name) to the family instead of losing a member (in name). My family seemed to have the opposite reaction. I suppose the real "loss" was theirs (at least to their minds), for instead of gaining another Hightower, they lost half a Hightower. What privilege have they lost in this transaction that they should look so hurt at the thought of it? Could it be that the old system of patriarchal dividends and linear inheritance is alive and kicking, still fueled by the system of marital name changing? Or could their concern be more genuinely altruistic, wanting us — as they say — not to have the trouble of explaining it to others who might not understand, not to have the drudgery of making our names impossibly long, and not to have to ever face a situation in which a child of ours would also want to hyphenate his or her married name thus making a three part last name? Altogether, the hurdles — legal haggling, faulty forms, and social pressuring — make the choice to change one's name a difficult one. Thus the gender status quo remains unchallenged.

* * *

Please submit a 5x7 or smaller, black-and-white or color glossy photo, *of the bride only*, to be used with the wedding write-up. Please be sure to write the *last name of the bridegroom first*, and the last name of the bride on the back of the photo.

> — Directions for submitting marriage announcements to the *Post and Courier* Newspaper (Charleston, South Carolina); emphasis added.

***

You're going to wear a skirt?!

> — a learned colleague upon hearing that kilts would be worn at my wedding

I am torn by the contradictions and ironies entailed by being a groom. On the one hand, one finds the joy of sameness, of fitting in, being a part of a tradition handed down and formulated and enacted by successive generations. Great pleasure goes into putting on a big party, having people accept and congratulate you for fitting in, for validating *their* choices by making them yourself. Pleasure for the bride and groom resides in this, and the congregation and well-wishers garner pleasure from it, too. Sameness. I have bought into some of the practices that I know are wrong, ultimately regressive, for this reason.

Such drive for similarity filters into many aspects of the wedding practice. We wear the proscribed outfit. And, though we have heard the explanations that all the groomsmen and groom dress alike to confuse evil spirits who would steal the bride (Editors of *Bride's*, 1999), we know that there are other reasons we all dress alike, too. Fitting in. Not taking attention away from the bride. Avoiding aesthetic dissonance.

So what about the men who, like me, wear kilts? Who wear yarmulkes? Who wear African stoles? Who wear kimonos? Who wear wedding dresses themselves (Dennis Rodman wasn't the first or last, you know)? These differences are missing in the discourse, too. They are missing from *For the Groom*, they are missing in the etiquette books, and they are missing from the television shows. How does one learn to be different and learn the price for difference? Why, indeed, do we follow the paths that we know are wrong?

Sexing the Groom

Joke from the Internet: Scientists have discovered a food that diminishes a woman's sex drive by 90% ... wedding cake. (Http://www.womensuck.org/jokes.html; last accessed on May 15, 2001)

I have spent a good deal of time thinking, researching, and writing on the subject of male teachers and the particular difficulties that they face in a "feminized profession" (e.g., Apple, 1986; Williams, 1992). I am especially intrigued that sexuality often gets sutured to the male body as it engages in the teaching act (see Johnson, 2000; King, 2000). Quite simply, where females are cast into the perpetual role of sex object, the one looked at (Berger, 1972; Mulvey, 1991), males are often cast into the perpetual role of, as I term it, the "sex subject." In any situation, male bodies are dangerous, sex-seeking, untamable, polluting. Given the disproportionate representation of the male body amongst rapists, sexual predators, and sexual harassers, such a moniker is not altogether undeserved, yet this suturing has painfully negative consequences for those men who are not rapists, assaulters, molesters, or harassers. As Jones (2001) has persuasively shown, the dangers men represent extend beyond the bounds of teaching, into nearly any situation (in her case, department store Santa Clauses) in which the male body comes into contact with a potential sexual object.

Many see marriage as such a site, where, until the twentieth century, marriage and sex were not considered separate (Lehman, 1993). In the popular imagination, the male impulse to marry revolves on the honeymoon and the promise of sex (a fiction for most people since the sexual revolution). *FTG*, in both of its issues, featured stories about sex during and after the honeymoon, with plenty of advice about how to be more equitable in lovemaking (from advice on sex on the wedding night to how to keep sex interesting — and plentiful — during married life). Both also have advice for the hapless first-time lingerie buyer amongst its readership. The groom, for his part, learns to be the appropriate sex subject. Magazines for brides do not focus so heavily on sex but focus instead on appearance — being an appropriate sex *object*. We might call this a lesson in the hetero-normative romance.

Along with the re-entrenchment of sexual divisions of labor and sexuality that each repetition of this trope entails, there coincides a repetition of an imaginary relationship, a romantic deception about the true meaning of the wedding and what weddings portend. Marriage, that is, at its most basic, does not revolve on having copious amounts of sex or on manufacturing one's body to create desire for sex in another. It revolves on a social relationship, (sometimes) a religious relationship, a consumer relationship, a relationship to the state, and a personal contract fraught with tensions, contradictions, and disagreements. The survival of such a tenuous, distributed relationship can never be assured. To prepare men and women as they are now (to make them sex subjects and objects, respectively), means to train them for a fantasy and to keep them unprepared for the true difficulties of marriage. Some of the interviews Mayerson (1996) shares show sex to be a shaky ground on which to build a marriage.

> Eighty percent of married men cheat in America. The rest cheat in Europe.
>
> — Jackie Mason

Such a process of sexing brides and grooms inevitably cycles back and disperses itself into other realms of life. Partly because we believe that men marry (partly) for sex, we believe that men are unable to restrain themselves sexually — the honeymoon, within this ideology, stands as just one more example to prove the rule. The rule, then, applies to men generally. Men only think with their dicks, the saying goes. Thus, male teachers, department store Santas (Jones, 2001), and other males who interact with children are suspect. Those men who use touch as part of care lose their ability to do so, lose in fact one of the aspects of their humanity: physical interaction with other humans (Johnson, 2000). Slowly we wall off men onto islands of themselves, their only foray out being through sex. Many men, though, actively work to fit the stereotype, to fit the expectation that to be men they must always already want sex. They are structured, but they in turn create the structure (see Bourdieu's [1977] concept of "habitus"). Such a cycle comes to haunt women, too, in their acceptance of/coercion into the sex object role. They are cast into the role by men, other women, even themselves, and the expectations and self-pressuring works much as it does with male sexuality. The structure works to constrain women, but women must help create the structure.

Thus, to put on a white wedding dress or a tuxedo is *not* an apolitical act. What politics the person wearing it chooses to invest in it, however, are not necessarily pre-determined. There are ways to rupture, interrupt, and resist.

* * *

The word *honeymoon* first appeared in print in the middle of the 16th century. Richard Huloet in his *Abecedarium Anglico Latinum* 1552 defined it as 'a term proverbially applied to such as be new married, which will not fall out a the first, but the one loueth [sic] the other at the beginning exceedingly, the likelihood of their exceeding love appearing to assuage, the which time the vulgar people call the honey moon.' His description suggests not only that the term had already been around for some time by the 1550s, but also that it was probably inspired by the notion that

although married love was at first sweet as honey, it soon waned
like the moon. (Ayto, 1990, p. 285)

In the premier issue of *FTG*, the text of the column "Ask an Old
Married Guy" lies under an illustration of a older man sleeping stretched
out on a couch, his rotund, undershirt-clad belly sticking up, holding a remote control, the ruins of a TV dinner lain on the floor by his head. I wonder
as I read if this fate lies ahead for me, too.

Here lies another rupture in the romance of weddings. Different wedding story lines broadcast at such a pitch that perhaps only the groom can
hear them. One story line features the bumbling and incompetent husband,
fiddling with this and that in the garage. One foretells the diminishing of sex
after marriage (a threat to the "sex subject"). Another tells the tale of never
seeing one's friends, or at least not without "permission." One particularly
gruesome story line warns of messy divorces that leave the man economi-
cally gouged and bereft of his children. The groom cannot take in only the
fantasy discourse of weddings unadulterated by these alternate discourses.
What wonder can we have, then, that the fear of commitment discourse per-
vades our culture and our lore about the male sex? Why would men want to
do something like getting married?

Men from the ages of 45 to 64 who live with wives are twice as
likely to live ten years longer than are their unmarried counterparts. (Sheehy, 1999, p. 261)

It may sound like cowboy movie wisdom, but the love of a good woman
can do a lot for a man. He will likely live longer and, most women would argue, better. But why? And despite the myths of the horrors of marriage
(those above), why do men continue to marry and stay married after many
years? I shall not attempt to gloss the millennia of love poetry that describes
the wonders and beauty of woman. I will resist the belief that just going
along with what everyone else does provides sufficient justification. I will
hope that, as I have sometimes heard argued, having slave labor legally
bound to serve them in the kitchen, the bedroom, the nursery, and now in
the work force proves a false reason. I hope something more lies behind it,
something hopeful. Perhaps the answer lies in the symbiotic relationship
that develops in the day-in, day-out fusing of two souls (though that sounds
like the love poetry lying to me after all).

We have, all in all, done an admirable job in training men to do nothing
but show up, wear a tux, say "I do," and then enjoy the honeymoon sex. We
have done a similarly adequate job of training women for every detail up to
and including the honeymoon. We have yet to accomplish training men and
women for the life after, for the struggle to have more equitable relationships.

Most men [surveyed] liked marriage for the domestic warmth
and security, and the stability and regularity of home life, having
someone there to help and care for them; sex was mentioned only
infrequently, and then as a minor reason.... . (Hite, 1981)

Grooming the Groom: Why it Matters Anyway

Princess for a Day Weddings and Special Occasions, "certified" wedding consultants in Texas, offer a number of consultation packages for brides who need help in planning and organizing their weddings. Their website (http://www.princess4aday.com) lists four packages, with one to fit nearly every need and budget. The premier package, and the most expensive, they call the "Princess Diana Wedding Package." Diana's image, bepearled and tiara-crowned, smiles out from the computer screen. If you want to be the ultimate princess — the one you watched all those years ago living out every girl's (and boy's?) Disney-sanctioned dream — simply buy this package. The bridal industry is always ready to sell back to you the desires they instilled in you in the first place.

What power resides in picking out flowers? This is a good question. I cannot pretend that men are somehow disadvantaged in the larger society because of their participation (or lack thereof) in planning and executing a wedding. Overall, knowing how to pick floral arrangements, knowing that the squiggly lines decorating cakes are called "cornelli," or knowing how to make birdseed bags with tulle will not garner one much cultural, economic, or symbolic capital (Bourdieu, 1977). In fact, given that these skills and knowledges are associated with the feminine, the reverse likely holds true for grooms who *do* have them. So, no, I do not argue that men are somehow left out of a vein of power that attends these knowledges. However, not participating or being structured out of participating leaves in place social relations which harm (at least in some ways) everyone, especially women.

Male absence from the marriage process harms women because weddings symbolically reenact the unequal division of labor. As largely symbolic and ephemeral as the practice of "wedding" may be, such a highly meaningful ritual creates and reflects the beliefs and larger practices outside of itself. Interrupting the symbolic is not a hollow act, but rather has the potential to shift those larger beliefs and practices which inform and create the symbolic and which it creates and informs. If that were untrue, why has the practice of "giving the bride away" largely been altered to be a "pledge of support" from parents? Why, then, has the word "obey" been almost universally stricken from wedding vows? Yes, the symbolic holds important sway; the symbolic can be a place for interruption.

Just what ought we interrupt, though? If we want to live more equitable, just lives with true partnerships, we must live that ideal in the symbolic and in rituals. Men should be expected to contribute equally. Men who already want to should be allowed to do so, but that requires teaching them and providing information on how to participate. No reason can be given for why a man cannot learn to pick out flowers, except that social mores have told him not to want to. No reason exists for why a woman cannot plan the honeymoon except that tradition delegates that to the groom. I do not suggest the bride take on even more. I suggest, rather, that this prelude to the most important partnership two people will enter should reflect the true nature of cooperation and sharing required of a marriage. Cooperation, both before and during the marriage, ensures the equitable survival of us all. The result could well be the living of fuller lives by both men and women.

At a more theoretical level, a person learns yet more facets of one's gender by getting married. Learning gender (and performing it for others) does not stop after the teenage years, but instead occurs across the entire trajectory of life, from birth to death. Remember Jack Palance's 1992 Academy Award acceptance speech in which he, at age seventy-seven, dropped to the floor to do one-armed push-ups and told the crowd he could "still get it up" because he wanted to prove he was not too old to play tough movie roles (see Kimmel, 1996b)? One never really stops learning gender. Because one learns critical facets of how to "do" gender in male-female relationships by going through the process of getting married, changing its script and making the process more equitable can change the very gender relations that both men and women learn to embody. They are unavoidably going to learn something about gender by getting married; what should it be that they learn? We have an opportunity to allow men and women to live fuller, more satisfying lives in which they can take pleasure in whatever they desire (even if they do not know they desire them yet), whether picking out flowers or making travel plans.

Two cautionary tales are in order, however. Change must be on more than an individual level to be effective. As R. W. Connell (1995) argues, "the project of remaking the self may represent containment, not revolution, in relation to the patriarchal gender order" (p. 139). Instead of fixing individuals one at a time, we need, he argues, "Collective projects of transformation [that] work at the level of the social" (p. 141). One couple changing their ceremony to reflect equality is not enough. Nor is it enough for one minister to refuse to conduct "giving away" rites. It takes organized couples, organizations of religious leaders, producers of literacy materials like magazines and etiquette books, and service providers together changing the symbolic politics of weddings on a large scale.

Second, be wary of the power of capital. The bridal industry — primary, secondary, and tertiary (Ingraham, 1999) — has a huge part to play in the creation of our cultural models of weddings. They sell us back the desires they help create in us. Too, though, they have a part to play in changing the cultural models and practices of weddings, through the images, advice, products, and service they offer. Danger lurks here, though, as many social movements all too easily become co-opted for capital's profit (think of the way Virginia Slims advertisements have coopted feminist messages or the way the tobacco industry tries to soften its image through bragging about its public service efforts). DeBeers getting Western women to buy diamond engagement rings for their fiancés will not serve the interest of equality. A bevy of new products to help the groom with his new share of the work load may be helpful, but ultimately may do good for profit but harm for the cause of equity. Great vigilance must be maintained to ensure that people, not just companies, benefit from expanding the "getting married" discourse.

Real change in wedding preparation may already be happening, as signaled in part by the appearance of a magazine for grooms, however briefly. While some may believe the changes stem from the changing social and economic roles of women (who need more help with weddings since they have increasingly taken on careers), I believe these changes signal that male desires and responsibility are on the rise as well. Much remains to be done, though. Schools and educators have a part to play. Though marriage seems unrelated to the mission of schools (since it usually happens physically and temporally outside of the K-12 setting), schools do indeed have social missions that can contribute to the changing of weddings and their attendant gender relations. Schools can teach media literacy and other methods of critical literacy, giving students the tools necessary to critically view advertising, reporting, and fictionalizing of weddings. Schools can make structural changes that demonstrate commitment to equality of the sexes, changes concerning, for example, discipline codes, pedagogy, material selection, hiring and promotion practices, course enrollment, and student-teacher relations. Yes, schools have many roles to play in this process, many tasks to accomplish. Let these tasks be undertaken *not* in the spirit of the self-interest that characterizes the bridal industry, but in the joy that comes from imagining new possibilities, new and better ways of being and loving in the world.

Acknowledgments

I am indebted to numerous people for help in the preparation of this chapter, but all remaining flaws are my own. Thanks to David Bloome for his help with the initial ideas that form the basis of the chapter. Thanks to François Tochon and my colleagues Gloria, Sabine, Jung Euen, Amy, Liz, Hyo-Kyung, and Mary for sharing their stories and focusing mine. Thanks, most especially, to Rebecca Weaver-Hightower for help in preparation of the manuscript and for sharing a life that I could use as data.

Families of the Soul: The Truth on Method

François V. Tochon

I. Meeting Notes

January 7 "Plumes au Vent" Daycare Center

She's talking about her new family and the dozen people present are holding their breath: this mother hasn't talked much at past meetings. She's a single parent who had given us an idea of how hard she found it to manage her daily life. This evening, she opens up. She has only recently been coming to meetings with her companion. Now, suddenly, she's telling us about herself. He bends his head a little shyly, sweetly, with a tender smile. The woman is young and energetic. She says her life has been hell. Today, Monday, her kids are back home after a weekend with their father. He had asked the children "how the crazy lady was." She bends her head as she says this and then raises it with a smile: "Marc and I are engaged." A quiet stirring reveals that we're touched by this news.

We're seated in a circle on the daycare center's small wooden chairs. The center is in a spacious red-brick house and we're upstairs in the children's playroom. Although some toys are still scattered here and there, everything is in order and it's the end of the day. Two daycare teachers have come in to replace the ones from the day shift, who are taking part in the meeting with parents. The kids are eating supper first, and from a distance we can hear the sounds of children and mealtime. This is the first time our circle has been so perfect. The arrangement of the chairs produces a sense of complicity, fosters sharing, and gives us the strong feeling that each of us is attentive to the others. Outside, the temperature is zero degrees; it's windy and snowy. But inside, in the room with blue walls, silence reigns; a few words are exchanged here and there. With depth.

Discovering Love

Her face has brightened. She's tanned and has broad cheek bones, sparkling eyes, and a mischievous air. She's about thirty. "The neighbor thinks I'm a crazy lady too; I like acting crazy when I play with my kids. It's so good to dance and sing with them, you forget everything. This summer we laughed so hard when we fell into the pool with our clothes on." Tonight's theme: "What is the family and what makes the difference?"

She has three children aged from three to five, and now she's taking her companion's daughter into her home. The girl is twelve years old. She's fallen in love with both of them — it's a package deal. And the things they're going through lead to thoughts about love. Imperceptibly, we enter a circle of feelings. "She's going to stay with us." She's surprised by the emotions the young girl's questions are triggering, she's surprised to be encountering an unspoiled, unexpected friend in this child who's opening up.

"I talked with her till midnight about all kinds of things. We were alone during the night, and she told me...lots of things, the kinds of things I told my friends when I was twelve, and I plunged right into the world of the pre-teen, with all its worries and questions and enthusiasms." Her companion bends his head still lower, as though he were holding back a silent smile; there is love in this restraint. Our circle has drawn closer, bound together by attentiveness.

"It was three in the morning, she was asking questions about everything, and sometimes I was embarrassed, I didn't dare answer, or sometimes they were things I hadn't thought about." She takes a breath and sits up straight. Her friend has pushed up the sleeves of his pullover — it's a close fit; he's wearing jeans; we can't see much of his face. He has an aquiline nose, a nice smile; he's looking, he's looking at his hands again. "Her body hair is growing in,...she's feeling things, she's amazed, and I don't know what to tell her, I just don't remember! The other day, she asked me to wash her back. I came close to her — that was the first time. Before that, she'd always refused. I realized...she has breasts now. She wanted to show them to me."

As he expresses it, this is his daughter, and he's happy, happy like a father, a father who's proud of his daughter, filled with a happiness he doesn't dare express, a happiness that shows in his restraint and his love for the woman who loves his daughter the way he loves his daughter, the woman who has welcomed her and loves her unreservedly, the way he would have liked to be loved. She steals a look his way, a smiling look, her eyes creased with mischief, and goes on: "Since it was three in the morning, I said, get dressed. We went out and went running on the skating rink. We laughed so hard, we fell down and couldn't get up again. It was seven o'clock when we came home and we slept all day."

January 14 "Trois Pommes" Daycare Center

Her son sees angels. "What am I to do? He describes every friend's own angel — his brother has the most beautiful angel!" The theme of this evening's discussion is the phenomena associated with transitions. For example, the mother-child separation when a young child is left at daycare. This mother, still a teenager, confides, "The first time, I stayed behind for twenty minutes; when I left we were both crying. I cried for three days, huddled up in my bed. I cried because I had to leave him every morning. I'd come home from the daycare center, go to bed, and cry until five o'clock. Then I'd go pick him up."

This is a former school that's been turned into daycare centers; our discussion groups are scattered in two large rooms. We passed out colored pieces of cardboard to all the participants, and everyone wrote down their names. The color coding will allow us to re-form groups and change groups from one session to another. Groups are organized by color, and in two weeks' time we'll suggest that each group comprise participants of all colors. That way, every member will have been through a different experience. At that stage, we'll mark a letter on each piece of cardboard to allow for further variation among the groups, unless the parents express the wish to stay in stable groups. It's the parents who decide on the topics discussed and the method of organization, working from a range of options that we bring.

No two sessions are the same. This evening, sixteen parents with varied backgrounds are present. At our last session, we observed that dads talked more than moms, so this time around we suggested that the four dads present form their own group. This evening, the session has been organized as "a pub conversation," with refreshments tailored for every group. The cook has prepared dishes for the groups, and a low table has been set up, with the circles of chairs radiating away from it. The parents asked for mealtime to double as a time for small-group conversation on the theme of the day, because they wanted more time to visit with each other. Sessions begin at 5:30 p.m. and end at 7:40 p.m. Usually, meals are taken in a large group, but this cuts off the discussions (although it has the benefit of prompting new ones). The idea of pub conversations was submitted to a vote, and this evening we're giving it our first try. At the end of the evening, we'll take stock and vote on how to organize our next session.

Inner Reality Is Not Unreal

Valériane, a daycare teacher, is watching this mother attentively. Eric sees angels and describes them to his little friends. Does he have a proper sense of reality? Does he have a sense of a different reality? "Is it true that it may all be unreal?" asks his mother, suddenly worried. She hadn't thought about this possibility. Eric and his brother are her cherished treasures, she says. Our conversations soothe her fears and make clear the implications of taking a firm position, no matter what it may be. "Inner reality is not unreal: it positions the child in relation to values that comfort him."

Eric has lost his father. "He's seen his father and he's also described his (deceased) aunt." These episodes could be transitory. The child needs to involve himself in action and access the objective world in order to broaden his ability to change the world. There's a moment of silence. Outside, it's snowing. The crunching of celery stalks, carrots, and green pepper can be heard: raw vegetables have been placed on the tables as an appetizer. The coffee maker is boiling. Valériane takes this opportunity to restart the conversation. Loud voices can be heard coming from where the men's group is seated. I've withdrawn momentarily to the back of the room to write, with a big blue cup of hot coffee by me. In the group next to me, Diane has just shared her perception of a transition situation.

Our team consists of individuals of various nationalities.[1] Our views differ and our interests are diverse, but we all share a baseline belief in the importance of an open approach in education. We're interested in differences in language and culture and how they affect communication. We believe that many problems can be solved by means of in-depth, honest conversations on the events of everyday life. Nevertheless, we're not therapists but educators. We take an educational perspective on the events that unfold during our sessions. The research project under way is being conducted in the province of Quebec, in disadvantaged bilingual settings, in networks of daycare centers and pre-kindergartens. Some of the parents involved are immigrants or refugees; their mother tongues include Serbo-Croatian, European French, and English. Some come from Asia or Africa. Many of the families in which the parents come from overseas live in a single room.

The Rituals of Communication

In Diane's group, one mom is talking about the transition rituals she and her child have devised when she leaves him at the daycare center in the morning. This child can only feel safe if he imports a piece of home, a stuffed bear, to the daycare center. He only feels good at the daycare center if his bear is there too. When his mom leaves, he goes to the north window to signal to her, then he makes two hand signals from the east window, and last he waves his arms hard from the third window as he watches his mother slowly leave, her car window down despite the cold. For a week now, this mom has been in crisis, she says. Her child forgot to carry out the ritual three times, and she was all alone waiting for her little guy to signal to her. But, as she puts it, the little guy had discovered his pals and forgotten his mom. The result was a family scene that she describes. So this morning he went back to signaling his mother with a slightly sad smile; she noticed his heart wasn't in it.

The group of fathers call themselves a team. "Our team." The problem the team is facing is how to build a relationship with your child. This concern contrasts with that of the mothers. Whereas the fathers are engaged in discussion about rituals for building a relationship, the mothers are reflecting on the rituals they set up to mitigate separation. One father exclaims, "We have to forge the bond that biology hands to mothers." But in both cases, the question of permanence arises. Family rituals constitute landmarks. They affect timetables, a relationship's rhythms, and constancy of affection.

"After washing his hands, my father used to gently place his hand on the nape of my neck and say, 'See, it's cool!'" "Do we allow men the space to create a relationship?" says Valériane, from the other end of the room. Paul has had enough: "My child is three years old and he's in crisis." Behind this revelation, we see his helplessness. A sturdy, red-haired man, he's shaken by his wife's almost pathological attachment to her son. She experiences distress from the moment she leaves him behind. The child is developing an acute, unbalanced sense of their relationship and can no longer bear to see his father approach his mother. He positions himself between them and tries to separate them. This father expresses the feeling that his spouse tries to prevent him from establishing a sense of complicity with the child. This evening she stayed home with her son because he's sick. They're spending the evening in bed whispering words of comfort to each other, he adds.

Telling the Truth about Communication

At the end of the session we're in the big empty room, going over the things that were said. Our goal is to review the way the evening was organized, but it's also to review our own selves: were our reactions suitable in every case, was it appropriate to offer such-and-such an answer in such-and-such a situation? This process constitutes the professional development phase of the evening. The daycare teachers join our team for this part. They're close to the parents, and they were part of the parents' groups during the evening. They too have children and they talk about their own child-rearing experiences. Besides, they deal with lots of kids and can contribute useful advice.

Our review of the evening leads us to reflect on ways to help some of the parents. Marie-Pierre, the daycare teacher, had noticed this mother's problems right from the start, she says. She clung to her child. "She had a long rubber band that brought her and her child back together every time she had to distance herself from him a little." The father understands that something's not going right and it causes him pain, but he's at risk of developing resentment that will result in violence sooner or later, says Marie-Pierre. The daycare teacher intends to tell the child that he has a good father. She wonders what means could be used to calm this mother when she attends parental sessions again. How can we help her see her relationship in a more balanced way? This issue is touchy as it relies on Marie-Pierre's interpretation of the situation, and we have first to see what data support this interpretation.

"We Can Do Without Men!"

The discussion broadens to consider the men's group. At the end of the session, we asked the parents if they wanted to vary the organizational principle (by forming groups with several colors of cardboard) and if they wanted to mix the men with the women again or maintain a separate group for fathers. Several women reacted strongly: "We can do without them!" Jean-Marie refers back to this reaction. At the first session men and women mingled, then it was suggested there be only one man in any group, so that they wouldn't monopolize the mother's attention. Men talk more than women. But rejection of men has found virulent expression here, remarks one daycare teacher.

One father reacted: "There were five men, and we didn't talk about sex at all!" The mothers burst into laughter. In their groups, they had reproached themselves with being mother hens and voiced the importance each one gives to expressing her emotions. Their rituals mitigate the effects of separation, but they are not absolute. "That ritual of the three kisses exchanged before parting — he refused to do it, just to set up a bit of blackmail: by refusing to carry out the ritual, he wanted to create a feeling of lack. I left without the kisses, I didn't make a big scene about it, and he understood that this ritual is not an absolute." Sometimes rituals take on too much importance. If the ritual is initiated by the child, the parent has to preserve a bit of space. Before going along with it, it's best to be sure you'll be able to keep it up. Otherwise, as one mom reported, you'll be stuck lying down next to your child every night, and he'll never be able to go to sleep alone. Ritual can lead to independence: it's important to see that it evolves.

Seduction and Power

There is one man in particular that Valériane, the daycare teacher, finds quite charismatic and who tends to occupy center stage. (In fact, he literally works in the theater.) He's open, but he finds he's obliged to discipline his son, who repeatedly makes scenes. This very significant challenge to his values shakes his self-perception, and he has spent two of our evenings monopolizing the conversation with his problem. Finding himself among men, he's adjusted his way of intervening and his place within the group. He begins to listen to the others and observes that, even though others don't talk much, they have problems that are far more painful than his, he expresses. Valériane notes that the relations that form between men oblige him to drop the strategies of seduction that he deploys to monopolize the attention of women listening.

As we go back over the evening, the discussion strays off topic for a moment. Valériane observes with a smile, "He's a seducer. You should just see him getting into things in my office." "But I'm a seductress myself, and I know how to treat seducers!" The daycare teachers now make comments. "Just let me take the first seat in the room and you'll see who sits next to me!" Since I'm sitting on her left, I remark that I sat down first; then Jean-Marie and I broach a short discussion, while Valériane continues. Later on, as we drive back to the university, this episode will be rediscussed with Diane in the research team: we're looking for neutral ground but there's no such thing. Seduction and power are often linked in human relations, Diane remarks. Our sessions draw us so close to the parents and daycare teachers that we're looking at life in ways we'd forgotten about — as freedom, as a choice, as a decision. Working close to the parents and the daycare teachers, we're also working on ourselves. No topic is innocent; we're trying to be truthful.

January 15 "Sur une Patte" Daycare Center

France has replaced Mimi as the head of the daycare center. She's somewhat overwhelmed by this new responsibility (the buck stops with her), but it's also opening up new horizons for her. It represents a change of identity. She meets us on our arrival an hour before the session and we discuss the evening's theme. The parents had asked that we review the holiday season.

One mother will not be here tonight: her little boy is sick. Experiences in other daycare centers have heightened our alertness to the use of pretexts, and we worry about the mother's health. I had met with this mother in mid-December to inform her of her test results. Could there be a connection? Participants in our sessions take a battery of tests at the start of the project and at its completion. This is a condition for funding for the activity. Given that our activity is part of a research project, it's only reasonable that we justify the moneys spent on meals, evening child care, and so on. It's also a good thing to provide an account of the sessions' usefulness on a broad scale. Nevertheless, our preferred approach is a qualitative analysis of situations. So that everyone can have a grasp of the usefulness of the tests, we provide one-on-one reports on the profiles obtained from them during clinical interviews with a child-rearing focus.

Respect for Privacy

Providing test results was what we had done at our last session. One young mother had been recommended to us by the Community Health Center through the daycare center's coordinator a she was recovering from a suicidal period. This young mother's profile showed marked improvement after a year of involvement in our sessions, and she was finally freeing herself from feelings of persecution that had led her to want to take her own life. She was looking for small jobs and regaining courage. I had talked to her about the importance of this progress and added that it would be good for her to have a yearly check-up to be sure her physical health was okay. Her response was that she had too much to do to see a doctor, but that she'd think about it in early January.

At the end of the evening, as we were conducting an overview of the main events of the session, I informed Mimi, the daycare center's coordinator who was in touch with the Community Health Center for regular reports (and the participant agreed), that it was important for this mother to consider contacting a physician in early January for a check-up. Indeed the test results relating to physical health suggested high risk. Mimi would inform the community health center that was following this mom. There was no procedural problem with this, but it was clear that things should be handled with discretion and tact. There was nothing exceptional in suggesting an annual check-up. This mother knew we were in touch with her health advisors as they had recommended her to us, and she had agreed to this relationship. Then the daycare center coordinator changed. France, a well-trained daycare teacher, replaced Mimi who retired after thirty years in nursing and early childhood education.

On arriving at the daycare center an hour before our session, we had run into this mom, and she didn't appear very happy to see us. She was leaving with her little boy, who didn't look poorly. France, the new daycare center's coordinator, explained to us that when she'd conveyed the information to the community health center, the worker who follows this mom had suggested a three-way meeting to strongly urge her to get medical tests. These social service specialists had been trained in the hard intervention approach and were accustomed to confronting resistant individuals in a group.

The Dynamics of Friendship and Comfort

Listening to this, I was pained and struck: a hypersensitive person was placed in a confrontational situation. Just as she was getting stronger emotionally and mentally, she was plunged into a dynamic of revolt, risk taking, and disgrace. When this mom was thus confronted, it became clear she was refusing to see a doctor because she's afraid she has AIDS. A diagnosis of AIDS would disgrace her. Clearly, if we didn't defuse the situation, she might find it preferable to walk out rather than face humiliation. A medical diagnosis might put an end to doubt and point to areas of need where attention might lead to greater well-being. But the social action to be taken would have had to be conducted within a dynamic of friendship and comfort. In contrast, some psychosocial workers cut themselves off from these feelings of closeness: "It's your problem," they say. A social worker who's responsible for social protection services has told me how she was trained to maintain her morale: "Your first job is to determine whose problem it is. Then you delegate it and forget about it!"

"Let's Drop the Masks!"

We haven't yet had the time to think in depth about the things we've just found out, and here we are meeting the parents who are arriving for tonight's session, to be held in one of the daycare center's small playrooms. About fifteen small blue and yellow chairs have been placed in a circle. Jean-Marie conducts the session and I take notes. He and I are placed at either end of the room. About a dozen mothers aged between twenty and thirty are present. Then a father arrives, the former companion of a mother who's especially demanding about the quality of intervention. "We have no time to waste," she says, "let's drop the masks: let's tell it like it is." At this center our sessions with parents have always been very intense, sometimes overwhelming. The shared reflections about things lived through has brought the members of this group close together.

Jean-Marie suggests that each person make a drawing to show how they perceived the Christmas holiday period. The suggestion may come across as childish, and two mothers give us looks that suggest they don't want to be led down the garden path. Despite this, everyone goes into an adjacent room with reasonably good grace to draw on sheets of paper supplied by us. I stay behind in the first room to finish writing up my notes. Alternately, I could have gone with the others to draw and share my perceptions. Which is better: a non-participatory, half-participatory, or fully involved attitude? Increasingly, I favor an attitude of full involvement in activities. Note-taking has more than one purpose: it offers the basis for giving feedback to the facilitator; it serves as a record of sessions that have taken place; it allows you to provide an account of the experience; and the subsequent write-up based on the notes constitutes an educational and professional development tool.

When everyone walks back in with their pictures, the atmosphere has grown lighter. Drawing is pleasant. As adults we generally have no time to do it. Each person shows her or his drawing and talks about it. The only dad who's present that evening goes first. He's a tall, thin fellow with a moustache, and he wears a tiny crucifix earring in one ear. He's drawn two big rounded, pink hills, with a red ball between them representing the sun. Above, a star. On the rounded hills, some fir trees scattered here and there. He tells us that he loves nature, pointing to the little solitary man perched between the two hills. His father died last November. "The star is the one who's supposed to watch over us. These hills give me a feeling of a unity."

A mother begins to speak. In her picture, gifts have been opened and lie in disorder, her daughter is seated on the couch alone with lots of room to her left. The mother is standing up behind her and to her right, next to the Christmas tree. She doesn't look pleased. "My mother was supposed to be in Florida over the holidays. We started unwrapping the presents and my ex-husband turned up; at one point, he told me to go look in the closet. It seemed like a funny thing to suggest. I thought I'd find a gift there. When I opened the closet I found my mother inside. She was hiding there. I was so rattled to see her that I went upstairs and cried. She spoiled my whole evening."

"Well, If You Feel Like Burying Your Heads in the Sand…"

The next drawing seems calm. Pictured in it is the peacefulness of a cottage. Inside, things are not so quiet. "My boyfriend and I generally get together with our families two evenings a month. All of a sudden, we had spent seventeen days in a row cut off from the world in this cottage buried in the snow, which explains the snow surrounding the whole scene." At left, we see a blue-haired girl all made up in blue. The mother continues: "The girl wearing the navy blue lipstick was my Christmas present: Look Mom, I'm so beautiful! I start up a relationship with the blue-haired teenager's dad and she's the free gift that comes with him. He's a bit old fashioned and the teen's view is, 'You're not cool!' What a holiday! She wanted to press our buttons. It didn't work with me. She led off like this: 'I'm not sure if I can tell you everything, because I don't know if you're going to be on my side or my dad's.' 'Why should I be on one side or the other?' So then she got started telling me about everything that bothers Jacques, using hair-raising language. 'Okay, if you guys feel like burying your heads in the sand that's fine with me! I wanted to introduce you to my boyfriend, show you his car, he's nineteen, I'm taking the pill, we use condoms, we do both, don't worry, and if you'd rather not meet him, I'm leaving with him.' And besides all that, the atmosphere in the cottage was full of the competition between the kids; they were ready to kill each other because they didn't all have the same number of presents."

We spend a short time on a mom's picture that shows nothing but harmony: first the parents' gifts, then the children's, with everything being videotaped and everyone happy. Another picture shows a Christmas tree, a tall girl, a big bottle of wine and a half-full wine glass. "There are a lot of people missing from this picture. A lot have died; people were away, the family has to be built up again. I was alone all through the holidays. It was sad more than anything else, and I didn't control my feelings, I cried and cried. It was quiet."

Another mother talks to us about her enjoyment of choral singing: "The best part was singing in the choir. We really got off on the mass for the old people. We sang really hard. It did everyone good. On Christmas Day I felt like I was suffocating. My aunt stuck to me, she'd become a stranger. Every five minutes she asked the same question: 'So how are the kids?' I drowned my sorrows in coffee and went off to one side; an abyss had opened up, contact was broken. My cousin helped me save face; she and her partner are cool, they have teenagers, they're interested. After that, I spent time with my new boyfriend. He came over for New Year's Eve. We started to eat and then suddenly his parents phoned, they didn't know we were together. They insisted on his coming over and he went to join them at around eight to see in the New Year. He left me alone with half the bottle. It really wasn't a family evening! I'm already getting ready for next year, I'd like to have thirty friends over. My father's family are all dead, so family holidays are just an existential void. Gifts are unexciting. What I used to like was seeing children's eyes sparkle, seeing them happy at this time of year. That's over. It's loneliness and silence."

There's a lull in the conversation. Then a mom breaks the silence: "I spent Christmas with my new boyfriend and my three daughters. We opened presents, there was the bell ringing and all that, all the magic — it's exhausting. You run from one place to the other, Christmas is cameras and pictures. I was disappointed in Hélène. My little girl was counting her presents. It made me feel bad. She was comparing herself to others. So I decided to let off steam. My boyfriend doesn't dance, so I just let loose and at last I had fun. I found my old boyfriend, who likes dancing, and I let off steam all night long. The next day was hard."

"This Is the First Time I've Slept with My Mother"

In the next picture, there's a bed with three people in it, a child and two adults. The bed is inside a large circle that represents the world, and the world is surrounded by little dancing figures. "We spent the night in the country. The house was made of wood; we were on the first floor and suddenly we heard cracking noises from the second floor in the middle of the night. My son said it was ghosts and went to take shelter in my mother's bed because he was scared. I was alone for an hour. There were more cracking noises and I was scared. So I went to take shelter in my mother's bed too. The three of us protected ourselves together. That's the first time I ever slept with my mother." The picture shows the ghosts colored yellow: they're part of the family circle.

The last picture shows a Christmas tree and an almost empty couch. "On Christmas Eve evening, we opened presents, nothing happened. There was room for someone else on the couch. My daughter and I rented movies. I never liked the holidays. On Christmas Day I went to eat at my mother's; five minutes into it, I felt bad, I couldn't wait for it to finish." We go round the table. "Christmas isn't the same any more. We always liked traditions: cookies, a glass of milk, a little bell going dingalingaling, and Santa Claus would come by, like a fairy tale. Santa Claus doesn't come any more; I miss it." We tell each other about happy Christmases. "One year there were fifty-eight of us in the house and two girls trapped Santa Claus so they could get all the presents. That year, Santa Claus couldn't join the family: he couldn't get away!"

Families of a New Kind

"Is it possible there are new ways to form families?"

"No, no one will ever make a mother out of a friend!"

"Just like my boyfriend's not my children's father; it can't be replaced."

But isn't the family a fiction? "I was invited to my cousins'. I'm thirty. I hadn't seen them since I was twelve. They're also thirty. I was really disappointed! It was a real show. Inside the huge house, my mother did everything she could to get people to calm down, but they would only get together in cliques: Baptists, Catholics, Jehovah's Witnesses; laborers in one corner, rich folks in another, it was a real masquerade. There were invisible walls everywhere."

"People ask you what you're going through and you know ahead of time that you can't answer because the other person isn't experiencing the same things. They can't understand. There are people who just can't understand when you're spontaneous."

"There's no model of the family any more. The family has turned into a big show. Families now are reconstituted on the basis of friendship."

The daycare teacher asks, "Could it simply be that you've grown up?"

"No, I think it's because we're getting away from artificiality: we need authentic relationships, we can't stand the masks any more."

"Do you think they realize they're wearing masks?"

"The teenaged girl who wears blue hair to create a shock because she doesn't believe in the family, that creates a distance too."

"In our sessions, we're building something: we've taken off our masks, we've reached an agreement to drop that for a while. This is a family of the soul."

II. A Letter on Method

April

Encounter Groups

For two evenings now, I've been struck by the truthfulness of the frame in which our settings can unfold. The daycare teachers, some of the parents, and we ourselves in the research team seem to be approaching the functioning used in encounter groups, where there's very little use of facades and a great deal to understand. Each of us brings a specific dynamic to our interventions, and the way these dynamics interact seems to me to promise complementarity, if only we can manage to get in training.

Journals: A Two-Way Correspondence

I've begun to wonder if one way of eliciting meaningful conversations — to use the term Daniel Walsh adopted from Jerome Bruner — regarding valid, concretely based data might be to engage in two-way correspondence in the form of a journal kept by everyone involved in the research project. This correspondence would be based on our field notes, and the sender would sometimes be a daycare teacher, sometimes a session facilitator, sometimes a researcher, sometimes even a father or a mother, or for that matter a child helped out by her mother or daycare teacher. We are in the process of conducting research on the active relationship between families and daycare centers even as we create that relationship. Our wish is to engage, during sessions, lucidly and transparently with the narratives of experience. Monday evening, I was struck by the children's excitability (which could be accounted for by the snowfall, the recent change to daylight saving's time, or the encounter between two groups of children who didn't know each other). Their excitement vibrated through the house, and in such a climate it seemed hard to calm the interactions of individuals. Our initial investigation of our intervention should emerge from such a process of calm.

Silent Intervention

In this tiny room, with the daycare teachers, we tried to calm our relations; we sought this calm, a calm like a silence that needs to be established so that everyone will feel good, and from which our reflections, our listening, and our creation can originate. And the time needed to calm things down led us to encroach on the time reserved for receiving parents. Marie-Ange went to meet them alone, and then I asked Diane and Touriya (who, though they were present as researchers, have children attending this daycare center) to help Marie-Ange conduct the large-group session while we finished up informing the daycare teachers of the nature of the intervention. Certain important issues had emerged with the parents: on one occasion, they should not have been separated from the daycare teachers they were familiar with (the insecurity of some parents came through). On another, we were unable to come together to provide them with an answer and convey a sense of consistency. We were divided, and events determined our intervention instead of the other way around. Certainly, in taking action with such different sets of groups simultaneously (parents, daycare teachers, researchers, and facilitators), role assignment needs to be at least well thought through and consistent, even if not rigid, to ensure everyone involved is satisfied.

Working Together for Understanding

My basic assumption is that a consistent approach to research on intervention can be developed empirically, provided precise timetables are respected and team discussions are followed through as the project unfolds. I realize further that we must let each other know what the limits of our expectations are regarding others' contributions. Gestures have as much of an impact as words. We have to deal with the dilemma of working together on lived experiences, while creating a climate in which we ourselves don't seek out or prompt the emergence of these lived experiences, but rather where parents and daycare teachers are involved in a natural relationship and live out the emergence spontaneously. That is, a climate in which they don't view us as voyeurs or even researchers, but accept us as fellow travelers who have come together to understand.

Intervention, Responsibility, and Undesired Effects

The discussions I had with Jean-Marie and Gilbert helped me see other possible points of view. Initially, in observing Nora's reaction, I was shattered by the hurt we caused her (or perhaps the hurt we revealed) by opting to invite her to take part in the intervention. I was shocked by our flagrant involvement in the coming about of a tactless, insensitive meeting, during which this mom may have acquired true information, but in a context that gave the information a false implication.

In short, concern over detail in launching a project like this one seems to me to be a key requirement, not for the project's success, but for the early mitigation of inevitable undesired effects. As Gilbert had observed, parents aren't blind when they're invited to participate in an intervention-research program and told that pre-selection has been conducted on the basis of a test. The point of departure for communication between the family and the daycare center is the recognition that there is something to be done and this something is worth discussing. After several years' experience, I've given up diagnostic tests in favor of making sessions optional and basing them on parents' free involvement. In these circumstances, dialogue has a more honest basis.

Short Term Problems

At the same time, just this lightness of structure in our preventive, pedagogical intervention-research project reveals that we consider problems of home-to-daycare transition and the improvement of home-to-daycare communication to be things that can be addressed within the short time period allotted for our sessions. This should in itself reassure anxious parents, since it means we view the cases analyzed as being resolvable simply through meetings and the alignment of the child's two care settings. Information provided by Catherine reveals that my thoughts along these lines make sense. Catherine observes that, when parents maintain regular contact with the daycare center and its various committees, problems relating to their children may arise but are settled rapidly, because the problem is discussed by the daycare teacher and the parents. I find this input valuable, because it shows that diagnosis of a mild integration problem (such as shyness, uncommunicativeness in the group, rowdiness) can be rapidly resolved using the solution we're proposing, without stigmatizing the child or identifying him or her as different.

A Pedagogical Sample

The best way to explain the choice of participants in this first phase of the intervention-research project is the following. We are engaged in preventive pedagogy. Certain mild integration problems can be handled through discussion between parents and the daycare teacher, providing the matter in question is broached calmly and in depth. To test this principle on a large scale, [2] we turn to families whose children don't present serious disorders, but who are chosen rather on the basis of the daycare teachers' representations of them in filling out a social integration test. If we chose children who had no problems, we would not be able to infer that they benefitted from the intervention. If their problems were serious, we could not suppose this kind of intervention would be adequate. The children chosen are ones whose relationship with the daycare center merits increased attention and discussion, and this attention is expected itself to constitute most of the solution to the problem. That is why the intervention-research project can and must take place in a serene climate.

The test used has limitations integral to the nature of the daycare teacher's knowledge of any given child, because this knowledge may be only recently acquired and thus limited and may be further restricted by the very kinds of traits, such as silence and uncommunicativeness, that constitute mild integration problems. Two daycare teachers told me that the test had not allowed for the choice of two children who might have benefitted from the intervention, because, since these children hardly expressed themselves, the teachers had too little information about the children to answer the test questions; and yet this very handicap revealed an integration problem. Besides this, the conditions in which the test was conducted could vary from one daycare center to another. Last, verification of the value of the tests used for participants revealed that, for twelve scales out of twenty, representativeness[3] was lower than 30%. All this goes to show that a test serves above all as a tool for reflection. Its scientific value should not be overestimated.

Marie-Ange Takes Flight

At our last session, Marie-Ange overstepped her role as facilitator. Several times, she took strong positions in intervening, expressing bold and highly personal judgements and interpretations and putting herself forward as the person with answers to everything because of her abstruse knowledge. I want to broach the delicate matter of this unrestrained approach to intervention, not in order to rebuke it, but so that among us we can determine what we want to define as professionalism in intervention. This particular intervention was lacking in professionalism, and discussing it will enable us to come to an agreement on the ethics of our behavior. Or at least on the ethics we would like to aspire to, it being understood that nobody is immune to slips of this kind. Having defined ethics as the art of behavior, we begin by trying to give an account of what had happened. Give an account, not explain, was how we put it. In the reflections that follow, I will be situating our shared search as the quest for an art of right behavior in the home-daycare center relationship and thus as a quest for an ethics of intervention.

When Deconstruction Fossilizes

Nobody is immune to acts of excess, nor to the progressive hardening of attitude that reaches complete fossilization just when the attitude in question has triggered a response from the environment. We are working on lived experiences and narratives of experience with the goal of understanding them. Possibly, we will be able to draw conclusions from them that will be useful in education, or in educating educators who will be able to replicate this experience in other settings and other networks. It is all this that gives the present reflections their likely value. Every preventive measure has undesired effects, just as every gaffe can have a positive side.

During the session, Marie-Ange had revealed personal information. In revealing herself and in unveiling an important aspect of another daycare teacher's private life, she created a momentary loss of balance whose negative effects might have caused the parents to label daycare teachers in general and our intervention team in particular. One beneficial effect of this unveiling is that, over the course of a complex process of adjustment that followed this "intervention," the feeling was restored to certain parents that they weren't guinea pigs ("Poor things, they have a child with integration problems, the assessment will show whether things are going better"), but rather participants in an experience whose joys and occasional vicissitudes were shared by everyone involved.

When Marie-Ange suddenly began talking about her own life in a blended family — making no connection to what had preceded — and made reference to the private life of another teacher by asking her to confirm what she herself was saying, this confessional gesture, with the potential to prompt a generalized public confession, triggered simultaneous interest and embarrassment. Marie-Ange's backing parents into a corner led one father to reveal in fits and starts that he had never known whether his daughter was really *his* daughter, and to ask, five minutes later, when things had calmed down, if Marie-Ange's own child was among the sample chosen for the intervention.

Diagnosis is Power

This "We are all equal" might have meant that the momentary imbalance produced by the public confession had subsided as a new feeling arose: "You may have chosen us because of a problem that makes us feel anxious, but you've just shown us that, even though you're acting as case workers, you have problems too." From this flows a new feeling of unity for some ("We're on the same side"); but is this feeling shared by all? Handing out a diagnosis remains a deployment of power. If we maintain mutual respect, we should be able to increase the professionalism of our research on intervention to the point where everyone feels comfortable, not man-handled, when personal issues are put on the table without constraint, because one wants to reflect on them with one's daycare teacher because this will be useful to one's child. It's a fine line that draws pedagogical intervention. Pedagogy is not a therapy.

The Temptation to Explain

In dissecting cases this way, I try to describe situations and as far as possible avoid the tendency to explain. It's true that explanation is almost embedded within the interpretation of the events described. To avoid an excess of interpretation and explanation, you have to go back to the data. During the second stage of the writing process, having reread what I've just written, I may come to realize where I've introduced an explanation into my reflections that shouldn't be there. What we're trying to do is narrate.

In describing our experiences as agents for social change, we are probably enhancing our own professionalism, i.e., our ability to confront professional events appropriately. Thus the process of intervention research includes analysis of experiences specific to the process of transition from home to daycare that children and parents undergo, and of our own experience in intervening. These narratives of experience provide the grounding for our action, our internal regulation. These two types of narrative support each other, partly because we are interacting with parents.

Deproblematizing the Lack of Understanding

I am struck by the fact that whenever we're sure we've understood, we're overlooking what's essential. I thought I had understood parents' anxiety on receiving the news that their child had been chosen for the study. I had talked to the daycare teachers about it ahead of time, and we wanted to avoid misunderstandings on this score. But, to some extent, events overtook us on that first evening (the snow, the daycare teachers' lateness), and Nora magnified an issue that we could have resolved with her without incident, had we had the grasp on things that was available to us the second evening, following this event. Nora asked in a vehement tone about the criteria for choosing her child. She stated that the elements the intervention addressed were culturally biased. When our group of project workers came together at the end of the evening, the focus was on Marie-Ange's intervention. The fact is, when you look at it closely, what may have annoyed Diane, what prompted Jean-Marie's frown, what made Touriya shake her head, and what motivated me to speak up was that problematic attitudes were being deproblematized by Marie-Ange by means of justifications that showed she refused to hear how we had perceived them. In insisting she understood, she was failing to listen to us. Similarly, we ourselves, in understanding "the problem for parents of having their child chosen," risked missing the whole human dimension.

May

Journals and Teamwork

I'd like this journal to be focused on teamwork and on the role played by reflection in refining our actions during the first months of the intervention-research project. All our roles grew clearer and were fine tuned. Each one of us has found her or his own niche for participation, reflection, and writing. I didn't want to interfere in this process of progressive situatedness, which occurred in small steps, and which continues to unfold through a series of mutual adjustments, some of which are produced by the reflection group that meets following every session in the daycare centers, and some of which are produced by reading other participants' journals during our journal exchange periods.

At this point, I identify a potential reader for myself, someone I would like to tell about our project, our shared action, our experience. I've suggested that every member of the team do the same thing when they write up a clean version of their field notes and make entries in their journals. I'd been struck by the fact that early journals were decontextualized; they were modeled on ethnographic note-taking, which the researchers had indeed been trained in. But ethnographic field notes, which record no more than the basics of the essential, objective information obtained during interaction, are poorly designed to reflect the density of reality and the complexity of the interactions we experience during our sessions.

Adopting the Narrative Writing Technique

Objectivizing note-taking aims to yield a corpus for subsequent content analysis. Content analysis deals with the frequency and kind of certain meaningful occurrences in a corpus and thus decontextualizes information. The perspective of content analysis is taxonomic; that is, it classifies and it compares. For example, one might compare occurrences of a specific kind of content across several daycare centers or among several parents.

Without excluding the possibility of content analysis or of thematic results analysis, our narrative orientation aims to offer a fleshed-out account of events and of the feelings and perceptions expressed during our sessions. We reveal our reactions, feelings, and perceptions as participatory researchers, as observers involved in the actions unfolding. To this end, we adopt a wholly different type of writing, writing that is nuanced and allusive and that incarnates the complexity of real situations.

Situated Notes

That's why decontextualized note-taking could not suffice. The context has to be reported, and the conceptual links that enable a given participant to conceive of the issues at play during discussion require the writing to incorporate an interpretive dimension. They require, too, the reporting of those links between events that make the intervention relationship comprehensible. This kind of report, being highly situated and sticking close to events, necessitates a narrative writing mode. Often, metaphor serves to pinpoint subtle perceptions allusively to better effect than discarnate, informative writing whose sole aim is rational explication, which strips the report of the feelings one experienced at the time.

Creating the Setting and Describing Your Feelings

Even when one adopts an informative style, there is real involvement by the individual who observes, takes notes, and chooses information to report. A process of selection takes place, leading the person to choose some events that she or he finds more striking than others. Why are they striking? What prior knowledge, what conceptual links, what emotions lead one to report this fact and not that? I invited members of our team to reflect on this, pointing out that, whatever the standard view on this may be, so called "objective" and "informative" writing employs methods of selection and expression that give the contents a subjective impact.

You could say the limitations of narrative writing constitute its virtue: by putting the writer on stage and situating her or him in time and space, it creates a setting, a context for interpretation, and describes the process of choosing information as an intersubjective intervention.

Objectivity is Multireferential

We work to build objectivity through discussion, by means of the plurality of perspectives. Our writing is functional: its goal is to enhance our understanding of the process under way. It's aimed at optimizing action, but also at conducing to generalization, because the cases discussed are representative. In the social sciences, it was long believed that generalizability was a function of the typological representativeness of a study. In other words, one needed to have enough points of comparison to reach a threshold of probability that allowed for generalizing the research results. This assumption led members of the research community to believe that clinical case study results lacked general applicability. Looking more deeply at this matter, one sees that generalizability of experimental research relates to the possibility for replicating results. The logic of replication has hitherto led to the design of top-down change imposed on practitioners and often out of tune with practitioners' reality. These top-down models for change work badly because they do not take account of the logic proper to the players involved.

Our Results Can Be Replicated

Replicability does exist in intervention research focused on human experience, but it serves as the basis of bottom-up change founded on different principles than previous models for innovation. When research reports adopt a narrative approach, the goal of replicability is satisfied, because the narrative of lived experience allows readers of the narrative to link those experiences to their own and draw conclusions that are valid in their own sphere of action. Thus the results of an intervention-research project take on generalizability to the extent that readers, keeping in mind the specifics of the context described and the fact that participants are subjective, mentally recreate the conditions for action that we worked with and insert the appropriate modifications to productively adjust this kind of action to their own context of practice. We formulate few general rules, but we report on events we lived through, specifying the emotions and perceptions those events elicited and the conclusions we reached in our discussions. Readers can then insert themselves into the multiple, nuanced perception of the circumstances and interpretations that prompted our action. Further, they can graft their own situated knowledge onto these narratives, making it possible to integrate them into fresh contexts.

Making Stories Agree

This is why we take detailed notes. Our task is to recount the many levels of the reality that has been experienced, so that we can reach agreement on our stories. I experienced this first stage of our action research as a tuning process, as though we were tuning a piano. It's conducted small step by small step, and it takes time. For it to work, we have to take the time to call to mind each setting and our own individual perceptions, as well as taking the time to listen to each other. And the time we have is never sufficient, because there's always more to learn. On this score, I was surprised to realize that the guidelines we settled on together are often forgotten almost immediately. And then we find ourselves discussing the ways to do things as though we'd never discussed them before, and we look for a scapegoat. Luckily, the scapegoat changes from one session to another. That's a somewhat piquant comment — note how an anecdotal style spices up a text.

Specifying Roles

After much discussion, we reached agreement on certain guidelines, which I then wrote down. Weeks passed and, the guidelines notwithstanding, roles were established and took hold almost naturally: it may be assumed that this development had not been foreseen. It's true that, in the workings of a group, time brings consensus in through the back door and practices take root before you even know it. This process occurred, for example (examples are always necessary), in connection with such commonplace-seeming things as the group organization of research notes and each person's way of keeping her or his journal.

On this score, extremely specific work methods were negotiated and discussed right at the outset. And then I was amazed to find everyone, myself included, adopting a particular approach that was often different from the one suggested or the one we'd actually agreed on. When I go back over journal entries for the first sessions, I find that they're strictly informative. I can scarcely discern a narrative dimension. We discuss this as a team: Touriya and Diane hold the view that neutral writing is more serious; it focuses on the facts. In my opinion, the researchers have been bludgeoned into accepting this decree of scientific objectivity — they've been subjected to objectivist brainwashing: Doesn't anybody know how to tell a story any more? We have so much to unlearn!

Adopting a Letter-Writing Style

In narrative writing, it's important to provide the context. Context includes intention, space and time, and intended readers. So this evening, as a team — in a daycare center on Sainte-Jeanne Street, after the cook and the three daycare teachers had gone and left us the key (which we were instructed to leave in the letter box) — we agreed that each one of us would specify a real or fictional recipient for our narratives, so that we could write them in a style more like letter writing. It was agreed that Touriya would address a recipient in her native country, Algeria, in order to convey her cultural perceptions about the situations we were experiencing; that Diane would allow herself a militant, feminist approach to her writing and not adopt disguise, but be herself, when she wished to criticize a particular action or attitude; that Nancy would reveal her methodological doubts and quests and her conceptual struggles in order to take a stand against the hegemony of positivism. We're talking about sharing the novel of our lives, the narrative of our encounters; a part of each one of us lives and breathes beneath these texts: let's make them personal.

Formalizing Note-Taking

One of the suggestions that got us started was in formalizing our personal note-taking related to margins (two inches at left) and to the systematic subtitling of paragraphs so that information could be easily located and indexed from one journal to another. The headings could thus serve in the preliminary organization of notes related to key events and major processes of reflection. These basic suggestions were incorporated into extremely diverse texts, with each writer focusing her or his reflection on a specific level of the intervention and on factual occurrences, without prior consultation, and with each one choosing options that struck her or him as wholly natural. I, for instance, realized that it's sometimes more effective to place the synthesizing subtitle or key sentence after the relevant paragraph rather than before it — it provides an opportunity to engage in reflective rereading.

Without realizing it, then, we ended by specializing in specific options. For example, Touriya opted for a broken-up description organized around each evening's main moments: time spent with the daycare teachers, time in the parent/teacher group, the time before supper, the time after supper, and the period at the end of the evening when our group reflected on action. Touriya finds it hard to subtitle her paragraphs with a succinct statement of the theme discussed. In contrast, Diane, Jean-Marie, and Marie-Ange find this an effective way to organize their self-expression. I as reader find it easy to locate the key components of texts whose theme-based subtitles turn up at regular intervals. But on reflection, Touriya's method of presentation strikes me as offering a difference that complements this approach and possibly serving different goals at the point when the project report will be prepared. As I record entries in my journal, I am already forming mental representations of the techniques and organization to be used in the final report.

Levels of Narrative Specialization

In my own narrative writing, I tend to specialize in matters that only I can talk about, because of my prior knowledge, my contacts, and the responsibility I carry as principal investigator. These consist of the development of the methodology used and of the operational framework for our intervention-research activities. Although the project's innovative orientation gives it a mixed rather than top-down nature, it can't be denied that some people have more responsibility than others for constituting the framework for the intervention. To carry this responsibility out, you have to have a vision of the project as a whole and a vision of the direction it's taking, both as intervention and as research. You also need the time to make systematic links between the suggestions and interactions arising in each venue and stage. This knowledge organizes one's responsibilities in spite of oneself.

Our intervention-research project is organized heterarchically rather than hierarchically. A heterarchy is a hierarchy whose headship is variously filled according to need and can be filled turn and turn about by individuals with different roles. Certainly, those who were present from the inception of the process occupy a privileged position because they constitute the project's "memory." They contribute to the process of weaving continuity into the narrative thread of our experience as relayed to other key individuals, and pass along the shared intentions whose cohesion and implementation we are building together. We are engaged in intervention within a network, and information ripples out informally through the daycare centers.

Defining Your Own Narrative Niche

Everybody has her or his own niche. It's desirable for each niche to become more formally defined as the weeks pass, so that our perspectives may be intentionally diverse and complementary and the internal consistency of each niche better defined. The idea is not for each person to restate what the others have written; the point is for each person to specify his or her own angle of vision. This process has already begun, but so far, the differentiation took place more or less intuitively. Now, let's define our niches, specify our roles within the narrative of experience, and affirm the nature of the difference. Let's each situate ourselves. Our roles were carved out during the process of intervention and group facilitation. Let's carve them out for the process of narrating our experience.

I'm inclined to specify my narrative niche as recounting the operations of the team, in strict relationship with the reflection groups we conduct at the end of our intervention evenings. Your journals don't have to recreate or depict reality in the same way. Choose a specific level of the narrative of experience. What would you like to focus on in your narrative?

We discussed a possible intercultural focus with Touriya: if her intended recipient is North African, her analysis of the intervention experience will be situated in terms this reader will be able to understand, highlighting, perhaps, contrasts between the two cultures as regards elements specific to our own focus of concern, namely the transition from home to daycare. Regarding questions like these, there is much we can analyze and reflect on in relation to our own specific prior knowledge.

The Politics of Narrative Experience

Our narrative writing could adopt various frameworks. The framework of feminist reflection seems particularly appropriate for our locus of intervention. An in-depth narrative about the possible split between home and daycare or the role of women professionals, whether mothers or daycare teachers, in the transition to daycare, would be very enlightening. An appropriate critical analysis would enable one to take a position on the fact that the professionals in charge of handling this most critical period in human development receive the lowest salaries our society offers and, in the private sector, the most cursory professional training. This point of view is not lacking within our project, with women predominating within the team; but it needs to be present within "the politics of experience," to use R.D. Laing's expression. In these sessions, a space is created for action and speech. Individual initiative is encouraged, so long as it doesn't violate another person's private space. You must make the connection between intervention-research and your own motivations and life interests. This narrative could become your struggle.

Towards Methodological Correspondence

I'd like to close by placing an emphasis on the distinctiveness of our action-research project. Reflection on a narrative approach as conducted during our project is relatively new to the sphere of daycare work. In settings where narrative of experience is used (I think in particular of teachers' education and professional development), it is not being used to obtain simultaneous, ongoing feedback within the team; intervention is rarely paired with research *on* intervention. Embedding several levels of simultaneous action and research — with parents, children, and teachers; and among members of the intervention team — is probably without precedent in this context: our experience is unique. It deserves our full attention, the people we're encountering need us to make both an intellectual and a personal, socioaffective (which is not to say emotional) investment. I await your reactions to this "letter on method."

Notes

[1] The author of this chapter conducted work on pedagogy in bilingual settings in Manitoba and Quebec before coming to work at the University of Wisconsin-Madison. The research and intervention team in Quebec involved one specialist of early childhood education (now a faculty professor advising daycare reforms in Quebec), four experienced social workers specialized in early childhood and parental education (with Masters in Psychology, Social Work, Education or Bilingual Education), three graduate students in Education, and one field worker. Our background countries were Switzerland, Romania, Morocco, and Canada. For other publications on this study, see Tochon (1997), Miron & Tochon (1998), and Tochon & Miron (2000).

² This intervention-research project involved close to two hundred families over four years.

³ i.e., the percentage of variance explained by the first factor in refactorization.

Acknowledgments

The study reported on in this chapter was supported by a research grant. I am grateful to the Social Research Council of Quebec (CQRS) for enabling me to contribute to the study of educational partnerships with families in bilingual settings.

References

Agar, M. (1994). *Language shock: Understanding of the culture of conversation*. New York: William Morrow.

Ahlberg, M. (1991). Concept mapping, concept matrices, link tables and argumentation analysis as techniques for educational research on textbooks and educational discourses and as tools for teachers and their pupils in their everyday work. In M.L. Julkunen (Ed.), *Research on texts at school* (pp. 89-154). Joensuu, Finland: Joensuun Yliopiston Monistuskeskus.

Alrichter, H., & Posch, P. (1989). Does the 'Grounded Theory' approach offer a guiding paradigm for teacher research? *Cambridge Journal of Education, 19(1)*, 21-31.

Apple, M.W. (1986). *Teachers and texts: A political economy of class and gender relations in education*. New York: Routledge & Kegan Paul.

Auerbach, E., & Burgess, D. (1985). The hidden curriculum of survival ESL. *TESOL Quarterly, 19 (3)*, 475-495.

Ayto, J. (1990). *Dictionary of word origins*. New York: Arcade.

Bakhtin, M.M. (1968). *Rabelais and his world*. Cambridge, MA: M.I.T. Press.

Barnes, M., & Berke, J. (1973). *Mary Barnes: Two accounts of a journey through madness*. New York: Ballantine Books.

Becker, H.S. (1982). *Art worlds*. Berkeley, CA: University of California Press.

Berger, J. (1972). *Ways of seeing*. London: British Broadcasting Corporation & Penguin.

Belsey, C. (1980). *Critical practice*. London: Methuen.

Bialystok, E., & Hakuta, K. (1994) *In other words: The science and psychology of second-language acquisition*. New York: Harper Collins.

Bourdieu, P. (1977). *Outline of a theory of practice* (R. Nice, Trans.). Cambridge, England: Cambridge University Press. (Original work published 1972)

Bourdieu, P. (1991). *Language and symbolic power*. Cambridge, MA: Harvard University Press.

Bourdieu, P. (1998). *Practical reason*. Stanford: Stanford University Press.

Bremer, et al. (1996). *Achieving understanding: Discourse in intercultural encounters*. London: Longman.

Brown, D.H. (1994). *Teaching by principles*. New Jersey: Prentice Hall.

Bullough, R.V., & Pinnegar, S. (2000). Guidelines for quality in autobiographical forms of self-study research. *Educational Researcher, 30(3)*, 13-21.

Bremer, K., Roberts, C., Vasseur, M-T., Simonot, M., & Broeder, P. (1996). *Achieving understanding: Discourse in intercultural encounters*. London: Longman.

Brookfield, S.D. (1995). *Becoming a critically reflective teacher*. San Francisco: Jossey-Bass.

Calderhead, J. (1989). Reflective teaching and teacher education. *Teaching and Teacher Education, 5*(1), 43-51.

Calderwood, P. (2000). *Learning community: Finding common ground in difference*. New York: Teachers College Press.

Calgren, I. (1999). Professionalism and teachers as designer. *Journal of Curriculum Studies, 31*(1), 43-56.

Carr, W, & Kemmis, S. (1986). *Becoming critical: Education, knowledge and action research*. London: Falmer.

Carter, S., & Sokol, J. (2000). *Men who cannot love: How to recognize a commitmentphobic man before he breaks your heart* (Reissue ed.). New York: Berkeley Publishing Group.

Chambers, B.G. (1945). *Color and design in apparel*. New York: Prentice-Hall.

Charmaz, K. (2000). Grounded theory: Objectivist and constructivist methods. In N. Denzin & Y. Lincoln (Eds.), *The handbook of qualitative research* (pp. 509-536). Thousand Oaks, CA: Sage.

Clough P., (1999). Crises of schooling and the "crises of representation": The story of Rob. *Qualitative Inquiry, 5(3)*, 428-448.

Color Tables. (1999). Color tables. Pittsburgh: PPG Architectural Finishes, Inc.

Color Wheel. (2000). Color wheel. The Color Wheel Company.

Connell, R.W. (1995). *Masculinities*. Berkeley, CA: University of California Press.

Cox, M., Pagliarini, I., & Assis-Peterson, A. (1999). Critical pedagogy in ELT: Images of Brazilian teachers of English. *TESOL Quarterly, 33(3)*, 433-452.

Cummins, J.P. (1989). *Empowering minority students*. Sacramento, CA: California Association for Bilingual Education.

Cummins, J.P. (1994). The Socioacademic Achievement Model in the context of coercive and collaborative relations of power. In R.A. Devillar, C.J. Faltis, & J.P. Cummnis (Eds), *Cultural diversity in schools: From rhetoric to practice* (pp.363-390). Albany: SUNY Press.

Cummins, J.P. (2000). *Language, power, and pedagogy: Bilingual children in the crossfire*. Buffalo, NY: Multilingual Matters.

Danesi, M. (1999). *Of cigarettes, high heels, and other interesting things*. New York: St. Martin's Press.

Daniels, H. (1994). *Literature circles: Voice and choice in the student-centered classroom*. York, MA: Stenhouse.

de Beauvoir, S. (1967). *The ethics of ambiguity* (Bernard Frechtman, Trans.). New York: The Citadel Press. (Original work published 1947)

DeVault, M. (1997). Personal writing in social research: Issues of production and interpretation. In R. Hertz (Ed.), *Reflexivity and voice* (pp. 216-228). Thousand Oaks, CA: Sage.

Dewey, J. (1933). *How we think. A restatement of the relation of reflective thinking to the educative process*. Boston: D.C. Heath & Co.

Diaz-Rico, L., & Weed, K. (1995). *The crosscultural, language, and academic development handbook*. Boston: Allyn & Bacon.

Dominique, P., Girardet, J., Verdelhan, M., & Verdelhan, M. (1989). *Le nouveau sans frontières, level 2* [The new without frontiers]. Paris: *CLE International.*

Dominique, P., Girardet, J., Verdelhan, M., & Verdelhan, M. (1998). *Le nouveau sans frontières, level 1* [The new without frontiers]. Paris: CLE International.

Dwyer, F.M. (1972). *A guide for improving visualized instruction.* Pennsylvania State College: Learning Services.

Eagleton, J. (1983). *Literary theory: An introduction.* Minneapolis, MN: University of Minnesota Press.

Editors of Bride's Magazine. (1999). *Bride's book of etiquette* (Revised ed.). New York: Perigee.

Edwards, T. (1997). *Men in the mirror: Men's fashion, masculinity, and consumer society.* London: Cassell.

Elbaz, F. (1988). Critical reflection on teaching: Insights from Freire. *Journal of Education for Teaching, 14(2),* 171-181.

Ellis C. (1997). Evocative autoethnography: Writing emotionally about our lives. In W.G. Tierney & Y. S. Lincoln (Eds.), *Representation and the text: Reframing the narrative voice* (pp.115-139). Albany: State University of New York Press.

Ellis, R. (1997). *Second language acquisition.* New York: Oxford University Press.

Evans, M.A., Watson, C., & Willows, D.M. (1987). A naturalistic inquiry into illustration in instructional textbooks. In H.A. Houghton & D.M. Wilows (Eds.), *The psychology of illustration 2* (pp. 86-115). New York: Springer-Verlag.

Fairclough, N. (1989). *Language and power.* London & New York: Longman.

Fairclough, N. (1995). *Critical discourse analysis: The critical study of language.* London: Longman.

Faltis, C. J., & Hudelson, S. J. (1998). *Bilingual education in elementary and secondary school communities: Toward understanding and caring.* Boston, MA: Allyn and Bacon.

Fehrman, K.R., & Fehrman, C. (2000). *Color: The secret influence.* Upper Saddle River, NJ: Prentice-Hall.

Fendler, L. (2000). *Teacher reflection in a hall of mirrors: Epistemological and political reverberations.* East Lansing, MI: Unpublished manuscript.

Finders, M. J. (1997). *Just girls: Hidden literacies and life in junior high.* New York: Teachers College Press.

Foucault, M. (1972). The discourse on language. In *The archeology of knowledge and the discourse on language* and *The discourse on language.* (pp. 215-237). New York: Pantheon.

Foucault, M. (1980). *Power/ knowledge: Selected interviews and other writings, 1972-1977.* (Colin Gordon (Ed.) New York: Pantheon Books.

Foucault, M. (1997a) Subjectivity and truth. In P. Rabinow (Ed.), *Michel Foucault: Ethics, subjectivity and truth* (Volume 1 of *Essential works of Michel Foucault 1954-1984* (pp. 87-98). New York: New York University Press.

Foucault, M. (1997b). Technologies of the Self. In P. Rabinow (Ed.), *Michel Foucault: Ethics, subjectivity , and truth* (Volume 1 of *Essential works of Michel Foucault 1954-1984* (p. 222-255). New York: New York University Press.

Foucault, M. (1998). The thought of the outside. In J.D. Faubion (Ed.), *Michel Foucault: Aethetics, method, and epistemology* (Volume 2 of *Essential works of Foucault 1954-1984* (pp.140-172). New York. New York University Press.

Frankenberg, R. (1996). "When we are capable of stopping, we begin to see": Being white, seeing whiteness. In B. Thompson, & S. Tygai. (Eds.), *Names we call home; Autobiography on racial identity* (pp. 3-17). New York: Routledge.

Freire, P. (2000). *Pedagogy of the Oppressed, New Revised 20th Anniversary Edition.* (Myra Bergman Ramos, Trans.) New York: Continuum.

Freire, P., & Shor, I. (1987). *A pedagogy for liberation.* London: Bergin & Garvey.

Freud, S. (1923). *The Ego and the ID.* New York: Norton. http://www.loc.gov/exhibits/freud/ex/73a.html

Freud, S. (1926). Psychoanalysis: Freudian school. *Encyclopedia Britannica*, 13th ed. See http://www.haverford.edu/psych/ddavis/p109g/freud.psa

Freud. S. (1938). *An outline of psycho-analysis.* New York: Norton.

Galisson, R. (1980). *D'hier à aujourd'hui la didactique des langues étrangères.* [Foreign language didactics from yesterday to today.] Paris: CLE International.

Gee, J. P. (1996). *Social linguistics and literacies: Ideology in discourses.* Bristol, PA: Falmer Press.

Gee, J. P. (1999). *An introduction to discourse analysis: Theory and method.* London: Routledge.

Genesee, F. (1987). *Learning through two languages: Studies of immersion and bilingual education.* Cambridge, MA: Newbury House Publishers.

Gergen, K. J., & Gergen, M. M. (1997). Narrative of the self. In L.P. Hinchman & S.K. Hinchman (Eds.), *Memory, identity, community* (pp.161-184). Albany: State University of New York Press.

Gibbs, J. (2000). *Tribes: A new way of learning and being together.* Sausalito, CA: CenterSource Systems, LLC.

Girardet, J. (1988). *Le livre du professeur du nouveau sans frontières.* [Instructional manual for teachers of the new frontiers.] Paris: CLE International.

Goffman, E. (1976). *Gender advertisements.* New York: Harper Colophon Books.

Good, T. (1990). Building the knowledge base of teaching. In D. Dill (Ed.), *What teachers need to know.* San Francisco: Jossey Bass.

Gore, J., & Zeichner, K. (1991). *Action research and reflective teaching in preservice teacher education,* 7(2), 119-136.

Gore, J., & Zeichner, K. (1984). On becoming a reflective teacher. In C. Grant (Ed.), *Preparing for reflective teaching.* Boston: Allyn and Bacon.

Groddeck, G. (1923). *The book of the it.* New York: International Universities Press.

Hall, G. (1985, April). *A stage of concern approach to teacher education*. Paper presented at the annual meeting of the American Educational Research Association (AERA), Chicago, IL.

Harvard, G., & Hodkinson, P. (1994). *Action and reflection in teacher education*. Norwood, NJ: Ablex.

Hite, S. (1981). The Hite report on male sexuality. New York: Alfred A. Knopf.

Hodge, R, & Kress, G. (1988). *Social semiotics*. Ithaca, NY: Cornell University Press.

Hutchby, I. (1999). Power in iscourse: Arguments on talk radio. In A. Jaworski & N. Coupland (Eds), *The discourse reader* (pp. 576-588). New York: Routledge.

Hymes, D. (1974). *Foundations in sociolinguistics: An ethnographic approach*. Philadelphia: University of Pennsylvania Press.

Ingraham, C. (1999). *White weddings: Romancing heterosexuality in popular culture*. New York: Routledge.

International Olympic Committee. See www.olympic.org/ioc/e/news/index_e.html.

Jameson, F. (1981). *The political unconscious: Narrative as a social symbolic act*. Ithaca, NY: Cornell University Press.

Johnson, R. T. (2000). *Hands off!: The disappearance of touch in the care of children*. New York: Peter Lang.

Jones, A. (2001). Self-surveillance and the male teaching body. In A. Jones (Ed.), *Touchy subject: Teachers touching children*. Dunedin, New Zealand: University of Otago Press.

Jung, C.G. (1973a). *Collected works of C.G. Jung*. Princeton, NJ: Princeton University Press.

Jung, C.G. (1973b). *Dialectique du moi et de l'inconscient* [Dialectic of the ego and the unconscious]. Paris: Gallimard.

Kimmel, M. (1996a). Integrating men into the curriculum. *Duke Journal of Gender Law and Policy, 4*, 181-195.

Kimmel, M. (1996b). *Manhood in America: A cultural history*. New York: Free Press.

King, J. R. (2000). The problem(s) of men in early education. In N. Lesko (Ed.), *Masculinities in school* (pp. 3-26). Thousand Oaks, CA: Sage.

Kohn, A. (1996). *Beyond discipline: From compliance to community*. Alexandria, VA: Association for Supervision and Curriculum Development.

Kramsch, C. (1996). Whem gehört die Deutsche Sprache? *Die Unterrichtspraxis, 29*, 1-11.

Kres, G. (1985). *Linguistic processes in sociocultural practices*. Oxford, UK: Oxford University Press.

Kruks, S. (1990). *Situation and human existence: Freedom, subjectivity, and society*. New York and London: Routledge.

Kruks, S. (1999). Panopticism and shame: Reading Foucault through Beauvoir. *Labyrinth, 1*(1). See laybrinth.iaf.ac.at/1999/Kruks.html.

Laing, R.D. (1960). *The divided self*. London: Tavistock.

Laing, R.D. (1967). *The politics of experience*. New York: Pantheon.

Laing, R.D. (1969). *The politics of the family*. London & Toronto: Tavistock/ CBC.

Laplanche J., & Pontalis, J.-B. (1973). *Vocabulaire de la psychanalyse* [Language of psycho-analysis]. Paris: Presses Universitaires de France.

Larousse (1996). Le Petit Larousse Compact (New edition). Paris: Larousse.

Larsen-Freeman, D. (1991). Second language acquisition research: Staking out the territory. *Tesol Quarterly, 25(2),* 315-341.

Lee, D. (1992). *Competing discourses: Perspective and ideology in language.* London: Longman.

Lehman, P. (1993). *Running scared: Masculinity and the representation of the male body.* Philadelphia: Temple University Press.

Levie, W.H. (1987). Research on pictures: A guide to the literature. In H.A. Houghton & D.M. Wilows (Eds.), *The psychology of illustration 1* (pp. 1-50). New York: Springer-Verlag.

Lurie, A. (1981). *The language of clothes.* New York: Owl Books.

MacDonnell, D. (1986). Theories of discourse: An introduction. Oxford, UK: Blackwell.

Macedo, D. (1994a). *Literacies of power: What Americans are not allowed to know.* Boulder, CO: Westview Press.

Macedo, D. (1994b). English-only: The tongue-tying of America. In D. Macedo *Literacies of power: What Americans are not allowed to know* (pp. 125-136). Boulder, CO: Westview Press.

Martin, M. (1986). *Self-deception and morality.* Lawrence, KA: University Press of Kansas.

Maslow, A.H. (1968). *Toward a psychology of being.* New York: Litton Educational Publishing.

Matoon, M.A. (1994). *Jungian psychology after Jung.* New York: The Round Table Press. See http:/www.cgjungpage.org/mattooncplex.html

Mayerson, C. (1996). *Goin' to the chapel: Dreams of love, realities of marriage.* New York: Basic Books.

Mayes, L. (2000). Sit down and shirt up. *For the Groom, 1(1),* 39-41.

McKeon, D. (1994). Language, culture, and schooling. In F. Genesee (Ed), *Educating second language children: The whole child, the whole curriculum, the whole community* (pp. 15-32). New York: Cambridge University Press.

McNamara, D. (1990). Research on teachers' thinking: Its contribution to educating student teachers to think critically. *Journal of Education for Teaching, 16(2), 147-160.*

Miron, J.M., & Tochon, F.V. (1998). *Parents experts* [Expert parents]. Sherbrooke, QC: CRP, University of Sherbrooke Publishers.

Mulvey, L. (1991). Visual pleasure and narrative cinema. In R.R. Warhol & D.P. Herndl (Eds.), *Feminisms: An anthology of literary theory and criticism.* New Brunswick, NJ: Rutgers University Press.

Mulcahy, P., & Samuels, S.J. (1987). Three hundred years of illustrations in American textbooks. *The psychology of illustration, 2,* 1-52. New York: Springer-Verlag.

Munby, H., & Russel, T. (1989). Educating the reflective teacher: An essay review of two books by Donald Schon. *Journal of Curriculum Studies, 21(1),* 71-80.

Narayan K., (1997). Introduction. In K. Narayan & U.D. Sood (Eds), *Mondays on the dark night of the moon* (pp.3-21). New York: Oxford University Press.

Nguyen, T.C.P. (1999). The epistemic map to organize references and auto-evaluate conceptual change. *International Journal of Applied Semiotics, 1,* 127-133.

Ortega, L. (1999). Rethinking foreign language education: Political dimensions of the profession. In K.A. Davis (Ed.). *Foreign language teaching and language minority education.* Honolulu: University of Hawaii.

Orwell, G. (1961). *1984.* New York: New American Library.

Pamphilon, B. (1999). The Zoom Model: A dynamic framework for the analysis of life histories. *Qualitative Inquiry, 5*(3), 393-410.

Pantone. (1998). *Pantone solid start guide.* NJ: Pantone.

Pastoureau, M. (1989). *Couleurs, images, symboles.* Paris: Le Léopard d'Or.

Peeck, J. (1987). Role of illustrations in procession. In H.A. Houghton & D.M. Wilows (Eds.), *The psychology of illustration 1* (pp. 115-151). New York: Springer-Verlag.

Peck, S.(1999). Recognizing and meeting the needs of ESL students. In M. Celce-Murcia (Ed.), *Teaching English as a second language* 2nd ed. (pp. 363-371). Boston: Heinle & Heinle.

Peirce, B.N. (1989). Toward a pedagogy of possibility in the teaching of English internationally: People's English in South Africa. *TESOL Quarterly, 23* (3), 401-420.

Pennycook, A. (1994). *The cultural politics of English as an international language.* London: Longman.

Pennycook, A. (1998). *English and the discourses of colonialism.* London: Routledge.

Pennycook, A. (2001). *Critical applied linguistics: A critical introduction.* Mahwah, NJ: Lawrence Erlbaum.

PPG Architectural Finishes (1999). *Color tables.* PPG.

Personal Narrative Group. (1989). Forms that transform. In Personal Narrative Group (Eds.), *Interpreting women's lives: Feminist theory and personal narratives* (pp. 99-102). Bloomington: Indiana University Press.

Post, P. (1999). *Emily Post's weddings (3rd ed.).* New York: Harper Collins.

Rasbridge, L. (1996). An anthropological approach to Cambodian refugee women: Reciprocity in oral histories. In G. Etter Lewis & Michelle Foster (Eds.), *Unrelated kin: Race and gender in women's personal narratives* (pp. 201-213). New York: Routledge.

Réquédat, F. (1966). *Classement des exercices structuraux* [Classification of structured exercises]. Paris: Hachette-Larousse.

Richie, D. (1996). *The films of Akira Kurosawa.* Berkeley: University of California Press.

Riley II, C.A. (1995). *Color codes.* Hanover & London: University Press of New England.

Ricoeur, P. (1984). *Time and narrative. Volume 1.* (Kathleen McLaughlin & David Pellauer, Trans.) Chicago: The University of Chicago Press.

Ricoeur, P. (1985). *Time and narrative. Volume 2.* (Kathleen McLaughlin & David Pellauer, Trans.) Chicago: The University of Chicago Press.

Ricoeur, P. (1988). *Time and narrative. Volume 3.* (Kathleen McLaughlin & David Pellauer, Trans.) Chicago: The University of Chicago Press.

Ricoeur, P. (1990). *Soi-même comme un autre.* [Self as another]. Paris: Seuil.

Rogers, L. (1998). *Wish I were: Felt pathways of the self.* Madison, WI: Atwood Publishing.

Santos, B. de Souza (1997). Toward a multicultural conception of human rights. *Zeitschrift für RechtsSoziologie, 1/97,* 1-15.

Sapon-Shevin, M. (1999). *Because we can change the world: A pracitical guide to building cooperative, inclusive classroom communities.* Needham Heights, MA: Allyn & Bacon.

Schon, D. (1983). *The reflective practitioner: How professionals think in action.* New York: Basic Books.

Schon, D. (1987). *Educating the reflective practitioner toward a new design for teaching and learning in the professions.* San Francisco: Jossey-Bass.

Schon, D. (Ed.). (1991). *The reflective turn: Case studies in educational practice.* New York: Teacher College Press.

Schultz, R.A. (1990). Bridging the gap between teaching and learning: A critical look at foreign language textbooks. In S. Sieloff Magnan (Ed.), *Challenges in the 90s for college foreign language programs.* Boston: Heinle & Heinle.

Selander, S. (1991). Pedagogic text analysis. In M.L. Julkunen (Ed.) *Research on texts at school* (pp. 35-88). Joensuu, Finland: Joensuun Yliopiston Monistuskeskus.

Sheehy, G. (1999). *Understanding men's passages.* (Revised ed.). New York: Ballantine Books.

Shulman, L. (1987). Knowledge and teaching: Foundations of a new reform. *Harvard Educational Review, 57*(2), 1-22.

Smith, D. (1991) Educating the reflective practitioner in curriculum. *Curriculum, 12* (7), 115-124.

Smyth, J. (1989). Developing and sustaining critical reflection in teacher education. *Journal of Teacher Education, 15*(3), 2-9.

Stake, R.E. (2000). Case studies. In N.K Denzin & Y.S. Lincoln (Eds.), *Handbook of qualitative research,* 2nd ed. (pp. 435-454). Thousand Oak, CA: Sage Publications.

Tabachnick, B.R., & Zeichner, K.M. (1991). *Issues and practices in inquiry-oriented teacher education.* London: Falmer Press.

Thompson, J.B. (1984). *Studies in the theory of ideology.* Berkeley, CA: University of California Press.

Tierney, W.G. (2000). Undaunted courage: Life history and the postmodern challenge. *Handbook of qualitative research,* 2nd ed. (pp. 537-553). Thousand Oak, CA: Sage.

Tochon, F.V. (1990). Heuristic schemata as tools for epistemic analysis of teachers' thinking. *Teaching and Teacher Education, 6,* 183-196.

Tochon, F.V. (1994). Presence beyond the narrative: Semiotic tools for deconstructing the personal story. *Curriculum Studies 2*(2), 221-247.

Tochon, F.V. (Ed.) (1997). *Éduquer avant l'école: l'intervention préscolaire en milieux pluriethniques et défavorisés* [Educate before school: Preschool actions in multiethnic and low-income setting]. Montreal, Bruxels, & Paris: Montreal University Press & De Boeck University.

Tochon, F.V. (1998, October). *From symbolic interaction to the culture of emotions: "Non-intrusive action" as a means to cooperating with parents and children in bilingual settings.* Paper presented at Working with Challenging Students in Schools: A Cross-Cultural Perspective Conference. Spurwink Institute, Lewiston, ME.

Tochon, F.V. (1999a). *Video study groups for education, professional development, and change.* Madison, WI: Atwood Publishing.

Tochon, F.V. (1999b). Myths in teacher education: Towards reflectivity. *Pedagogy, Culture, and Society, 7*(2), 257-289.

Tochon, F.V., & Miron, J.-M. (2000). *Parents responsables. Rapport de recherche présenté au Conseil québécois de la recherche sociale* [Accountable parents: Research report to the Quebec Councel for Social Research]. Sherbrooke, QC: CRP Publishers, University of Sherbrooke, Canada.

U. S. Bureau of the Census. (1996). *Statistical abstracts of the U.S.* Washington, D.C.: Government Printing Office.

Usher, R.S., & Edwards, D. (1995). Confessing all? A postmodern guide to the guidance and counseling of adult learners. *Studies in the Education of Adults, 27*(1), 9-23.

Valli, L. (1992). *Reflective teacher education: Cases and critiques.* Albany, NY: State University of New York Press.

Valli, L. (1990, April). *The question of quality and content in reflective teaching.* Paper presented at the annual meeting of the American Educational Research Association (AERA), Boston, MA.

Wildman, T., & Niles, J. (1987). Reflective teachers: Tensions between abstractions and realities. *Journal of Teacher Education,* July/August, 25-31.

Williams, C.L. (1992). The glass escalator: Hidden advantages for men in the "female" professions. *Social Problems, 39,* 253-267.

Wisconsin Department of Public Instruction. (1997). *Wisconsin's model academic standards for foreign languages.* Madison, WI: Author.

Wortham, S.E.F. (1994). *Acting out participant examples in the classroom.* Philadelphia, PA: John Benjamins.

Yule, G., & Tarone, E. (1991). *Focus of the language learner.* Oxford: Oxford University Press.

Zeichner, K.M. (1990). Changing directions in the practicum looking ahead to the 1990's. *Journal for Teaching, 16*(2), 105-131.

Zeichner, K.M. (1994). Research in teacher thinking and different views of reflective practice in teaching and teacher education. In I. Carlgren, G. Handel, & S. Vaage (Eds.), *Teacher's minds and actions: Research on teacher's thinking and practice.* Bristol, PA: Falmer.

The

COLLABORATIVE

ADMINISTRATOR

Working Together
as a Professional
Learning Community

Austin Buffum

Cassandra Erkens

Charles Hinman

Susan Huff

Lillie G. Jessie

Terri L. Martin

Mike Mattos

Anthony Muhammad

Peter Noonan

Geri Parscale

Eric Twadell

Jay Westover

Kenneth C. Williams

Solution Tree

Introduction by Richard DuFour   Foreword by Robert Eaker

Cover design by Grannan Design, Ltd.

Printed in the United States of America

ISBN 978-1-934009-37-6

Other Resources on Professional Learning Communities

The Collaborative Teacher: Working Together as a Professional Learning Community

Getting Started: Reculturing Schools to Become Professional Learning Communities

A Leader's Companion: Inspiration for Professional Learning Communities at Work™

Learning by Doing: A Handbook for Professional Learning Communities at Work™

On Common Ground: The Power of Professional Learning Communities

Passion and Persistence: How to Develop a Professional Learning Community

The Power of Professional Learning Communities at Work™: Bringing the Big Ideas to Life

Professional Learning Communities at Work™: Best Practices for Enhancing Student Achievement

Professional Learning Communities at Work™ Plan Book

Pyramid Response to Intervention: RTI, PLCs, and How to Respond When Kids Don't Learn

Revisiting Professional Learning Communities at Work™: New Insights for Improving Schools

Through New Eyes: Examining the Culture of Your School

Whatever It Takes: How Professional Learning Communities Respond When Kids Don't Learn

Table of Contents

Foreword

Robert Eaker

I read *The Collaborative Administrator* with great anticipation and high hopes for a number of reasons. First, I am personally familiar with and have tremendous admiration for the work of each author. Second, I have often thought that the insights and ideas of these highly successful practitioners should be shared with others. Well, I was not disappointed. Simply put, this book is a jewel!

Each chapter reflects both breadth and depth in their understanding of professional learning community concepts and practices. The authors have a broad spectrum of experience, ranging from the world of the classroom teacher to the culture of a district office. They represent rural schools, urban schools, and suburban schools. Some work in large districts, while others work in smaller ones. Some chapters focus on broader, more affective subjects, such as building trust and commitment, while others discuss very specific strategies for critical tasks, such as creating school schedules and negotiating teacher contracts in a professional learning community.

A number of important themes emerge from the writing of these experts. The dominant theme is the critical importance of effective leadership. If nearly 3 decades of effective schools research has taught us anything, it is this: Without strong leadership, the disparate elements of effective practices cannot be brought together and maintained. It is virtually impossible to reculture schools or school districts into high-performing professional learning communities without widely dispersed, high-quality leadership.

However, simply recognizing the power of professional learning communities, or the critical role leadership plays in them, isn't enough. The challenge facing administrators is not just understanding or exhibiting effective leadership practices. The excitement of administrators hoping to transform their school or school district into a professional learning community is often tempered by the nagging question, "What do I do?"

Fortunately, the professional learning community concept itself contains the answer. In a professional learning community, leaders first seek to gain *shared knowledge* by seeking *best practices*. *The Collaborative Administrator* is a treasure trove of "what to do's" and "how to do's" from highly successful administrators who not only possess a deep, rich understanding of professional learning community concepts and practices, but equally important, have actually done it!

Another theme that permeates each chapter is the importance of getting started—of doing the work. While knowledge of what to do is essential, knowledge alone is inadequate. Effective administrators move from *knowing* to *doing,* and *The Collaborative Administrator* is loaded with practical, proven practices that readers will find invaluable. If implemented, these practices will drive the professional learning community concepts deep into the culture of districts, schools, teams, and classrooms.

Of course, becoming a professional learning community is more than simply "doing." Effective leaders do the right things. Just what are the right things? The reflections and suggestions of the authors connect with the "big ideas" that form the framework of a professional learning community—an intense focus on learning, the use of high-performing collaborative teams, and a focus on continuous improvement and results.

While the authors address issues related to each of these big ideas, they lay heavy emphasis on creating a collaborative culture. The word *collaborative* is at the center of the title of *The Collaborative Administrator* for a reason. Effective leaders of professional learning communities embed a collaborative culture into the day-to-day life of their school. Want to know how to *collaboratively* address the critical issues of learning? Want to know how to *collaboratively* develop and use common formative assessments? Want to know how to *collaboratively* develop plans to provide students extra time and support or enrichment within the school day? Answers to these questions, and more, are found in chapter after chapter of *The Collaborative Administrator.*

However, it is misleading to represent *The Collaborative Administrator* as a mere collection of practical suggestions for reculturing districts and schools into professional learning communities. The authors clearly possess a deep, rich, and broad understanding of the research that forms the framework for their practice. In fact, the issues and ideas each writer examines represent an essential requirement for successful school improvement—a merger of the world of research and best practice with the world of the practicing, successful administrator.

The Collaborative Administrator takes the excuses off the table. Yes, reculturing schools to function as professional learning communities is difficult, incremental, and complex work, but it can be done, and this book shows how. When I came to the end of this book, my thoughts were simply these: "The professional learning community concept—*powerful*. The ideas in this book—*priceless!*"

Introduction

Richard DuFour

Americans have a fascination with the strong, charismatic, take-charge, heroic leader who single-handedly saves the day by virtue of imposing his or her will on a difficult situation. These leaders are not deterred by the inadequacies and mediocrity of the mere mortals who surround them. They apply their personal insights and assert their unique talents to overcome all obstacles. These rare individuals are born, not made, and their special gifts set them apart from those whom they lead. They determine the success or failure of most collective endeavors.

This tradition is illustrated beautifully in the movie *Lean on Me,* Hollywood's tribute to the leadership of principal Joe Clark as he took on the challenge of improving a troubled school in Paterson, New Jersey. According to the film, Clark, a former Army Drill Sergeant, set the tone for his leadership at his very first meeting with the faculty. "There is only one boss in this school, and that's me," he thunders at his staff. "There will be no talking at my meetings. I will talk and you will listen. You take out your pencils and write. This is not a damn democracy. I have one year to turn this school around." Those who may not like the message (or the messenger) are told they can quit, and approximately 100 faculty members did over the course of the next few years. On his first day in the position, Clark threw 300 students out of the school, referring to them as "leeches and parasites." "In this building," Clark boasted years later, "everything emanates and ultimates (sic) from me. Nothing happens without me" (Bowen, 1988).

In 1985, within 2 years of his taking the position, the U.S. Department of Education named Clark one of the nation's top 10 principals. Secretary of Education William Bennett praised Clark as a tough educator for tough times, commenting that "sometimes you need Dirty Harry" in the principalship. President Reagan cited Clark as an exemplar of the principalship, and Clark was offered a position as a White House policy adviser (Bowen, 1988). By 1989, *Lean on Me* hit the silver screen, advertised as "a true story of an American hero" and "the feel-good story of the year."

And now, as Paul Harvey would say, "the rest of the story." Although Clark removed hundreds of the most disruptive and low-performing students from "his" school, student achievement remained stagnant over his 6-year tenure and remained in the bottom third of the nation. The dropout rate at Paterson actually increased from 13% to 21% (Bowen, 1988). But why bother with the rest of the story, when Clark's persona offered such a perfect fit for the mythology of effective leadership that continues to permeate this country?

The authors of *The Collaborative Administrator* offer a different view of leadership. Although they explore the topic from different perspectives, they consistently call for leaders who share authority, empower others, and assess their effectiveness as leaders on the extent to which they create the conditions that result in higher levels of learning—both for students and adults. Rather than disparage and demean their teachers, they love them, and see them as the solution to, not the cause of, the problems of education. They recognize and value the collective wisdom residing within the school, and they create the structures and culture to allow staff members to tap into that wisdom. They are religiously attentive to establishing positive relationships with and among teachers.

The leaders they describe do not, however, simply delegate authority to others and hope for the best. They are eager to listen to the perspectives of others in an effort to find common ground, but they are also skillful in communicating and building consensus around shared purpose and priorities. Both their words and their actions convey what must be "tight" in their schools and districts—those imperatives that all staff members are expected to observe and honor. Furthermore, they do not hesitate to insist that staff act in accordance with the purpose and priorities of the organization. They are vigilant in protecting against the erosion of core values and willing to confront those who violate those values. They are emphatically assertive when necessary. They are not weak leaders, quite the contrary. They are strong leaders who demonstrate a different kind of strength than the authoritarian control of traditional hierarchies. They enlist colleagues in a fundamentally moral endeavor—making a difference in the lives of students—and then work with those colleagues collectively and collaboratively to succeed in that endeavor.

Finally, these leaders are courageously patient. They resist the temptation to pursue each new initiative touted to resolve the problems of education, and they focus instead on the slow, steady work of building the capacity of the staff to solve the unique problems of their school and their students. They don't dabble in innovation. They embody the level-five leaders described in *Good to Great* who persisted in "a quiet deliberate process of figuring out what needed to be done to create the best future results and then taking those steps, one after another. By pushing in a constant direction over an extended period of time, they inevitably hit a point of breakthrough" (Collins, 2001, p. 169). They demonstrate consistent, coherent effort over time and the resilience necessary for moving forward during the tough times that accompany any substantive improvement initiative.

An important step in creating schools that are successful in helping all students learn at higher levels is to recognize this challenge requires more than a heroic individual leader whose will and skill compensate for the deficiencies of the staff. If school or district improvement initiatives rely solely on the charisma or energy of an extraordinary principal or superintendent, initiatives will come and go as leaders come and go. Sustained and substantive school improvement will require leaders who are committed to empowering others, to dispersing leadership, and to creating systems and cultures that enable ordinary people to accomplish extraordinary things. Schools need strong leaders more than ever, but not the autocratic authoritarian that has symbolized strong leadership in the past. They don't need Joe Clark. They need men and women who recognize their ultimate legacy will be determined by developing other leaders throughout the school and district who can take the organization even further after they have gone.

The authors of *The Collaborative Administrator* embrace this image of leadership, but more importantly, they present specific, practical, and proven strategies that can help hard-working administrators transform their schools. They are convinced educators can create the conditions to help students learn at higher levels because, as some of the most effective school practitioners in America, they have successfully led the collective effort to create those conditions. Readers will recognize these authors offer the conviction, wisdom, and insight that can only come with "learning by doing" in the real world of schools.

Chapter Overview

Mike Mattos points out in chapter 1 that in order for schools to improve student achievement, they must do more than call themselves professional learning communities (PLCs): They must align the culture and practices of their schools with all the vital elements of a PLC. He describes the common mistakes leaders make in attempting to implement this powerful school improvement process, characterizing those mistakes as the selective approach, the managerial approach, and the "sacred cow" approach. Mike then provides an excellent overview of the characteristics of PLCs, emphasizes the need for an honest assessment of a school's current reality, and provides specific examples of how educators can create and implement an ongoing process to align the practices of their schools with the essential characteristics of a PLC. His chapter also includes tools to help school leaders both assess current practices in their schools and align those practices with PLC concepts. Finally, his chapter is filled with specific questions to help a staff begin the dialogue essential to improving student achievement.

In chapter 2, Cassandra Erkens calls for school leaders who serve others, who model what they expect of others, and who celebrate the small wins necessary to sustain improvement initiatives. She recognizes that meaningful improvement is all about shaping the culture of the school, and she suggests ways leaders can help foster a culture of safety, questioning, and risk-taking. She argues persuasively that teachers are inherently leaders—that great leaders teach and great teachers lead. She concludes by calling upon leaders at all levels of a school district to recognize their ability to empower others to lead and to create the conditions that make widely dispersed and shared leadership the norm for their schools and districts.

Although I have never found anyone opposed to a climate of trust, in many schools trust is like the adage about the weather— everyone talks about it, but no one does anything about it. In chapter 3, Austin Buffum does more than talk about trust: He offers concrete recommendations on how to build, maintain, and repair trust in a school setting. After identifying the most common barriers to trust, he cites the specific things principals must do to build a foundation of trust in their schools. He also explores the issue of trust between teachers and how leaders can strengthen trust at that level. There is far more to building trust than simply establishing congenial relations, and Austin cautions that principals who fail to confront adult behavior that violates the purpose and priorities of the school actually reduce levels of trust throughout the building.

In chapter 4, Ken Williams explores how principals help move stakeholders from compliance to commitment. Ken offers four strategies, and for each strategy he presents a quote to establish its theme and the direction, questions to help the reader reflect upon the strategy, the mindset supporting the strategy, the specific outcomes to be achieved through implementation, and examples of concrete, actionable steps principals can take to begin the journey from compliance to commitment. He calls upon leaders to assume good intentions on the part of the staff and to approach early implementation problems as evidence of the need for additional support and clarity. Like almost all the authors, he too calls upon leaders to model priorities by "getting close to the work" and engaging in the same activities they ask of their staffs. Ken provides ideas for dispersing leadership and regards dispersed leadership as essential to strengthening commitment. Finally, he offers excellent ideas for making frequent celebration an important part of the school culture.

In *Influencer,* Patterson, Grenny, Maxfield, McMillan, and Switzler (2007) contend the first issues that must be addressed in efforts to persuade others to change are the questions of desirability and feasibility: "Is it worth it?" and "Can I do it?" In chapter 5, Chuck Hinman, George Knights, and Jeffrey Hubbard acknowledge that in many schools teachers have lost faith in their ability to impact student learning, and thus leaders must help restore teachers' sense of self-efficacy if they are to succeed in changing the culture and structures of schools. The authors offer a series of activities and questions to help people throughout the district establish the clarity of purpose and collective commitments essential to creating a professional learning community. They remind us that while professional learning communities are results-oriented and hungry for data and information regarding their effectiveness, they are also very intentional in their efforts to touch the heart and stir the emotions of people throughout the organization. This chapter offers tools and ideas designed to make "a direct connection with the heart, where purpose and passion live."

Lillie Jessie devotes chapter 6 to presenting five "principal principles" to help school leaders create professional learning communities.

Those five principles include: 1) personal mission must precede organizational and school mission; 2) monitor what matters, when it matters; 3) engage in the principle of caring; 4) teach what you preach; and 5) respond when children are not learning . . . even when it threatens your popularity. Her entire chapter is underscored by the imperative of principals demonstrating an unrelenting personal commitment to the moral purpose of helping all students learn. There are many responsibilities and tasks a leader may delegate to others, but modeling this commitment is not one of them. Lillie writes with humility, acknowledging the times when her own practices were less than effective; however, principals who consider the strategies she presents and the conviction with which she presents them will be better positioned to be "principals of principle."

In chapter 7, Anthony Muhammad reminds us of a central fact of school improvement—teaching matters. While this common-sense observation sounds unassailable, he also reminds us that as products of schools that were designed to sort and select students on the basis of aptitude or ability, contemporary teachers "are now mandated to do something they have never done and have never witnessed; to not just measure but ensure proficiency for all students." Anthony argues that the key to improved learning for students is a commitment to the ongoing, job-embedded learning of the adults who serve those students. He then presents a very personal story of how he and the staff of Levey Middle School in Southfield, Michigan transformed the culture of their school through shared leadership; faculty-wide analysis of student achievement; limited, focused, and results-oriented goals; collective inquiry into best practice, and purposeful collaboration. Educators who are prone to the "yeah-but" syndrome—"Yeah, but our kids come from poor homes," or "Yeah, but our union contract limits what we can demand of staff"—may be troubled by the success story of this award-winning, nationally recognized school that refused to make excuses for low student achievement. Educators committed to helping all students learn will find valuable information and insights for bringing that commitment to life in their daily work.

All of the authors stress the importance of promoting adult learning in our schools, but in chapter 8, Terri Martin examines how skillful leaders establish the culture and structures that contribute to the ongoing, job-embedded professional development of their staffs. As she writes, "Once the culture of learning together has been embedded, professional development is not something to attend; it is a way of doing business." The process begins when teams of teachers analyze the existing evidence of the learning of their students to identify areas of concern. These concerns then become the focus of either schoolwide or team-specific professional development that utilizes both external and internal expertise. Terri calls upon leaders to tie staff development directly to the needs of learners (both students and adults) and to structure professional development to ensure the learning is collective, collaborative, and social.

As long ago as 1994, the National Education Commission on Time and Learning reported that traditional school structures made both students and educators "prisoners of time." In chapter 9, Peter Noonan offers ideas for escaping that prison. Like most of the authors, he advises principals to engage staff in the consideration of "why" before "how" when it comes to changes in traditional practice, and to begin the dialogue with probing questions rather than definitive answers. He calls for empowering staff to make important decisions, but he also cautions principals to identify a few "non-negotiables" that establish the parameters essential to effective empowerment. For example, Peter asked the scheduling committee for his high school to create a schedule that set aside time during the regular school day both for teachers to collaborate and for students to receive additional support for learning. Peter offers three different schedules that could be used to provide high school students with time for systematic interventions. More importantly, his chapter illustrates the importance of small group dialogue and personal conversations when building consensus for change. Peter makes it clear that while a principal can impose a new schedule, it takes shared leadership to shape the assumptions, beliefs, and expectations that constitute a new culture.

In chapter 10, Geri Parscale contrasts the traditional school response to students who experience academic difficulty with the timely, directive, and systematic response of a professional learning community. She cautions that before a staff can create an effective pyramid of interventions to provide students with additional time for learning, teachers must be clear on what they want their students to learn and how they will monitor that learning. She then offers a four-step process a school might use to create a system of interventions and questions to assess the effectiveness of that system. Geri offers an important caution: No system of interventions can compensate for ineffective teaching. Thus, at the same time the collaborative administrator engages staff in the plan to provide struggling students with additional time and support, he or she must also address the need to provide teachers with the time and support to assess and improve their instructional practice.

Susan Huff describes how professional learning communities convert data into information as a catalyst for improvement in chapter 11. She describes various kinds of assessments and how the information from those different assessments can assist the school-improvement process. For example, she draws distinctions between summative and formative assessments and describes in detail how collaborative teams of teachers in her school used frequent and timely information from common formative assessments to respond to the needs of individual students and to improve their individual and collective practice. Susan also describes how the school used data to assess the impact of varied action research projects aimed at helping more students learn. She concludes by pointing out how schools can gather and use data that go beyond student achievement to inform the professionals within the building, and she suggests questions principals can use to help the staff explore the data.

In chapter 12, Eric Twadell argues that a district asking teachers to focus on learning, to build shared knowledge as part of their decision-making process, to collaboratively engage in collective inquiry, to disperse leadership, and to make decisions based on evidence should model what it asks of others. He contends that the collective bargaining process provides a wonderful opportunity for such modeling and then describes how win–win bargaining can promote the high-trust, participatory relationships that characterize effective organizations. He describes the impact of the win–win process in two award-winning school districts in suburban Chicago. Eric also identifies the agreed-upon protocols and procedures that have been instrumental to the success of the process. He emphasizes that the focus of the negotiations must move beyond topics that benefit adults to issues that specifically support the primary purpose of the district—improved student learning. His chapter explains how the win–win negotiating process was used to address issues such as providing time for teachers to collaborate, creating systems of interventions for students, and helping teachers engage in professional development that was directly tied to their students and their school.

Jay Westover addresses the role of the central office in building professional learning communities in chapter 13. He argues that the central office is most effective in accomplishing this goal when it utilizes *"loose-tight practices* characterized by *strategic focus*—clear parameters and priorities—that create *collective efficacy* by directly empowering individuals to work within established boundaries in a creative and autonomous way."* Jay outlines a framework to help central office leaders create these conditions. The framework includes: 1) building shared knowledge through strategic focus on team products and student results, 2) developing common beliefs through widely distributed leadership, and 3) establishing collective commitments through collective efficacy. He then presents examples of school districts that model the elements of the framework and poses guiding questions to help a central office implement the framework.

I highly recommend *The Collaborative Administrator* to all those who are sincerely interested in making their schools and districts more hospitable places for student and adult learning. It is, without question, the best single collection of advice for improving schools from successful practitioners that I have ever read. I urge you not only to read this book but, more importantly, to put its wisdom into practice in your schools and districts.

References

Bowen, E. (1988, Feb. 1). Getting tough. *Time*. Accessed at www.time.com/time/magazine/article/0,9171,966577–1,00.html on April 1, 2008.

Collins, J. (2001). *Good to great: Why some companies make the leap . . . and others don't.* New York: HarperCollins.

National Education Commission on Time and Learning. (1994). *Prisoners of time.* Washington, DC: U.S. Government Printing Office.

Patterson, K., Grenny, J., Maxfield, D., McMillan, R., & Switzler, A. (2007). *Influencer: The power to change anything.* New York: McGraw-Hill.

MIKE MATTOS

The leadership of Mike Mattos, principal of Pioneer Middle School in Tustin, California, has resulted in consistently outstanding student achievement. Based on standardized test scores, Pioneer ranks first among middle schools in Orange County and in the top 1% of the state. In 2007, Pioneer was named a California Distinguished School. For his excellent leadership, Mike was named the Orange County Middle School Administrator of the Year by the Association of California School Administrators. Previously, as principal of Marjorie Veeh Elementary School in Tustin, Mike helped create a nationally recognized PLC that greatly improved student learning for all students, with a significant impact on the large population of youth at risk. Mike is the coauthor of *Pyramid Response to Intervention: RTI, PLCs, and How to Respond When Kids Don't Learn* (Solution Tree, 2008).

ONE

Walk the 'Lign:
Aligning School Practices With
Essential PLC Characteristics

Mike Mattos

Never have the demands on our educational system been greater or the consequences of failure so severe. Beyond the high-stakes school accountability requirements mandated by state and federal laws, the difference between success and failure in school is quite literally life and death for our students. Today, students who graduate from school with a mastery of essential skills and knowledge are prepared to compete in the global marketplace, with numerous paths of opportunity. For students who fail in our educational system, however, there are few paths to success. Traditional manufacturing and agricultural jobs that require minimal skills yet provide sufficient wages and benefits are either nonexistent or fail to pay above poverty-level compensation. Subsequently, the likely pathway for these students leads to an adult life of hardship, incarceration, or dependence on welfare systems. With such high stakes, school administrators today are like tightrope walkers without a safety net, responsible for meeting the needs of every child with little room for error.

As educational leaders, this stark reality that we are responsible to lead critical, lifesaving work can be both daunting and inspiring. Fortunately, we now possess research-based best practices that are proven to meet this need. Conclusive, compelling research confirms that becoming a professional learning community (PLC) is the most powerful and effective process to systematically change school culture and ensure high levels of learning for all students. As Mike Schmoker states, "There are simple, proven, affordable structures that exist right now and could have a dramatic, widespread impact on schools and achievement—in virtually any school. An astonishing level of agreement has emerged on this point" (2004, p. 1). Equally important, there is no ambiguity regarding what school leadership must do to achieve these "dramatic, widespread" results. To ensure high levels of learning for all students, we must align our school culture and structures to the essential characteristics of being a PLC. These characteristics are:

- Common mission, vision, values, and goals

- Collaborative culture

- Collective inquiry

- Action orientation

- Continuous improvement

- Focus on results

Considering that all school leaders have access to this research-based, proven "roadmap" to closing the achievement gap, why are so few schools achieving significant, sustained school improvement? We understand why schools and districts that haven't embraced the PLC movement are not improving. But what about schools that claim to be PLCs? Why are many of these schools still struggling? More often than not, the problem is that their administrators failed to align their schools' culture and practices with *all* the essential PLC characteristics, for without a deep implementation of all six characteristics, a school will not achieve learning for all. This chapter will explore the common mistakes that leaders make when implementing PLC practices, will suggest key questions for administrators to evaluate the site's current level of implementation, and will provide practical implementation tools.

Ineffective PLC Leadership

Without question, the extent to which administrators align site beliefs and programs with all essential PLC characteristics will directly determine a school's ability to improve student achievement. Administrative ineffectiveness in implementing these critical characteristics can be attributed to three ineffective leadership approaches: the Selective Approach, the Managerial Approach, and the "Sacred Cow" Approach.

Problem 1: The Selective Approach

> The administrator "picks and chooses" to implement some essential PLC characteristics, while disregarding or avoiding others.

Some administrators begin to learn about PLC concepts and conclude, "We have collaborative teams, [*or* We use common assessments], so we are a PLC"—as if one or two traits are sufficient to "raise the banner" of being a PLC. This superficial approach to PLCs creates a façade of implementation, but fails to create the deep, systemic change that is necessary to dramatically improve an organization. As Jim Collins says in *Good to Great and the Social Sectors,* "In building a great institution, there is no single defining action, no grand program, no one killer innovation, no solitary lucky break, no miracle moment" (2005, p. 23). So, too, becoming a great school does not consist of implementing one essential characteristic.

Another common problem occurs when administrators choose to implement only the characteristics that they favor or find expedient, while choosing to disregard or avoid others that they do not support or find too difficult to address. For example, one superintendent announced that all schools in his district would become PLCs, then started by implementing a districtwide benchmark testing program to ensure a "Focus on Results." Because the superintendent had a strong background in assessment, he viewed PLCs as a perfect vehicle to promote a stronger district assessment program. Unfortunately, he gave almost no attention to creating a common mission and vision, ensuring site collaborative time, and building shared knowledge regarding essential learning. In reality, the superintendent's goal was not to become a PLC, but instead to use PLC research to support his assessment goals. While district benchmark tests can be a helpful "means" to achieve an "end" of learning, in this case the benchmarks alone were the superintendent's desired end.

Conversely, another principal delayed implementing common assessments at her school because the staff found student assessment results to be threatening and uncomfortable. Not wanting to upset her staff nor hurt school collegiality and buy-in for PLCs, this principal avoided focusing on results. Unfortunately, this decision also made it nearly impossible for her site to accurately assess the effectiveness of the school's instructional program, set SMART goals, and create effective site interventions for struggling students.

Whether due to a lack of deep understanding, a desire to focus on favorable characteristics, or a lack of conviction to address the more difficult ones, the results are the same: If at least one essential characteristic is missing, the entire system will collapse. This selective, partial approach to implementation may be the most widespread misapplication of PLC philosophy.

Problem 2: The Managerial Approach

> The administrator views the six essential PLC characteristics as an implementation checklist.

Too often, administrators believe that by writing a new school mission statement or renaming department meetings as "PLC time," they have completed an item on the PLC to-do list. As Rick DuFour states, "This checklist approach can sharpen our focus on what must be done. But we also must recognize the inherent dangers in efforts to simplify complex tasks" (DuFour, 1998, p. 1). Implementing PLCs with a managerial leadership style lacks a deep understanding of the six essential PLC characteristics and how they work interdependently to create an ongoing *process* to improve student learning.

For example, a principal who was just starting to implement PLCs asked a colleague to review his agenda for an upcoming staff development day. The agenda looked like a grocery list:

1. Write a mission and vision statement.

2. Write team value statements.

3. Write team SMART goals.

4. Create action plan to implement goals.

5. Identify common assessments.

When the colleague questioned the ambitious plan for the day, the principal said his goal was to "address all the essential PLC characteristics." Unfortunately, the principal viewed each characteristic as a distinct act to be accomplished, instead of as *guiding principles* to be considered in all acts. When writing a mission and vision statement, for example, wouldn't the staff want to use collective inquiry to build shared knowledge about the traits of effective schools, or consider their students' needs by focusing on current assessment data? And once the mission is written, would it not make sense to create action steps to begin making the mission statement a reality? Ultimately, an effective administrator cannot view the essential characteristics as singular actions to be accomplished, but as ongoing goals that must continually be reconsidered and embedded within all the school's beliefs and procedures. This is the difference between "doing" PLC practices and "being" a PLC.

Problem 3: The "Sacred Cow" Approach

> The administrator fails to apply the six essential PLC characteristics to *all* school practices.

When a school accepts high levels of learning as their fundamental purpose, the staff must be willing to examine *all* practices in light of their impact on learning (DuFour, DuFour, Eaker, & Many, 2006). Because the six essential characteristics are necessary to ensure student learning, examining school practices is an ongoing process of aligning all school practices with these characteristics. But just as some administrators implement only *some* of the characteristics, others apply the characteristics to only *some* school practices. Due to a lack of awareness or conflicting priorities, these administrators allow "sacred cow" school practices that are actually counterproductive to student learning to continue.

In one case, for example, a principal met with a student at risk of failing science. It was the end of the first quarter, and the principal stressed to the child that there were still 9 weeks to improve his grade, so he had to get to work. The boy leaned back in his chair and announced that he was not going to try until February, at the beginning of the new semester. The principal was shocked, so he reminded the child of the importance of passing science. The student responded, "You just don't get it. I *can't* pass this semester. I have a 22% in science right now, and my teacher allows no make-up work, no extra-credit, and no make-up tests. If I earn every point possible for the second quarter, I still can't pass, so why try?"

Unfortunately, the student was right. If the purpose of a professional learning community is to ensure student learning, then why would we implement grading practices that are so counterproductive? Besides grading policies, some of the most prevalent educational sacred cows include teacher evaluation procedures, master schedules, school calendars, and athletics. By failing to align the sacred cows, these administrators "talk the talk" of being a PLC, but don't "walk the walk."

Powerful PLC Leadership

While these misguided administrative approaches are highly ineffective, there are powerful practices that school leaders can use to successfully implement all six essential characteristics. These include developing a deep understanding of all six characteristics, assessing a site's "current reality" in relation to these traits, and creating an ongoing process to align school practices with the essential characteristics.

Understand the Essential Characteristics and Assess Current Reality

To avoid the selective, managerial, or sacred cow approach to PLC implementation, it is vital to develop a deep understanding of the essential characteristics and how they work interdependently to create an ongoing process to improve student learning. Only by developing this understanding can an administrator accurately assess his or her site's current level of alignment and effectively take steps towards continuous improvement. To this end, consider the following descriptions and key questions related to each essential characteristic.

Shared Mission, Vision, Values, and Goals

All too often, administrators begin PLC implementation by jumping directly into forming collaborative teams, identifying essential standards, and creating common assessments, while failing to first build the vital consensus on a common mission of learning. As *Learning by Doing* states:

The very essence of a learning community is a focus on and a commitment to the learning of each student. When a school or district functions as a PLC, educators with the organization embrace high levels of learning for all students as both the reason the organization exists and the fundamental responsibility of those who work within it. (DuFour, DuFour, Eaker, & Many, 2006, p. 3)

This seismic shift from a focus on teaching to a focus on learning is far more than a school slogan or catchy "Learning for All" motto on a school's letterhead. In a PLC school, there are two underlining, fundamental assumptions inherent in the mission of high levels of learning for all students: 1) The educators in the organization believe that all students are capable of high levels of learning, and 2) they assume the responsibility to make this outcome a reality for every child. These fundamental assumptions are the foundation upon which all PLC practices are built and the reason why PLC educators feel compelled to implement the essential characteristics. Administrators who want to build support for a PLC should ask the following key "current reality" questions:

- Has your site collectively determined that high levels of *learning* for *all* students is the fundamental purpose of your school?

- Does your site take responsibility to ensure that all students learn?

- What proof do you have that your mission is being put into action?

Collaborative Culture

The second essential PLC characteristic is a collaborative culture. Because no single teacher could possibly possess all the knowledge, skills, time, and resources needed to achieve the mission of high levels of learning for all students, educators at a PLC school work in high-performing, collaborative teams. Collaboration does not happen by invitation or chance; instead, frequent collaborative time is embedded into the teacher contract day, allowing disciplinary teams to work interdependently to achieve common goals linked to their collective mission of learning (DuFour, DuFour, Eaker, & Many, 2006). PLC collaboration goes beyond mere congeniality to dig deeply into learning. It engages in disciplined inquiry and continuous improvement in order to "raise the bar" and "close the gap" of student learning and achievement (Fullan, 2005, p. 209). To this end, team collaborative time almost exclusively focuses on four critical questions:

1. What is it we expect students to learn?

2. How will we know if our students are learning?

3. How will we respond when students don't learn?

4. How will we respond when students have learned? (DuFour, DuFour, Eaker, & Many, 2006)

These essential questions help a team focus their collaborative efforts on their fundamental purpose—learning.

Because the elements of a collaborative culture are simple, logical, and universally accepted as best practice, it would seem that this essential characteristic would be an unlikely stumbling block to implementing PLC practices, but surprisingly, this is not the case. Thus, when assessing a site's current reality in creating a collaborative culture, consider the following key questions:

• Does your staff meet frequently, during the professional day, in collaborative teams?

• Are your teams configured to best address the four critical learning questions?

• Do your teams focus their collaborative efforts on learning?

• What current site practices do or don't promote/support collaboration?

Collective Inquiry

Roland Barth says, "Ultimately there are two kinds of schools: learning enriched schools and learning impoverished schools. I have yet to see a school where the learning curves . . . of the adults were steep upward and those of the students were not. Teachers and students go hand and hand as learners . . . or they don't go at all" (2001, p. 23). In a professional learning community, teams engage in collective inquiry to continually learn about best practices in teaching and learning. Teams do not make decisions merely by sharing experiences or averaging opinions, but instead by building shared knowledge through learning together. This collaborative learning enables team members to develop new skills to better meet the learning needs of their students.

The initial process of building collaborative teams creates opportunities for learning, as teachers who traditionally worked in isolation begin to benefit from the collective knowledge of their peers. If a collaborative team does not create a continuous process of learning, however, at some point the team's effectiveness will be restricted to the limits of the team's collective knowledge. To assess a site's current reality in this area, consider the following key questions:

- How are decisions made at your site?

- Are decisions made after building shared knowledge?

- How do you know that you are implementing research-based best practices?

- What topics and issues are you currently learning about?

Action Orientation and Continuous Improvement

Members of a professional learning community are action-oriented: They move quickly to turn aspirations into action and visions into reality.

—Richard DuFour, Rebecca DuFour,
Robert Eaker, & Thomas Many

All collaborative learning, planning, and goal-setting is useless until put into action. Unless staff members are willing to try new things, improvement in student learning is impossible. Additionally, this action orientation provides staff learning opportunities, as there is no better way to learn than by doing. PLC educators do not view experimentation as a singular task to be accomplished; rather, they embrace experimentation as "how we do things" every day. Human nature tends to view change as an uncomfortable process, but in a PLC, the team should feel uneasy *without* change, for without change, there is no opportunity for improvement. To assess these characteristics, consider the following key questions:

- Are your site goals and intentions put into action?

- Does your site embrace change or fight it?

- Does your school's culture allow, support, and promote risk-taking and experimentation?

- What new practices are you currently implementing?

Focus on Results

Members of a PLC school realize that all their efforts to achieve the mission of high levels of learning for all students must be assessed on the basis of results rather than good intentions. A PLC school has a "thirst" for information about their school. This focus on results leads each collaborative team to create a series of common, formative assessments to measure each student's progress towards mastery of essential learning outcomes (DuFour, DuFour, Eaker, & Many, 2006). This steady flow of student assessment information is the "life blood" of a PLC, as it is used to set goals, identify students in need of additional time and support, and confirm which instructional strategies are most effective in meeting the needs of students. To measure progress towards implementing a culture that has a focus on results, consider the following key questions:

- How does your site know that your students are learning?

- What does your site regularly assess, monitor, and celebrate?

- What does your site do with assessment information?

Tools for Self-Assessment

Assessing your site's progress toward implementing the essential PLC characteristics should be a collaborative process. Included in this chapter are two resources to assist you:

1. Essential Characteristics "Current Reality" Staff Survey (page 32)

2. Current Reality and Steps to Success Planning Chart (page 34)

By having every staff member take the "Current Reality" survey, leaders can secure vital information on the culture and perceptions of the school. Use this information to identify program strengths and weaknesses, as well as to set goals for improvement. Expect differing levels of success in implementing each characteristic, but insist that all six characteristics are addressed. Figure 1-1 shows the results if even one characteristic is skipped.

As Figure 1-1 demonstrates, the ultimate cost of avoiding or disregarding an essential characteristic is to lose all the benefits of becoming a professional learning community—hardly a price that an effective administrator should be willing to pay.

Aligning School Practices With the Essential Characteristics

In addition to assessing current progress towards implementing the essential characteristics, it is equally important to create an ongoing process of aligning individual school practices with the critical outcomes. Because these characteristics serve as defining elements of educational best practice, the more aligned school procedures are to these ideals, the more likely it is that high levels of learning will take place. To this end, there is a simple, yet powerful process that school leaders can utilize to align practices. This process is centered on the graphic organizer in Figure 1-2 (page 26).

	Common Mission, Vision, & Goals	Collaborative Culture	Collective Inquiry	Action Experimentation	Continuous Improvement	Focus on Results
Missing Common Mission, Vision, Values, & Goals	**Staff efforts do not focus on student learning.**	Staff works collaboratively to achieve school mission.	School practices are grounded in research-based best practices.	School puts its mission, vision, values, and goals into practice.	Essential PLC characteristics are continually reviewed and implemented.	Progress towards meeting school mission, vision, and goals is monitored, assessed, and celebrated.
Missing Collaborative Culture	Staff efforts focus on high levels of learning for all students.	**Staff works in isolation to achieve school mission.**	School practices are grounded in research-based best practices.	School puts its mission, vision, values, and goals into practice.	Essential PLC characteristics are continually reviewed and implemented.	Progress towards meeting school mission, vision, and goals is monitored, assessed, and celebrated.
Missing Collective Inquiry	Staff efforts focus on high levels of learning for all students.	Staff works collaboratively to achieve school mission.	**School practices are not based in research-based best practices.**	School puts its mission, vision, values, and goals into practice.	Essential PLC characteristics are continually reviewed and implemented.	Progress towards meeting school mission, vision, and goals is monitored, assessed, and celebrated.
Missing Action Orientation	Staff efforts focus on high levels of learning for all students.	Staff works collaboratively to achieve school mission.	School practices are grounded in research-based best practices.	**School mission, vision, values, and goals are not implemented.**	Essential PLC characteristics are continually reviewed and implemented.	Progress towards meeting school mission, vision, and goals is monitored, assessed, and celebrated.
Missing Continuous Improvement	Staff efforts focus on high levels of learning for all students.	Staff works collaboratively to achieve school mission.	School practices are grounded in research-based best practices.	School puts its mission, vision, values, and goals into practice.	**Essential PLC characteristics are viewed as a singular act. Improvement stops.**	Progress towards meeting school mission, vision, and goals is monitored, assessed, and celebrated.
Missing Focus on Results	Staff efforts focus on high levels of learning for all students.	Staff works collaboratively to achieve school mission.	School practices are grounded in research-based best practices.	School puts its mission, vision, values, and goals into practice.	Essential PLC characteristics are continually reviewed and implemented.	**School has no information to measure student learning or program effectiveness.**

Figure 1-1: Effects of Missing a PLC Essential Characteristic

Focus Area: _____		
Current Outcomes	**Current Practices**	**Desired PLC Outcomes**

Figure 1-2: An Alignment Tool

To align a particular school practice or program, start by identifying a focus area, then list all the existing steps or procedures in the center column titled "Current Practices." For example, one of the sacred cows mentioned previously was teacher evaluation practice. Often, traditional teacher evaluation procedures are counterproductive to PLC characteristics. School leaders can begin the alignment process by listing their current teacher evaluation procedures (see Figure 1-3).

Focus Area: Teacher Evaluation		
Current Outcomes	**Current Practices**	**Desired PLC Outcomes**
	Identify/Review Evaluation Standards and Process	
	Goal-Setting Conference	
	Formal Observation(s)	
	Postobservation Conference	
	Final Evaluation Process	

Figure 1-3: Step One

Next, ask the following guiding questions about each listed procedure:

1. Does it promote/ensure high levels of learning for all students?

2. Is it in alignment with our site mission, vision, values, and goals?

3. Does it support and promote collaboration?

4. What evidence do we have that it is best practice?

5. How will results be measured and evaluated?

Record answers to these questions in the left-hand column, titled "Current Outcomes."

Focus Area: Teacher Evaluation		
Current Outcomes	**Current Practices**	**Desired PLC Outcomes**
• Administrator reviews evaluation process and teaching standards with teachers. • Process focuses on teacher's instructional practices and meeting individual responsibilities.	Identify/Review Evaluation Standards and Process	
• Every teacher writes his or her own goals for the year. • Goals focus on teaching.	Goal-Setting Conference	
• Administrator observes teacher. • Observation(s) focus on teacher's instructional practices.	Formal Observation(s)	
• Administrator and teacher meet to review observation. • Focus is on teacher's instructional practices.	Postobservation Conference	
• Administrator and teacher meet to review final evaluation. • Focus is on teacher's instructional practices. • The entire process happens annually or biannually.	Final Evaluation Process	

Figure 1-4: Step Two

In this case, the current teacher evaluation program can be characterized as an individual process between a teacher and administrator that focuses on teaching practices. Once this step is completed, turn to the right-hand column, titled "Desired PLC Outcomes." Reviewing the guiding questions again, identify the desired outcomes you would expect if the focus area was aligned with PLC essential characteristics.

Focus Area: Teacher Evaluation

Current Outcomes	Current Practices	Desired PLC Outcomes
• Administrator reviews evaluation process and teaching standards with teachers. • Process focuses on teacher's instructional practices and meeting individual responsibilities.	Identify/Review Evaluation Standards and Process	• Administrator works with a collaborative team to review the evaluation process and identify teaching standards that are aligned with PLC practices.
• Every teacher writes his or her own goals for the year. • Goals focus on teaching.	Goal-Setting Conference	• Principal works with collaborative team to review previous year's assessment data and develop team SMART goal(s) for the current year. • Teacher teams use collective inquiry to identify best instructional practices to achieve the team SMART goal(s). • Team SMART goal(s) are selected as the goals for teacher evaluation.
• Administrator observes teacher. • Observation(s) focus on teacher's instructional practices.	Formal Observation(s)	• Administrator and collaborative team select observation opportunities that directly relate to team SMART goal(s).
• Administrator and teacher meet to review observation. • Focus is on teacher's instructional practices.	Postobservation Conference	• Administrator and collaborative team meet to discuss instructional practices. • Teams may provide student learning data to demonstrate teaching effectiveness.
• Administrator and teacher meet to review final evaluation. • Focus is on teacher's instructional practices. • The entire process happens annually or biannually.	Final Evaluation Process	• Final evaluation focuses on achievement of team SMART goal(s) and student learning. • If a teacher is in need of assistance, fellow team members can be a resource for model lessons, peer tutoring, and mentoring.

Figure 1-5: Step Three

Once all three columns are complete, the final step is to compare the outer columns. If entries under "Current Outcomes" and "Desired PLC Outcomes" are the same, then the focus area is highly aligned with PLC essential standards. But if the outer columns differ significantly, then current practices should be revised to align with the essential characteristics—or eliminated—because they are counterproductive to student learning.

In our example, the school's current teacher evaluation process was significantly misaligned with PLC characteristics. Figure 1-6 shows how, within the terms of the existing district/teacher contract, the school leadership team revised their process to better align with PLC characteristics.

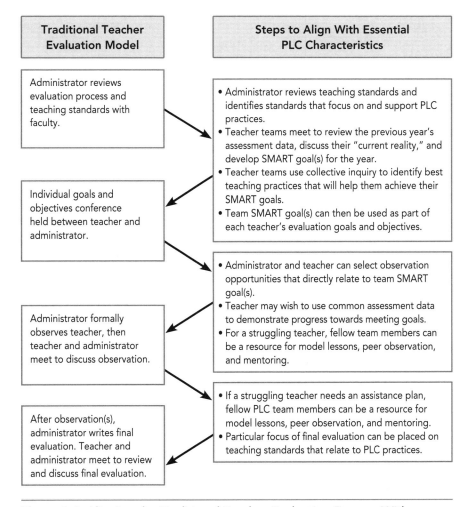

Figure 1-6: Aligning the Traditional Teacher Evaluation Process With Essential PLC Characteristics

By making a few targeted revisions, the teacher evaluation process now supports a focus on learning and collaboration. Considering the amount of time, effort, and emphasis placed on teacher evaluation, it only makes sense to have procedures that complement a school's fundamental purpose.

Final Thoughts

In *Good to Great,* Jim Collins says, "Greatness is not a function of circumstance. . . . it is largely a matter of conscious choice, and discipline" (2005, p. 40). As school leaders, we cannot leave student learning up to luck, hope, or chance. If we want to be a great school, our primary administrative responsibility is to create the necessary conditions upon which high levels of learning for all students are inevitable. This can be achieved if, and only if, we are willing to align all of our organization's practice, procedure, and disposition to achieve the same outcome—learning.

Yet while it is important to learn how to implement PLC practices, we must never lose sight of why we are doing this work. If we embrace that our fundamental leadership responsibility is to promote, defend, and ensure learning for all students, we will understand that implementing PLC practices is not an end in itself, but instead a means to achieve this mission. The six essential PLC characteristics are not tasks be accomplished, but a way of thinking, acting, and being that guides our efforts. For in the end, our effectiveness in implementing PLC practices will not be measured in standardized test scores or meeting federal mandates, but rather in the life-ending failures or lifelong successes of our students.

References

Barth, R. (2001). *Learning by heart.* San Francisco: Jossey-Bass.

Collins, J. (2005). *Good to great and the social sectors: A monograph to accompany* Good to Great. New York: HarperCollins.

DuFour, R. (1998, Spring). You won't find this on any checklist. *Journal of Staff Development, 19*(2), 57–58.

DuFour, R., DuFour, R., Eaker, R., & Many, T. (2006). *Learning by doing: A handbook for professional learning communities at work.* Bloomington, IN: Solution Tree.

Fullan, M. (2005). Professional learning communities writ large. In R. DuFour, R. Eaker, & R. DuFour (Eds.), *On common ground: The power of professional learning communities* (pp. 209–224). Bloomington, IN: Solution Tree (formerly National Educational Service).

Schmoker, M. (2004, February). Tipping point: From feckless reform to substantive instructional improvement. *Phi Delta Kappan, 85*(6), 424–432.

Essential Characteristics "Current Reality" Staff Survey

Survey Directions: If the question is a statement, please use the following scale to indicate the extent to which each of the following statements is true for you and/or your department team:

1	2	3	4	5
Not very true		Partially true		Very true

- If the question is open-ended, please share your thoughts.

- Honesty is essential!

List your Department/Team(s): _____

Common Mission, Vision, Values, & Goals

- ❑ I know our school's mission and vision.
- ❑ I believe in our school's mission and vision.
- ❑ Our mission and vision were created collectively.
- ❑ My efforts are vital and essential to making our mission and vision a reality.
- ❑ Our team has identified team norms to guide us in working together.
- ❑ Team members consistently adhere to our team norms.

Collaborative Culture

- ❑ Our team meeting time is focused and productive.
- ❑ My input is valued and respected by the team.
- ❑ Team collaboration has improved student learning in my classes.
- ❑ Our team works interdependently to achieve our goals.

Setting Goals/Collective Inquiry

- ❑ Each team member is clear on the essential standards of our course(s).
- ❑ We have identified course content and/or topics that can be eliminated so we can devote more time to essential standards.
- ❑ We have agreed on how to best sequence/pace the course content.
- ❑ We have aligned our essential standards with state/district standards and the assessments required of our students.
- ❑ We continually revise and re-evaluate what is essential for students to learn.

(continued)

The Collaborative Administrator • © 2008 Solution Tree
www.solution-tree.com

Essential Characteristics "Current Reality" Staff Survey (continued)

Focus on Results

- ❏ Our team has developed common assessments to determine each student's mastery of essential standards and to assess strengths and weaknesses of our program.
- ❏ Our team regularly analyzes common assessment data.
- ❏ We have established the proficiency standard (rigor level) we want each student to achieve on our essential standards and assessments.
- ❏ We have taught our students the criteria we will use to judge their work.
- ❏ We have agreed on the criteria we will use in judging the quality of student work related to essential standards, and we practice applying those criteria consistently.
- ❏ We use the results of common assessments to assist each other in building on strengths and addressing weaknesses to help students achieve at higher levels.
- ❏ We use common assessment data to identify students who need additional time and support to master essential standards.

Targeted Interventions

- ❏ Our team discusses how we can respond when students have not learned essential standards.
- ❏ The Pyramid of Interventions effectively helps my students at risk.

Administrative Support

- ❏ Our site administration adheres to our site norms, vision, and mission.
- ❏ Our site administration provides me the support I need to do my best.
- ❏ Our site administration is approachable and responsive to my concerns.
- ❏ Key decisions are made collectively at our school.

Additional Questions

List the three best things about our school: What's working?

List three suggestions to improve our school.

(Adapted with permission from *Learning by Doing*, DuFour, DuFour, Eaker, & Many, 2006, Bloomington, IN: Solution Tree.)

Current Reality and Steps to Success Planning Chart

Potential Bump	Essential Questions	Your Current Reality	Desired Outcome (Long-Term Goal)	First Steps (Short-Term Goal)
Common Mission, Vision, Values, & Goals	• Has your site collectively determined that high levels of learning for all students are the fundamental purpose of your school? • Does your site take responsibility to ensure that all students learn? • What proof do you have that your mission is being put into action?			
Collaborative Culture	• Does your staff meet frequently, during the professional day, in collaborative teams? • Are your teams configured to best address the four critical learning questions? • Do your teams focus their collaborative efforts on learning? • What current site practices do or don't promote and support collaboration?			
Collective Inquiry	• How are decisions made at your site? • Are decisions made after building shared knowledge? • How do you know that you are implementing researched-based, best practices? • What topics/issues are you currently learning about?			
Action Experimentation and Continuous Improvement	• Are your site goals and intentions put into action? • Does your site embrace change or fight it? • Does your school's culture allow, support, and promote risk-taking and experimentation? • What new practices are you currently implementing?			
Focus on Results	• How does your site know that your students are learning? • What does your site regularly assess, monitor, and/or celebrate? • What does your site do with assessment information?			

The Collaborative Administrator • © 2008 Solution Tree
www.solution-tree.com

Aligning School Practices With Essential PLC Characteristics

Guiding Questions

1. Does it promote/ensure high levels of learning for all students?

2. Is it in alignment with our site mission, vision, values, and goals?

3. Does it support and promote collaboration?

4. What evidence do we have that it is best practice?

5. How will results be measured and evaluated?

Focus Area: _____

Current Outcomes	Current Practices	Desired PLC Outcomes

Part One

LEADING A CULTURE OF COLLABORATION

CASSANDRA ERKENS

An independent consultant and recognized leader in education, Cassandra Erkens shares her expert knowledge with teachers and administrators throughout the United States and Canada. Cassandra is the president of Anam Cara Consulting, Inc., and has served as a high school English teacher, district-level director of staff development, and state-level educational effectiveness regional facilitator. Cassandra has authored and co-authored several formal education-based training programs for Solution Tree and other national service providers. She trains all Solution Tree presenters, as well as other education experts.

TWO

Growing Teacher Leadership

Cassandra Erkens

Any successful school reform effort is the result of the work of teachers who transformed the educational experience within their classrooms. While this has always been the case, our history with "top down" reform efforts suggests we've not always tapped into the amazing synergy of creative classroom teachers operating in professional learning communities. In fact, our reforms almost always involve a few remarkable teacher leaders *leaving* the classroom to accept additional responsibilities, take on temporary roles, help implement lengthy strategic plans, and institutionalize change.

Today we understand that our strongest teacher leaders must remain *inside* the classroom to respond to gaps in student learning and to empower their colleagues to explore and master the art of teaching and learning. Teacher leadership is critical to successful school reform. Systems-thinking expert Michael Fullan states, "Broadening teacher leadership until it becomes the norm is the sine qua non of educational reform" (1997, p. 34). We must create the conditions in which both the depth and the breadth of teacher leadership develop to become the very culture in which we conduct our day-to-day work within classrooms and schools and districts.

It is fair to conclude that empowering teacher leaders in classrooms changes how we as administrators must understand, identify, and empower teacher leadership within our educational organizations. Without question, leadership in such a model must be shared: "Widely dispersed leadership is essential in building and sustaining professional learning communities, and it is important that individuals at all levels lead effectively" (DuFour, DuFour, Eaker, & Many, 2006, p. 185). Whether we work at the building or central office level, we must understand our own role as administrators in developing shared and empowered leadership through professional learning communities.

The architects for professional learning communities remain clear on this point: Becoming a PLC changes everything and "everyone. Every educator—every teacher, counselor, principal, central office member, and superintendent—will be called upon to redefine his or her role and responsibilities. People comfortable working in isolation will be asked to work collaboratively. People accustomed to hoarding authority will be asked to share it. People who have operated under certain assumptions their entire careers will be asked to change them" (DuFour, DuFour, Eaker, & Many, 2006, p. 286). In order for education to transform, *we* must be willing to transform ourselves and our roles as leaders.

Redefining Our Roles as Leaders

While the world of work has changed and will continue to change dramatically over time, Noel Tichy asserts that "the job of a leader has not changed. Enhancing the value of assets and sustaining growth are still the ultimate goal" (Tichy & Cardwell, 2004, p. 10). Defined, leadership is the practice of guiding and inspiring others to journey willingly toward an identified target; done well, it nurtures a culture of risk-taking and learning, thereby creating the opportunity for meaningful changes in the direction, beliefs, values, practices, and skills of the individual, group, and organization. Far more than a series of strategies to lead change and a practice of monitoring the effectiveness of our efforts, leadership is about relationships. It requires *heart*. Exceptional leaders understand that leadership is not facilitating a series of activities, but rather guiding and encouraging *people* on the journey. We must both *be* that exceptional leader for others and *evoke* the exceptional leader in others. To do that, we must serve, we must model, and we must celebrate.

Serving

Traditionally, administration has been a role of "leading from the front" with answers to inquiries and clear directions for next steps. But school reform happens in the heart of the classroom, not in a strategic plan. In a collaborative culture, we must both lead *and* serve so that others might lead. As we establish the direction, our job is to anticipate the teams' needs and remove barriers. Our mantra must be *How can I help?*

When we lead as a facilitator, we help individuals co-create the answers rather than provide the answers. Though we might feel we already have the solutions and providing the answers would seem far simpler and more expedient, we must resist the urge. We must even resist the *request* for answers by staff members who prefer we simplify and abbreviate their work with our solutions. In fact, it's often best not to have the answers formed in advance in order to allow for deep exploration and creative responses as we engage our staff in inquiry.

But this is not to say we are disengaged; in fact, the opposite is true. We are most likely more engaged, more visible, and more accessible than we may have been in the past. We are pushing up our sleeves joining difficult conversations; we are stepping in to cover a periodic class so an important classroom intervention can take place; we are monitoring learning in classrooms daily; and we are anticipating next steps and preparing necessary materials so teams have what they need for addressing issues or concerns.

The moment we become aware, for example, that the practice of using common assessments has generated staff readiness for conversations about grading, we gather the relevant materials, launch a guiding coalition to lead the exploration, and create the space and the desired climate for the impending conversation. When it's time for the conversation, we have prepared all that teams need for the discussion:

- Current, and relevant best-practice research on grading
- Listings of current and varied grading practices and policies in the building
- Copies of the current report card
- District expectations and policies for grading
- Feedback, if possible, from key stakeholder groups—including staff—regarding concerns with current practices

If we want to maximize the effectiveness of our professional learning communities, then we must anticipate needs and find ways to remove barriers. As much as possible, we are proactive rather than reactive as we set teams up for success. We *serve* so that our teams can better help us lead the necessary changes in our work.

Modeling

One of the most significant things we can do as leaders is model that which we expect of others. As Kouzes and Posner (2002) note, "Exemplary leaders know that if they want to gain commitment and achieve the highest standards, they must be models of the behavior they expect of others. Leaders model the way" (p. 14). If we want collaboration, we ourselves must be willing to collaborate. If we want staff to challenge the system, then we ourselves must not only be willing to challenge the system, but also accept *being challenged* as part of the system.

Administrators must practice the same tenets of inquiry and reflection. In their book *Hard Facts, Dangerous Half-Truths and Total Nonsense: Profiting From Evidence-Based Management* (2006), authors Pfeffer and Sutton state:

> One of the most crucial chores of leaders is to display and promote curiosity. . . . Leaders breed such curiosity by having both the humility to be students and the confidence to be

teachers. When we think of managers and leaders who best exemplify the mind-set required for practicing evidence-based management, a deep belief and commitment to teaching is usually a big part of the story . . . great leaders are great teachers. (p. 236)

Reflective practitioners tend to share common habits and beliefs about themselves as learners. First and foremost, they constantly study their craft through any and all available mediums. What does it take to lead well? They turn to the literature, to the research, to the gurus, to the workshops. They do whatever it takes to understand the best ways to serve. Moreover, they make their learning public, sharing with others their current book list, their struggles, and their insights along the way. They take risks and acknowledge their mistakes. They participate.

Mr. Gonzales, a principal, was so impressed by the depth of conversation and high levels of learning his staff experienced each time they gathered to examine student work that he decided to try the process. In the absence of student work, he gathered his staff meeting agendas and brought them to the table. He told the team that he'd noticed the staff meetings were rather boring and ineffective, and he asked them to examine the agendas as if they were student work. Mr. Gonzales listened carefully to their discussion regarding his agendas and made instant changes based on their feedback. Today, staff enjoy attending his staff meetings.

Strong leaders like Mr. Gonzales seek feedback on their own effectiveness and adjust accordingly, working to assure their efforts are supportive of individuals and the organization at large. The gift of their reflection is both their vulnerability and their courage. Our strongest leaders are an exploration in duality (Collins, 2001).

Our work in a collaborative and empowered culture requires modeling: "Leaders' deeds are far more important than their words when determining how serious they really are about what they say. Words and deeds must be consistent" (Kouzes & Posner, 2002, p. 14). We model to share in the work. We model to exemplify organizational values. We model to lead the way to change. We model to create new leaders.

Celebrating

In a professional learning community, we also lead by cheering. We celebrate small wins along the way, attending to cultural impact and organizational values as we determine what and how to celebrate. The role of celebration cannot be taken lightly, especially as we nurture risk-taking and challenges to the status quo. "It's part of a leader's job to show appreciation for people's contributions and to create a culture of celebration," Kouzes and Posner remind us; "Encouragement is curiously serious business. It's how leaders visibly and behaviorally link rewards with performance" (2002, pp. 19–20).

In all of her work to implement professional learning communities consistently across her school, Ms. Brown noticed that although she had pockets of excellence, no team was fully utilizing the PLC process. She decided to ask each team to share their greatest learning and success as a PLC at the upcoming professional development day for a staffwide celebration of their progress. To her surprise and delight, the sharing was rich, complete with data charts and common assessment examples. Teams asked questions and took notes regarding how colleagues were handling things in other teams. Soon they shared intervention strategies, agenda templates, data protocols, and other such helpful tools and strategies. Best of all, the teams shared stories that caused great laughter and helped to create a culture of learning through practice. Ms. Brown believes engaging her staff in this process of celebration did more to move her staff forward to full implementation than another formal workshop might have done on that day.

Preparing the Culture for Shared Leadership

Often times when we talk about quality leadership, we strategize from the place of effective tactics and plans. But followership is an active process. We must attend to what it would take in order for others to *follow* our best efforts successfully. When we do that, we can clearly see the significance of attending to culture (see Figure 2-1).

If leaders want to:	Then followers must:	And followers will require:
Establish a guiding coalition . . .	. . . participate in leadership effort.	Peer acceptance for risk-taking and leading
Identify essential learner outcomes . . .	. . . challenge each other's thinking.	Open and honest dialogue
Create and implement common assessments . . .	. . . share personal achievement results.	Trust
Challenge practices that interfere with mission and vision . . .	. . . explore beliefs.	Safety
Solicit feedback regarding current plans . . .	. . . provide honest input.	Administrative receptiveness to feedback

Figure 2-1. Leadership Strategies to Create Active Followers

As Hargreaves and Fink (2007) point out, "The most important contribution that senior leaders can make to the development of emergent distributed leadership is to create an inclusive, purposeful, and optimistic culture in which initiatives can easily come forward." Creating the conditions for empowerment and ultimately the success of transformation within classrooms requires us as leaders to attend to culture.

A Culture of Safety

Collaboration is founded on safety and trust. Individuals cannot collaborate successfully, challenge the status quo, or take risks if they do not feel safe. We as leaders can do much to create an environment of safety—including simple acts like creating group norms to guide our discussions and holding teams accountable to those norms.

Ultimately, however, safety will be hinged on how we respond to given situations:

- Do we support staff in difficult situations?

- Do we respond with an open mind to challenging news?

- Do we address negativity and unprofessional conduct quickly?

- Most importantly, do we act as a buffer for our teams and our schools striving to recreate themselves?

Strong leaders "look out the window to apportion credit to factors outside themselves when things go well (and if they cannot find a specific person or event to give credit to, they credit good luck). At the same time, they look in the mirror to apportion responsibility, never blaming bad luck when things go poorly" (Collins, 2001, p. 35).

A Culture of Questioning

Today, schools are predicated on having the "right answers," from classroom to classroom and building to building. This approach to learning confines our thinking and erroneously sets us up to view mistakes as detrimental to our learning. Our entire culture must shift from "What did you learn in school today?" to "What questions did you ask in school today?" As leaders, we can open the doors to this change by creating good questions, welcoming staff questions, and celebrating the questions themselves. It is fair to expect that educators become learners and researchers of their own craft—a pathway filled with ready-made questions: Will that best practice work with my kids? With my standards? Will formative assessments increase student motivation and productivity? Is there a better alternative to the way we currently manage report cards and conferences? The opportunities for meaningful questions that can lead to our transformation are limitless. As leaders, we can begin the process by posing some of our own rich and meaningful questions and inviting new questions from others. Encourage inquiry-based responses that provide multiple creative responses, then ask which of the responses might best meet our needs. In the end, the answers to one good question should naturally lead to new questions.

A Culture of Risk-Taking

> *To learn is to risk; to lead others toward profound levels of learning is to risk; to promote personal and organizational renewal is to risk. To create schools hospitable to human learning is to risk. In short, the career of the lifelong learner and of the school based reformer is the life of a risk taker.*

> —Roland Barth

As we work to transform our schools, the opportunities for risk-taking are boundless. We must ourselves be willing to take risks and share our efforts with staff. We must encourage their risk-taking and celebrate their findings—even when the results did not turn out as desired. Mistakes are an inherent part of the learning journey. In the absence of mistakes, we can limit ourselves to transactional rather than transformational learning. This is not to say that we celebrate failure—rather, we celebrate the efforts to succeed. We frame problems as opportunities, and we encourage divergent thinking. We cannot have learning without risk-taking.

Empowering Teacher Leaders

Can teachers become leaders? Without formal training? Phil Schlechty, educational author and creator of the Center for Leadership in School Reform, claims teachers already *are* leaders: "Teachers . . . are leaders, and what they do should be understood in terms of theories of leadership, as opposed to most existing theories of teaching and learning" (1997, p. 185). Better still, Noel Tichy, business author and leadership expert, suggests that today's business leaders must learn to function more *as* teachers: "Teaching is at the heart of leading. In fact, it is through teaching that leaders lead others. . . . Leading is getting others to see a situation as it really is and to understand what responses need to be taken so that they will act in ways that move the organization to where it needs to be. . . . Simply put, if you are not teaching, you are not leading" (1997, p. 57). Teachers already bring much to the table as leaders. Our administrative work isn't as much about *creating* leaders as it is about *leveraging* teacher leadership to transform our schools.

Teachers as Leaders

We must begin to build capacity for a system of shared and dispersed leadership: "Developing others to be leaders, creating leaders at every level, and getting them aligned and energized is how you get there" (Tichy & Cardwell, 2004, p. 10). Who are the teacher leaders in our organizations? Are they the ones who always share their opinions? Who inform policy? Who seek roles outside the classroom?

While the teachers who adopt roles outside the classroom are often perceived as leaders by their peers, they are not necessarily the teacher leaders to whom staff turn with educational questions or concerns for classroom application. In most buildings and districts, we can easily identify the master teachers who are well-respected by colleagues because they regularly demonstrate integrity, openness, ingenuity, competency, and trustworthiness. These individuals are often quiet and sometimes resist the urging of others to accept more formal opportunities to lead. However, their colleagues have already acknowledged them as leaders by frequently turning to them for guidance—even in the absence of a positional leadership title. Such teacher leaders are deemed by Doug Reeves to be the "super hubs" of our organizations, and we need to identify and empower the super hubs in our teacher networks: "Understanding, identifying, and deploying networks for positive results is the central challenge of leaders who seek to transform the status quo. Rather than trying to contrive networks through organizational charts or rigid hierarchies, school leaders should harness the power of the networks that they already have by listening to their key members—which is the greatest leadership technique of all" (2006a, p. 37). If we are to empower teacher leadership in our schools and districts, we must first identify the individuals functioning as leaders and formally engage their leadership within their professional learning community in a manner that influences the expertise of their peers and exacts collaborative leadership from the entire team.

Beyond finding the leaders who can share in the responsibility of dispersed leadership in our organizations, we must do the work of empowering them. We can't have all of the answers. If we truly wish to support the work of professional learning communities, we will need to build capacity and nurture the collective efficacy of our staff. Professional learning communities engage in inquiry regarding their own effectiveness; they challenge the status quo; they generate collective responses to students who aren't learning; and ultimately, they transform their understanding of education and their capacity as teachers who impact learning. All of that work involves risk-taking on behalf of the community and encouragement on behalf of administrators.

Leading With Yes

To encourage is to foster, promote, approve, or advance an idea, an individual, or a group. This means we learn to lead with the word *yes* when approached with a request to try something new or explore alternatives. When we reply initially with the more comfortable, "safe," controlled response of *no,* we send the message that we are more about controlling for consistency than we are about exploring possibilities.

This does not mean creating a free-for-all approach to supporting change in our schools. In fact, Dr. DuFour and his colleagues state, "Educators ask, 'Will you support me?' as a litmus test for their leaders, assuming a 'good' leader will assure them of unwavering support. Effective leaders, however, will not support ineffective practice, cruel comments, or deliberate violations of collective commitments. In those instances, support would be no virtue" (DuFour, DuFour, Eaker, & Many, 2006, p. 191). This juncture of our decision-making requires clarity on our vision, mission, values, beliefs, goals, and operational commitments to each other. These pillars serve as both our foundational anchors and our navigational stars. They help us to be clear on what we will be "tight" about in the moments when we are asked to allow for risk-taking. Leading with *yes* can and often might need to be qualified:

> "Yes, you may consider creating tiers of performance expectations in your common assessments for differentiated ability groups—if you can demonstrate how that decision will help your team meet its SMART goal and our organization move toward its vision of all students achieving at high levels."

> "Yes, we can change the process and format for parent/teacher/student conferences—after we explore best practices in the ideal process and engage our community as stakeholders in the outcome."

> "Yes, it's possible to invest in developing a July study skills program—once the team helps me resolve transportation and accessibility issues so struggling learners have equitable access."

Even with qualifiers, the first thing our staff hears is openness in our response: They hear us lead with *yes,* and with that, we have sent a message that we acknowledge and accept their efforts to reinvent a practice or a policy or an outdated understanding. But we are tight about our values and beliefs and direction, and if the request at hand is not in alignment, the team has a responsibility to reconsider its request to achieve alignment. The team is empowered and even encouraged to do so, but the charge is placed entirely in the team's capable hands.

Trusting the Journey

Finally, when we allow for risk-taking, we must create a culture in which mistakes may well occur—in fact, might even be anticipated in advance of the activity itself. Benefits of the learning far outweigh the costs of the mistake.

For example, in the early stages of one team's efforts to regroup children during a weekly planned intervention period, the team decided to automatically place all learners with special needs in Mr. Borough's classroom, where they were already receiving special education services. Their principal, Ms. Cunningham, anticipated that such a predictable and patterned response on their part would "sell their learners short" of their potential and would fail to allow the team to be truly responsive to their data. When approached, however, Ms. Cunningham empowered the team to try it—with the caveat that they monitor their own results and respond accordingly to their findings. She was able to do so for the following reasons:

- She believed that the team would discover the weakness in their plan and would adjust accordingly.

- She trusted that no child would be harmed in the process.

- She understood that to block their decision would send the message that she was still the "keeper of the answers" and their empowerment did not extend beyond her own comfort zone as the leader.

As Ms. Cunningham predicted, a few weeks into the process, the team discovered that the learners they'd identified for consistent placement during intervention time didn't always need to be in the remediation group. Rather, sometimes these learners needed to be in the "achieved" and even the "enriched" groups. Their new insight was far more powerful and convincing for their own understanding than Ms. Cunningham telling them that their plan wouldn't work. Pleased with their findings, Ms. Cunningham celebrated their learning and facilitated their ability to make changes in their own plans so soon after they'd begun the process.

The work of professional learning communities requires an entrepreneurial spirit. It is a journey of learning for everyone in the system: students, staff, and administrators alike. Learning involves risk-taking and mistake making and ultimately leads to transformational insights. We must create a formative culture in which we work together to find our answers.

Sharing the Work of Leading

Sharing the work of leadership is as much about empowering others as it is about empowering ourselves to do *great* work. Too often, leaders throughout school systems express frustration that they are "unempowered":

"We would do that," teachers say, "if our principal would just give us clear direction and step out of our way."

"I could support that," the principal proposes, "if time permitted and the district would allow it."

"I would help with that," the program director responds, "if I had any clout or authority with the schools."

"I could change that," the superintendent offers, "if state mandates or teacher unions would grant it."

At some level, all of us can feel overwhelmed and unempowered. But in reality, no one is coming to bestow more power upon us. The truth is *we* are the ones to champion the causes that we can see require attention. We cannot wait for others to empower us. And we cannot hold back from empowering others.

To change our understanding of educational organizations as hierarchies, to relinquish our sense of order and control as leaders, can be difficult and even painful for the organization *and* the leaders making the changes. But it is precisely the disequilibrium that renders status quo useless and allows for insight and learning to evolve. In such apparent chaos, a new order and a shared equilibrium emerge. True educational reform can happen in that space. This is not to say we proceed with reckless abandon; rather, we take calculated risks. We navigate chaos because it is the only thing that can truly lead to synergy, collaborative innovation, and collective wisdom. We alter our understanding of leadership and ourselves as leaders. Growing teacher leaders moves us from transactional change efforts to truly transformational change.

References

Collins, J. (2001). *Good to great: Why some companies make the leap . . . and others don't.* New York: HarperCollins.

DuFour, R., DuFour, R., Eaker, R., & Many, T. (2006). *Learning by doing: A handbook for professional learning communities at work.* Bloomington, IN: Solution Tree.

Fullan, M. (1997). Broadening the concept of teacher leadership. In S. Caldwell (Ed.), *Professional development in learning-centered schools* (pp. 34–39). Oxford, OH: National Staff Development Council.

Hargreaves, A., & Fink, D. (2007). *Sustainable leadership.* San Francisco: Jossey-Bass.

Kouzes, J., & Posner, B. (2002). *The leadership challenge* (3rd ed.). San Francisco: Jossey-Bass.

Pfeffer, J., & Sutton, R. (2006). *Hard facts, dangerous half-truths and total nonsense: Profiting from evidence-based management.* Boston: Harvard Business School.

Reeves, D. (2006a, May). Challenging the status quo: Of hubs, bridges and networks. *Educational Leadership, 63*(8), 32–37.

Reeves, D. (2006b). *The learning leader: How to focus school improvement for better results.* Alexandria, VA: Association for Supervision and Curriculum Development.

Schlechty, P. (1997). *Inventing better schools: An action plan for educational reform.* San Francisco: Jossey-Bass.

Tichy, N. (1997). *The leadership engine: How winning companies build leaders at every level.* New York: Harper Business.

Tichy, N., & Cardwell, N. (2004). *The cycle of leadership: How great leaders teach their companies to win.* New York: Harper Business.

AUSTIN BUFFUM

Austin Buffum, Ed.D., is retired as the senior deputy superintendent of the Capistrano Unified School District, which serves more than 50,000 students in South Orange County, California. For his excellent leadership, Dr. Buffum was selected 2006 Curriculum and Instruction Administrator of the Year by the Association of California School Administrators. During his 37-year career in public education, Dr. Buffum has been a music teacher and coordinator, elementary school principal, curriculum director, and assistant superintendent. In addition to articles published in the *Journal of Staff Development, American School Board Journal,* and *Leadership,* he is the coauthor of *Pyramid Response to Intervention: RTI, PLCs, and How to Respond When Kids Don't Learn* (Solution Tree, 2008). He now shares his in-depth knowledge of building and sustaining PLCs with schools, districts, and state departments of education throughout North America.

THREE

Trust: The Secret Ingredient to Successful Shared Leadership

Austin Buffum

> *The leaders who work most effectively, it seems to me, never say "I." And that's not because they have trained themselves not to say "I." They don't think "I." They think "we"; they think "team." They understand their job to be to make the team function. They accept responsibility and don't sidestep it, but "we" gets the credit. This is what creates trust, what enables you to get the task done.*
>
> —Peter Drucker

Professional learning communities are driven by the work of high-performing, collaborative teams—the "engine" of the PLC. Dukewits and Gowin (1996) concluded that effective teams are characterized by high levels of trust that result in open communication, mutual respect for people, and a willingness to participate in the work of the team. In the decades of literature on school reform, words like *trust, collegiality,* and *buy-in* appear frequently. Rebecca DuFour framed it this way:

> Trust is built over time. It goes back to the idea of leaders modeling their priorities through their behaviors. Teachers learn to trust their leaders when leaders do the things they are asking others to do. People, over time, will see that the norms leaders set and the commitments they make really do drive the work. They must recognize that leaders are going

to do what they say they'll do, rather than just talk about it. (Eaker, DuFour, & DuFour, 2002, p. 89)

This chapter will help principals and teachers identify the barriers to building trust between teachers on collaborative teams and between teachers and school administration, as well as offer concrete recommendations on how to repair, build, and maintain trust in a school setting.

Barriers to Building and Maintaining Trust

There are many scenarios that can destroy trust rather quickly in a school: salary negotiations that become embittered, press coverage that pits administration against teachers, controversial attendance boundary decisions, and the endless accountability struggles that consume teachers and administrators alike. While the list of potential threats to trust is nearly endless, Brewster and Railsback (2003) identified the following as the most common obstacles to building and maintaining trust in schools:

- Top-down decision-making that is perceived as arbitrary, misinformed, or not in the best interests of the school

- Ineffective communication

- Lack of follow-through on or support for school improvement efforts and other projects

- Unstable or inadequate school funding

- Failure to remove teachers or principals who are widely viewed to be ineffective

- Frequent turnover in school leadership (Brewster & Railsback, 2003, p. 10)

Perhaps the greatest obstacle to building trust in a school is the residue, regardless of its cause, from past issues. These take on "a life of their own" and are often exaggerated as they become part of the folklore of the school. As Jennifer James (2004) cautions us, "It becomes very hard to adapt, to tell the new stories, the ones you need to fit into the real world, if you cannot take apart the old stories." It is important for a staff to identify those stories from the past that are now obsolete or even destructive—to expose the fact that at best, they are no longer true, and at worst, they never were. It may take years for a faculty, accustomed to dictates issued from "on high," to fully receive and embrace the empowering message of the PLC—namely that the new knowledge needed to improve teaching and learning in a school best comes from a collaborative team of teachers deeply engaged in collective inquiry. It may take years for a faculty to forget a single instance in which common, formative assessment data was used solely to evaluate a teacher rather than to help them learn. Old stories must be challenged for their veracity or at least their timeliness and then replaced with new stories that fit the current reality and are believable.

Trust Between Principals and Teachers

There is nothing more important to the building of trust that will lead to highly effective collaborative teams than the relationships that exist between a school's principal and its teachers. "As it goes between teacher and principal," Boyd suggests, "so will it go in other relationships in the school. If the teacher-principal relationship can be characterized as helpful, supportive, trusting, so too will relationships between teachers, students, and parents" (1992, p. 6). According to Goodlad (1984), "a bond of trust and mutual support between principal and teachers . . . appears to be basic to school improvement" (p. 9). Who can deny that we live in a time of great cynicism about our leaders, our government, and even each other? If we are to experience a true sense of community, one in which we are looking out for the well-being of others as well as ourselves, then trust must become an important commodity in our schools. What, then, should a principal do to lay a foundation of trust in a school?

Operate With Honesty and Integrity

Highly respected principals demonstrate honesty and follow-through on commitments (Barlow, 2001; Blase & Blase, 2001; Sebring & Bryk, 2000). DuFour and Eaker (1998) described it this way: "Principals of professional learning communities acquire trust the old-fashioned way—they earn it. They deliver on promises. They impose on themselves the highest standard of congruence between their words and deeds" (p. 194).

While the ideal circumstance would find teachers and administrators alike operating with integrity and honesty, it is the responsibility of the principal to first set the tone for the ethos of the school by adhering to the "golden rule of leadership . . . do what you say you will do" (Kouzes & Posner, 1996, p. 107). A large measure of the cynicism in schools is created by the administrator who, like a politician, makes many promises, says what people want to hear, and then ignores much of what has been promised. Teachers at a middle school, for example, will watch carefully to see if their new principal will follow through on discipline referrals or will instead slowly gravitate toward the patterns of past principals who in a few months became too consumed with paperwork and parent complaints to follow up on promises made at the opening staff meeting.

Make Yourself Available

Principals earn trust—from teachers, students, and parents—by making themselves available. This goes beyond merely being "seen" or "management by walking around." Barlow (2001) states, "Once the leader takes the risk of being open, others are more likely to take a similar risk—and thereby take the first steps necessary to building a culture of trust" (p. 26).

As a new principal in a new school in a new town, Suzanne Michelony naturally took over the former principal's office at Little Chico Creek School without much thought. During her 12-year tenure at her former school, she had maintained an open-door policy; she expected the office staff and teachers to "pop in" to discuss whatever needed to be fixed, shared, and so on. Her new office at Little Chico Creek School was located off a narrow, poorly lit corridor that was out of the way of normal staff traffic. During her first month, Suzanne left the door to her office open, as usual, but few entered. Those that did gave her an apologetic look followed by, "I'm sorry for disturbing you. . . ." She felt left out, distanced from her new staff. She reasoned, "If I feel left out and distanced, what is my staff feeling?"

Principal Michelony noticed a conference room in the main office. It was directly in the traffic lane of teachers doing business with the office staff and close to the public entry door and staff mail room. Over a weekend, she moved all the contents from her office to the conference room. She left the large desk behind and instead found a round table for meetings.

On the following Monday, an hour before school started, the first of several teachers and staff stood at the door to comment on her new "digs." Weeks later, she reflected:

> It's been 2 months since the change, and I feel very connected to the staff. I know when people arrive. I have my usual staff visitors who plop down and relate school or personal information. I've learned of family celebrations, joys, and tribulations. I've learned of health difficulties, partner difficulties, and student difficulties. Staff are on the ready to assist me. One teacher even related that it was important for the staff to help me succeed. The secretary and clerk appreciate that I'm within "earshot" of parent interchanges giving me the ability to assist when necessary. The office procedures are no longer foreign. I feel comfortable jumping in and answering phones or answering a question from a community member or parent. I truly believe that it's not only an

open-door policy that is effective, but it's where that "open door" is situated.

Demonstrate a Caring Attitude

Principals earn the respect and trust of teachers when they demonstrate an authentic concern for the well-being of others on the staff or in the school community at large. This concern must not be surface or insincere—principals need to go beyond a question asked in passing to true concern (Sebring & Bryk, 2000). Kevin Rafferty from Chaparral Elementary School in Ladera Ranch, California, shared but one of many such stories in which principals have demonstrated true caring and concern:

> A former parent contacted me on behalf of a neighbor. The mother of one of our first-grade students is in and out of the hospital and hospice care dying from cancer right now. After appeals from the family to help the first-grade child with transportation home from school each day were met with a deaf ear by his previous school and the district office, I worked things out with a cadre of volunteers at our school to get the first-grade child home every day.

Listen

A principal who is unwilling or unable to listen to what others have to say reduces trust and makes others feel more isolated as well as frustrated (Blase & Blase, 2001). At R.H. Dana Elementary School in southern California, principal Chris Weber and his staff had good reason to celebrate. The percent of student subgroups scoring proficient or above had more than doubled in 2 years, and the achievement gap had decreased by 30 percent. Despite this success, Chris sensed that he wasn't communicating effectively with his staff. Morale wasn't as high as he would have liked, and teachers seemed anxious about their work. Chris decided to take three steps to improve the situation. Here's how he describes his plan:

1) Once a month, I host voluntary lunch meetings with one grade level a day. I have no agenda; teachers bring questions and concerns. Their suggestions often lead to their presentations about innovative ideas during staffwide collaboration time. And I provide the cookies. Participation on the part of teachers is nearly 100%.

2) I added recognition to my daily email to staff. I made a real effort to acknowledge the exceptional work, some of it relatively mundane and some of it incredibly progressive, that teachers were doing daily in their classrooms. I was neglecting this. . . . People want to be appreciated.

3) Lastly, I realized that the best way I communicate is informally and one on one. I made an effort to find teachers in the classrooms for a few minutes before or after school to simply chat and touch base. I can often get a pulse of the staff and address questions. I was always out and about, but I now make an effort to stay for 5 to 15 minutes (or longer) instead of 30 to 60 seconds.

Chris says, "While trying to change the world and progressively transform my school, I can't forget a very simple concept: Communication is key."

Encourage Risk-Taking

If we want teachers to be "learners," principals must provide a safety net for those teacher teams trying new things that don't work as hoped (Blase & Blase, 2001). When teachers are "left hanging in the wind" as a result of trying something new, experimentation and action research are set back for years to come.

Consider Mrs. Rodriguez, a third-grade teacher who approaches her principal, Mr. Franklin, about a field trip involving a boat that she wants her students to experience. After bringing up every reason not to allow the excursion, Principal Franklin concludes the conversation by saying, with a furrowed brow, "Well, let me think about it. Get back to me in a couple of weeks." If Mrs. Rodriguez should somehow return undeterred in a couple of weeks, his response is apt to be, "Okay, you may take the field trip, *but* if anything happens, I want you to know it's *your* responsibility." The Chinese use the same ideograph for both danger and opportunity, which suggests that a good question for Principal Franklin to ask would be, "What do you think the children might learn?" Then, after considering the real safety concerns of such a trip as well as the benefit to the students, if the trip is approved, he should convey to Mrs. Rodriguez that he will share responsibility for the decision—the ultimate safety net every teacher deserves.

Share Decision-Making

If we want teachers to behave and regard themselves as professionals, the principal must establish authentic processes to involve teachers in decision-making (Black, 1997). These opportunities must not be perceived as "pretend" participation in which the principal solicits input and then goes ahead with whatever he wanted in the first place. Roland Barth (1990) argues, "Without shared leadership, it is impossible for a shared culture to exist in a school" (p. 172). Schools can be a place in which everyone becomes a school leader in some way, especially when we recognize the relationship between leading and learning. Our most powerful learning occurs when we tackle an assignment we don't know how to do, when we want to know how to do it, and when what we do will impact others with whom we work. When teachers take leadership in something they care deeply about—piloting a new science curriculum, setting up a new software program for scoring common formative assessments—they have the opportunity for powerful learning. In this way, teacher leadership provides many occasions for teacher growth. When teachers are leading, they are learning—and thus we become a "community of learners."

Value Dissent

Teachers need to be able to share concerns and voice disagreement without fear of reprisal (Lien, Johnson, & Ragland, 1997). Blase and Blase (2001) recommend that principals "welcome and embrace conflict as a way to produce substantive, positive outcomes over the long run. Regarding conflict as potentially constructive helps build supportive human relationships because it allows us to deal with our differences in win–win ways" (p. 29).

Most successful relationships require productive conflict; however, in many work environments, conflict is seen as something to be avoided at all costs. It's important to differentiate between conflict that centers on personalities and that which centers on ideas. In all too many schools, teachers go to great lengths in avoiding any hint of conflict with another teacher over pedagogy or discipline, let alone challenging the administration over such issues. In his book *The Five Dysfunctions of a Team,* Patrick Lencioni (2002) directly links trust with the fear of conflict, reasoning that teams that lack trust are incapable of "engaging in unfiltered and passionate debate of ideas. Instead they resort to veiled discussions and guarded comments" (p. 188). Principals who model openness to healthy debate over ideas help to create a collaborative environment that encourages meaningful discussion and values dissent—keys to a functional team.

Don't Allow Accountability to Consume Teachers

Principals need to do everything possible to protect teachers from the negative aspects of accountability systems, especially those that fail to take into account progress in student achievement that is significant, yet falls short of a politically established standard: "As public criticism focuses on schools' inadequacies, teachers need to know that their principal values their efforts and senses their good intentions" (Bryk & Schneider, 2002, p. 129). When teachers feel unsupported by the principal, mistrust is likely to grow.

Principal Johnson worried all weekend about how he was going to frame for the staff the fact that his school had failed to make adequate yearly progress (AYP). Despite tremendous growth, two subgroups had fallen just short. What he decided to do really paid off. He committed to finding something good to celebrate every week at the school, rather than making everything revolve around AYP. Principal Johnson was highly strategic in identifying those things to be celebrated, always looking for behaviors consistent with those of collaborative teams within a PLC. For example, he spent the next year consistently celebrating teacher teams who had identified essential learnings, built common assessments and used them to inform their instruction, and provided timely systematic interventions to those students who didn't learn. By focusing on these small incremental steps and celebrating the teams exhibiting these kinds of PLC behavior, the end-of-year summative assessment took care of itself. One year later, the school made AYP and then some!

Make Certain That Teachers Have What They Need to Teach

When teachers know that their principal will fight to ensure that they have the basic books, supplies, and other materials—and that they don't have to wait for someone to realize they don't have what they need—their trust in and respect for that person grows (Kratzer, 1997). Teachers are also more willing to try new things when the administration is effective at finding the necessary resources to turn a new idea for teaching into reality. When teachers engage in collective inquiry and begin to ask for new resources based upon their research, administrators build trust by writing grants, providing teachers the opportunity to observe other classrooms or schools, asking the PTA to help purchase math manipulatives, and so on.

When teachers make such requests for new materials, it is also important for the principal to act *quickly* and to help teachers cut through the "red tape" so often found in school district purchasing offices. Teachers usually need supplies now, not in 4 months, and when they see the principal battling the bureaucracy to get them what they need quickly, trust grows.

Be Prepared to Confront Ineffective Teachers

A principal's unwillingness or inability to confront teachers who are obfuscating the will of the other teachers—or who are widely acknowledged as incompetent—will undermine the trust the principal is trying to build with the staff at large (Bryk & Schneider, 2003). Of course, this kind of action should be undertaken with great care and forethought; however, simply looking the other way or ignoring the "elephant in the room" will only serve to weaken the trust so necessary to building a culture of collaboration.

This also applies to districts unwilling to confront principals whose management style is anathema to the shared leadership necessary to facilitate PLCs. The following story comes from the assistant superintendent of instruction in a school district implementing PLCs districtwide:

> As I work with the Teacher's Association and teachers in general, I sometimes hear comments questioning the district's commitment to PLCs. As a cabinet we are struggling as we look at principals within the district and asking ourselves if each of them demonstrate a leadership style that facilitates the development of PLCs.
>
> We have one principal in particular that different staff members have come to me and shared stories of how he is dictatorial, doesn't follow through on his promises, and doesn't welcome the opinions of others. Last year I dealt with three sets of parents over concerns about this principal not listening and not appearing to genuinely care about their child. The superintendent and I have made a commitment that we will work with him this year to try to change some of this behavior, but that we will release him if he cannot or is not willing

to practice a more collaborative leadership style with his staff and community.

We believe that our behavior will demonstrate to "the troops" that we truly are committed to working collaboratively for the good of the children and want principals that demonstrate the behavior we are asking of teachers.

Trust Between Teachers

The previous section focused on how the principal and other school administrators can foster the development of trust. While the responsibility for building trust among teachers falls first upon the principal, "the behavior of teachers is the primary influence on trust in colleagues" (Tschannen-Moran & Hoy, 1998, pp. 348–349). If trusting relationships are needed to support the work of collaborative teams, teachers must also assume responsibility to identify barriers to trust and to work to improve or repair their own relationships. Following are some ideas that may help.

Make Relationships a Priority

There are numerous questionnaires and surveys that would help a faculty better understand the extent to which teachers trust each other in a building. At Whitaker Middle School in Portland, Oregon, teachers took responsibility for measuring, understanding, and then improving the level of trust between teachers. Plagued with low test scores, low staff morale, and high staff turnover, Whitaker applied for and received a Comprehensive School Reform grant in 2002. As part of the reform process, the school formed a Trust Evaluation Committee. The committee was comprised of 10 teachers, one school psychologist, one classified staff member, four support staff members, and seven community volunteers. They met for 5 months to analyze the results of several trust surveys and review the research on trust. Eventually, the committee recommended that two cofacilitators be employed to work with the entire staff to increase trust levels. As a result of these efforts, collaborative teams began to flourish at the school, and the teachers committed to a 5-year plan to continue addressing the all-important issue of trust between teachers.

Promote Relationship-Building Through Staff Development Models

Professional learning communities provide multiple opportunities for staff development; staff development in a PLC is deeply embedded in the work of teams as they answer the four essential questions of the PLC. Other models such as peer coaching, mentoring, and critical friends also bring teachers together in a way that can serve to strengthen relationships. Teachers at Southridge High School in Beaverton, Oregon, chose to implement PLC by using Critical Friends Groups (as developed by the Annenberg Institute for School Reform). In 2002, Southridge High School was recognized as an Exemplary Smaller Learning Communities Project site by the U. S. Department of Education. Principal Sarah Boly commented, "We had all of these wonderful smaller learning communities in place, but we didn't have staff-to-staff relationships built upon trust" (as quoted in Brewster & Railsback, 2003, p. 38). Boly believed that Critical Friends Groups would help teachers develop the emotional safety necessary to holding honest discussions about teaching and learning. State assessment results show continued gains for all subgroups at Southridge, and the school continues to gain recognition as a leader in developing smaller learning communities.

Involve the Staff in Discussions That Focus on the School's Mission, Vision, and Values

Trust among faculty members is built when teachers believe that everyone is acting upon the same mission, vision, and values. It is "grounded in common understandings about what students should learn, how instruction should be conducted, and how teachers and students should behave with one another. For teachers to sense integrity among colleagues, a faculty must not only share these views but also perceive that the actions taken by other teachers are consistent with them" (Bryk & Schneider, 2002, p. 130). Most of us express strong feelings about caring for and protecting children; it's one of the reasons we entered the profession. A few instances of flagrant disregard for children—even if only by one or two teachers—can have a disastrous impact on trust. Teachers are probably not going to collaborate openly about essential learnings and common formative assessments if unprofessional behavior about the safety and well-being of students goes unacknowledged and unchallenged.

Create Frequent, Meaningful Opportunities for Teachers to Work Together Collaboratively

Meaningful opportunities and authentic, trust-building relationships "are fostered by personal conversations, frequent dialogue, shared work, and shared responsibilities. As individuals interact with one another, they tend to listen across boundaries—boundaries erected by disciplines, grade levels, expertise, authority, position, race, and gender" (Lambert, 1998, p. 79). Beyond making time in the schedule for teachers to work together collaboratively, principals can help build trust between teachers by providing training to teachers on how to effectively lead and participate in team meetings (Blase & Blase, 2001). Principals would be well advised to heed the following advice from DuFour and Eaker (1998, p. 125):

> Providing teachers with time for collaboration does not ensure that they will engage in deep discourse about how they can achieve the goals of the school more effectively. . . . In the wrong school culture, the time set aside for educators to work together will simply reinforce the negative aspects of that culture.

Laying Tracks of Trust

This chapter has provided some working definitions of trust and made a number of recommendations on how principals can work to build and maintain trust within a school. It is important to remember, however, that we must not wait for everyone in a school to have established trust before we begin the essential work of the professional learning community. Robert Eaker (Eaker, DuFour, & DuFour, 2002, p. 89) put it this way:

> I simply don't think it makes sense to wait until everyone trusts each other, and then take off on our mission to become a professional learning community. Trust is something that's built incrementally over time. Of course, this puts tremendous responsibility on the part of leaders to continually manage their own behavior so that they can build trust and lead others. I think that the first time that the leader's behavior is incongruent with what they've been professing, it tends to just wipe out any trust that's been built. So you have to be very, very careful to make sure that your behavior is congruent with those values and commitments you've made.

The leader's buying doughnuts for meetings might encourage a feeling of collegiality and esprit de corps, but it doesn't build trust. School leaders need to see trust as the bridge that PLC reform must travel across, and that bridge is built incrementally through carefully made decisions and constant modeling by the leader.

So, as principals ask how to move forward with the important work of professional learning communities at our schools, we must not wait until everyone at the school trusts each other. On the other hand, we should heed the words of Karen Seashore Louis (2007), who cautions us not to proceed blindly without considering and attending to the important issue of trust: "The chronic individualism and isolation of the 'egg carton school' is currently viewed as an impediment to school reform and improvement, but simple initiatives to create professional learning communities in schools that are characterized by coherent distrust may be destined to fail if underlying issues contributing to that distrust are not addressed" (p. 20). If we truly believe that the collaborative team is the "engine" of the professional learning community, then spending time "laying tracks of trust" upon which that engine can propel itself forward is indeed time well-spent.

References

Barlow, V. (2001). *Trust and the principalship.* Unpublished manuscript, University of Calgary, British Columbia, Canada. Accessed at www.ucalgary.ca/cll/resources/ on October 5, 2007.

Barth, R. (1990). *Improving schools from within: Teachers, parents, and principals can make a difference.* San Francisco: Jossey-Bass.

Black, S. (1997). Creating community [Research Report]. *American School Board Journal, 184*(6), 32–35.

Blase, J., & Blase, J. R. (2001). *Empowering teachers: What successful principals do* (2nd ed.). Thousand Oaks, CA: Corwin.

Boyd, V. (1992). *School context: Bridge or barrier to change.* Southwest Educational Development Laboratory. Accessed at www.sedl.org/change/school/preface.html on October 22, 2007.

Brewster, C., & Railsback, J. (2003*). Building trusting relationships for school improvement: Implications for principals and teachers.* Portland, OR: Northwest Regional Educational Laboratory.

Bryk, A. S., & Schneider, B. (2002). *Trust in schools: A core resource for improvement.* New York: Russell Sage Foundation.

Bryk, A. S., & Schneider, B. (2003). Trust in schools: A core resource for school reform. *Educational Leadership, 60*(6), 40–45.

Chapman, R., Hinson, R., Hipp, K. A., Jacoby, C. L., Huffman, J. B., Pankake, A. M., Sattes, B., et al. (2000). *Multiple mirrors: Reflections on the creation of professional learning communities.* Austin, TX: Southwest Educational Development Laboratory.

Collins, J., & Porras, J. (1997). *Built to last: Successful habits of visionary companies.* New York: Harper Business.

Drucker, P. (1990). *Managing the non-profit organization.* New York: HarperCollins.

DuFour, R., & Eaker, R. (1998). *Professional learning communities at work: Best practices for enhancing student achievement.* Bloomington, IN: Solution Tree (formerly National Educational Service).

Dukewits, P., & Gowin, L. (1996). Creating successful collaborative teams. *Journal of Staff Development, 17*(4), 12–16.

Eaker, R., DuFour, R., & DuFour, R. (2002). *Getting started: Reculturing schools to become professional learning communities.* Bloomington, IN: Solution Tree (formerly National Educational Service).

Goodlad, J. (1984). *A place called school: Prospects for the future.* New York: McGraw-Hill.

James, J. (2004). *Telling a new story.* Accessed at www.jenniferjames.com/forum/telling.htm on October 22, 2007.

Kouzes, J., & Posner, B. (1996). Seven lessons for leading the voyage to the future. In F. Hesselbein, M. Goldsmith, & R. Beckhard (Eds.), *The leader of the future: New visions, strategies and practices for the next era* (pp. 99–110). San Francisco: Jossey-Bass.

Kratzer, C. C. (1997, March). *A community of respect, caring, and trust: One school's story.* Paper presented at the annual meeting of the American Educational Research Association, Chicago, IL. (ERIC Document Reproduction Service No. ED409654).

Lambert, L. (1998). *Building leadership capacity in schools.* Alexandria, VA: Association for Supervision and Curriculum Development.

Lencioni, P. (2002). *The five dysfunctions of a team: A leadership fable.* San Francisco: Jossey-Bass.

Lickona, T., & Davidson, M. (2005). *Smart and good high schools: Integrating excellence and ethics for success in school, work, and beyond.* Cortland, NY: Center for the 4th and 5th R's (Respect and Responsibility), and Washington, DC: Character Education Partnership.

Lien, L., Johnson, J. F., & Ragland, M. (with Anderson, K., Asera, R., Ginsberg, M., et al.). (1997). *Successful Texas school-wide programs: Research study results, school profiles, voices of practitioners and parents.* Austin: University of Texas, Charles A. Dana Center. (ERIC Document Reproduction Service No. ED406084).

Little, J. (1990). The persistence of privacy: Autonomy and initiative in teachers' professional relations. *Teachers College Record, 91*(4), 509–536.

Louis, K. S. (2007). Trust and improvement in schools. *Journal of Educational Change, 8*(1), 1–24.

Sebring, P. B., & Bryk, A. S. (2000). School leadership and the bottom line in Chicago. *Phi Delta Kappan, 81*(6), 440–443.

Tschannen-Moran, M., & Hoy, W. K. (1998). Trust in schools: A conceptual and empirical analysis. *Journal of Educational Administration, 36*(3/4), 334–352.

KENNETH C. WILLIAMS

With 14 years experience in public education, Kenneth C. Williams, M.S. Ed., has provided enthusiastic leadership in a variety of ways. Skilled in developing productive, student-focused learning environments, Ken is a distinguished teacher, mentor, public speaker, and school leader. He fills his presentations with the same intelligence, energy, and humor that have made him such a positive presence in the lives of his students and colleagues. Ken was the hands-down selection for the principalship of Damascus Elementary School in Damascus, Maryland. His leadership was crucial to creating a successful professional learning community at Damascus, a challenged school that needed a new direction. The results of his efforts can be seen across all grade levels. Over a 2-year period, the school's state standardized test scores revealed a significant increase in the percentage of students performing at proficient and advanced levels. He is the principal of The Learning Academy at E. J. Swint Elementary in Jonesboro, Georgia.

FOUR

From C to Shining C: Relational Leadership Practices That Move Teachers From Compliance to Commitment

Kenneth C. Williams

> *It is possible to be tough-minded and adamant about protecting purpose and priorities while also being tender with people.*
>
> —Richard DuFour, Rebecca DuFour,
> Robert Eaker, & Thomas Many

A growing research trend identifies leadership as a relationship—a relationship between those whose goal it is to lead, and those whose desire it is to follow. The PLC movement has charged school leaders all over the world to lead and facilitate a process of school improvement that ensures learning for all. Ensuring the learning of every student requires more than *compliance,* however. Learning for all students requires deep levels of *commitment* from all stakeholders, and that commitment is nurtured through principals developing relationships with teachers that foster trust, integrity, collaboration, and ownership. The ambitious mission of learning for all can only be accomplished through the deep commitment of teachers. Successfully leading a school through the process of becoming a professional learning community is a function of how much we focus on people and relationships as an essential component of attaining results. This style of leadership is not aligned with quick-fix command and control measures that typically yield brief spurts of improvement. Professional learning communities require sustained leadership and a sincere and genuine connection with teachers.

What Do We Mean by *Compliance* and *Commitment*?

First, we must clarify that this is not a metaphor describing good versus evil, effective versus ineffective, or right versus wrong. Moving from compliance to commitment is a developmental journey that every school experiences. Before we fully understand, embrace, and implement a professional learning community, we start with a list of goals to accomplish. It is my contention that aspects of relational leadership provide the bridge between teachers accomplishing tasks out of compliance and teachers embedding PLC practices out of commitment. So compliance is a necessary stage along the journey; the goal is to take steps each day to work toward committed behaviors and a learning culture.

Each leader has to assess where the school is with regard to its learning culture. Some leaders will find that they are starting at compliance. Others will start with compliance as an early goal. Schools with well-established learning and performance cultures will enter the journey further along the compliance and commitment continuum. For example, in my first year as principal of The Learning Academy at E. J. Swint, I inherited a school with a known record for academic failure—the worst-performing elementary school in our district. The school's culture was toxic, and the need for leadership was clear. We had adult attendance issues that mirrored our student attendance issues. Our effective teachers were overwhelmed by the entrenched culture of negativity, blame shifting, low expectations, and failure. So as ambitious and far-reaching as my vision was for E. J. Swint, my first goal was staff compliance. The continuum for our school started long before compliance, and in fact, for a good portion of my first year, compliance was actually the result we worked for. We celebrated, learned from, and built upon compliance.

Four Strategies for Building Commitment

This chapter will address four strategies leaders can apply to capitalize on relational leadership opportunities. Each of the four strategies will be addressed from five different angles.

The Quote: Each strategy will open with a quote to "set the stage." Quotes are often memorable not only for *what* they say, but also *how* they say it. The quote at the opening of each section will underscore the theme and direction of the section. It is meant to remind, provoke, engage, and inspire you to take action in the direction of building commitment.

The Question: Because relational leadership does not always lend itself to concrete and quantifiable data, it is easy to read a list of leadership behaviors and conclude that we do most or all these things. To get the most out of this chapter, take the time to really consider the question for each strategy—as a tool to prompt self-reflection or to elicit feedback from teachers and peers. A simple awareness of the questions as you go about the work of leading a professional learning community will improve your results.

The Mindset: Unlike traditional top-down, command-and-control approaches to leadership, relational leadership in PLC has many layers and multiple roles. There are times when your leadership will be "out in front," times when your leadership is "behind the scenes" in a more supportive role, and times when your approach will be collaborative or directive. Clarifying your mindset will help you support teachers and students more effectively.

The Mission: Here we will clarify outcomes. In my leadership, I work daily to be results-oriented and outcomes-focused. Every conversation I initiate, every meeting I have, every task that I ask of our staff, and every type of support I provide has a clear outcome—outcomes that I have identified beforehand. This focus on outcomes helps to keep all activities and interactions on a productive path. The truth is that every action, interaction, and circumstance has an outcome. The more intentional we are about the outcomes we desire, the more likely that we will bring those outcomes into being.

The Motion: The architects of the PLC movement tell us, "When people begin to act, people begin to hope. When people begin to gain hope, they begin to behave differently. When people behave differently, they experience success. When people experience success, their attitudes change. When a person's attitude changes, it affects other people. This is the essence of reculturing schools into professional learning communities" (DuFour, DuFour, Eaker, & Many, 2006, p. 6). Motion is where the "rubber meets the road." Recommended strategies only have meaning when we take action. In this section I will provide some examples of concrete, actionable steps a principal can begin taking *tomorrow* to build the relationship bridge from compliance to commitment. The suggestions are those that worked at my school. They may or may not work in your situation. The intended outcome of explaining these strategies is to:

- Provide you with a place to start taking action.

- Activate your thinking about your own school's culture.

- Generate ideas and opportunities that will work with your school.

Please note: If you are looking for a quick fix for earning and building the commitment of teachers, you won't find it in this chapter. In my experience, there is no such thing. It takes an action-oriented commitment to create positive transformation. May your practice be positively affected through your engagement in the following strategies.

Strategy 1: Lead With a "Can't Do" Attitude

Effective school cultures don't simply encourage individuals to go off and do whatever they want, but rather establish clear

parameters and priorities that enable individuals to work within established boundaries in a creative and autonomous way. They are characterized by directed empowerment or a culture of discipline with an ethic of entrepreneurship.

—Richard DuFour, Rebecca DuFour,
Robert Eaker, & Thomas Many

> **The Question:** How important is it to allow for a growth period of mistakes, misunderstandings, and misfires when building commitment? As the leader, what should be my approach to this growth period?

The Mindset: Most challenges with implementation can be looked at through two different lenses.

1. Is this a "won't do" issue? (The team or individual knows what to do and deliberately chooses not to.)

2. Is this a "can't do" issue? (The team or individual needs more support, clarification, questions answered, templates, tools, information, and so on.)

I address a majority of our PLC implementation challenges with a "can't do" approach. Regardless of how clear you believe your communication and support to be, there are always instances when what you say is interpreted differently than you intended. A can't-do approach lends itself to several potential positive outcomes:

- You are instantly in a supportive role.

- You have given teachers the benefit of the doubt that they, too, want to achieve the desired results.

- You allow people who "won't do" to "save face" in a supportive and positive environment.

- Your supportive approach has the potential to yield more positive strategies and ideas for improvement than a confrontational approach.

Leading with a can't-do attitude begins with a results-oriented and outcomes-focused mindset. As the principal, I take 100% responsibility for everything that happens at my school . . . *everything*. All problem-solving begins with me reflecting on how I could have contributed to the outcome.

> **The Mission:** To move teams and individuals to achieve desired results by giving the benefit of the doubt when results have not been achieved; to move teams forward in as productive and positive an environment as possible

The Motion: Look for opportunities to confront issues that seem to show noncompliance. Begin with the assumption that the team or individual requires more support, additional information, templates, or tools. Ask what *you* can do to help them meet the expectation. As the leader, you have to take the position that you have always had the power to make it different, to get it right, and to produce desired results. Regardless of the issue, ask yourself a battery of questions such as:

- How did I create this situation?

- How have I contributed to this situation?

- What was I thinking with regard to that situation?

- What did I say or not say?

- What did I do or not do to create that result?

- How did I get the team (or person) to act that way?

- What can I do differently next time to get the results I want?

- What does this situation say about me as a leader?

Strategy 2: Get Close to the Work

Titles are granted, but it's your behavior that wins you respect.

—James Kouzes & Barry Posner

> **The Question:** How can I as the principal deepen the level of buy-in and commitment of teachers?

The Mindset: There is a lot to be said for communicating a strong vision, providing time and resources for teachers to collaborate, and supporting all of the initiatives related to the development of a professional learning community. However, few things have the impact, speak as loudly, or build as much leadership credibility as when the principal gets involved hands-on in any aspect of implementation. When the principal gets close to any part of the work, he can be a direct support to the improvement efforts. When the principal takes on responsibilities involving initiatives that he has asked teachers to be responsible for, his credibility grows in the eyes of teachers.

My only caution to principals is to keep things in perspective with regard to how much you take on. It's not necessarily *how much* you do, but *that* you do. This is a judgment call you need to carefully consider depending on the size and leadership culture of your school. Regardless of the size of the school or the scope of responsibilities, all principals can find at least one area to contribute *along with* teachers. Your understanding of the day-to-day work will deepen, allowing you to more effectively support teams of teachers, and you will communicate by deed what your school holds as high value and high priority. Moller and Pankake (2006) note that "the principal's presence signals that the work being done is important, and teachers perceive this as an acknowledgement that their efforts are being recognized and appreciated" (p. 80).

The Mission: To walk your talk; to better understand adult and student learning on a daily basis; to serve as a support for teams; to build credibility in the eyes of your teachers

The Motion: Look for opportunities to get closer to where the work is happening. The bonus is that very often verification and monitoring take care of themselves as you get close to the work, without the trust-busting practice of "snoopervision."

Following are opportunities to be visibly hands-on with PLC implementation.

- Mentor a student in your Save One Student program or another mentoring program that may be part of your pyramid of interventions. Ask every staff member to mentor one student.

- Attend one collaborative team meeting per assigned grade level per week—as an observer. When we don't take the traditional, sometimes invasive supervisory approach, we seek to be seen as an asset to the team dynamic.

- Attend and participate in all professional development activities and in-services. Your presence sends the message that professional learning is important.

- Participate in your school's learning support programs. In our school, Success Street is a 30-minute block to provide students with extra time and support on a daily basis as part of our pyramid of interventions. Every staff member not already assigned to homeroom is assigned a classroom to support on a daily basis. My assistant principal and I combine to provide Success Street tutoring to one of our kindergarten homerooms. When teachers see us working on a daily basis with a small group of learners, it sends a message of collective commitment, shared values, and shared responsibility.

Strategy 3: Give Others a Reputation to Uphold

The essential challenge of the leader is not attaining perfection but acknowledging imperfection and obtaining complementarities. Rather than developing what they lack, great leaders will magnify their own strengths and simultaneously create teams that do not mimic the leader but provide different and equally important strengths for the organization.

—Douglas Reeves

The Question: What steps can I take to use the diverse talents of teachers and teams to embed many of the practices of a PLC?

The Mindset: The best leaders believe that no matter what their role, or where they are with regard to performance level, people can achieve the high standards that have been set. It's called the Pygmalion effect, and it's a belief so strong that even if others don't believe in themselves initially, the leader's belief—or the teacher's or parent's or colleague's—gives rise to new self-confidence, to a belief that "yes, I *can* do it." Your belief becomes a self-fulfilling prophecy of success.

I have always held in high regard those influential people in my life who saw more in me than I saw in myself and who challenged me to stretch and get better. In a PLC, part of the principal's role is to look for, discover, and tap into the gifts and talents of the teachers on staff. Connecting with people often requires principals to once again tap into the visionary side of leadership—to see beyond a person's self-imposed limitations and expectations. Just as teachers see the potential in students, principals have to see the stretch potential of every teacher, hold that crown of vision and achievement above their heads, and as Howard Thurman once said, "challenge them to grow tall enough to wear it." Do more than settle for compliance. Intentionally look for and find opportunities to utilize the talents and strengths to move the professional learning community forward.

See more in others than they see in themselves, guide them to and through successful pursuits, and you will build a coalition of teacher leaders poised to answer the call of learning for all.

It takes just as much vision to recognize and embrace our own shortcomings and to use them as the lens by which we cultivate and develop other leaders. Showing vulnerability is one of the most powerful tools in the development of collective leadership; it takes the conversation beyond "you can do it" and into the often awkward realm of "I need you." Demonstrating the need for someone's skills and talents due to your own skill deficits is a powerful building tool. It not only speaks to the innate human need to feel a sense of purpose, but it also humanizes you as a leader, debunking the myth of the all-knowing leader. Showing vulnerability is a tremendous risk. In admitting shortcomings, you are exposing powerful information about yourself to others. I have found that when I reveal my vulnerabilities and communicate need, leaders from all areas will line up to engage, participate, and give assistance.

> **The Mission:** To build trust by making yourself vulnerable; to capitalize on the leadership potential of your vulnerability by developing and distributing leadership opportunities that bolster your shortcomings or areas of deficit

The Motion: Be visible. Visibility and credibility can go hand in hand. The ability to influence teachers to improve their practice through participating in a professional learning community depends a lot on how teachers view the principal in terms of her competence, credibility, and approachability. Much of this is positively enhanced by visibility. Visibility not only keeps you in touch with what is going on, but shows teachers how much their work is valued. With the minute-to-minute changes in a leader's day, it's easy to stay busy and relatively invisible, so schedule for visibility. Once I made being visible a part of my daily calendar, it became a priority. Schedule for visibility with students as well as with teachers during professional learning activities.

- Offer to facilitate the development of team norms.

- Attend collaborative team meetings.

- Attend a professional development session when able.

- Make yourself vulnerable, and be the first to trust. Vulnerability is the foundation of trust. According to Kouzes and Posner (2002), trust is built when we make ourselves vulnerable to others whose subsequent behavior we cannot control. If principals of a PLC want the high levels of performance that come with trust and collaboration, then they must first show trust in others before asking trust from others (Kouzes & Posner, 2002).

- Keep a running list in your PDA or organizer of opportunities to say thank you or to celebrate. Often, the moment at hand isn't ideal for recognition or celebration. Maintaining a running list of people to thank and recognize increases the chances of you showing gratitude and recognizing accomplishments when time permits.

- Carry notecards. I make it a practice to keep several notecards on my person in the event that I see something that I can respond to immediately or find myself with some time to review my running list of people to thank and recognize. A handwritten personalized note card is a low-cost, highly valued practice. In light of instant communication, a handwritten note of thanks and appreciation is often regarded as a cherished symbol. Its impact is not to be underestimated.

Strategy 4: Search for Opportunities to Celebrate

If people know there's a caring leader in their midst, patrolling the organization in search of achievements to celebrate, it only stands to reason that they'll be stimulated to show you something you can honor and celebrate. They relax and want to offer the best of themselves. This positive focus on behavior and performance, linked to goals and values, significantly improves morale as it moves the company toward higher levels of performance and increased productivity.

—James Kouzes & Barry Posner

The Question: How can I use celebration as a powerful tool for communicating what is valued in a professional learning community?

The Mindset: The most high-leverage mindset to adopt regarding celebrations is that there is a continuum of celebratory opportunities, from a thumbs-up to a fireworks display and everything in between. Often people associate celebration with the accomplishment of an ambitious goal. While this is true, principals in a professional learning community should also take advantage of the countless smaller opportunities along the journey of becoming a PLC. All celebration should be aligned with the larger vision and with student achievement.

Early in my tenure at The Learning Academy at E. J. Swint, I thought of celebration as a far-off target we would eventually hit. I had to learn to embrace the idea that our daily work presents us with opportunities for sincere praise and recognition along the way, eventually leading to us fulfilling our ultimate vision. No matter what stage of development your school culture is in, you can find reasons to celebrate. In the beginning, celebration at my school began as recognizing the completion of tasks and products related to PLC implementation. Based on the cultural changes we were experiencing, completing anything in a timely manner was an accomplishment. This recognition of relatively small victories provided an opportunity to reinforce highly valued behaviors that I expected others would eventually emulate. As time progressed, we slowly raised the expectation bar for celebrations, aligning them more directly with student achievement results. The bottom line is that you have to go looking for reasons to celebrate. You must then make the celebration public as often as possible. For those you celebrate, this will create the desire to succeed again. For others, it will create a desire to join the recognized.

> **The Mission:** To take every opportunity to remind everyone of what is most important on this PLC journey; to recognize individual and team excellence; to let the recognized behavior be a model for others

The Motion: Early in the PLC implementation process, recognize teams for taking risks, accomplishing tasks, and meeting deadlines:

- Recognize teams for honoring the process of developing norms and protocols.

- Recognize teams for identifying essential learnings and developing common formative assessments.

- Eventually, raise the performance standard, and recognize the application of these products and the resulting student and adult learning.

- Plan for a celebration-focused walkthrough. Make looking for any opportunity to celebrate the focus of your visits. Carry a large (5" x 5") pad of sticky notes, and leave encouraging notes on learning-centered bulletin boards or on exemplary student work.

- Make celebration everyone's responsibility. Form a staff celebrations committee. Provide opportunities for every staff member to publicly recognize when they admire the work of a teammate or colleague.

- Create opportunities for many winners.

An Enduring Foundation

In the end, success in a professional learning community is directly correlated to how well people work together. An effective PLC leader builds a bridge between teacher compliance and teacher commitment through relationships. While there is irrefutable evidence that PLCs are driven by the work of collaborative teams, the relational leadership practices of principals cannot be discounted. Building and sustaining strong, productive, and viable human relationships will enable you to bring forth and nurture your staff's gifts and talents, for the benefit of student learning. Effective relationships that lead to better achievement results take place in direct proportion to the willingness of the principal to stretch. In a professional learning community, leadership competencies must begin with the individual and grow from the inside out. As Doug Reeves tells us, "Relational leadership does not depend on false affirmations provided in vain attempts to build the self-esteem of subordinates, but rather on the trust and integrity that are at the foundation of any enduring relationship" (2006, p. 39). *Regate a fronte* is Latin for *lead from the front*; model what you expect, and "be the first to trust" (Kouzes & Posner, 2002).

Leadership consists of a set of learned skills that with practice can be utilized successfully to improve individual human effectiveness and to build lasting relationships. We must move from the narrow view that leadership is about efficiency, control, and stability in maintaining the status quo toward an understanding of leadership as encompassing effectiveness, continuous improvement, innovation, empowerment, and relationships. Our largest renewable resource and most important asset is decidedly the teachers we work with, support, and serve.

References

DuFour, R., DuFour, R., Eaker, R., & Many, T. (2006). *Learning by doing: A handbook for professional learning communities at work*. Bloomington, IN: Solution Tree.

Fullan, M. (2001). *Leadership in a culture of change*. San Francisco: Jossey-Bass.

Fullan, M. (2006). *Turnaround leadership*. San Francisco: Jossey-Bass.

Kouzes, J., & Posner, B. (2002). *The leadership challenge*. San Francisco: Jossey-Bass.

Moller, G., & Pankake, A. (2006). *Lead with me: A principal's guide to teacher leadership*. Larchmont, NY: Eye on Education.

Reeves, D. (2006). *The learning leader: How to focus school improvement for better results*. Alexandria, VA: Association for Supervision and Curriculum Development.

CHARLES HINMAN

 Charles Hinman, Ed.D., has 15 years' experience as a high school administrator and is assistant superintendent of education in the Newport Mesa Unified School District in Costa Mesa, California. An innovative leader who constantly challenges himself, his staff, and his students, Dr. Hinman carefully researched the Professional Learning Communities at Work™ model for school improvement before successfully implementing the concepts at San Clemente High School in the Capistrano Unified School District, where he served as principal for 5 years. Through implementation of a PLC, San Clemente High School saw improvement in virtually every measurable category and became a California Distinguished School. Dr. Hinman received his doctorate in educational administration from the University of Southern California.

George Knights

As principal of Newhart Middle School in the Capistrano Unified School District (CUSD) of Orange County, California, George Knights demonstrates a leadership style that exemplifies his commitment to professional learning communities. Previously, George played a key role in building a PLC that reversed a trend of underperformance at San Clemente High School (also in the CUSD), and ultimately landed the school in the top 2% of America's best-performing high schools, as reported by *Newsweek* (May 16, 2006).

Jeffrey Hubbard

Dr. Jeffrey Hubbard is superintendent of the Newport Mesa Unified School District and previously served as superintendent of the Beverly Hills Unified School District. He is a strong advocate of professional learning communities and believes PLCs hold the key to educational reform. Dr. Hubbard is a member of the USC Dean's Superintendent Advisory Group, Pepperdine University Dean's Superintendent Advisory Group, the Association of California School Administrators, and the California School Boards Association.

FIVE

A Passion-Driven Professional Learning Community: Putting Faith Into Action

Charles Hinman
With George Knights and Jeffrey Hubbard

"It's not about you." This is the opening sentence and basis of Rick Warren's bestselling book, *The Purpose Driven Life* (2001). The book's premise is that the true purpose of life is found not in self-absorption, but through faith in action. As educators, our true purpose is to ensure all children learn at higher levels, and our educational faith is measured by the actions we take to ensure our purpose. Unfortunately, while most educators enter the profession with conviction of purpose, many lose faith. Countless internal and external factors convince them to accept the norm: educational social Darwinism.

As administrators, we must not only help build the foundation of a professional learning community; we must also help those who have lost the passion for our purpose. We must rebuild their willingness to put faith into action. This chapter will provide activities designed to help administrators drive this renewal process to become a passion-driven professional learning community.

Renewing the Heart

The power of the heart is not something that one manufactures; rather, it is something that one discovers, or better yet, recovers. Renewal is the process of striking a chord in the soul—giving an emotional reminder of the passion that drew us into education in the first place. Tapping into the power of purpose and faith to fuel a professional learning community can help change even the most hardened soul. In a profession in which compliance has taken the place of creativity, appealing to the heart might be one of the most overlooked yet effective tools a leader has to impact change.

Fear of Resisters

Resisters are one of the biggest obstacles to the cultural changes required to become a professional learning community. Many administrators will not even attempt change for fear of a battle of wills with resisters. But this battle is unnecessary. When Jim Collins (2001) asked great businesses, "How did you address resisters during your transformation from good to great?" he found that successful CEOs could not even understand the question. Addressing resistance was not a key challenge in building commitment (Collins, 2001):

> Clearly, the good-to-great companies did get incredible commitment and alignment—they artfully managed change—but they never really spent much time thinking about it. It was utterly transparent to them. We learned that under the right conditions, the problems of commitment, alignment, motivation, and change just melt away. They largely take care of themselves. (p. 178)

For these companies, there was no "miracle moment." Rather, greatness came gradually as a result of hundreds of seemingly insignificant pushes. Discipline, passion, and unrelenting purpose made the difference.

A passion-driven professional learning community develops in the same way. Through a constant mantra about our purpose, and through the consistent evaluation of our faith in action, our leadership becomes transparent to followers and resisters alike. Emotional intelligence research tells us that it is not what you do, but rather how you do it that makes all the difference. Consider this quote from *Primal Leadership:*

> Great leaders move us. They ignite our passion and inspire the best in us. When we try to explain why they are so effective, we speak of strategy, vision, or powerful ideas. But the reality is much more primal: Great leadership works through emotions. No matter what leaders set out to do, whether it's creating strategy or mobilizing teams into action, their success depends on how they do it. Even if they get everything else just right, if leaders fail in this primal task of driving emotions in the right direction, nothing they do will work as well as it could or should. (Goleman, Boyatzis, & McKee, 2002, p. 3)

The following activities help educators recover their passion and fuel the momentum to become a purposeful learning community. These are just a few of countless possible activities. Start somewhere, anywhere, with any activity or strategy that will remind teachers why they became teachers in the first place, and the results will speak for themselves.

The Fundamental Belief

Before you begin the process of implementing a professional learning community—before you talk about what it is you want children to learn, how you know if they have learned it, and how will you respond if they do not learn—you and your staff need to identify your core beliefs. Through this simple activity, you can begin the process of defining the core values of your team. **Note:** While the questions in this activity have been tested in workshops throughout North America, you may want to change them slightly to best fit your situation.

Here's How

At a teachers' meeting, talk about the importance of understanding our fundamental beliefs about our roles as educators. Tell the teachers that you are going to lead them through a series of questions that are intended to help in the process of identifying the *organization's* core beliefs. Your role will only be as a facilitator; do not comment on or judge their responses. The power of this activity lies in participants' free responses and in their ability to reflect on those responses.

Question 1: *Why did you go into this profession? Please take a moment to discuss with the person sitting next to you.*

After 3 or 4 minutes, ask for a few volunteers to share their stories. You will likely hear similar messages about wanting to help and teach children.

Question 2: *Is it okay for a 13-year-old student to choose to fail? Please take a moment to discuss with the person sitting next to you.*

After 3 to 4 minutes, tell the staff that you are going to walk around the room and randomly select teachers to answer the question. The only answers that you will accept are Yes, No, or I Pass. Some will want to explain their answers. Do not let them; hold them to the three options. Move quickly throughout the room, and randomly point to teachers. Periodically repeat the question, and always repeat the answer to ensure it is heard. You will likely get a good ratio of each response. Without judgment, ask: "Is it fair that students have classes from teachers with different values?" Do not allow discussion. Move on quickly.

Potential follow-up to Question 2: *Should 13-year-olds select their own courses and levels?*

Question 3: *Which is more important, student learning or teaching responsibility? I realize that the true answer is a certain combination of both, but for this process, you must pick one. Please take a moment to discuss with the person sitting next to you.*

After 3 to 4 minutes, tell the staff that you are going to walk around the room and randomly select teachers to answer the question.

The only answers that you will accept are Learning, Responsibility, or I Pass. Some will want to explain their answers. Do not let them. Move quickly throughout the room, and randomly point to teachers. Periodically repeat the question, and always repeat the answer to make sure it is heard. You will likely get a good ratio of each response. Without judgment, ask: "Is it fair that students have classes from teachers with different priorities?" Do not allow discussion. Move on quickly.

Question 4: *Consider this scenario. In a first-semester freshman English class, a student has a score of 45% going into the final. This student has been a discipline problem the entire semester and has not done much homework. No matter what score this student receives on the final, he cannot pass. The entire semester was designed so that students understand the fundamentals and concepts of writing a five-paragraph essay; the final is the culmination of that effort. Since you do not trust this student, you stand over him and watch him write his essay so you know he did not cheat. When you grade the essay, you find that it is perfection. He learned every first-semester English standard. What semester grade do you assign? Take a moment and discuss it with the person sitting next to you. [Modify the example for your school's grade level if necessary.]*

After 3 to 4 minutes, tell the staff that you are going to walk around the room and randomly select teachers to answer the question. The only answers that you will accept are A, B, C, D, F, or I Pass. Some will want to explain their answers. Do not let them. Move quickly throughout the room, and randomly point to teachers. Periodically repeat the question, and always repeat the answer. You will likely get a good ratio of each response. Without judgment, rhetorically ask: "Does anyone see a problem here? Is it fair that a student doing the same work in Teacher A's classroom gets a significantly different grade in Teacher B's classroom?"

Then ask these important follow-up rhetorical questions:

What class should this student be placed in next year, remedial or honors? What class would our current system assign?

Here's Why

This activity is designed to take teachers out of their comfort zone of isolation. It creates a purpose-filled debate about how we measure student success and the consistency of our assessment practice—how our policies reflect "faith in action."

The Results

During this activity, emotions will probably run high. This is why your role is only to mediate, not to judge. Through discussion, even the most hardened positions begin to soften.

Follow-up rhetorical questions will allow the conversation to continue beyond the general meeting. At the conclusion of the meeting, give a copy of the activity to your leadership team, department chairs, or team leaders, and ask them to discuss the additional questions in a smaller forum with their teams. The next time you meet with the leaders, see if you can come to consensus on the staff's core values.

Is This Acceptable?

There is tremendous power in combining data with the right question. Simply put, are the results of your data acceptable to your staff? This idea first came to us from Rick DuFour when he stated that part of becoming a PLC was making public what had traditionally been private. In this era of compliance, we have become adept at celebrating our successes—pass rates, standardized proficiency rates, school rankings, and so on—yet we typically do not make public our areas of concern—dropout rates, truancy rates, failure rates, below-proficiency rates, and so on. This strategy challenges a staff to examine all the data.

Here's How

The easiest way to start this activity is to create a simple bar graph of students who have received one or more F grades (or equivalent for primary grades) in a given school year (see Figure 5-1 for an example). Another easy way to start is with state test results that show the percentage of students below or far below proficient (see Figure 5-2, page 96). Once you show the data, give your staff time to think about it. Then ask: "Is this acceptable? Is it acceptable that this many of our students are failing or are below/far below proficient?"

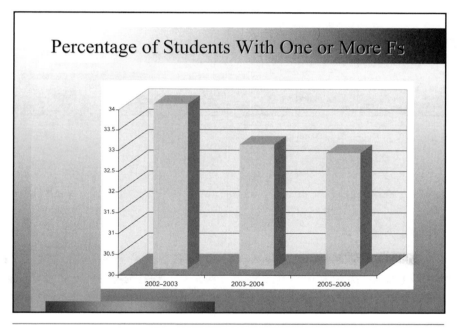

Figure 5-1. Percentage of Students With One or More Fs

CST Score, Third-Grade Language Arts

- **24% advanced**
- **30% proficient**
- **20% basic**
- **16% below basic**
- **10% far below basic**

Figure 5-2: State Test Results

It is best to have very little conversation about what data you are going to make public until it is put up on a screen for all to see.

Here's Why

Making public what has traditionally been private will challenge the naturally competitive nature of the staff. While it is vital to celebrate your successes, it is just as vital to share where improvement is needed.

The Results

When a staff sees this type of information, they often become defensive. Be strong. Continuously remind teachers that no indictment is meant or implied by data.

Seeing the F data generates questions such as:

- How many of those Fs are truancies?

- How many of those Fs are nonsuits?

- How many of those Fs are students who don't do their homework?

- How many of those Fs are students who don't care?

The answer to each of these responses should be "I don't know." The initial point of this exercise is to reflect on the data and to ask whether it is acceptable. The staff will likely conclude that it is not. At this point, the power of purpose turns to faith in action: They will want to dig deeper to find out who, find out why, and then find a solution!

Impact Assignment

To gather momentum in a nontraditional way, consider this strategy. It seems to be only a team-building activity, but it builds purpose behind the scenes. This activity was inspired by Denny Bellesi, a former pastor of Coast Hills Church in Aliso Viejo, California. He once called 100 parishioners up to the stage and gave each a $100 bill. Their "Kingdom Assignment" was simple: Go out into the community, and do as much good as possible. The results of this experiment literally changed a congregation and community (Bellesi & Bellesi, 2003), and they can change your school, too.

Here's How

Write a series of simple team-building tasks on slips of paper, and put them into envelopes to pass out at a staff development meeting. Here are a few activity examples:

- Find two new teachers, introduce yourself, and discuss why you became a teacher.

- Tell two people about your favorite teacher growing up; describe why he or she was your favorite.

- Start a conversation with someone you have never spoken with at length.

- Say thank you to someone who you know has done a great job for our school and may have otherwise gone unnoticed.

- Choose an administrator, and share an idea to help students feel more connected to school.

- Initiate a discussion with a colleague regarding best practice. Continue the conversation until you each discover a valuable method or practice that you haven't tried in your classrooms. Agree to provide supplemental materials to each other to help implement the new practices.

- Think of someone who has positively impacted your teaching, and let that person know specifically what it was and how he or she made a difference to you.

- Share a program or idea that you have observed at another school that you feel could benefit our school. Talk about what it would take to implement the idea at our school.

Stuff an envelope for each teacher (duplicating tasks is fine). However, in some of the envelopes, instead of the task, insert a $20 bill with a note saying, "Use this $20 bill to make a difference in the life of a student. You are free to use it in any way you wish. Nobody knows that you have it. If you like, please send me an anonymous note and let me know what happened and the impact that you made." Distribute the envelopes, and explain that some contain money instead of a task; reiterate that this is confidential and that no one knows who received the money. **Note:** Funding for this project can be handled in varying ways, but initially, the most powerful impact is if the administration donates to this activity.

Here's Why

The current staff development event will buzz with the audacity of this "pay it forward" activity, and later, emails and personal accounts of the compassion teachers have for students will extend the buzz long past the initial investment. In some cases, the full impact takes months to develop, but the impact is deep, especially for those who serendipitously receive the charge to make a difference.

The Results

The results are amazing. One teacher, Wendy, stood up in a faculty meeting and shared that she was initially angry about receiving the impact assignment. After all, she taught honors classes, and her students were all disciplined and stable. She then related her experience with the ninth-grade girl she chose for the impact assignment. After noticing that this student's grades were slipping, Wendy purchased a simple make-up kit and gave it to her after class. Through the joy of learning that someone cared, the teary-eyed girl shared that her father had been put in prison and she had been removed from her home. The two cried together for some time, and Wendy began mentoring the student from that point on. Through this simple impact assignment, a life was changed. As Wendy related this story to the staff, there was not a dry eye in the room.

Jeff, a math teacher, took a different approach. He left the $20 bill in his wallet for months—to remind him to care for kids at every opportunity. He intends never to spend it, and his stories of caring acts of impact keep multiplying yearly. Mike, an English teacher, bought two books and started a lunch book club just to get the "damn money spent." That book club is in its fourth year!

As your team begins to develop professional learning communities, the third critical question will naturally become the most thought-provoking: How will you respond when children are not learning? Many of the intervention strategies you develop to respond to this question will be both traditional and broad-based. The impact assignment is a reminder that while intervention must be systemic, it must sometimes be individualized as well. PLC educators stop at nothing to reach their students.

The Reality Check

Teachers have been inundated with new leaders, reforms, and initiatives promising to bring educational nirvana, yet rarely bringing results. With each failure, a new layer of skepticism separates us from our purpose and creates resistance to anything new or different. In this environment of this-too-shall-pass mentality, education has become one of the most cynical professions.

Here's How

Call it like it is! Concede that it would be very difficult to believe in any new reform or change in pedagogy based on the recent history of education. Ask teachers to consider the following:

Realities of the Superintendent: Odds are the superintendent will be replaced, leave, or retire in a short number of years. With a new superintendent will likely come new reforms.

Realities of the Principal: Odds are the principal will be replaced, leave, or retire in a short number of years. With a new principal will likely come a new vision for the school.

Realities of Politics: Odds are that whoever is not in power is working hard to get elected. Once in office, the new party will put into effect new and promised educational reforms.

Realities of Reforms: Odds are the latest reform movement will be gone in short order just like its predecessors.

Put the list of reforms and nomenclatures on pages 102–103 in a PowerPoint to the tune of "The Way We Were." Before you hit "play," take a survey of teachers who have been in the profession for 5, 10, 15,

20, 25, 30 years, and so on. Veterans will really understand your point. This also is a great opportunity for your staff to recognize those who are at the twilight of their careers.

Read the following excerpt from the book *Accountability for Learning* (Reeves, 2004, p. 2):

> If only the presentation is persuasive enough, if only the rewards are great enough, if only the sanctions are tough enough, the reasoning goes, then the staff will see the light and they will at last comply with the wishes of those giving instructions. If sincere intentions were sufficient for success, then the landscape of educational reform would not be littered with frustrated leaders and policy makers who noticed that, after rendering a decision about something that seemed momentous, absolutely *nothing happened in the classroom*. The board adopted academic standards and solemnly vowed that all children would meet them. *Nothing happened in the classroom*. The superintendent announced a new vision statement; along with core values and an organizational mission that the entire staff would enthusiastically chant. *Nothing happened in the classroom*. Millions were spent on new technology. *Nothing happened in the classroom*. Staff development programs were adopted so that teachers, like circus animals, would be "trained" to perform new feats. Although seats were dutifully warmed during countless training, *nothing happened in the classroom*.

Spend some time talking about and sharing memories of each of these initiatives from the past.

Here's Why

As the instructional leader, you need to break down the cynicism that has built up over the years. Acknowledge there are good reasons why many staff members feel betrayed by the very system

Memories of the Way We Were:
Reforms and Nomenclatures in the Last 30 Years

- ECE—Early Child Education
- SIP—School Improvement Program
- RISE—Reform of Intermediate and Secondary Education
- EIA—Economic Impact Aid
- Challenge Districts
- Rainbow Curriculum
- Miller-Unruh Reading
- Mentor Teaching Program
- Ready or Not Here They Come
- It's Elementary
- Caught in the Middle
- Charter schools
- Head Start
- Healthy Start
- SCANS—Secretary's Commission on Acquiring Necessary Skills
- National Service Program
- Governor's Commission on School Reform
- Nation at Risk
- TQM—Total Quality Management
- CETA—Comprehensive Employment and Training Act
- Outcome-based education
- America 2000
- Goals 2000
- Bilingual Education
- Model Curriculum Standards Guide
- State frameworks
- PPBS—Planning Program Budgeting System
- ELP—Extended Learning Program
- MGM—Mentally Gifted Minors
- GATE—Gifted and Talented Education

- First Class—A Guide for Primary Education
- Team teaching
- Sensitivity training
- Integrated curriculum
- Spiral curriculum
- Whole language
- New math
- New new math
- Reform
- Restructure
- Decentralize
- Vision
- Networking
- Mission statement
- Performance-based assessment
- Strategic planning
- No Child Left Behind
- Intelligence Rearmament
- Core curriculum
- Systemic change
- Sex respect
- Downsize
- Programmatic change
- Affirmative Action
- Intellectually challenged
- Portfolio assessment
- Shared decision-making
- Brain-based learning
- RSP
- SDC
- ROP
- LDS
- School within a school

(continued)

Memories of the Way We Were: Reforms and Nomenclatures in the Last 30 Years	
• Interdisciplinary team • Teacher empowerment • High-performance schools • Site-based management • Collaborative management • Collegial evaluation • Interest-based bargaining • Win-win negotiations • Articulation • Authentic assessment • Cognitive behavior modification • Construct • Path-goal theory • Constructivism • Multicultural education • Conflict resolution • Redesign • Horizontal enrichment • Cooperative learning • Meltdown • Interface • Summative teacher evaluation • Formative teacher evaluation • Intergenerational education • Clinical supervision • Least restrictive environment • Developmentally appropriate practices	• Block scheduling/Flex scheduling • Thinking curriculum • LEP • FEP • NEP • EL • ESL • ELD • ELL • IEP • ILP • ITP • CCR • PQR • CCR • CSR • SSR • DELAC • EDY • FRISK • FEP • IASA • MOU • PSAA • OS • SBCP • SSP • WASC

they have dedicated themselves to. Recognize that not only has there been a history of reform, but with that history comes the realities of bureaucratic compliance. While federal, state, and local agencies require only compliancy, a professional learning community promotes creativity and student learning. In a PLC, compliance is the baseline, and creativity is the model of growth.

The Results

The point of the exercise is that the change process lies with the people in the room. No matter what external forces exist, your staff has the power to make a commitment to become a professional learning community, to be passion-driven, and to have faith in action. This is a great opportunity to begin identifying the core values your team will commit to and be willing to reflect upon year after year.

New Teacher Oath

Building a culture of support for new teachers is an important and commonly overlooked instructional responsibility. The following strategy is a ceremony that instills in veteran teachers the responsibility to nurture a culture of new teacher support.

Here's How

Bring all the new teachers up in front of the entire staff, introduce them, and facilitate the following new teacher tradition. Substitute your school or mascot name for those used in the example.

After introducing the "new to us" teachers, say, "I'm going to assert several statements of particular value to this staff. When I'm finished with all of the statements, and you agree, please respond by saying, 'We *will*.'"

New-to-us teachers: *Will you . . .*

- *Care about our Cougar students?*
- *Be committed to the idea that we are about student learning— not just teaching or covering the material?*
- *Seek out wise advice from those who have been around the learning block a few times?*
- *Act professionally?*
- *Be continuous learners, and share with your colleagues what you know?*

- *Seek to set learning results measured through shared data, common assessments, and team analysis to help all students learn?*
- *Accept "helpful advice" when given without offense?*
- *Be committed to intervening when a student is struggling in his or her learning—even the hardest to teach?*
- *Represent Cougar Valley High School both at school and in the community?*
- *And, finally, become part of the Cougar culture?*

If you will . . . respond by saying, "We will."

Staff: *Will you . . .*

- *Support your new-to-us colleagues?*
- *Care about them?*
- *Share your resources, knowledge, and understanding of the profession?*
- *Welcome them into your class to observe on a moment's notice?*
- *Take the time to say, "Hi, how are you?"—and stop long enough to hear the answer?*
- *Have the "difficult" conversation when you know it is in their best interest?*
- *Practice random acts of kindness towards them?*
- *Collaborate with them and treat them as professionals?*
- *Clear a seat at the table when you see them coming, and invite them to sit?*
- *Be interested in the new ideas they bring?*
- *And, finally, impart to them the Cougar culture?*

If you will . . . respond by saying, "We will."

Instruct the entire staff to come forward in a reception line and shake each new teacher's hand. Encourage them to make a short statement of support in any way they wish. This works best if it is the conclusion of the meeting.

Here's Why

There is more at stake with this activity than simply generating the commitment to support new teachers. This activity has tremendous power to invoke powerful, beloved ceremonies such as weddings, communion, bar mitzvahs, Hippocratic oaths, community service oaths, and so on. Tap into that power to initiate change throughout your organization.

The Results

This activity is not really about the new teachers. In fact, the most common result is the recommitment by veteran teachers to foster a culture of care for *all* colleagues. One of the foundations of a professional learning community is in the ability to work in highly effective teams. Teacher trust is a significant part of this process. There is no better way to build trust among teachers as a commitment to each others' success. Be prepared for conversations with tearful teachers who will volunteer to organize efforts to promote a culture of support for new teachers!

The Heart of a PLC

Why do so many well-intentioned leaders fail to bring about school improvement even when they are advocating all the right ideas? So much critical time, energy, and resources are poured into making the case, reviewing the literature, and proving the point, and yet "nothing happens in the classroom" (Reeves, 2004). The reality is that the majority of our teachers have become disconnected to our instructional leaders. Who can blame them, considering all the "reforms o' the day" that have come and gone promising to "fix" education. This chapter didn't set out to "wow" you, the reader, with a body of research to logically convince you that the heartful way is the better way to lead. Rather, we hope these strategies and activities will bypass the formal part of the brain altogether and make a direct connection with the heart, where purpose and passion live. There is nothing more powerful to move a group of educators to action than to remind them of why they entered the profession in the first place: helping all children learn at high levels. In our experience, the path to educational redemption runs straight through the heart of a professional learning community. Teachers on that path see the wisdom of working in collaborative teams and being data-driven; they focus on learning, because they have faith in their power to change students' lives. Teachers need that faith to sustain them on the journey—and so do administrators.

References

Bellesi, D., & Bellesi, L. (2003). *The kingdom assignment: What will you do with the talents God has given you?* Grand Rapids, MI: Zondervan.

Collins, J. (2001). *Good to great: Why some companies make the leap . . . and others don't.* New York: HarperCollins.

Goleman, D., Boyatzis, R., & McKee, A. (2002). *Primal leadership: Realizing the power of emotional intelligence.* Boston: Harvard Business.

Reeves, D. (2004). *Accountability for learning: How teachers and school leaders can take charge.* Alexandria, VA: Association for Supervision and Curriculum Development.

Warren, R. (2001). *The purpose driven life: What on earth am I here for?* Grand Rapids, MI: Zondervan.

LILLIE G. JESSIE

Lillie Jessie has provided award-winning leadership throughout her 17-year tenure as principal of Elizabeth Vaughan Elementary School in Woodbridge, Virginia. Her innovative, proactive approach has raised the school to unprecedented levels of success. Locally recognized in 2003–2004 as a School of Excellence, Vaughan was honored in 2006 as one of 69 schools in Virginia to close the achievement gap between low- and middle-income students. The school also opened the first student-run bank in an elementary school in Prince William County Public Schools (PWCS), and received the performance-based PWCS Business Partnership Award. For achieving amazing goals using the Professional Learning Communities at Work process, Vaughan is one of eight schools featured in the video *The Power of Professional Learning Communities at Work: Bringing the Big Ideas to Life*. It is also listed as an Evidence of Effectiveness school on the website www.allthingsplc.info.

SIX

The Principal's Principles of Leadership in a Professional Learning Community

Lillie G. Jessie

Because my husband is a former Marine Corps officer, when I think of the role of a principal, several military quotes related to leadership come to mind. One is, "Respond to what you see on the ground." Another reminds us, "Never go into battle without your troops." Marzano, Waters, and McNulty's (2005) meta-analysis of school leadership reminds us that principals not only have to respond to what they see "on the ground," but also what is "under it." Of the 21 leadership responsibilities Marzano lists, situational awareness is listed as having the highest correlation on student achievement. A lack of situational awareness—an inability to read undercurrents, a pervasive feeling that you are in a battle for the hearts and minds of staff—is one of the greatest challenges of leadership.

In order to create and sustain a learning environment, a principal must consider certain critical factors. Those factors are building leadership capacity from within, monitoring what matters, and having that personal moral compass so frequently referred to by Fullan (2005), Collins (2001), and Senge (2005). Rick DuFour (2004a) refers to this type of leadership as an "affair of the heart." The common thread in their observations of leaders of great organizations is that they have principles that are so deeply embedded that failure is not an option for them or for those working under their leadership. Ron Edmonds notes that although an effective school must have a strong instructional leader, "There are many schools out there that have strong instructional leaders, but are not yet effective" (Lezotte & McKee, 2002, p. 17). In order for others to follow your lead, you have to have a mission and vision that others embrace and are excited about.

Researchers also warn us about the short-term effects that a charismatic leader can have, however. Doug Reeves defines true leadership as an individual who is a "leader of leaders": "Great leaders magnify their own strengths and simultaneously create teams that do not mimic the leader but provide different and equally important strengths to the organization" (Reeves, 2006, p. 23). There was a time early on in my career when I felt that I had to be an expert at everything. I have since learned that my job is not necessarily to *be* the expert, but rather to *find* the experts in my organization. The leader of any organization has the difficult task of not only making the impossible seem possible, but also helping others believe in their own possibilities. They look for talented individuals and nurture their leadership abilities.

This chapter is devoted to what I perceive to be the five principles that underpin successful school leadership in a professional learning community. I have identified only five of what I call the Principal's Principles, but I could have listed more. As I share these principles, I will also share some of my personal successes and defeats. Do not lose sight of what was said at the beginning of this chapter—respond to what you see on the ground. Your ground surface will be different from mine; only you know the soil content, only you can sort the weeds from the grass, and only you can provide the right nutrients for growth. Create your own garden of hope.

Principle 1: Personal Mission Must Precede Organizational and School Mission

Changing the hearts and minds of teachers and even parents who do not believe in the abilities of students from "disadvantaged"

backgrounds is not a job for the faint of heart. You must *believe* that regardless of income, educational background, race, and environment, every child not only has the ability, but also the *right* to learn. Additionally, you have to believe that every child has the right to learn *at high levels.*

For me, belief came not as a result of Marzano's meta-analysis, but rather from more than 35 years of experience and daily self-reflection. My personal experience made it easy to believe that children from homes where they were not read to each night could still demonstrate an ability to learn. You see, I was one of those kids. Not only did I lack books in my home, but I was denied access to public libraries. I grew up in the segregated South during the era of Brown versus Board of Education. My parents did not read to me because they lacked the skills and the materials. In fact, I read for them once I acquired the skill. The irony is that I see this same scenario being played out every day in my school. Students from second language homes, for example, are in many instances the readers for their families. Our job is to find the sometimes invisible gift and desire for learning that we know exist inside these students.

Despite my personal experience, it was not until I saw two videos, one on effective schools and one on professional learning communities (DuFour, 2003), that my belief that all students could learn was confirmed by educational research. This was my "aha" moment. I recall thinking, "Wow, I have finally found someone who believes what I believe." Both videos outlined processes that made us as educators rethink our views on student learning. One would think that these simple, cost-effective changes would dramatically change practices in our schools. There is a plethora of research that indicates professional learning communities will enhance learning in our schools. Why then has such a simple and commonsense strategy not been embraced by every school in North America? I see thousands of educators at the PLC institutes and summits. What happens to all of that enthusiasm when they return to their schools? In my mind, it has to do with a lack of personal mission or what Michael Fullan (2001) calls a moral purpose.

For some, moral purpose is a matter of birthright. For example, the Kennedys are known for their public service; it is a family legacy. Jacques Cousteau passed his love of the undersea world to his son Jean-Michel. Martin Luther King, Jr., was born into a family of ministers. For others, events in our lives shape who we become—or who we do *not* want to become. Growing up, I knew that I did not want to be a maid in someone's home, the major source of income for African American women in the South at that time. As a principal, I see parents everyday who have what I call "not" goals. They may not have a goal for their children to become doctors or lawyers, but they know that they do *not* want their children to become teenage parents, the victims of crime or criminals, or hourly wage earners. They want more for their children, and to that end, they are willing to do laborious jobs that many professionals would not think of doing. These parents have a moral strong purpose.

Moral purpose may develop during what Morris Massey (1986) refers to as a Significant Emotional Event (SEE)—those circumstances that shake us to our very core, after which we are never the same again. One of my SEEs was growing up in the South and having a sixth-grade teacher believe in my ability. Sharing her belief in the ability of all kids is my way of showing my gratitude; because of her belief in me, it is impossible for me to turn my back on children who aren't learning. I do not want my students to achieve anything less than greatness. A SEE in my education career happened when my school was on the front page of the newspaper; the headline read, "Vaughan Elementary Has the Lowest Math Scores in the County." My school's demographics had changed from the "lucky" middle-class school to the "losing" low-income school Doug Reeves (2006) talks about, but we had not changed our practices.

Some of you reading this book may not have had a SEE in your lives similar to my two experiences, but many of you, like me, grew up in homes where you were the only person in your family to receive a higher education. You cannot allow yourself to buy into the belief that children from poor families have less ability than those from middle-class homes. You know better! Others of you may be thinking, "I haven't had a SEE." Yes, you have! If you are in education today, you have had a SEE. It is called No Child Left Behind.

One would think that having a SEE would make us more willing to respond in a positive way to change. But change is hard. I cannot tell you how many workshops I attended where I heard the words *mission*, *vision*, and *goals*. During one PLC workshop, I heard Rick DuFour refer to a book called *The Knowing-Doing Gap* by Pfeffer and Sutton (2000). I read the book, and like most principals, lamented about *my staff* needing to close this gap. I am embarrassed to say that it was not until recently that I fully understood the impact of having a meaningful mission statement. After seeing a video (DuFour, 2003) on professional learning communities, for example, I still allowed my staff to write a long, too-detailed mission statement. Why? Because like many of you, I found that it is easier to go along if you want to get along. All of that moral purpose and SEE stuff that I referred to earlier went right out the window. I was a part of the knowing-doing gap.

Ron Edmonds was known to say we already know what to do, but that it is a question of having the will to do it. Maybe some of you are like me: It just takes a while before we get it! It is my observation, after more than 35 years of listening to principals, that the desire for approval by our staff and those above us tempts us on a daily basis. Implementing a PLC is not a matter of "knowing," it is truly a matter of "doing," and that's the hard part. Let your personal mission trump your need for personal approval.

Principle 2: Monitor What Matters, When It Matters

Rick DuFour laughingly talks about the 30-minute teacher observations that principals engage in and why they do not yield the results we need to truly monitor student success. If we want students to succeed, what do we monitor? That was my question for several years. I now know that we should monitor real data on a frequent basis, including student conversations, student responses to test format, teacher and student body language, and staff personal situations that can adversely affect learning. Monitor what is beneath the pretty graphs and charts provided to you. Monitor what your staff says, how they say it, and what they do not say. In other words, monitor staff *silence!* There is usually a powerful message hidden in the silence.

One of the researchers who had a great influence on my practice is Mike Schmoker (1996). I read his book *Results* and viewed his video with staff. Afterwards, we began a quarterly session I called the Day of Dialogue. The teachers secretly called it the Day of Death. I now realize these quarterly chats made us a data-driven school, but not a professional learning community. I was monitoring what Doug Reeves (2006) would call tests instead of assessment. Monitoring tests in quarterly data sessions provided little information to guide our instructional practices, because it was too late to provide interventions. Moreover, the tests we used were not really aligned with the curriculum. The Day of Dialogue did, however, create a forum of discussion. The long mission statement mentioned earlier served as a jumping-off point for our present statement; Day of Dialogue served also as a jumping-off point for how we monitor assessments today—on a weekly basis, using the information to guide our practice, in alignment with the PLC process.

Thursday is my data chat day with staff. I am addicted to this day. If I do not talk to a grade level for a couple of weeks, I feel that I do not know what is going on—good, bad, or ugly—at that grade level. This weekly sharing of information also allows me to reach another

PLC objective of building leadership from within. Every facet of this meeting is organized and presented by teachers. The Communication Lead sits at the head of the table. I am a member of the outer circle. There are loose and tight elements to this meeting. The tight element is that the agenda each week must relate to Big Idea #1, assurance that students are learning. The four critical questions that drive a PLC (DuFour, DuFour, Eaker, & Many, 2006) must be answered:

1. Are the children learning?

2. How do you know?

3. What are the plans for those who are not learning?

4. What are the plans for those who already know it?

Weekly student responses to common assessments are presented by either the Communication Lead or the person assigned to the specific content area being presented. Items of concern are discussed on a weekly basis, including the collaborative process. Dispersed leadership is the goal.

What is loose, you ask? How the teachers present the information is loose. Some use historical graphs, while others use bar or line charts. Loose also are grade-level plans for students not mastering the objective. Some grades use 1 day a week for a language arts intervention group; others use temporary reassignments of teachers or students. Still others use the daily intervention time in our schedule.

In my responsibilities as principal, I am tight on looking at teachers who have mastered the objectives at high levels instead of focusing all of my energy on teachers whose students are performing poorly. My goal is to reinforce the interdependence that comes with the collaborative process of a PLC. The conversation is not about why one person did so poorly, but rather, what is the high-performing teacher doing that can be shared? It is the principal's role in a PLC to remind teachers to eliminate the fear of humiliation.

The role of a principal during assessment discussion, as Rick DuFour often says in his keynotes, is to ask the right questions and know when to probe further. I recall once asking why a large percentage of students failed an open-book science test in one classroom. The answer was, "They didn't study. They watched television instead." Boy, was I ready to go into that classroom and give those students the old one-two! Then when I asked how could this be, how could they possibly fail an open-book test, the teacher responded, "Oh no, their *books* weren't open, just their *notes.*" Upon inspection, the teacher and I realized that the students had poorly written notes. Instead of fussing at the students, we discussed the need to implement Marzano's effective teaching strategy of how to take notes.

We still have our quarterly data reports, but they are used to determine our status in relationship to pacing and to celebrate our success as a staff. The weekly sharing is within grade levels, but the quarterly sharing is in front of the entire staff. Rick and Becky DuFour talk about the need to deprivatize practices, and they also remind us that we need to celebrate small wins. This process does both. I am frankly amazed at what happens when you ask teachers to brag about their performance in front of their peers! The pride they display is unbelievable. I borrowed this idea from a newly appointed vice president of a well-known technology firm. She talked about meeting with various departments of her engineering firm on a weekly basis and how they displayed their prized projects. I thought if this works for business, maybe it would work for schools. I modified her idea. Remember, very few of us have original thoughts. My hope is that some of my experiences will ignite a concept or response that will change your school in a positive way.

Principle 3: Engage in the Principle of Caring

"Success is like a vitamin, a child needs at least one a day!" These were the words of Mel Levine (2002) during his appearance on *The Oprah Winfrey Show*, as he promoted his bestselling book *A Mind at a*

Time. Later, during the summer of 2007, I had the pleasure of visiting Adlai Stevenson High School, where Rick DuFour was previously principal. I was struck by the beauty of the school in general. One knew right away this school valued its customers. The gardens were manicured and well-kept, as was every aspect of the building. But the most striking and lasting image in his school were the thousands, yes, there had to be thousands, of awards on display. Plaques were lined up on every wall. In some instances, they reached the ceiling. Students' names were engraved on bricks as you entered the building. It reminded me of Dr. Levine's admonition, and I thought, "The vitamins are on display for all to see on a daily basis."

When I think about it, my journey to become a PLC started 16 years ago when I became principal of Vaughan. I am a reader of the research, and somewhere I had read about the importance of student celebrations. I bought pom poms for every classroom and asked teachers to bring them to each honor celebration. I was ready to celebrate, but the staff was not. They would bring the pom poms but refused to shake them. You haven't lived until you are in an auditorium full of lifeless pom poms. I used to call those celebrations the "pepless" rallies. Today the pep rallies not only have pep, they have step. The staff, not I, determines what will be on the agenda. When we learned that my assistant principal, Stephanie Sanders, had been promoted and would be leaving in a week, the staff and students put on a pep rally that brought tears to her eyes and to the eyes of her parents. My role? Just do what they had assigned to me on the agenda. Remember, never go into battle without your troops.

We have given many awards in my school over the years, though not as many as Stevenson High. I was astonished by the positive response to a simple $5 cup, referred to as the Principal's Cup, given to a staff member for going above and beyond and announced over the personal address system each week. Equally well-received was a visit by the ice-cream truck for staff and selected students who had scored 500 or above on the Virginia Standards of Learning test. Teachers seemed to enjoy it even more than the kids, and it became our least costly and favorite celebration—and spread to other schools in our area. A fellow principal told me, "I spent over $1,000 on a faculty breakfast and got no response, but I received numerous written and verbal thank-you responses to the arrival of the ice-cream truck." A final example: Honor-roll students in my school have received an engraved brick encased in a sidewalk around our flag pole since 1992. It is not unusual to see them—the "Brick Kids," a name they gave to themselves—return as young adults during the holidays with family members to see their brick. One of my Brick Kids passed away several years ago. He was a senior in high school. At the funeral, I was stunned to see all of his Vaughan Elementary honor certificates on display. His family referenced his having an engraved brick at my school. We now have a memorial brick on our sidewalk. The depth of gratitude expressed by his family during the installation ceremony was overwhelming.

I once heard a national consultant named Jackie Wuertenburg say that everyone has to have what she called a "tah-dah." My daughter was a student at Virginia Tech, where there was a mass shooting in 2007. I wonder how many times do we have to hear the same phrases—"He was quiet," "He was a loner," "I don't recall seeing him in my class"—before we realize that kids need the vitamin of success or a tah-dah. It does not take an expensive or huge gesture to give the one thing most of us crave in life: recognition.

Principle 4: Teach What You Preach... Touch a Child's Life!

The literature is replete with principals who brag about knowing each student's name. To know the names of many is admirable, but in my estimation, to know why a small cluster of students is not learning is as or more important than knowing every child's name. Demonstrate your passion for learning by working directly with students; you'll be surprised at what you will learn.

How many times have you heard, "It's all about the kids?" In reality, principals spend little time in conversations with students that are not punitive in nature. We spend more time talking to adults *about* kids than we do talking *to* kids. In the business world, when we want to know how we are doing, we ask the customer (Collins, 2001). In education, we spend a great deal of time looking at grades, bar graphs, and charts, and talking to teachers and parents, but little or no time talking to our customer, the child. If you want to know if a child has learned a concept, ask him. Remember, two of the big ideas in a PLC are a focus on learning and a focus on results. This may come as a shocker to some of you and a reminder to others; sometimes those beautiful graphs and charts do not reflect the "real deal."

One way to interact with students is by going into classrooms and conducting mini lessons. These are not done to demonstrate your teaching skills. Frankly, my teachers are so much better than I am at the daily craft of teaching. I am there for a far more important reason: to let the students know that I know, value, and care about what they are learning. I also want them to know that I enjoy being in a classroom with them. We need to know more about each other, and student interaction is the only way you can achieve this objective. The mantra from a principal to students should be: "I am expecting great things!" It's a mantra because it must be verbalized, and they have to hear it more than once before belief sets in. You cannot believe how much power the voice of a principal has in the minds of students. If you don't believe me, relive one of those social gatherings where someone introduces you as a principal to a group; inevitably, someone confesses that years ago, she was sent to your office for misbehavior.

How will you know if you have been successful with this strategy? You will know by the content of the informal conversations children have with you in the hallway. I was so honored when one of my students interrupted me during a conversation about the Virginia Standards of Learning test by saying, "Enough already! I'll pass the thing!" If you want to move a child from the bottom of the bell to the top of the J curve (Lezotte & McKee, 2002) or to the top of the mountain curve (Reeves, 2006), say something like, "I am expecting great things from you!" Say it over and over until belief sets in. Recently I said, "Thank you, PLC," when one of my former students returned to a Title I Family Night with his younger sister. The previous year, a teacher and I had prodded him from failing to honor status using this "expecting" strategy, and he had successfully moved on to middle school. From the back of the room where I was serving pizza, everyone else in attendance heard him announce, "Mrs. Jessie, I made four As and one B." A principal cannot buy the feeling that happens inside.

Principle 5: Respond When Children Are Not Learning… Even When It Threatens Your Popularity

I saved the best for last! I don't know how many times I have heard the joke about the mom who told her son that he had to go to school, even if he did not want to . . . because he was the principal. There have been times in my career when I really did not want to come to school because I had to confront an issue. Recently, when I was troubled over a student learning situation, my husband actually stood over the bed and said, "It's going to work out, Jess. Just think how great it's going to be when you solve this problem."

My response was laced with sarcasm and little confidence in his prediction: "Sure it will." Of course, he was right; it did work out. That was last school year. This year has started off with the usual things that confront principals, and again, my husband has had to remind me that things would work out. One of my friends said some things are like "nailing Jell-O to a wall." In the business of education, Jell-O slides are the norm.

"Professional learning community! Professional learning community!" There is something about that phrase that sounds so optimistic. You can almost see Julie Andrews on that hill singing, "The hills are alive with the sound of music." It just sounds like everything is going to be wonderful, everyday! You think you should be able to say, "Embrace learning and results," and teachers will respond, "We would love to." In reality, it does not happen that way. It is truly a process. In a professional learning community, you don't get to say, "I'm done!"

Unfortunately, the more savvy you become at identifying problems, the more you see. I was relieved when I read that one of Gardner's (2004) seven "acceptable" ways of persuasion included confrontation. Rick DuFour says, "Perhaps there are schools that made the transition to a professional learning community without conflict or anxiety, but I am unaware of any . . . how we react when immersed in the conflict that accompanies change" is what is important (DuFour, 2004b, p. 64). Gary Reglin (1995) said we should not label the students "at risk" but instead should call them students "placed at risk" because of our teaching practices. Ron Edmonds says that a happy school is not always an effective school. In other words, there are educators who are turning their backs and sometimes embracing ineffective practices at the expense of students in order to maintain friendships or adult approval. Why? In some instances, it is a result of mandated central office survey results. As principals, we want to achieve high scores on anonymous surveys *and* maintain a vigil on low-performing individuals. It is a virtual tight rope for many. The key to keeping your balance is knowing your purpose: high student performance.

There are days when the staff will put their pom poms on the floor and refuse to cheer. This is their way of drawing a line in the sand. You have to have the courage to step over the line, but it is just as important that you carry people with you. Your job will be to make sure the "show goes on" with those who want to participate. Your job also requires you to do something that is even more challenging: You have to talk to those who are not participating and determine their strengths. Doug Reeves says you go on a "treasure hunt" and find pockets of excellence . . . then you document . . . and replicate those practices (Reeves, 2006, p. 135). Leadership must be dispersed if we want to achieve sustainability.

There is a fire-building contest during the tie-breaker ceremony on the television show *Survivor.* Inevitably, the winner of the ceremony is the individual who realizes that the more intense and longer lasting fire must be built from the bottom up. This is also true for sustainable school improvement efforts. Sometimes your leaders are not the ones who are highly visible. They are the ones at the "bottom" of the pile. Make invisible excellence visible to all. Some of the greatest leaders at Vaughan are nondegreed staff, such as our teacher aides and media specialist. When the degreed staff see them excelling, it puts a fire to achieve beneath them. My experience is that people cannot stand the "heat of success" when it is all around them. They want to be a part of the excitement. Some of those people who called my Day of Dialogue the Day of Death are the same people now proudly displaying their data during our annual data dinner. They proudly tell other teachers who fear accountability, "We've being doing this for years." Did some teachers leave? Yes. Following their departure, some of them have become accountability advocates in their new settings. Others continue to resist change. Education is no different than any other field. You can't change the hearts and minds of everyone.

In the end, it always comes back to the first principle: personal mission. Why are you in this? Are you willing to risk your popularity for student achievement? Ironically, a staff accepts confrontation when its members share your mission and vision . . . when they know the mission is not about you or them, but about kids and their learning. There is absolutely nothing like success. The staff is looking to you to lead them. In fact, they *expect* you to confront and take on the difficult issues that impede their plans to reach a goal. Stand up for your principles, principals!

Acknowledgment

I want to thank Dr. Rick DuFour for successfully implementing the expecting strategy with me. He sat down at a table with me in 2007 and said, "You need to write." This statement of expectation scared me to death. Now you know this strategy works with adults, too! I hope this chapter lives up to his expectation.

References

Collins, J. (2001). *Good to great: Why some companies make the leap . . . and others don't*. New York: Harper Business.

DuFour, R. (2003). *Through new eyes: Examining the culture of your school*. Bloomington, IN: Solution Tree (formerly National Educational Service).

DuFour, R. (2004a, Winter). Leadership is an affair of the heart. *National Staff Development Council, 25*(1), 67–68.

DuFour, R. (2004b). Leading edge: Culture shift doesn't occur overnight . . . or without conflict. *Journal of Staff Development, 24*(4), 63–64.

DuFour, R., DuFour, R., Eaker, R., & Many, T. (2006). *Learning by doing: A handbook for professional learning communities at work*. Bloomington, IN: Solution Tree.

Fullan, M. (2001). *Leading in a culture of change*. San Francisco: Jossey-Bass.

Fullan, M. (2005). Professional learning communities, writ large. In R. DuFour, R. Eaker, & R. DuFour (Eds.), *On common ground: The power of professional learning communities* (pp. 209–224). Bloomington, IN: Solution Tree (formerly National Educational Service).

Gardner, H. (2004). *Changing minds: The art and science of changing our own and other people's minds*. Boston: Harvard Business School.

Lencioni, P. (2002). *The five dysfunctions of a team: A leadership fable*. San Francisco: Jossey-Bass.

Levine, M. (2002). *A mind at a time*. New York: Simon & Schuster.

Lezotte, L., & McKee, K. (2002). *Assembly required: A continuous school improvement system*. Okemos, MI: Effective Schools Products, Ltd.

Marzano, J., Waters, T., & McNulty, B. (2005). *School leadership that works: From research to results*. Alexandria, VA: Association for Supervision and Curriculum Development.

Massey, M. (1986). *What you are is where you were when: The Massey triad* (Rev. program.). Lakewood, WA: The Richardson Company.

Pfeffer, J., & Sutton, R. (2000). *The knowing-doing gap: How smart companies turn knowledge into action.* Boston: Harvard Business School.

Reeves, D. (2006). *The learning leader: How to focus school improvement for better results.* Alexandria, VA: Association for Supervision and Curriculum Development.

Reglin, G. (1995). *Achievement for African-American students: Strategies for the diverse classroom.* Bloomington, IN: Solution Tree (formerly National Educational Service).

Schmoker, M. (1996). *Results: The key to continuous school improvement.* Alexandria, VA: Association for Supervision and Curriculum Development.

Senge, P. (2005). *The fifth discipline: The art and practice of the learning organization.* New York: Currency, Doubleday.

Part Two

LEADING A CULTURE OF LEARNING AND RESULTS

ANTHONY MUHAMMAD

Dr. Anthony Muhammad's experience ranges from classroom teacher to principal to champion of effective learning environments. In 1995, he cofounded a nationally recognized charter school, the Sankofa Shule Public School Academy in Lansing, Michigan. The progress realized at Sankofa Shule was documented in *U.S. News & World Report* and the *Wall Street Journal*. In 1999, Sankofa Shule's students scored higher than all other students in Ingham County in the areas of math (94.5% proficiency) and writing (92.9%). As the former principal of Levey Middle School and Southfield High School in Southfield, Michigan, Dr. Muhammad used the Professional Learning Communities at Work school improvement model to address troubling issues. At the time of his arrival, Levey had a history of poor scores on state academic assessments and more than 3,000 disciplinary referrals and suspensions the previous year. Dr. Muhammad's progressive approach to leadership resulted in measurable gains in student achievement, both in academic performance and in decreased disciplinary referrals. His efforts earned him the state's top award for middle school principals, and Levey is now recognized as a National Exemplary School by the U.S. Department of Education.

SEVEN

Teaching Matters: Leadership That Improves Professional Practice

Anthony Muhammad

Administrators who are anxious to improve the quality and level of learning of the students in their schools should remember one thing: Teaching matters. Leaders cannot forget this critical fact. The most important interactions in our schools take place daily, within each and every classroom, between teacher and students. School leaders have an infinite list of responsibilities, but providing direction and leadership in the area of classroom instruction and good professional practice has been proven to be a great use of our limited time and resources.

Teaching has 6 to 10 times as much impact on student achievement as all other factors combined (Mortimore & Sammons, 1987). Mike Schmoker (2006) points out that changing to teaching proficiency, a focus on the precise academic needs of each individual student as opposed to teaching to the classroom norm and expecting a normal distribution of achievement, does not have to be revolutionary. Continuous commonsense efforts to even roughly conform to effective practice and essential standards of quality instruction will make a life-changing difference for students across all socioeconomic levels. The evidence is clear. If we want to make our schools centers for high levels of learning, we must address the skill of our teaching staff—and address it with vigor.

Since the passage of the Elementary and Secondary Education Act in 2001, more popularly referred to as No Child Left Behind (NCLB), the accountability movement has mandated student proficiency on state standardized tests. Historically, schools have never been held responsible for *demonstrated* student proficiency. In fact, as students themselves, most teachers were socialized in a tracking system that sorted students into levels of "natural" talent and effort; students may or may not have been at the proficient level. If they weren't, it was the students' responsibility to perform better. Educators form their ideas about teaching when they themselves are children in school. The 13 years of K–12 education that today's educators spent as children observing practitioners helped to shape their "norms" of teaching (Lortie, 1975). In essence, teachers are now mandated to do something that they have never done and have never witnessed: to not just measure, but *ensure* proficiency for all students.

We would be naive to believe that a simple mandate unaccompanied by training and guidance can lead to the universal proficiency in math and reading mandated for every student in the United States as outlined in NCLB, which does not mandate a method to improve student learning, only the results. In her study of school reform implementation, Mary Kennedy points out that "teachers need more knowledge or guidance in order to alter their practices" (2005, p. 17). Kennedy's argument makes perfect sense. How can teachers make the necessary changes in practice to achieve new heights in student achievement, if they do not have the knowledge to accomplish this end? Many schools are turning to the professional learning community (PLC) model of school reform.

In a 2006 article, Richard and Rebecca DuFour write, "PLCs operate under the assumption that the key to improved learning for students is continuous, job-embedded learning for educators" (p. 3). This statement makes a direct correlation between the knowledge of teachers and the academic growth of the students that they serve. In fact, the DuFours make a point to identify educator growth as the *key* to improved learning for students. So, if school leaders truly want to transform their schools into communities that focus on student learning, they must first focus the school community on learning for the *adults*.

Creating an Internal Focus

It is understandable if school leaders get a migraine headache when thinking about the task of convincing educators that they need to improve their levels of knowledge and skill. Traditionally, the teacher is the authority in his or her classroom. Students are responsible for listening to the teacher's instruction, participating in the teacher's activities, and performing tasks outlined by the teacher, all with the goal of pleasing the teacher. The students who do this well are generally rewarded with pleasing evaluations, while the students who do not are punished through feedback that summarizes the displeasure of the teacher. This system creates a polarized effect that creates a group of "winners" and "losers" based on compliance with teacher expectations, which may not always be centered on learning.

The traditional paradigm demands that *student* behavior adjust to better fit the teachers' expectations (Cuban & Tyack, 1995). This rigid system has been the guiding educational paradigm for over a century, and there have been many attempts to alter it, with little to no success. Administrators have traditionally managed the school with the agreement that the teachers lead their classrooms, and the administrators manage the organization. This unspoken pact is deeply rooted in the culture of the traditional school.

In some schools, leaders face additional, institutional barriers. Many collective bargaining agreements restrict the focus of school meetings and professional development days set aside for teacher improvement. In fact, many collective bargaining agreements allow educators to use sick days or personal days to opt *out* of bargained professional development. In other cases, leaders have limited human and financial resources for professional development. Leaders in areas with high percentages of minority and socioeconomically disadvantaged students face the added challenge of high teacher turnover—even more than the average school, which experiences a teacher exodus of 50% within the first 5 years of classroom practice (Emerick, 2005). So how does a leader demonstrate instructional leadership when organizational structure is inflexible, funds are low, and a constant stream of new teachers must be retaught the skills lost when experienced staff leave the school community?

All of the barriers listed above, both cultural and institutional, make the job of leading schools very difficult. It is easy for school leaders to be sidetracked by all of the management tasks that cross their desks on a daily basis. It is easy to become distracted by parental issues and managing the many mandates handed down by state and federal agencies. But the overwhelming body of knowledge available in the educational research community dictates that a focus on adult learning is a non-negotiable, necessary component of improving student learning.

The Courage to Move Forward

As the newly hired principal of Levey Middle School in Southfield, Michigan, in 2001, I faced many of the obstacles faced by my peers. On the state of Michigan academic assessment, our students scored far below state average in every area. Sixty-five percent of the professionals on my staff had been practicing for 3 years or less. Our collective bargaining agreement was very specific about what could be demanded of teachers during their planning period. If the building's union representative did not agree to the staff meeting agenda and sign off on it, staff members were not required to attend scheduled staff meetings.

These challenges alone can discourage a school leader from implementing standards for adult learning, but to add insult to injury, I was the third principal hired to lead my school within less than 3 years. The culture of autonomy and isolation at Levey was even more pronounced because of the unstable history of school leadership; educators had been forced to depend on their own ability to survive an unhealthy culture. Despite these obstacles, we were able to create an environment where teachers engaged in an ongoing system of professional development that targeted our areas of need, which led to phenomenal gains in student achievement and improvement in school culture.

Getting Started

As an educator, my personal commitment to learning for all students was very important. That desire guided me to do some things that many of my colleagues felt were unorthodox or "taboo." I knew that our students had the capacity to be superstars, and we needed to find the key to unlock their potential. Because I was hired to be the principal at Levey 2 months before I officially began, I took the opportunity to visit the school several times; I talked with the outgoing principal, met with key teachers, and reviewed data and documents about school performance. After each visit, I left with a bigger headache than I had on the previous visit. The issue that concerned me most was the large number of novice teachers and their skill level. How could they be the catalyst to transform a school if they were just familiarizing themselves with the basics of teaching?

I kept asking myself this question until an idea generated. I asked myself, "If we have a curriculum and learning outcomes for students, why can't we have them for teachers?" If students have an organized and viable curriculum to guide their development in critical areas, the teachers who guide them should embrace a similar system. I consulted some of my colleagues about my idea—and they all laughed at me. I had a choice: Do I let conventional wisdom guide my decisions, or do I let my core beliefs about students and learning guide me? I chose to let my conviction for students be my guide, and I ignored the advice of my colleagues.

Organizing a Leadership Team

Upsetting teacher autonomy is a dangerous endeavor. I was trying to build a culture of collaboration that had not been built before, so organizing a leadership team was very important. *What areas should we focus on? How do we choose the curriculum for our adult learners? Where will we find the time? How will we structure our learning activities?* These were important questions that I did not feel qualified to answer alone.

In many schools, the school improvement team provides the structure for making collaborative decisions about school policy and direction. When I examined the composition of our team, I was concerned. The school improvement team was composed entirely of sixth- and seventh-grade teachers. All of the educators on the team were dedicated and knowledgeable, but there was no representation from the eighth grade, support staff, special education, electives, or administration. How could this team function properly if it did not fully represent those it was charged to lead? A new structure and team was in order. I organized a more balanced, comprehensive body of leaders that included the administrative staff, counselors, and the chairs of academic departments, special education, and electives. The new team adequately represented the diverse needs of the staff, and I would heavily rely on the expertise of this team to do the "heavy lifting" of shared decision-making.

After assembling this powerful team, I had to organize and focus our work—and we had a lot of work to do! We held two summer meetings, one in early July and the second in early August. Our job was to pinpoint the areas of need for our school and set goals for improvement—while simultaneously developing a course of study for our educators to improve their skills in our weak areas.

Planning for Change

Change is a difficult process for any human being, but it is even more challenging for teachers who had become increasingly pessimistic over the past 10 years due to unstable school leadership and poor student performance. It was very difficult for them to accept change and to have confidence in a progressive plan because of their past struggles. The process for the implementation of the teacher's curriculum had to be organized and nearly flawless to have the desired effect of changes in pedagogical practices. We started our first meeting with a review of data.

Let Data Show the Way

Data give a realistic, unbiased view of school performance. As school leader, it was my responsibility to provide the team members with a comprehensive set of data that accurately described our school. The results of state standardized tests were just one part of our data packet. Our data packet also included information about teacher grading practices, student discipline, student attendance, teacher attendance, parental involvement, and other quantifiable information on our school performance from the previous school year.

As we collectively reviewed this critical data, we could have easily identified hundreds of areas of need. But we had the added job of prioritizing our needs. Milton Friedman, one of the pioneers of American school reform, points out that there are many things that can be emphasized and identified for school improvement, but the best schools realize that they have limited resources, and they focus on the most urgent issues. In an interview conducted by Nick Gillespie, Friedman argued that "the modern reform movement is too ambitious and in order to make substantive, long-term progress, we need to narrow our focus" (2005, p. 18). Instead of overwhelming our teachers with an unfocused push to improve a hundred different areas of performance, we chose to identify the four or five *most critical* areas of need and set measurable improvement goals for those areas of need.

Support Professional Learning

After identifying those essential needs, we had to find resources to support our learning. Is it logical to set goals for improvement without supporting the growth necessary to achieve those goals? Of course it is not. Unfortunately, that is the historical approach to school improvement: It is mandated, so it must happen! We felt that this was not a healthy approach, so we spent the second half of our first meeting scanning databases to find the best professional literature on our areas of need.

For example, one of our goals for the 2001–2002 school year was *Decrease the number of student suspensions for the 2001–2002 school year by 40% by utilizing a whole-school approach to improving student behavior.* I believe that this is a good and reasonable goal for any school having a difficult time with student violence and student disruption of the educational process. At Levey, we all agreed this issue needed to be attacked in a *collective* manner. To do so, our educators needed to learn new strategies in classroom management, student/teacher relationships, teacher/parent relationships, and other areas. Each team member spent the second half of the day scanning the educational databases (ERIC, Google Scholar, and so on) to find books, articles, and research reports that would support targeted growth toward our goal. We made a commitment to one another to read the literature over the next month to identify the pieces that were most useful to our cause.

We reconvened in early August. The focus of our second meeting of the summer was to identify a universally approved body of literature to present to our staff to familiarize them with strategies to improve their practice. Each team member would stand before the leadership team and report on the literature that he or she felt was essential for us to examine in order to grow. In most cases, each team member identified 20 to 25 pieces of literature during the initial research, but after reviewing the actual literature, most found only 3 to 5 worthy of sharing with the entire school community. After each member gave a report, he or she placed the recommended literature in the center of the table; at the conclusion of the report, the pile on the table became our collective reading assignments for the entire upcoming school year.

Clarify Outcomes

At the conclusion of this exercise, we had one more task: to identify what we wanted our staff to take away from the reading. So we examined each piece of literature and collectively developed study questions for our staff to consider while reading. Later, we used staff answers to this critical inquiry to shape collaborative discussions focused on the literature. Each question on the study guide was carefully prepared to avoid conversations centered on *frustration* and to encourage conversations focused on *improvement.* The following questions are excerpts from questions developed for a staff reading of a book by Robert Green (2005) called *Expectations: How Teacher Expectation Can Increase Student Achievement and Assist in Closing the Achievement Gap:*

1. Researchers have proven that a student's level of education is best predicted by his/her zip code. Why do you think that this present reality exists? Does this have any impact on your expectations of students in your classroom?

2. Please examine the seven characteristics of Effective Schools (pgs. 14–18). After reviewing them, identity the one characteristic that we need to improve most, and give suggestions about ways that we can improve this component.

As you can see, the questions had the goal of challenging our teachers to use the literature to reflect on past and current practices. In addition, the inquiries focused the educators on finding solutions to issues instead of dwelling on the seemingly overwhelming nature of the issues that we faced.

After we identified critical literature and developed disciplined and focused inquiries on the literature, we created a binder for each teacher. The binder contained three sections. The first section contained the critical data that compelled us to choose the areas of focus for school improvement. These data were also a helpful tool to use with resisters, who would question the rationale of activities focused on improving teacher proficiency. The second section of the binder contained the measurable improvement goals. The third section contained copies of the literature, along with the study questions, divided into biweekly reading assignments. The collective work of this leadership team identified exactly what we needed to improve, selected specific literature to provide us necessary guidance to achieve improvement goals, and created focus questions that maximized the benefit for each professional.

After organizing our adult learning system, the next challenge was finding the time within an already packed teacher schedule and inspiring teachers to internalize the goals envisioned by the administration and the leadership team.

Remove Barriers

Anyone familiar with the struggles of Levey Middle School would not disagree with the fact that the school needed improvement, and improvement that focused on increasing teacher proficiency. The idea was solid, but how do you implement such a drastic change of focus and behavior within a system that is full of teacher requirements and mandates that allow little structural "wiggle room" for change? Richard DuFour and Robert Eaker note that "simply declaring a new vision is not sufficient. The organization must make every effort to remove the structural and cultural barriers that threaten to impede the implementation of that vision" (1998, p. 64). In other words, if the change is important and vital, leadership must find a way to make it happen, regardless of the number and power of the obstacles.

A professional learning community must first examine practices that the organization should consider *abandoning* before considering *additional* functions for the organization to adopt (DuFour & Eaker, 1998). The leadership team at Levey referred to this process as "addition by subtraction." We understood that to become an exemplary school, a targeted system of teacher skill development was a prerequisite. Following the addition by subtraction paradigm, we understood that our job was not to add more time commitments and demands to teachers' existing requirements. Instead, our job was to find slots of time and commitments that were disconnected from our vision for the school and eliminate those practices by replacing them with more effective practices.

After spending hours conversing and reviewing every aspect of the scope of teacher responsibility, we found our "golden nugget." Our collective bargaining agreement required teachers in our district to attend two staff meetings per month, the second and fourth Monday of every month. Instead of using those meetings to make announcements or hear scantly prepared presentations on various topics, we restructured these mandatory meetings and renamed them *Learning Centers*.

Learning Centers

Learning Centers allowed us to focus on building our professional skills. As the school administrator, I declared that Learning Centers were to be used for the sole purpose of professional growth; professional growth would be our only agenda item. Our school had a professional staff of 51, including counselors, social workers, and school psychologists. Each professional staff member was assigned to one of five learning teams, and they would stay with that team for the entire school year. Staff members were not allowed to pick their teams; the leadership team made that decision based upon our desire to make sure that diverse points of view would be represented during discussions. Therefore, each group was a microcosm of the diversity represented in our staff. Teams met simultaneously in different parts of the school library or cafeteria to share their perspectives on their reading assignments and discussion questions.

Staff members agreed to read the literature chosen by the leadership team over the summer and answer the student questions prior to attending the Learning Center. They agreed to be prepared to discuss and share their perspectives on how we could use the information taken from the literature to improve our school. How did I get them to agree to make this commitment? At our first staff meeting, I outlined the current condition of our school, focusing on the need for change as a *moral imperative* as opposed to a *compliance imperative*. We needed to change for the sake of our students and community, and to do so, we needed to develop knowledge of alternative methods of practice through a focused system of collective study. The staff agreed on the first day of school to do their part and give the literature and the Learning Center a fair chance. I banked on the assumption that if teachers were connected with best practice on an ongoing basis and experienced some success, they would eventually intrinsically embrace this concept. Sometimes school leaders have to depend on their ability to motivate and inspire in order to encourage people to do things outside of their normal realm of consideration (Eaker & Gonzalez, 2006).

Each team was assigned a *learning leader* who was also a member of the leadership team. He or she was responsible for making sure that the group focused on the assigned reading and the corresponding study questions to find *solutions* and ways to *apply* the research principles.

The conversations were rich and meaningful. Teachers compared their real-life experiences from the classroom to the research on good professional practices. The literature sometimes caused some healthy disagreement, challenged some long-held assumptions, and provided an empirical foundation for change and improvement. Staff members were required by contract to stay at these meetings for 1 hour, but because the educators found this exercise so beneficial and enlightening, many would stay for up to 3 hours. The willingness of veteran teachers to try new things was shockingly high, and the learning curve for new teachers became smaller and smaller. This focus on the proficiency of the educator would eventually pay big dividends for our students.

The Benefits

What benefits did we experience as a result of these Learning Centers? First and foremost, we developed a shared sense of knowledge. Our entire vocabulary changed, and our teachers became a walking body of professional knowledge. When referring to a concept like *differentiated instruction,* we could accurately assume that everyone had the same frame of reference and understanding of the concept because we studied and dissected this concept together. When we formed new collaborative teams, this common body of knowledge allowed us to move at a rapid pace without worrying about varied levels of knowledge on professional practice. This new vocabulary also transformed our informal teacher culture. When I would encounter teachers discussing students and their various problems, I no longer heard complaints and blame; instead, I overheard conversations focused on solutions and a willingness to experiment with new techniques learned during their Learning Center.

By 2005, our student achievement on our state assessment far exceeded the state average in each core academic area of instruction. The achievement gap associated with race and socioeconomic status was a nonissue at Levey. In fact, the gap had been reversed. Student violence and classroom disruptions greatly decreased as well and were not even issues of discussion and concern anymore. Teacher retention was no longer a problem, either. Between the years 2001 and 2006, there were no teacher resignations or transfers. The only changes in staff occurred as a result of six teachers accepting administrative positions.

School leaders interested in transforming schools into professional learning communities will eventually have to tackle this issue of adult learning. In a PLC, adult learning is as important as student learning. Some comfort zones may need to be challenged and some barriers broken, but the benefits associated with those risks can be potentially revolutionary. We cannot afford to ignore the principles of good leadership; strong *instructional* leadership is a major component of school effectiveness. If we are organized, intentional, inspirational, and lead by example, teachers will be willing to give up autonomy for methods that they are convinced are better for the students that they serve. The Learning Center serves as an example. I am forever thankful for the very professional and skilled staff of educators at Levey Middle School for their willingness to accept responsibility for their own development as professionals. As a result, our students are forever changed.

References

Cuban, L., & Tyack, D. (1995). *Tinkering towards utopia: A century of public school reform.* Cambridge, MA: Harvard University.

DuFour, R., & DuFour, R. (2006). The power of professional learning communities. *National Forum of Educational Administration and Supervision Journal, 24*(1), 2–5.

DuFour, R., & Eaker, R. (1998). *Professional learning communities at work: Best practices for enhancing student achievement.* Bloomington, IN: Solution Tree (formerly National Educational Service).

Eaker, R., & Gonzalez, D. (2006). Leading in a professional learning community. *National Forum of Educational Administration and Supervision Journal, 24*(1), 6–11.

Emerick, S. (2005, October). Teachers' working conditions as catalysts for student learning. *ASCD Infobrief,* 42–43.

Gillespie, N. (2005, December). The father of modern school reform. *Reason, 17*(2), 16–18.

Green, R (2005). *Expectations: How teacher expectation can increase student achievement and assist in closing the achievement gap.* Columbus, OH: SRA McGraw-Hill.

Kennedy, M. (2005). *Inside teaching: How classroom life undermines reform.* Cambridge, MA: Harvard University.

Lortie, D. C. (1975). *Schoolteacher: A sociology study.* Chicago: University of Chicago.

Mortimore, P., & Sammons, P. (1987, September). New evidence on effective elementary schools. *Educational Leadership, 45*(1), 4–8.

Schmoker, M. (2006). *Results now: How we can achieve unprecedented improvements in teaching and learning.* Alexandria, VA: Association for Supervision and Curriculum Development.

TERRI L. MARTIN

Dr. Terri Martin has dedicated herself to working with schools that have been slammed with demands from No Child Left Behind legislation. Her success as an administrator illustrates the effectiveness of the Professional Learning Communities at Work model for school improvement, and she draws from this proven experience to help others create sustainable PLCs. Time and again, she has witnessed positive results for students and substantial growth in academic achievement trends in schools and districts that have embedded this process. Terri uses her knowledge from being an administrator, a statewide professional developer, and the director of school improvement initiatives for the state of Missouri to assist others with their vision of creating a high-performance school or maintaining their current status of success.

EIGHT

Professional Learning in a Professional Learning Community

Terri L. Martin

One of the most powerful messages of the professional learning communities movement is that teachers can and do make the difference. For too long we have blamed the struggles of public education on the teachers. The reality is that schools are impacted by both internal and external factors, some of them beyond the control of educators, some not. If we want to improve schools, we must move away from placing blame and finding excuses. When implemented correctly, professional learning communities restore hope and self-efficacy by promoting the professionalism and expertise of teachers. Richard DuFour writes, "It should be self-evident that the quality of personnel is of central importance to a school, and that enabling individuals to improve their effectiveness is the key to any meaningful school improvement effort" (1991, p. 7).

We know that when schools are focused on learning for both students and teachers, our opportunity for success grows. We are getting increasingly sophisticated in understanding that learning is the primary purpose of schools. Many schools are now creating structures in which learning is the constant and time is flexible; systematic interventions for students are increasingly becoming the norm. Slowly, we are turning the corner. Educators are moving beyond just talking about focusing on learning for all students; they are moving toward ensuring that learning occurs for all students. But now we must realize that learning for all includes adults as well as students. Robert

Marzano suggests, "Perhaps the most obvious way to address the issue of professionalism is to engage teachers in meaningful staff development activities" (Marzano, 2003, p. 65). This chapter will explore how a professional learning community defines and utilizes high-quality professional development to support teachers as they strive to ensure high standards for all students. We can re-envision professional development to identify, embed, and support teacher learning to reach the same high standards we set for our students.

Understanding Professional Development

> *Skillful leaders establish policies and organizational structures that support ongoing professional learning and continuous improvement.*

> —National Staff Development Council

If we truly believe that teachers are central to improving student achievement, we have to also believe that they need the appropriate support and structures to be successful. We will have to go beyond the typical "sit and get" event that an educator attends in the hopes of gathering tidbits of information to take back to the classroom. While there is well-meaning intent on behalf of both those delivering the message and those receiving it, more often than not, traditional professional development only provides an inspiring and motivating moment. As Dennis Sparks, past president of the National Staff Development Council (NSDC) writes, "Even relatively well-executed 'pull-out' staff development seldom affects a school's culture, extends to the classroom, or is sustained over enough time to affect instructional practice. In most schools, a large gap exists between what is known about professional learning that affects teaching and improves student achievement and the professional development that teachers and principals regularly experience" (Sparks, 2005b, p. 85). Without a structure in place to allow teachers to share, practice, and implement their learning, new knowledge is rarely embedded in current classroom practice. In a very short period of time, teachers return to the historical way of doing business.

In an attempt to bring relevance and importance to professional development, there has been a shift to high-quality professional development (NSDC, 2003). High-quality professional development creates a context for improving student learning: That includes creating collaborative learning communities focused on continuous improvement. The content of this new professional development centers on research-based strategies that are historically proven to positively impact all students. Its process is built around using multiple sources of student data, setting goals, and applying new knowledge.

However, this new approach alone is not enough. Schools that are true professional learning communities, as defined by Rick and Becky DuFour, Bob Eaker, and Tom Many (2006), understand the power that comes with this kind of professional development. PLCs enhance the learning that occurs in their collaborative cultures through well-defined and focused adult learning. They define areas of growth through data analysis, and then they ensure that the adults receive the knowledge they need to make the necessary decisions for continuous growth. Through their structures and processes, these professional learning communities define, learn, and implement appropriate professional development: that which will positively impact student achievement.

Defining an Area of Focus

In effective schools, the shared vision of the school is centered on learning. This vision then drives the professional development opportunities. When schools create a vision that is results-oriented, they can use the vision to make decisions about adult learning (DuFour, Eaker, & DuFour, 2005). Written vision statements become the foundation for the work of the school when they are centered on curriculum, assessment, and instruction. It is this process of defining and documenting the direction of the school that provides direction for the learners and the learning.

Using the vision as a guide, administrators can start the process of ensuring alignment between the school's needs and the staff's growth and professional development opportunities. In the beginning, administrators are essential in defining what kind of professional development is necessary. As DuFour notes, "Principals typically function as gatekeepers for change and innovation, and the eventual outcome of a staff development initiative often rests upon the guidance and support furnished by the principal" (1991, p. 9). When this is done correctly, teachers receive the knowledge and support that allow a building to be continuously improving.

Data-Driven Decision-Making

To ensure that they guide their staff in the appropriate direction, effective administrators use data to develop a focus area. Massive amounts of data cross the desks of school leaders, and the time it takes to analyze and process all the data can in itself be a deterrent to developing high-quality professional development. It is imperative that leaders make decisions on *which* data to review; they must protect teacher time by narrowing the data that the teachers use. The National Staff Development Council (2003) suggests that "data on student learning gathered from standardized tests, district-made tests, student work samples, portfolios, and other sources provide important input to the selection of school or district improvement goals and provide focus for staff development efforts" (p. 176). As administrators view the available data, they do so with one key question in mind: "What area would allow the school to see the greatest gains in student achievement?"

Collaborative Decision-Making

Once a focus area has been chosen, schools use the structure of professional learning communities to allow teams of teachers to review the data to see where teacher learning needs to occur. This is a step that is often missed. While building-level data define the area of focus, classroom-level data drive academic improvement. Even in the infancy of professional learning communities, Rick DuFour (1991) wrote, "Since the ultimate success of a staff development initiative depends upon the willingness of teachers to commit to that initiative, the task of generating a sense of support and ownership among teachers must be a primary concern of the principal" (p. 63). Teachers are the ones who will be participating in the learning, so they must see the need for the learning to occur and understand that they are the ones who will make the difference. Leadership capacity is built and sustained in teachers. As Hargreaves and Fink (2003) note, "In a complex, fast-paced world, leadership cannot just rest on the shoulders of the few. The burden is too great. In highly complex, knowledge-based organizations, everyone's intelligence is needed to help the organization flex, respond, regroup, and retool in the face of unpredictable and sometimes overwhelming demands" (p. 696). It is time to stop looking outside for what will fix our schools and know that it is what we already have inside that counts.

Most schools identify learning needs related to curriculum, instruction, or assessment. A variety of guiding questions can assist teachers in determining the next steps in the process: "What are we currently doing?" "What is working?" "How do we know it is working?" "What isn't working, and how do we know that it isn't?" "What do we as teachers need to know in order to increase student achievement in this area?" These questions provide guidance while also protecting teacher autonomy in making decisions regarding professional development.

This process of defining professional development also sets the stage for the use of an inquiry process to examine current teaching practice and evaluate current achievement results. Defining professional development in this way helps teachers understand that it works best not as a one-time event, but rather as a continuous resource to improve what happens in their classrooms. As teachers engage in challenging dialogue regarding classroom practices and student achievement, they begin to see the value of professional development in supporting their own growth and responding to their individual and collective educational needs.

Providing Effective Professional Development

While defining an area of focus will help schools understand what professional development they need, they must still decide how best to provide it. Professional development follows two very different strands: learning that comes from outside the school environment and learning that comes from within. Both are important for adult learning, but each meets different needs of the learner. Professional development from the outside ensures that educators keep current with best practices and assists with gaps in the knowledge base of the learners. It also assists schools with creating a common knowledge and vocabulary in regard to a given practice. The new advocacy for collaboration, however, transfers well into the professional development arena. "Because learning has a strong social component," Dennis Sparks tells us, "and because synergy that comes from group problem solving often leads to innovative solutions, the most powerful forms of professional development are centered on teams within schools" (2005b, p. 91). When the emphasis on learning switches from isolation to a team approach, the structure of professional development moves from learning from the outside to learning from the *inside*. The key is in knowing when it is appropriate to go outside the district for knowledge and when it is best to capitalize on that which is well within our reach.

Professional Development From the Outside

Every school is filled with a variety of experts in a variety of fields. This expertise needs to be cultivated and shared. More often than not, schools simply do not utilize the expertise of the professionals within the building. In some cases, however, even the experts in the building do not have the knowledge they need or would like to have. When everyone needs to have the same level of knowledge and ✭ use the same language in regard to that knowledge, it is appropriate to bring in an outside expert for the entire group. This allows schools to "regroup" on a topic and ensures that teachers are at the same level of knowledge and feel comfortable with it. Learning becomes a collective experience in which everyone hears the same message, given in the same way, at the same time. After this grounding, people can take their new learning and process it in different ways, based on past experiences and their personal knowledge, to make it most meaningful for them.

When teachers know what they are looking for to further their knowledge, they can make educated decisions about where to look. Conferences, workshops, books, and articles can assist with filling the gaps. We all understand the value of time, and since the decision to utilize these resources comes after defining a need for them, teachers see the value in them and can define for themselves exactly what to look for and how to best use it, with no time wasted studying that which is irrelevant.

Educators also need to keep current on best practices. Education experts and researchers are continuously updating, refining, and even identifying new practices to be used in schools in order to meet the ever-changing societal needs of those who walk through the school doors. Effective schools create a system that connects this new knowledge, when relevant, to what is happening in the classroom. The system may be a sharing circle where learning articles are distributed around the staff; this works best if the administrator highlights the key points so that readers can use their time wisely. Schools might also have resident experts assigned to keeping up with defined trends. If the school need is in the area of literacy, for example, a person or group of people might meet once a month to share the newest learning and distribute that which is relevant to the rest of the staff. Using strategies that promote this type of learning in the most efficient manner possible provides benefits for everyone.

The bottom line is that although the newest trend in professional development is, as it should be, to use in-house expertise and grow knowledge from within, there are still times when it is appropriate to pull from the outside. The key is to make sure that the learning is relevant and that structures are in place to support the educator in applying the learning. All that being said, the greatest growth occurs when the adults within the building are defined and supported as the educational experts.

Professional Development From the Inside

The most powerful forms of staff development occur in ongoing teams that meet on a regular basis, preferably several times a week, for the purposes of learning, joint lesson planning, and problem solving.
          —National Staff Development Council

This list from NSDC is just a beginning of what teachers can do in collaborative teams. When used appropriately, collaborative teams move educators closer toward the goal of ensuring that best practices learned through professional development are embedded into the daily business of schools.

First, however, we must have clarity on what collaboration is. Collaborative relationships are about teachers supporting teachers in order to promote success for students. Unlike *collegial* relationships, in which the emphasis is on supporting teachers on a more personal and social level, collaboration is all about the *professional* side of teaching.

In *On Common Ground,* Mike Schmoker further illustrates this by stating, "The right kind of continuous, structured teacher collaboration improves the quality of teaching and pays big, often immediate, dividends in student learning and professional morale in virtually any setting" (Schmoker, 2005, p. xii).

To be successful, teams must have norms, agendas, and general meeting management skills. *Norms* protect the teams as they work; each team decides how they want to conduct business in meetings and uses these norms to continuously guide their work. *Agendas* assist teams with framing their work each time they meet, and meeting minutes help to maintain a record of the work that gets done. Meeting *management* ensures that the focus can be on the work that needs to get done, not on the meeting structure itself. While most teams center their work on a content area, knowledge of content is not as critical as understanding the educational process, as Marzano (2003) points out: "While subject-matter knowledge in itself might not be consistently associated with student achievement, pedagogical knowledge is" (p. 64). Thus, team meetings are structured and managed to get the most out of every minute and to keep the focus on learning. The only arenas to be addressed are those having to do with curriculum and instruction as they relate to learning.

How to define the work of teams often becomes a stumbling block for schools. Mike Schmoker wrote in *On Common Ground* that a professional learning community "starts with a group of teachers who meet regularly as a team to identify essential and valued student learning, develop common formative assessments, analyze current levels of achievement, set achievement goals, share strategies, and then create lessons to improve upon those levels" (Schmoker, 2005, p. xii). In the past, we haven't categorized this work as professional development, simply because it happens within the school.

All of these tasks and so many more can now be defined as professional development. The mindset used to be that for professional development to occur, an outsider must come in to deliver the message. What we know now as best practice in professional development is that what matters most is what happens *inside* our schools. Linda Lambert might say it best when she says, "The habits and conditions that allow a staff to work well as a unit contribute to a 'professional community.' Such communities are places in which teachers participate in decision making, have a shared sense of purpose, engage in collaborative work, and accept joint responsibility for the outcomes of their work" (1998, p. 11). This is true professional development.

The professional learning that occurs in collaborative teams drives continuous growth. While learning is more structured during collaborative team times that are embedded in the school schedule, in a professional learning community, learning begins to permeate the entire educational environment. It becomes a part of conversations between staff members at all junctures of the school day—before and after school, during faculty meetings and lunch times. Whether scheduled or spontaneous, this professional learning is ongoing, job-embedded, and very specific to the individual needs of the school. Teachers feel free to express both their strengths and weaknesses when they know that the ultimate goal is success for all. Once the culture of learning together has been embedded, professional development is not about something to attend; it is a way of doing business.

Shared Learning

Continuous improvement in teaching, student achievement, and the quality of relationships among all members of the community is based on a continuous cycle of teaching and learning and an openness by everyone in the community to learn from everyone else in the community—no matter what their title or status.

—Dennis Sparks

Administrative support for shared learning is essential. Schools that have embedded professional development into their everyday business do business differently; for them, professional development is not about adding activities or strategies. *High-quality* professional development requires a cultural shift in our understanding—a realization that learning is continuous and best done collaboratively.

Administrators can build support for this new culture in many ways. Communicate the expected behaviors on an ongoing basis by sharing the message verbally through conversations in the hallways, teachers' lounge, and classrooms to show that learning is important and pervasive. Model collaborative learning structures during faculty meetings by eliminating "administrivia" and using that time to focus on the learning needs of the building—show what this type of professional development looks like. Messages and items in weekly or monthly newsletters will highlight the positive work teams are doing. Share research articles that support the work of the school and teams and reinforce job-embedded professional development.

It is also imperative that leaders address issues that would distract teams from their work. While teams should self-monitor their effectiveness, administrators need to be "tight" about ensuring that teams will meet regularly. Team time needs to be protected from outside events that might have negative impact or erode the time that teams get to spend together. Issues that might arise should be addressed quickly and efficiently within the team itself or with administrative assistance, if necessary.

Allocating monetary and human resources to support the effort of shared learning also helps further the process. In fact, "many schools are finding that dollars spent on substitutes for teachers so that they can engage in professional development during the school day is money well spent. Sometimes many of the best educational practices are happening in a colleague's classroom just down the hall. Money that is spent to allow teachers to learn from each other in their own buildings helps to further collegiality and collaboration" (Martin & Brown, 2007, pp. 57–58). Reorganize human resources to allow time for teachers to work together on common issues or view each other in action.

Leadership support of teacher learning outside of the team structure is relatively new to most people. For years we have talked about peer and collegial coaching, but the most common structure of this utilizes just one teacher as the expert and the other as the learner. Coaching in a *collaborative* environment focused on professional development is more unilateral. In this environment, there is not necessarily one expert. Instead, a *team* of teachers works together to find a better way of doing business. In the traditional coaching experience, "having the ability to actually see a colleague teach and then have follow-up conversations affords teachers the opportunity to be reflective about their own teaching practices in relation to the teaching practices of others. Peer coaching promotes the idea of teachers learning together and bettering their teaching practices together" (Martin & Brown, 2007, p. 62). In the PLC coaching experience, we must imagine this same scene with *multiple* teachers observing the same experience and then coming together to discuss what they observed and how to make their practices more valuable to students.

Once again, it is the building leader who can set the stage for this type of learning to occur—by providing release time for teachers to be together in the same classroom at the same time, either by restructuring the personnel in the building or using funds to secure substitutes.

Celebrating Learning

Learning from and with each other is an integral part of improvement, both personal and professional, and definitely something to be celebrated. The celebration of this collaborative work can itself become a part of reflection and continuous growth. Teams need defined times throughout the year to report out to the collective group as a way of reflecting on and celebrating their progress—and ensuring that learning doesn't become "siloed." High-quality professional development that focuses on inquiry and action research throughout the school day is driven by a schoolwide effort for improvement, and the greatest benefits can only be reaped if that learning is shared and celebrated.

Leadership in Learning

The value of professional development reaches an entirely different level when it is tied directly to the needs of the learners, both student and adult, within a building. It is not about the next new thing or what someone heard someone else talking about. It is not about doing what the school down the street is doing. It is about the very definite needs of an individual building and the collaborative efforts of educators to meet those needs. Once we understand this key point, our opportunities for individual and collective growth are endless. Professional development changes from being an external component of a school to one that is integrated and embedded into the school's processes and values.

This new kind of professional development also becomes the catalyst for transforming the school from individuals working in isolation to groups working collaboratively toward a common goal. Creating professional development systems in schools, as described in this chapter, goes one step further—it develops individual leadership skills and promotes a sense of shared leadership. Developing leadership skills for all is an essential component of creating a continuously improving school: "While a school can be run by a single leader and managed pretty effectively, increases in student achievement come when that leadership is shared and is larger than a single individual. Leadership has moved far beyond one person in schools that are truly making a difference" (Martin & Brown, 2007, p. 66). Defined professional development gives teachers the knowledge and skills to feel assured of being successful in a leadership role.

As the learning experience moves teachers into becoming leaders in their own right, it also promotes a sense of *shared* leadership. Teacher leaders not only make the difference, they sustain the difference. Everyone helps everyone else to grow personally and professionally. As Linda Lambert reminds us, "School leadership needs to be a broad concept that is separated from person, role, and a discrete set of individual behaviors. It needs to be embedded in the school community as a whole. Such a broadening of the concept of leadership suggests shared responsibility for a shared purpose of community" (1998, p. 5). In a professional learning community, everyone benefits from adult learning. Students have a better educational experience due to the increased expertise of their teachers. Teachers have a support network of peers with whom they learn and grow. The school becomes a safe learning place for all—truly all, youth and adults alike.

References

DuFour, R. (1991). *The principal as staff developer.* Bloomington, IN: Solution Tree (formerly National Educational Service).

DuFour, R., DuFour, R., Eaker, R., & Many, T. (2006). *Learning by doing: A handbook for professional learning communities at work.* Bloomington, IN: Solution Tree (formerly National Educational Service).

DuFour, R., Eaker, R., & DuFour, R. (Eds.). (2005). *On common ground: The power of professional learning communities.* Bloomington, IN: Solution Tree (formerly National Educational Service).

Hargreaves, A., & Fink, D. (2003). Sustaining leadership. *Phi Delta Kappan, 84*(9), 693–700.

Lambert, L. (1998). *Building leadership capacity in our schools.* Alexandria, VA: Association for Supervision and Curriculum Development.

Martin, T., & Brown, T. (2007). *Improving student achievement: An educational leader's guide for developing purposeful schools.* Norwood, MA: Christopher-Gordon.

Marzano, R. (2003). *What works in schools: Translating research into action.* Alexandria, VA: Association for Supervision and Curriculum Development.

National Staff Development Council. (NSDC). (2003). *Moving NSDC's staff development standards into practice: Innovation configurations*. Oxford, OH: Author.

Schmoker, M. (2005). Foreword. In R. DuFour, R. Eaker, & R. DuFour (Eds.), *On common ground: The power of professional learning communities* (pp. xi–xvi). Bloomington, IN: Solution Tree (formerly National Educational Service).

Sparks, D. (2005a). Leading for transformation in teaching, learning, and relationships. In R. DuFour, R. Eaker, & R. DuFour (Eds.), *On common ground: The power of professional learning communities* (pp. 155–175). Bloomington, IN: Solution Tree (formerly National Educational Service).

Sparks, D. (2005b). *Leading for results: Transforming, teaching, learning, and relationships in schools*. Thousand Oaks, CA: Corwin.

PETER NOONAN

As assistant superintendent for curriculum and instruction in Fairfax County, Virginia, Peter Noonan ensures continuous improvement in academic performance for all students in the diverse school community. He also focuses on strengthening collaborative relationships with parents, and developing and promoting positive, capable, and diverse school leaders. Committed to meeting the needs of all students, Peter bases his professional philosophy on quality instructional practice, flexibility, creativity, and the use of formative data.

NINE

Breaking Through the Barriers of Time: How to Find Time to Support Struggling Students

Peter Noonan

There comes a time in the affairs of man when he must take the bull by the tail and face the situation.

—W. C. Fields

When I took the principalship at Centreville High School (CVHS) in 2004, I was very excited by how the former principal described it as an "established and high-functioning professional learning community." She assured me that not only were collaborative teams working well together, but the school had also built in extra time through the daily schedule to ensure that all students had an extra opportunity to learn. Further, the faculty had carved out time within the daily routines for all teachers to plan and collaborate together. To mark the success of the school's progress toward becoming a PLC, beautiful stationery and customized t-shirts had been printed with the PLC logo at the top. However, it quickly became apparent that Centreville High School was not a true professional learning community and in no way reflected the most fundamental tenets of a PLC. Yes, paper and shirts are nice, but they don't always symbolize what is real.

To gain a better understanding of the faculty's perceived strengths, weaknesses, opportunities, and barriers (SWOB), I scheduled meetings with departments throughout my first summer on the job. In addition to asking each department to converse about and populate the SWOB chart in Figure 9-1, I also asked the faculty where they truly believed they were on the continuum of becoming a professional learning community.

Strengths	Weaknesses
Opportunities	Barriers

Figure 9-1: SWOB Chart

As a consequence of these meetings, we discovered a great need for building foundational knowledge. Through a "creative" financing process (not an auditor's expression!), I was able to cobble together funds to send a few faculty members to professional development opportunities that included hearing Rick and Becky DuFour speak. Rick DuFour, coauthor of *Professional Learning Communities at Work* and former principal of a comprehensive high school, had "walked in our shoes" and knew what it meant to change the culture of a school and become a professional learning community.

During his keynote address, Dr. DuFour said something that stuck with me and helped shape the future work we did at CVHS: "When Moses came down from the mountain and arrived among the people, he didn't say, 'Ladies and gentlemen, we have a new 11th commandment, and that commandment is *Thou shalt not change the daily bell schedule.*'" I realized that the bell schedule was one thing our school could modify and adapt positively to ensure that all students had extra time and support for learning. Dr. DuFour's comments reinforced to me and the other staff present that the work we were about to engage in was the right work, and that it was imperative that we change to reflect the ideal that all students will learn, no matter what it takes. This became our collective mission and work for the next year.

Educators often speak about how to effectively translate theory into action. The experiences outlined in this chapter are not intended to serve as a cookbook, magic bullet, or panacea that will ensure success. Rather, this chapter will explore how to move a staff from the theory outlined in texts, rhetoric, and conversations to *action*. Considering the average tenure of a principal is less than 5 years, it is critical that we as leaders leverage the time we have, stop talking, start acting, and close the "knowing-doing gap" (Pfeffer & Sutton, 2000).

Making a Case for "Why"

I began by establishing a case for *why* we needed to modify our daily routines. A school faculty that engages in activities that require deep reflection about the collective culture for learning (or lack thereof) will experience some cognitive dissidence. Discussions are often difficult. This potential conflict can be further exacerbated when the person reflecting (often out loud and in public) is the new principal (me). Therefore, in an effort to mitigate potential problems, I wanted to create structured opportunities for the faculty to have conversations that not only allowed for reflection, but also provided time and space for the faculty to discuss why they went about their daily routines as they did. These conversations occurred throughout the first month of my tenure at CVHS.

The faculty was invited by department, to keep the number of participants under 20 and thus allowing a free flow of information and ideas. Throughout the conversations, I made a point to stay as objective and facilitative as possible so that I didn't become overly entangled in the conversation. In the book *Leadership on the Line* (Heifetz & Linsky, 2002), this important reflective and perspective-building practice is called "getting on the balcony." I believed then, as I still do today, that a new leader should always listen more than talk; that's why we have two ears and one mouth. However, to ensure that I received the information that I needed to make good cultural decisions moving forward, I did ask probing, often difficult questions. Following these exhaustive, meaningful, and healthy discussions, it was clear that we needed a new starting point; we needed to establish a new culture based on shared knowledge and quality data. We were truly starting at the bottom and building.

Making fundamental changes in schools is historically one of the most difficult tasks for any administrator. As educators, we are afraid of making mistakes that will negatively impact the next generation of kids. This is certainly a noble reason to slow down the process of change, but often results in the status quo and no movement forward. Consequently, we fall back to what we have always done. To break down the walls of fear and paralysis, we must create a new vocabulary laden with research, philosophy for the 21st century, and instructional best practice.

To make inroads around these ideals, we started to read common books and discuss them as a group. This simple act allowed us to develop shared knowledge and a common vocabulary. Additionally, it reinforced a common set of beliefs and collective commitments. To ensure a generalized understanding about what a professional learning community is and the potential power in collaboration, we read *Professional Learning Communities at Work* (DuFour & Eaker, 1998). Afterwards, we developed a mission and vision statement that reflected our high expectations for students. Additionally, we proposed a common set of values and goals that framed the work and laid the foundation for our next book study.

Classroom Instruction That Works (Marzano, Pickering, & Pollock, 2001) helped us further refine our vision of excellence as it related to the daily practice by teachers in the classroom. This broad look at how high-quality classroom instruction supported student learning fit perfectly into our commitment to do whatever it took to meet all of our students' needs. As we learned more about how to embed the Marzano strategies into our daily practice, however, it became clear that we needed to modify our learning communities to allow time for reflective conversations about what works. As one teacher asked, "When are we supposed to have these conversations as a team to determine what practices work best for our kids?" We also needed time to reinforce learning for students who were not succeeding—to implement those practices.

Good to Great (Collins, 2001) was the last selection for our "teachers as readers" group. Collins begins his book stating that "good is the enemy of great" (2001, p. 1). The word *good* was thrown around in the same breath as *CVHS* too often by the staff, students, and community. *Good to Great* provided us with a common framework for our new common mission: making CVHS *great*.

While these readings helped us build background knowledge and common vocabulary, one other piece of information proved most influential and codified that we were a good, but not great, school. This data point was our D and F grade-distribution list. This list was generated, aggregated, and disaggregated on a quarterly basis and was a solid reflection of a traditional bell curve. CVHS is a large comprehensive high school of nearly 2,400 students; at the end of the first quarter following my arrival, over 800 students had at least one D or F. This staggering statistic gave us an opportunity to discuss what high expectations for all students meant in terms of our budding vision of learning for all.

As a consequence of reading and sharing together, developing a common belief system, and examining data, we came to a realization: *High expectations are not measured when a student is successful*. Rather, the true test of a faculty's high expectations is evident in how we collectively respond when a student is failing (Lezotte, 1991). After many late-night conversations and thoughtful insights from teacher leaders, we achieved critical mass for change. We decided that a *great* school meets the needs of all students, and this can only be done by shifting the time schedule to allow for greater access (time and support) for students as well as an opportunity for teachers to collaborate. In 2003, the National Commission on Teaching and America's Future released a study that reminded us that we were on the right path. The Commission suggested that "quality teaching requires strong professional learning communities. Collegial interchange, not isolation, must become the norm for teachers. Communities of learning can no longer be considered utopian; they must become the building blocks that establish a new foundation" (National Commission on Teaching and America's Future, 2002, p. 17). We laid a new foundation at CVHS; our building blocks were predicated on the vision of becoming a great school.

Collaborating for Greatness

Changing the schedule was a collaborative effort. To ensure broad representation of those who were most impacted by the change in the daily schedule, we decided to develop a cross-functional and cross-departmental scheduling committee of 15 people. The committee studied the current schedule and considered options available to us. Then they began to build something new and different.

As administrator, my involvement in this committee was minimal; our foreign language department chair took the lead. I did, however, "weigh in" with a few non-negotiables that would frame the committee's work. First, the committee was tasked to build time into the school day for students who needed extra time and support for learning. Second, the committee was to ensure that teachers saw their own students during the extra block of time, as they were the experts on their students' needs. Additionally, there had to be an attendance function attached to the extra period so that there was accountability for students. Finally, the committee was charged to review the plan for collaborative time for teachers and provide feedback.

To effect change, it was vital that teachers and I lead this Herculean effort *together*. As Doug Reeves (2006) has pointed out:

> Vision is a necessary but inefficient condition for effective leadership. Leadership must be . . . distributed. Distributed leadership is not merely an exercise in participatory democracy, nor is it the popular but ineffectual therapeutic brand of leadership in which the earnest but incompetent leaders assure followers that they 'hear' us or 'feel' for us, but otherwise blithely ignore our wishes. Distributed leadership is based on trust, as well as the certain knowledge that no single leader possesses the knowledge, skills, or talent to lead an organization. (p. 28)

I must admit that it was difficult to give up control of the scheduling committee, because ultimately, I was responsible for what happened. In an effort to wield some influence, I decided to start the first committee meeting by sharing five of my "brilliant" ideas of what the new bell schedule could look like. This meeting turned out to be a humbling experience. Upon delivering what I thought was a well-thought-out and highly articulate presentation of ideas to the scheduling committee, they dismissed me—but in a nice way. This rejection turned out to be one of the best things that could have happened, as it forced me to step back and allow the staff and faculty leaders the chance to resolve the collective issue of failing students. It also reinforced for the staff that I trusted them, their judgment, and their ability to solve problems.

Four months later, the scheduling committee published the following purpose statement along with a proposed new bell schedule:

> Centreville High School is committed to meeting the needs of all of our students. In order to meet students where they are academically, it is vital that we have opportunities to meet on occasions outside of the regularly scheduled class time. Too often, because of the demands of a comprehensive high

school and the commitments of our students, we are not able to utilize after-school time effectively. Therefore, we have developed a new schedule that will provide students and teachers an extra opportunity to meet and extend their experiences beyond what they may have already received during the "regular" instructional time while still in school.

This purpose statement became a touchstone for our changing culture at Centreville High School. This was the first time that a cross-departmental team of teachers had come together and overtly stated their intention to meet the needs of all students.

In order to build in extra time and support for students that would be required rather than invitational, the committee developed a schedule that incorporated a "PLUS" period (see Figure 9-2).

A Day: Periods 1, 3(+), 4, 5, 7
B Day: Periods 2, 3(+), 4, 6, 8

Period	Time
1 or 2	7:25–8:52
3 (PLUS)	9:00–9:31
4	9:39–10:23
5 or 6 (and lunch)	10:31–12:35
7 or 8	12:43–2:10

Figure 9-2: CVHS Bell Schedule—An Alternating Day Block Schedule

As you can see in Figure 9-2, the PLUS period is from 9 A.M. to 9:31 A.M. every day; it is assigned on a rotating basis to each of the other seven academic class periods. This rotation provides each teacher with the opportunity to see their students for an extra 31 minutes every seventh day. For example, on the first day of the 7-day cycle, students report to their first-period class during first period *and* during the PLUS period. On the second day of the cycle, students report to their second-period class during its regular time *and* the PLUS period. On the third day of the cycle, students report to their fourth-period class during fourth period *and* the PLUS period, and so on. The 7–day cycle continues throughout the year.

To build in collaboration time for teachers, we decided to align planning periods by content area. For example, the entire English department had the first block off (no classes were offered in English in the building during first block) for teacher planning, and the math department had the second block off (no math classes were offered during the second block schoolwide). As difficult as this may sound for a school because of master scheduling conflicts (single-time offerings and specialty classes), we were able to successfully make it work. As a consequence, every other day, our teachers had 90 minutes of uninterrupted planning time with their content partners.

Listening to Feedback

Presenting this to the faculty was initially difficult and had our staff "twisted in intellectual and emotional knots." They said the rotating schedule was "confusing," "hard to understand," "not going to meet the needs of all students," and would "create chaos in our building." It was clear that we would need to spend a significant amount of time explaining the schedule and allowing the faculty a chance to provide feedback. One of the faculty's greatest concerns was whether students would understand where they were to be on a daily basis. Ultimately, the students proved the most resilient during our reorganization of time, and, in fact, faculty members were often overheard asking the students where *they* (the teachers) were supposed to be.

For any organizational change to be successful, thoughtful and cautious planning around communication must take place. At CVHS, the committee chair and I spent a good amount of time discussing how best to process the sharing of the schedule. We wanted to give every staff member an opportunity to express any concern. If information is shared only in a large group, the dynamics of a few people can monopolize the conversation while those who have the greatest concern remain silent. This effect can subsequently undermine any plan, because the silent minority can subvert even the best-laid plans. Our communication plan accounted for this as we scheduled small group discussions during teachers' planning periods and followed these meetings up with a big faculty meeting several weeks later.

Two days of the small group discussions were set aside as "open door" days that encouraged the faculty to come and discuss what they liked and didn't like about the proposed schedule. As an added incentive, we provided doughnuts and coffee. Over 2 days, faculty streamed in and shared very clearly with us excitement, enthusiasm, and trepidation. This feedback was precisely what we were hoping for so that we could modify, adapt, and incorporate their thoughts into what was ultimately presented in a large faculty meeting. These one-on-one meetings were extremely valuable in our success. Through the encouragement of feedback, the faculty became part of the process and developed a sense of ownership for the work.

Ironically, this simple leadership/management function—small group meetings—turned out to be diametrically opposed to the leadership style present prior to my arrival. This provided "political capital" and made the faculty's rapid move forward easier than I or anyone else anticipated.

After the one-on-one conferences, we had a full faculty meeting after school. The new schedule was presented to the faculty. They then broke into four large groups and completed an affinity diagram in an effort to make meaning from the diverse voices of the faculty.

Conducting an Affinity Diagram

Affinity Diagram: A group decision-making technique designed to sort a large number of ideas, process variables, concepts, and opinions into naturally related groups connected by a simple concept

Guidelines

- Ensure ideas are described with phrases or sentences.
- Minimize the discussion while sorting—discuss while developing the header cards.
- Aim for 5–10 groups.
- If one group is much larger than others, consider splitting it.

Directions

1. Conduct a brainstorming session on the topic under investigation.
2. Clarify the list of ideas. Record them on small cards or sticky notes.
3. Randomly lay out cards on a table, flipchart, or wall.
4. Direct participants as follows: "Without speaking, sort the cards into similar groups based on your gut reaction. If you don't like the placement of a particular card, move it." Participants continue moving cards until they reach consensus on placement.
5. Create header cards consisting of a concise 3–5 word description: the unifying concept for the group. Place header card at top of each group.
6. Discuss the groupings, and try to understand how the groups relate to each other.

Tips

- Inquire whether ideas are adequately clarified.
- Use only 3–5 words in the phrase on the header card to describe the group.
- While sorting, physically get up and gather around the area where the cards are placed.
- Do not start sorting until all team members are ready.
- If an idea fits in more than one category or group, and consensus about placement cannot be reached, make a second card and place it in both groups.

Five major themes emerged from our affinity diagram. These five themes gave us an opportunity to further investigate the issues raised by the group with the support and resources of the entire faculty. We put out the themes to the group and created task forces to provide solutions to the concerns. This allowed the faculty to problem-solve and think critically in support of their future rather than feel alienated and left out of the process.

This collaborative process could not have taken place if we had not begun to do the work essential to developing a high-functioning, collaborative PLC. The staff was able to reflect critically without fear of retribution by me or a team member; to think creatively without concern for having their ideas crushed; and to problem-solve with the support of action research. We had a problem to solve, and all of us came to it with strengths and deficits—*and* with the end in mind. We allowed for personal differences to ensure a positive outcome for our students. This is not unlike looking at formative assessment data and making good collaborative decisions about how to intervene on behalf of students and, further, how to refine our teaching to prevent failure in the future. These are the fundamental tenets of a PLC, and it was a terrific model and action process for us to reflect on as we continued to refine our work. Six months later, the faculty reached consensus, and the following year, we implemented the new bell schedule.

A PLC Schedule in Action

The following school year started, and all of the concerns the faculty had regarding changing our schedule were realized. There was "chaos," "confusion," and "delay" on a daily basis for the first 2 weeks. However, because we had a solid cultural foundation of creating the schedule together, these problems were not insurmountable; in fact, they allowed us to grow even stronger as a team. It was an exciting time to be at Centreville High School because we were acting in ways consistent with our beliefs.

Abraham Lincoln once exhorted Congress, "Still the question recurs 'can we do better?' The dogmas of the quiet past are inadequate to the stormy present. The occasion is piled high with difficulty, and we must rise to the occasion. As our case is new, so we must think anew" (Phillips, 1992, p. 137). Lincoln reminds us that doing things differently takes courage. I am also reminded that when we are creating anything new and "rising to the occasion," we make mistakes and missteps. As leaders, we must honor our past but look to the future; we must allow our creative energy to flourish, even in failure, in our drive to create something even better.

At first, the faculty was a little unsure about what to do during the PLUS period. Initially they used the time for "intervention-like" activities such as going over material that a student had missed due to absence, reteaching material that had already been covered, requiring students to make up tests and quizzes, and asking students to organize their materials. However, as time passed and teachers realized that not all students required intervention, the teachers became very creative in their approach to how to use this time more effectively for enrichment and flexible grouping.

It became clear, for example, that large groups of students in a classroom did not facilitate individual intervention easily. Therefore, if a student had an A or B in the class he was scheduled to rotate back to during the PLUS, he could instead be excused to attend one of four areas throughout the building (the cafeteria, media center, computer lab, or lecture hall). These "student choice" opportunities became incentives for many students and met the individual needs of successful students allowing for independent quiet study, cooperative group project work, integration of technology, and general social options—yes, sometimes high school students need "down time."

Because the new master schedule provided teachers time to collaborate with content partners, thoughtful discussions took place throughout the building about how the new found time (PLUS) could be used creatively to meet the needs of all students differently. Two content-area teams, math and history, were "early adopters" when it came to looking at time as a resource and flexibility. During their planning time, the algebra team hatched a plan to flexibly group students based on teacher strengths during the PLUS period. This meant that when students rotated back to their first-period algebra class, a struggling student might be sent to another algebra teacher's PLUS period to take advantage of that teacher's strengths. This simple concept became one of the most powerful strategies to engage and provide meaningful intervention for math students. Additionally, it created among our math team a collective ownership for the success or failure of all students.

The history department used a similar strategy by setting up content "houses" during the PLUS period. On any given day, there might be an extra classroom staffed for U.S. history support for students struggling in that content. This structure allowed students an opportunity to hear the class content from another teacher. The instructional impact of this model was great because it allowed students a chance to know, and learn from, another significant adult in the building. This, like the algebra team, also created a collective ownership among the teachers for other students' success.

The PLUS period had other benefits as well. Centreville's chapter of the National Honor Society (NHS) is among the strongest in the state. Our students have been highly successful looking for opportunities to earn volunteer hours, but often they are outside of school. The PLUS period allowed the NHS students an opportunity to support other students at CVHS who were struggling. A cadre of NHS volunteers was created, and they reported to our media center daily. If, during the PLUS period, a teacher had a larger group than they anticipated for intervention, a phone call was placed to the media center, and an NHS tutor was sent to the classroom as a support. This was a highly successful strategy and provided opportunities for all of our kids to engage in school differently than they had in the past.

The final, and possibly the most exciting, way that our faculty engaged our students during the PLUS was by sharing their personal talents and gifts with our student body. Of teachers who did not have students rotating back during the PLUS period, many decided that they would teach our students something they had a passion for. For example, we had teachers volunteer to instruct students about bicycle maintenance, financial management, backgammon, a trip to Machu Picchu, and the like. This gesture by our teachers also became a valuable motivator for students who were struggling and typically unable to leave their classes during the PLUS period. A schedule of activities was developed, published, and advertised schoolwide so that students knew in advance which teachers were sharing their passion. If a student who was not successful wanted to attend one of these exciting sessions, the student could make an individual strategic plan (which included rigorous intervention) to succeed and be present if he or she met the mark. We re-engaged many students by providing this different avenue for success and by allowing for celebrations when a student met a personal learning goal.

Reflections From Beyond the Barrier

In more than 20 years as a teacher, principal, and district administrator, I came to understand that the school improvement efforts that succeeded did so first and foremost because they were able to capture the devotion and enthusiasm of highly talented people. That led me to believe that we should be thinking less in terms of developing systems to hand down to schools, and more in terms of finding new and better ways to enlist talented teachers and principals — and helping them cultivate the potential within each student day by day.

—Gary Gordon

After a year operating under our new bell schedule, we learned many lessons. First and foremost, changing culture to improve student achievement through systematic intervention and extra time is hard work. We quickly learned that our teachers were not trained to operate in a model that provides intervention. Additionally, we learned that it takes time and effort to build a model for collaboration that allows for meaningful conversations to occur around student progress and our own teaching practices.

We found that when we raised the expectations for our struggling students by saying that we were going to do whatever it took to ensure their success, we forced students far outside of their personal comfort zones. It was, unfortunately, a new message for many students who had traditionally eased their way through school by following the path of least resistance. Our parents questioned what we were doing, because Centreville had traditionally been a "good" and "successful" school in the eyes of the community. There was great concern about "breaking something that wasn't broken." Throughout our conversations with the Parent Teacher Student Association (PTSA), I encouraged them to read the same books we were reading and routinely updated them on our progress toward embracing learning for all. The pushback we received from all constituencies was uncomfortable.

However, after the first year of living through our new schedule, our new data set painted a picture of a changing reality. Not only did we make adequate yearly progress (AYP) in every subgroup, we had an overall gain of greater than 10% in math and English in the aggregate on our state assessments. Additionally, we had a 15% gain among our special education, ESOL, and African-American subgroups. For the first time in many years, we made substantive progress in closing the minority student achievement gap.

Beyond our student achievement data, it is also important to note that teacher satisfaction increased. Studies suggest that teacher efficacy is rooted in the success or failure of the students they instruct

(Gordon, 2006; Fleming & Asplund, 2007). Our work supports this theory; there was a direct correlation between our students' academic growth and our own satisfaction. We learned where our strengths lie as a collective teaching organization and how to teach to those strengths. We also have a greater understanding of where our gaps reside, and because we talk to each other about those gaps, we are making quality decisions to systematically close them. The parents most concerned scrutinized our data results closely and in the end, were enthused by what they found.

Another outcome was a dramatic decrease in our D and F rate. This data point was important to us as it truly spoke to our collective successes with kids. The D and F rate was reduced by over 30% the first year we implemented the PLUS period. We were, and are, about learning for all and have not forsaken rigor one bit. Our enrollment in Advanced Placement (AP) increased dramatically, and in 2004, we were recognized by *Newsweek* as a top-100 high school in the United States. We believe that a driver for our AP enrollment increase was our proactive conversations with students who were first-time AP takers; we promised that they would not "sink or swim." Rather, we assured them that a quality support system would be in place to ensure their success.

After further review through a continuous improvement process, it is fair to say that there are other schedules available that have proven to work that can also be used as models. More and more schools are making a conscious decision to build in extra time, often more than the 30 minutes CVHS added. Thirty minutes should be the daily minimum to impact those that need the support. We are fortunate in our county (Fairfax County Public Schools) to have creative and thoughtful principals who all do what is best for student achievement. Figures 9-3 and 9-4 (page 176) illustrate two other scheduling models that provide extra time for students as well as built-in teacher collaboration time. These come from Fairfax and Chantilly High Schools.

School Day: 7:20–2:05

A Day		B Day	
1st Period	7:20–8:46	2nd Period	7:20–8:46
		R and R*	8:46–9:30
3rd Period	8:54–10:20	Pride Time**	9:37–10:20
5th Period/Lunch	10:28–12:31	6th Period/Lunch	10:28–12:31
A Lunch	*10:28–11:00*	*A Lunch*	*10:28–11:00*
A Class	*11:05–12:31*	*A Class*	*11:05–12:31*
B Class	*10:28–11:15*	*B Class*	*10:28–11:15*
B Lunch	*11:15–11:45*	*B Lunch*	*11:15–11:45*
B Class	*11:50–12:31*	*B Class*	*11:50–12:31*
C Class	*10:28–11:55*	*C Class*	*10:28–11:55*
C Lunch	*12:00–12:31*	*C Lunch*	*12:00–12:31*
7th Period	12:39–2:05	8th Period	12:39–2:05

* Time schedule rotates by period like the CVHS PLUS period.
** Flexible time to attend other classes that students are failing or use as quiet study.

Figure 9-3: Fairfax High School Schedule—An Alternating Day Block Schedule

School Day: 7:24–2:06

Monday–Thursday Schedule			Friday Bell Schedule		
1st/2nd Periods	7:24–8:53		Teacher Collaboration	7:10–7:50	
3rd/4th Periods/LS	9:02–10:29		1st/2nd Periods	8:00–9:02	
			3rd/4th Periods/LS	9:32–10:49	
Learning Seminar 1*	9:02–9:42		Learning Seminar 1*	9:32–10:07	
Learning Seminar 2*	9:49–10:29		Learning Seminar 2*	10:14–10:49	
5th/6th Periods	10:38–12:30		5th/6th Periods	10:38–12:30	

Class	Lunch	Class	Class	Lunch	Class
10:36–11:05	*A 10:29–11:03*	*11:03–12:30*	*10:56–11:20*	*A 10:49–11:23*	*11:23–12:40*
10:36–11:33	*B 11:05–11:35*	*11:35–12:32*	*10:56–11:48*	*B 11:20–11:50*	*11:50–12:42*
10:38–12:05	*C 11:33–12:03*	*12:03–12:32*	*10:58–12:15*	*C 11:48–12:18*	*12:18–12:42*
	D 12:05–12:39			*D 12:15–12:49*	

7th/8th Periods	12:39–2:06	7th/8th Periods	12:49–2:06

* Time schedule rotates by period like the CVHS PLUS period.

Figure 9-4: Chantilly High School Schedule—An Alternating Day Block

Schedule

I am more convinced now than ever that the most important aspect of bringing about change is establishing a culture that is ready for, and supports it. My experience at Centreville High School centered on changing a belief system that promoted teaching to one that makes learning paramount. This cannot be done by simply shifting time around during the day. People must work together, read together, and experience together their organization's current realities as well as its future possibilities. I am very proud of our school and community for taking a risk and ultimately understanding that we are here for the students first.

The experiences outlined in this chapter are by no means a recipe for success, and I hope that the reflections of cultural readiness make that abundantly clear. There is no "one size fits all" approach. However, I have been able to successfully navigate three separate, and distinctly different, schools using many of the approaches and tools shared. I am hopeful that you, as an emerging or veteran leader, can pull pieces of this successful model and transform your school to one that focuses on student learning above all else.

References

Collins, J. (2001). *Good to great: Why some companies make the leap . . . and others don't.* New York: HarperCollins.

DuFour, R., DuFour, R., Eaker, R., & Karhanek, G. (2004). *Whatever it takes: How professional learning communities respond when kids don't learn.* Bloomington, IN: Solution Tree (formerly National Educational Service).

DuFour, R., DuFour, R., Eaker, R., & Many, T. (2006). *Learning by doing: A handbook for professional learning communities at work.* Bloomington, IN: Solution Tree.

DuFour, R., & Eaker, R. (1998). *Professional learning communities at work: Best practices for enhancing student achievement.* Bloomington, IN: Solution Tree (formerly National Educational Service).

Eaker, R., DuFour, R., & DuFour, R. (2002). *Getting started: Reculturing schools to become professional learning communities.* Bloomington, IN: Solution Tree (formerly National Educational Service).

Fleming, J. H., & Asplund, J. (2007). *Human sigma: Managing the employee-customer encounter.* New York: Gallup.

Fried, R. L. (1995). *The passionate teacher: A practical guide.* Boston: Beacon.

Gordon, G. (2006). *Building engaged schools: Getting the most out of America's classrooms.* New York: Gallup.

Heifetz, R., & Linsky, M. (2002). *Leadership on the line: Staying alive through the dangers of leading.* Boston: Harvard Business School.

Lezotte, L. (1991). *Correlates of effective schools: The first and second generation.* Okemos, MI: Effective Schools Products.

Marzano, R. J., Pickering, D. J., & Pollock, J. E. (2001). *Classroom instruction that works: Research-based strategies for increasing student achievement.* Alexandria, VA: Association for Supervision and Curriculum Development.

National Commission on Teaching and America's Future. (2002). *Unraveling the "teacher shortage" problem: Teacher retention is key.* Washington, DC: Author.

Pfeffer, J. & Sutton, R. (2000). *The knowing and doing gap: How smart companies turn knowledge into action.* Boston: Harvard Business School.

Phillips, D. (1992). *Lincoln on leadership: Executive strategies for tough times.* New York: Warner Books.

Reeves, D. (2006). *The learning leader: How to focus school improvement for better results.* Alexandria, VA: Association for Supervision and Curriculum Development.

Sergiovanni, T. (1992). *Moral leadership: Getting to the heart of school improvement.* San Francisco: Jossey-Bass.

GERI PARSCALE

Geri Parscale is director of professional development and instruction for Fort Leavenworth Unified School District 207. Under her leadership, schools throughout the district have consistently earned the Kansas Standard of Excellence for student performance in reading and math at all grade levels. For more than 20 years, Geri has worked closely with educators in a united effort to continuously improve schools. As principal of Bradley Elementary School in Fort Leavenworth in 2002, Geri implemented collaborative teacher time across all grade levels. As a result, 25% of Bradley students have achieved "exceeds standards" scores in science, math, writing, and social studies, and less than 5% scored in the "academic warning" range.

TEN

Building a Pyramid of Interventions

Geri Parscale

Consider this familiar scenario: Ms. Fenley, a new principal, decides to begin her new appointment by introducing herself to parents. A week prior to the beginning of school, she sends a note to welcome all parents to visit. She mentions that class lists for the year will be posted on the front doors of the school at 10:00 a.m. on Friday. Friday comes, lists are posted, and Ms. Fenley spends the rest of the day meeting with parents who have concerns about their child's placement, having many conversations about reading and math skills, needs, and personalities. The last parent leaves Ms. Fenley's office at 5:45 that evening. She is exhausted.

Later, after some reflection, Ms. Fenley realizes that there are no "bad" teachers on her staff. Parents simply know that certain teachers are better at helping struggling students than others. Certain teachers seem to "intervene" to help kids reach their fullest potential, and those are the teachers who are the most "in demand."

Why do parents often look at student placement as "your child got the good teacher, and mine didn't"? Why are some interventions for struggling students better than others? How do we help all staff provide effective academic interventions for all students who need it? How do we hold all staff accountable for providing those interventions? This chapter will explore how a professional learning community responds to these questions by building a pyramid of timely, systematic interventions to help all students succeed.

A Short History of Interventions

In a traditional school, interventions typically occur as reteaching for the whole class. For example, if a third-grade teacher recognizes that some students did not master regrouping in double-digit subtraction, she teaches it again to the whole group, even though not everyone needs reteaching. In a professional learning community, however, interventions occur individually or with small groups of students. We hold discussions around what we want students to learn and then target interventions designed to help students achieve that goal. In a PLC, the third-grade teacher would examine data from her formative assessments, notice that only four students did not grasp the concept of regrouping, and tailor her instruction to meet the needs of those children in a small group.

In a traditional school, interventions occur when the teacher feels help is needed. Teachers are on their own in deciding the appropriate response to the student, and they respond in very different ways, as Ms. Fenley's parents recognized. In a professional learning community, interventions occur in response to student performance on common assessments. There is a systematic, directed, timely response for all students in the school, and each teacher knows all the interventions. It is not left to the individual teacher to "supply" a way to help this child. The system has a plan, and all are required to use it.

In a traditional school, failure *is* an option. Teachers believe that it is their responsibility to provide clear lessons and opportunities for students to demonstrate learning. Students are given choices and advised that they will be held accountable for their decisions. Students who do not take advantage of learning opportunities must "suffer the consequence." In a PLC, learning is *required:* "Professional learning communities create a systematic process of interventions to ensure students receive additional time and support for learning when they experience difficulty. The intervention process is timely and students are directed rather than invited to utilize the system of time and support" (DuFour, DuFour, Eaker, & Many, 2006, p. 71). Put another way, in a professional learning community, as many people have heard Rick DuFour say, we "harass 'em 'til they pass."

Restructuring Beliefs, Asking Critical Questions

Implementing a system of interventions requires us to think differently about education, about teaching, about learning. It requires us to begin to think "otherwise" about our schools: "Thinking otherwise does not necessarily mean thinking big rather than small about good education. It means thinking differently" (Barth, 1991, p. 124). A school must restructure its culture and its beliefs. As your staff begins this different way of thinking, answering the four critical questions to guide your PLC development will be key to the success of this shift in thinking.

There are four questions that should guide you in all you do as you restructure your beliefs: 1) What is it that we want our students to learn? 2) How do we know that they have learned it? 3) What are we going to do if students do not learn it? 4) What are we going to do if students do learn it? (DuFour, DuFour, Eaker, & Many, 2006).

Answering questions 1 and 2 is not only important to the work of a professional learning community, it is vital for the success of any school trying to restructure cultures and beliefs. We cannot develop and implement interventions for our children if we first have not made it clear as to what we want them to learn. We must remember that "the constant collective inquiry into 'What is it we want our students to learn?' and 'How will we know when each student has learned it?' is a professional responsibility of *every* faculty member" (DuFour, DuFour, Eaker, & Many, 2006, p. 46). Only when teachers have answered the what and how of questions 1 and 2 can restructuring move forward.

Do You Take Responsibility to Ensure All Students Learn?

As administrator, begin conversations by asking your staff if they believe that all students can learn at high levels: Is their focus on learning or teaching? Ask yourself if *you* have also taken responsibility for student learning: Do your teachers have frequent, collaborative time embedded in the professional day? Is the school culture one of collaboration or isolation? Eastwood and Louis (1992) write that a vital piece to school restructuring is to build a culture of collaboration that is focused on cooperation. Your culture needs to reflect that everyone on your staff believes that they are making a difference for each child.

Have You Clearly Defined What All Students Should Learn?

Have you identified essential outcomes, or is student learning "all over the place"? Before building a system of academic interventions for those who aren't learning, you must know what you wanted them to learn. As leader of the building, you must give the time, talents, and tools to make this happen. Consider using tools such as the three-part test offered by Doug Reeves (2002). He encourages teams to evaluate the endurance, leverage, and readiness that each learning standard provides for children. Work with your team as they use these questions in developing their essential outcomes, answering the first critical question of a PLC.

Do You Use Frequent Common Formative Assessments to Measure Student Learning?

Answering this question can cause even the most experienced educators to shudder. The response is often, "Well . . . I . . . Uh . . . We have always . . ." None of these comments help us in a professional learning community. In a PLC, we focus on results, on finding answers to the second critical question of a PLC: "How will we know if students have learned?"

Let's take a page from the first year of a baby's life: After a child is born, she has no less than seven doctor's appointments throughout her first year. These "well child check-ups" are designed to reassure parents, provide information about the child's health, identify problems, provide developmental testing, and increase preventive care for the child. As a parent of a young child, I appreciated receiving information and care *while* my child was growing rather than waiting for "surprises" at the year-end appointment. I felt more of a participant, a partner, in my child's development.

The same is true for our students. They want the results, and we need them. As Rick Stiggins (2004) reminds us, "The mistake we have made at all levels is to believe that once-a-year standardized assessments alone can provide sufficient information and motivation to increase student learning" (pp. 22–23) If we are able to implement assessment tools that give us a picture of what students are learning on a day-to-day basis, we are able create much more powerful interventions for children who aren't learning. *Remember: We cannot move forward with any kind of intervention if we do not have a clear understanding of what we are teaching and how we are assessing.*

Building a Pyramid, Step by Step

When it comes to student achievement, the principal should guide the process. The principal must be lead data-collector, lead problem-identifier, lead problem-solver, and most importantly, the leader in ensuring that all the professionals in the school are consistently administering timely interventions for all children. As the principal ensures that all staff know what is being taught and understands how it is being assessed, he helps his staff move forward in the steps of building and implementing a POI, ensuring that all students receive the interventions that they need to achieve. Above all, the principal is the *lead learner* of the school.

Step One: Assess Current Reality

Start by opening a conversation about how your school currently handles interventions. During a professional learning opportunity such as a staff meeting or in-service day, separate your staff into groups of teachers of like disciplines or grade levels. Using the two critical questions that have been answered as a springboard for discussion, teachers can begin to look at differences between traditional schools and PLC schools.

Consider the following real-life example: Larry Breedlove, principal at Piper Middle School in Kansas City, Kansas, began these discussions with his teachers in the fall of the 2006–07 school year. In previous years, Piper had used typical forms of intervention: Teachers offered remediation to students who struggled, after-school help was optional, and summer school was available if all else failed. Any classroom interventions were used at the discretion of individual teachers, who applied the techniques they knew, based on what they felt should be done at any given time for students. By most accounts, Piper operated as a traditional school.

When Larry examined test scores, he could see that while the scores were "okay," they weren't improving. Student achievement was "log jammed" at the middle and not going anywhere. There was another piece of data that weighed heavily on Larry's mind—and the minds of his teachers. Piper Middle School works with children in grades 6, 7, and 8. The entering sixth-grade class had struggled both academically and behaviorally before coming to Piper. Nearly 50% of the students entering sixth grade that fall had performed below the proficient level on the state assessment in reading and math. Office referrals for behavior had been plentiful every year. The Piper staff knew that to make a difference with these children, to help them learn no matter what, things had to change. As principal, Larry knew that he had to lead his staff in a new direction. He had to lead them through a paradigm shift from looking at teaching to looking at learning.

To begin your conversations with your school staff, ask teachers to examine what happens in your school when a student does not demonstrate success. How does the school respond? When does it become apparent that a student is not succeeding? As you help your staff move forward, it is critical that these talking points are addressed.

As the teachers at Piper Middle began to ask themselves these questions, other questions surfaced, such as "Whose job is it to ensure that students learn?" The answer seemed simple enough. It is the teacher who has that responsibility. However, in answering that question, teachers had to look deeper. Did they honestly believe that they had the capacity to help students achieve at high levels? What needed to be in place in the system to ensure that students can and will learn? Larry asked, "Does a child attending Piper Middle have a limit on how long it takes to learn a concept?" The teachers' response was a resounding no. However, they realized that message was not being sent consistently. They operated like Cole and Schlechty's (1993) description of a traditional school: Quality was considered a variable, and time was the constant. Students were given a set amount of work to do in a set period of time, and then graded on the quality of what was accomplished.

By asking these questions and being honest about their current reality, teachers at Piper realized that there were many ways of doing things at Piper that did not match what they said they believed: that all students will learn. Once conversations started, a natural progression was to begin discussing why, and how they could adjust their practice to align with their beliefs.

Step Two: List and Evaluate Interventions

Ask teachers to brainstorm, as they did at Piper Middle, listing all the interventions that are currently used in your school. What is being done for students who are not learning? Make sure to list all the interventions, leaving none out. During this process, encourage staff to think of these interventions in terms of cardiopulmonary resuscitation (CPR). CPR is an urgent, life-saving process. It is directive, timely, targeted, systematic, and administered by trained professionals. When someone collapses in the presence of one of these trained professionals, immediate action is taken to avoid permanent damage. Similarly, when children are dying academically, we must approach them with the same sense of urgency. As teachers are brainstorming, encourage them to ask the following important questions.

Are Our Interventions Urgent and Directive?

Is there a sense of "we must use this intervention immediately" so that no permanent damage is done to the learner?

Are Our Interventions Timely?

This is actually a two-part question. First, do the interventions provide for extended time to learn the essential standards? Second, is our data current so that our response when students do not learn can be timely?

Let's ponder this: Would you wait a year to help someone who needs CPR immediately? The obvious answer would be no, followed by a loud chorus of "Of course not!" Think of the power interventions could have if data could be used in the same way. Guide your staff members into asking: Are the data we are using to gauge student achievement from an assessment that was administered last year? Is there a way that we can use up-to-date data that give a current picture of our students and their needs? As administrator of the building, it is your responsibility to get teachers that timely data and help them use it.

Are Our Interventions Targeted?

Is the intervention specific to the needs of the student? There is a profound difference between sending a child who has a fundamental disconnect with the procedural understanding of multistep multiplication to a tutor and sending a child to that same tutor because he won't do the work. The data your staff is using will help guide which intervention would be appropriate.

Are There Trained Professionals to Implement the Interventions?

I am not trained in using CPR. I would hope, however, that if I ever needed the procedure, whoever performed it on me would be trained. The same is true with interventions. As your staff looks at current interventions, consider whether there are staff members who are going to be asked to implement something that they do not know how to do. If so, what courses or further professional development need to be offered to make sure that all are trained?

Step Three: Classify Interventions

At this point, your teachers are in possession of a laundry list of the interventions used at your building. They have had the opportunity to look at these interventions through new eyes by asking critical questions. The next step for teachers is to classify these interventions from least intensive to most intensive.

Personal Needs Activity

This activity helps teachers get in the right mindset to rank interventions. Divide the group into tables of six. Place 10 items that people use every day in the middle of each table. These could include a pen, cotton balls, mascara, diapers, scissors, a comb, a cell phone, or toilet paper, for example. Make the selection as varied as possible, limiting each table to 10 items.

Ask the groups to place each item on a continuum from most used by most people to least used by the least number of people. Each member of the group must participate, and each person's views must be taken into account. At the end, however, each table must reach consensus on each item's placement on the continuum.

After each table has been given a chance to share their continuum with the whole group, explain that the items in front of them are used by different people every day to help them improve in some way (such as personal hygiene, convenience, and so on). Each item could be looked at as an "intervention." Even though all interventions are available to everyone (a pen can be purchased in many places, for example), not everyone needs all of them—just as not everyone sitting at each table uses all the items there. This activity helps to clarify many of the points in a pyramid's development.

Afterwards, ask teachers to look at the list of interventions from Step 3 and to sort and classify interventions from least intensive to most intensive, just as they did in the personal needs activity.

As they classify each intervention, help your teachers to ask questions:

- Are the interventions automatic responses for all children in the class?

- Are the interventions systematic?

- Are the interventions applied as the result of assessment results?

- Are the interventions "opt-in" for parents and kids?

- Are the interventions mandatory courses of action prescribed by the school?

- Are the interventions individualized for specific student needs, such as an IEP or 504 Plan?

As the teachers discuss the existing interventions using the questions listed, be ready for some direct conversations and hard questions. At Piper Middle School, teachers became "territorial" about current interventions, at times even arguing that that intervention was a "seventh-grade" intervention and not to be used at any other grade level. Additionally, some teachers may feel a bit intimidated or ill at ease when speaking about an intervention that is a personal favorite. Comfort levels might be threatened if one teacher speaks disparagingly about an intervention. Be prepared to deal with conflicts that may arise.

Step Four: Analyze Strengths and Weaknesses

The final step is to identify the strengths and weaknesses of current interventions. This is a step that again can raise feelings among staff if not handled with care and dignity.

As you help your staff in identifying strengths and weaknesses of an intervention, keep the focus on the student. When implementing the intervention, what strengths are there *for the student?* What specific assistance does the child receive from this intervention? The same is true with weaknesses. Ask, Why doesn't this intervention help *the child?* What results does it achieve? Stress that the teacher implementing the intervention is not being judged; the success or failure of the intervention does not imply that the teacher is good or bad. The quality of an intervention is determined solely by its results for the child. Once you have made these distinctions, you may decide to exclude certain interventions that you deem as not benefiting the child.

Putting It All Together

So you have compiled your work. You have asked probing questions that have led your staff to make a difficult, yet honest, assessment of their current practice. You have identified the interventions you already use, and you have become an expert at the good, bad, and ugly in their implementation. Now what?

As you begin framing your system of interventions, examine its structure, and choose with your staff the best graphic organizer for your needs. If your staff find the traditional pyramid the most recognizable and understandable, use that. If another graphic organizer is more applicable, by all means, use it. For example, rather than using a traditional pyramid, your staff may place two pyramids with their bases touching. This configuration allows for a visual representation of interventions for students needing help in mastering the concept on one pyramid, with interventions for children needing further challenge on the other.

The important piece of putting together your system of interventions is not which organizer you use, but how you structure the levels of intervention: always from least to most intensive. Refer your staff back to the personal needs activity in which they placed the products (interventions) into a continuum from most used to least used.

In the pyramid model, for example, the least intensive interventions are placed at the bottom; as you move up the pyramid, each intervention has a higher level of intensity (see Figure 10-1). Your pyramid could include all base-level interventions at the bottom, or Tier 1, of a 3-tier framework. The interventions on the bottom should be those available to 100% of students. Interventions such as counselor watch, parent conferences, bullying prevention programs, preferential seating, and collaborative teaching might be included in this tier.

Tier 2 interventions provide supplemental instruction and are available to all students who need extra time and assistance beyond Tier 1 interventions. Approximately 20% of your students might need these interventions. Tier 2 interventions could include creative tutoring, frequent progress monitoring, one-on-one instruction, cross–grade level teaming, and specific student support groups, for example.

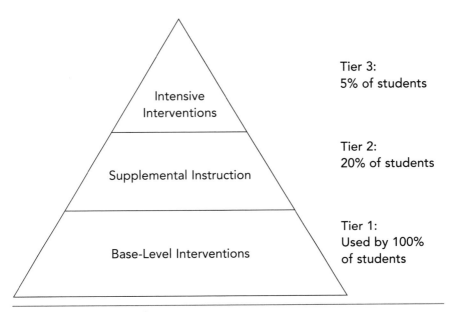

Figure 10-1: Pyramid of Interventions

Tier 3 interventions are much more intensive and will be utilized by only 5% of your students. You may include after-school tutoring, intensive parent/teacher conferencing, and, based on specific data generated in the first two tiers in response to interventions, special education services. Interventions in Tier 3 are those that are most intensive, used by the fewest number of students.

The configuration of your intervention system should be left up to your staff. It needs to be in a graphic organizer that they will understand, internalize, and use. It can include responses for both behavioral and academic needs, remedial programs as well as enrichment challenges. No matter what the language or configuration you use, the key is that it be developed locally so that teachers, administration, and parents are comfortable with it.

Adjusting and Evaluating Interventions

As you lead your staff in the development and implementation of your pyramid of interventions (POI), there are questions that must be continually answered to make certain that your interventions are being implemented systematically and in a timely manner. These questions include:

1. Are the interventions we are applying targeted and differentiated for the individual student?

2. Have we implemented the intervention in a timely manner?

3. Is the intervention targeted for the need of the student?

4. Is the intervention that we implement *different* than the instruction that has already been delivered?

Continually asking and answering these questions of your pyramid and its implementation (and other questions that are unique to your building) ensures that your interventions are providing children what they need to succeed.

Implementing Best Practice in the Classroom

As you lead your staff through the steps in building a pyramid and living as a PLC, you continually recognize what must be asked, identified, and addressed as you move forward in living as a PLC. You have asked your staff members to identify what a child is to learn, how they know it, and what they will do when students master these concepts. You have asked them to brainstorm interventions, to rate them according to their intensity. You have made sure that teachers have been trained to use these interventions. However, note one consideration as you move ahead.

As principal, you must ensure that in all classrooms, teachers teach using *best practices*. Do your teachers teach using research-based strategies? Do your teachers teach using the best procedures, the best approaches possible? Is the delivery of instruction solid? No support system in the world will compensate for bad teaching. As instructional leader, it is your responsibility to make sure that best practice is a way of life in your building—prior to creating a pyramid of interventions. As Austin Buffum said in a Pyramid of Interventions workshop in September of 2007, "A school can have the most 'whiz bang' programs out there. . . . If a school does not have a core curriculum that is solid and one that is delivered with fidelity, any system of interventions will collapse under itself."

Moving Forward

Any time we have new information presented to us, we feel a bit of uncertainty. As you move through the process of implementing high-quality interventions in your school, even the most solid teachers may express a certain level of apprehension. Leading your staff through this process may at times feel like you are trudging through tar pits. Continue to push, continue to persist, continue to persevere. Through your leadership, educators can help students to reach their fullest potential and beyond. And isn't *that* what we are here for?

References

Barth, R. S. (1991). Restructuring schools: Some questions for teachers and principals. *Phi Delta Kappan, 73*(2), 123–128.

Cole, R., & Schlechty, P. (1993). Teachers as trailblazers in restructuring. *Education Digest, 58*(6), 8–12.

DuFour, R., DuFour, R., Eaker, R., & Many, T. (2006). *Learning by doing: A handbook for professional learning communities at work.* Bloomington, IN: Solution Tree.

Duke, D. L. (2004). The turnaround principal. *Principal Magazine, 84*(1), 12–23.

Eastwood, K., & Louis, K. S. (1992). Restructuring that lasts: Managing the performance dip. *Journal of School Leadership, 2*(2), 213–224.

Portin, B. S., & Shen, J. (1998). The changing principalship: Its current status, variability, and impact. *Journal of Leadership Studies, 5*(3), 93–113.

Reeves, D. (2002). *The leader's guide to standards: A blueprint for educational equity and excellence.* San Francisco: John Wiley and Sons.

Stiggins, R. (2004). New assessment beliefs for a new school mission. *Phi Delta Kappan, 86*(1), 22–27.

SUSAN HUFF

Dr. Susan Huff is principal of Santaquin Elementary in Santaquin, Utah. During her former principalship at Westside Elementary, a Title I school in the Nebo School District, she developed innovative solutions to daunting challenges, including high mobility rates and the highest number of English-language learners in the district. In 2002, Susan began her study of the Professional Learning Communities at Work model for school improvement. She then led her staff in changing the culture of Westside. Teachers now engage in weekly collaborative meetings, follow curriculum maps, use common assessments, and learn by observing their colleagues. Westside students now perform well on standardized and criterion-referenced tests. In 2006 Susan was named Utah's National Distinguished Principal by the National Association of Elementary School Principals. In 2007 she earned her doctorate in education; her dissertation was on principal leadership in schools transforming as professional learning communities.

ELEVEN

Digging Deep Into Data

Susan Huff

Unless initiatives are subjected to ongoing assessment on the basis of tangible results, they represent random groping in the dark rather than purposeful improvement.

—Richard DuFour & Robert Eaker

In professional learning communities, schools measure performance with data and use data to make informed decisions to guide continuous improvement (Schmoker, 1999). Digging deep into data is the process of collaboratively analyzing data and changing it into useful information to improve teaching and learning: to check current reality and measure progress. Numbers alone mean nothing. The right numbers, interpreted well, provide information to evaluate the effectiveness of our improvement efforts, guide our practice, and ultimately transform even our lowest performing schools into places with high levels of learning for both students and adults.

With all the many sources of data available to schools, principals must decide what types and sources of useful data to collect and use. We must create processes to generate the right kind of data, and we must build our staff's capacity to interpret and apply that data. To change data to information, schools need a basis of comparison, and data that is easily accessible and openly shared (DuFour, 2007). Comparing data among similar students within a grade level or department, or across schools with similar students, provides meaning. Without a basis of comparison, we do not know if student performance was good or poor. This chapter will explore the various kinds of data: how to pro-actively generate truly useful data, how to identify the most meaningful information buried in the numbers, and how to apply that information to improve student learning.

Assessment Data

Data from assessments helps schools measure student learn-ing and measure progress toward achievement goals. School assess-ment data includes norm-referenced test results; criterion-referenced test results; data from concept tests, quizzes, and class assignments; anecdotal records and ongoing running records; and checklists and rubrics. School assessment data can be categorized as summative or formative.

Summative Assessments: Was the Standard Met?

Summative assessments (norm-referenced, criterion-referenced, end-of-unit, end-of-term, end-of-semester, or end-of-year tests) mea-sure whether a standard has been met (Stiggins & Chappuis, 2006). These tests all answer, "Was the standard met?" Both norm-refer-enced (NRT) and criterion-referenced (CRT) tests can be standard-ized. A standardized test uses uniform procedures for administration and scoring so that test results from different students are comparable (Bond, 1996).

Norm-Referenced Tests: How Do We Measure Up?

Many school systems administer summative norm-referenced tests as a general knowledge "checkup" to reveal how their schools com-pare to other schools on a large scale in assessing general knowledge in broad content domains (Stiggins, Arter, Chappuis, & Chappuis, 2004). These tests are designed to compare student achievement to that of other similar students. Digging deep into norm-referenced tests (NRTs) on a district or system level informs decisions to adjust instructional programs or purchase curriculum materials (Stiggins et al., 2004). On an individual student level, NRTs help schools identify students with special needs—students who may need gifted programming or students who may need remediation. On a school level, NRTs help schools view student learning on a broad scale.

As we began to implement improvement strategies as a professional learning community at Westside Elementary, we looked at trends over time in our NRT results as one piece of evidence of improvement. Over 5 years, our average norm-referenced test results increased from the 37th percentile to the 67th percentile—even though we had the largest number of English-language learners and the highest poverty in our district, as well as high mobility. We were once the lowest performing school in the district, but our NRT results showed improved student learning compared to other schools in the district, state, and nation. The NRT data showed general knowledge in broad domains was increasing as we used formative assessment data to target specific areas of the core curriculum where some students needed more time and support to reach mastery of state standards. It's important to note that improving NRT scores was not our goal; improved scores were a byproduct of our efforts with other data.

Criterion-Referenced Tests: What Did Students Learn?

A criterion-referenced test (CRT) sums up learning of academic content standards. CRTs are one indicator of how well individual students learned the knowledge and skills they are expected to master, and how well the school taught that curriculum (Bond, 1996). (For purposes herein I am restricting the definition of CRTs to state standardized tests administered toward the end of the school year to measure learning of state academic standards.)

Digging deep into CRT data on a district level provides comparative data for all schools within the district. This helps districts evaluate program effectiveness and identify schools that may need more district support for training or additional resources. As with

NRT data, digging deep into CRT data on an individual student level helps schools identify students for possible remediation or gifted programming.

Digging deep into CRT data on a school level is a process of looking back at the previous year's performance. The course or grade has ended; there is no opportunity for students to go back for additional learning from that teacher. So how can this "autopsy" of student learning prove useful? At Westside, computer-generated reports helped our teams look at their collective data to celebrate where they performed well and also to look for specific areas for future improvement. I modeled for teachers how to interpret and use the reports by starting discussions with teams of teachers and posing questions they could ask themselves individually and collectively as teams:

- Where does the data show our students performed well last year?

- In what specific content areas did our students not meet the standard or perform below our expectation?

- How will we change future instruction so that we get better results?

- How can our collective efforts improve student learning?

From CRT data, our teams then wrote SMART goals (Strategic and specific, Measurable, Attainable, Results-based, and Time-bound) for the new school year (O'Neill & Conzemius, 2006).

Disaggregated CRT data provides information to schools about the effectiveness of their programs for subpopulations. After we implemented a reteaching block for mathematics for students at Westside who needed more time and support, for example, we saw a 14% increase in 1 year in the math CRT scores of our students with limited English proficiency. At a neighboring school, the CRT data showed boys were 10 percentage points behind girls in performance.

The staff made adjustments in curriculum and instruction, and the school closed the performance gap for boys in a year.

End-of-Course, End-of-Unit, End-of-Semester, End-of-Year Tests

These teacher–initiated tests are summative when they are used to measure whether a standard has been met. Knowing whether students met the standard is important feedback for students and teachers, but there is more that can be learned at the end of a grading period from a summative teacher–initiated test.

Digging deep into data from teacher–initiated summative tests can impact future instruction. When these summative tests are team-made and administered across departments or grade levels with a common proficiency standard, comparing scores among the team allows teachers to see how their students performed in comparison to other similar students. When teachers have opportunities to reflect on their practice and dialogue with their collaborative team, they are able to make the connections they need to improve instructional practice in the future. Reflective dialogue helps teachers build on each other's ideas and expand their own learning in ways that they cannot do alone.

Digging deep into data at a nearby middle school helped math teachers analyze their individual and collective results. They administered their common team–made summative assessment. Answer sheets were scanned; a computerized test analysis showed the number of students who responded correctly to each test question. At their weekly collaborative team meeting, the teachers brought their test results and test analysis. Teachers engaged in reflective dialogue about their individual and collective results. They analyzed specific test questions where more students answered incorrectly. Was it a bad test question? Did the question measure the standard? Did the question match the instruction? Does instruction need to be improved? This reflective dialogue helped teachers make adjustments to the test and the instruction for the next time the unit will be taught.

Digging deep into data from summative tests that measure if a standard has been met is a way to improve future practice. Digging deep into data from *formative* assessments, however, is a way to improve teaching and learning in the present. Formative assessments have potential to impact teaching and learning along the way to meeting the standard.

Formative Assessments: Are We Making Progress?

While many critics charge that students are overtested, Doug Reeves (2005) contends that students are really underassessed. Effective school reform efforts include standards accompanied by frequent common assessments in the classroom. In a professional learning community, assessment is used to help all students meet a minimum standard of academic achievement, to help students understand the achievement target from the very beginning of the learning, and to help students watch themselves improve and then succeed (Stiggins, 2005). Assessments *for* learning occur *during* the learning process. These formative assessments ask students if they are making progress on their journey toward the standard, while summative assessments—assessments *of* learning—ask students at the end of the journey if they have met the standard (Stiggins, 2005).

Formative Assessments Inform Students

Because students can also be data-driven decision-makers, formative assessment results give students descriptive feedback that permits them to see where they are now and close the gap between where they are and the standard (Stiggins & Chappuis, 2006). Students need feedback and advice on what is wrong and how to make it right. Feedback must be timely and must help students learn through reflection so that they can close the gap between where they are and the standard (Senge, Cambron-McCabe, Lucas, Smith, Dutton, & Kleiner, 2000).

At Westside, along with receiving timely feedback on their formative assessments, all second-grade students graphed their own results. This not only provided feedback to students on their progress, but was a great motivator for students to apply greater effort to improve. As Rick Stiggins (2005) reminds us, "Success at learning becomes its own reward, promoting confidence and persistence" (p. 77).

Formative Assessments Inform Teachers

Teachers need to know how students are performing to adapt their own work to meet student needs (Stiggins & Chappuis, 2006). Informed decisions are made through the use of data (Schmoker, 1999), not by what teachers "feel" or "think" is best. Teachers adjust their instructional practices, their methods, and their materials as they monitor student progress through frequent formative assessment data.

In a review of 20 studies, Black and Wiliam (1998) found "all these studies show that innovations that include strengthening the practice of formative assessment produce significant and often substantial learning gains" (p. 139). Black and Wiliam contended that firm evidence shows that formative assessment can raise achievement. They boldly stated that they know of "no other way of raising standards for which such a strong prima facie case can be made" (p. 139). Although all students benefit from formative assessment, Black and Wiliam found that "improved formative assessment helps low achievers more than other students and so reduces the range of achievement while raising achievement overall" (p. 141).

In a study of low-achieving students with and without learning disabilities, the treatment that included formative assessment feedback resulted in greater effort and dramatically more learning for low-achieving students (Fuchs, Fuchs, Karns, Hamlett, Katzaroff, & Dutka, 1997). This same study, however, reported disappointing results where students with learning disabilities were concerned. The increased effort associated with formative assessment in students with learning disabilities "produced no discernable effect on learning. There were no statistically significant differences in achievement for LD children" (Fuchs et al., p. 535).

The results of the Fuchs study are significant. This study showed that *most* low-achieving students will have dramatically increased learning through formative assessments, but students with learning disabilities need more than measurement and feedback along the way to meeting the standard. At Westside Elementary we found that many low-performing students, including those with learning disabilities, needed more time and support, differentiated instruction, and interventions, in addition to formative assessment, to close that learning gap. Students with identified learning disabilities received special education resource pullout for 30 minutes per day for reading and/or math. This provided more time and support in addition to classroom instruction, in a small-group setting with differentiated instruction and frequent formative assessments several times each week. Students received continual feedback on their work; they monitored and recorded their own learning progress on their formative assessments. We saw positive results. During my last year at Westside, eight students were discontinued from special education because they had closed the achievement gap and were now on grade level; seven had discontinued the year before, and seven more the year before that. It was data that allowed us to target individual students who needed more time and support, and ongoing assessment data during reteaching that informed both students and teachers of student progress toward the standard.

Team-Made Common Formative Assessments

Common assessments guide the work of collaborative teams as they focus on results (DuFour, 2004). In a professional learning community, teams of teachers create and administer common formative assessments on an ongoing basis with the intention of collaboratively examining the results for shared learning, instructional planning for individual students, as well as curriculum, instruction, and/or assessment modifications.

A common assessment holds all students (and teachers on the team) to a common proficiency standard, which is set and agreed upon before instruction begins. Then the results of all assessments are compared among the team members. Each teacher has a basis of comparison of how individual students performed compared to the rest of the students in the same course or grade level. The teacher can then draw on the strength of the team for ideas, materials, and strategies to help each student reach mastery (DuFour, 2004). In a professional learning community, there is a sense of collective ownership for the learning of each student in that grade level or course, rather than just for the learning of an individual teacher's students. The collective focus is on the success of each student.

Common formative assessments provide data that is not available in any other way—information that serves as an "in-flight course correction" to modify teaching, improve assessment, and increase student learning. What makes an assessment formative? Rick DuFour (2007) provided a checklist:

1. Is it used to identify students who are experiencing difficulty in their learning?

2. Are students who are having difficulty provided with additional time and support for learning?

3. Are students given an additional opportunity to demonstrate their learning?

A key to successful use of common assessments is to frequently assess a few key concepts, rather than assess many concepts infrequently (Reeves, 2004).

When we first started using common assessments at Westside, I asked teachers to begin with five common assessments. We quickly realized we needed to *create* these common assessments as a team and give them more frequently. We found that a math chapter test, for example, was not a good common assessment because the chapter covered many concepts and 4 to 6 weeks of instruction. This was too long to wait to intervene for students who needed more time and support to learn a specific concept in a reteaching group. It was also difficult to pinpoint the precise concepts where individual students needed more time and support because the test assessed multiple standards at once. In the case of the chapter tests, more data did *not* equal more useful information. We needed data that was timely and linked to student mastery of key learning concepts. Our team-made common assessments proved much more effective for increased student learning.

Creating Processes to Generate Information-Rich Data

Collecting data as useful information is a thoughtful, ongoing process of selecting from available data as well as generating specific new data. Digging deep into data from common formative mathematics assessments followed this cycle at Westside (as principal, I guided all along the way until teachers could do this on their own):

1. Grade-level teams developed curriculum maps based on state standards that served as common pacing guides for instruction, which all team members agreed to follow.

2. Teams wrote common assessments that were aligned with state standards. They gathered test items from multiple sources, including parts of textbook assessments and parts of computer test-item pools. Tests were typically 10 to 20 questions and were administered every 1 or 2 weeks, depending on the length of time needed to teach the standard(s). Teachers agreed on a common proficiency level for each test.

3. At weekly team collaboration, teachers looked ahead on the curriculum map to see what concepts would be taught next.

They brought materials and collaborated on best practices to teach the upcoming concept, thus "front loading" their instruction.

4. Each teacher on the team taught the concept, continually assessing and checking for understanding during instruction, and then administered the common assessment during an agreed-upon window of time.

5. Teachers scored the tests and recorded the results on a common reporting form so that class results could be easily compared side by side among the team.

6. Teachers brought the recorded scores and the tests to collaboration, divided according to proficiency: one stack for nonproficient students who needed reteaching, one stack with students who needed enrichment, and one stack for students who met the standard but might benefit from some additional practice.

7. The team tallied the total number of nonproficient students and designated which member of the team (typically the teacher with the most proficient students) would reteach the students who needed more time and support. All the other students were quickly divided into enrichment or additional practice groups, with teachers assigned to each.

8. The team analyzed the assessment results by looking at the most frequently missed questions to see where nonproficient students were having difficulty. The team made a plan to help each student improve who had not yet met the standard. Test questions were analyzed to see if any changes should be made in the assessment for next year.

9. Whole-class instruction continued on with the next unit, according to the curriculum map, but an additional common 30-minute block was built into the daily schedule for "reteach

and enrich." During this time, students were grouped according to the last common formative assessment results. The length of time for this grouping was based on how much time was needed for students in the reteach group to obtain mastery of the standard. As students demonstrated mastery in the reteach group and were retested, they could move to a practice group, leaving a decreasingly smaller group for more individual attention in the reteach group.

The next common formative assessment started the cycle of digging deep into data all over again: diagnosing student learning deficiencies, prescribing a remedy, administering it through more time and support, and giving students additional opportunities to demonstrate their new learning.

Reflective Dialogue

Several studies showed strong professional learning communities are built on teachers who regularly engage in reflective dialogue about their practice (Kruse, Louis, & Bryk, 1994; Newmann & Wehlage, 1995; Bryk, Camburn, & Louis, 1999). Reflective conversations put practice and pedagogy under scrutiny—scrutiny that challenges any current teaching practices that do not produce evidence of student learning (Sebring, Bryk, Easton, Luppescu, Thum, Lopez, & Smith, 1995). Reflective dialogue around common formative assessment data causes team collaborations to focus on *results*.

I witnessed many examples of the power of reflective dialogue each week among collaborative teams at Westside, but one example stands out. Our schoolwide January reading benchmarks were complete; the data was entered; inverse rankings were ready for me to bring to each grade-level team meeting. When I looked at the data for second grade, one teacher, Melanie, had fewer than 50% of her students reading on grade level, while the other classes did much better. I was very nervous to share the results with the team; I was not sure how this first-year teacher would react. I passed out the data sheets. The new teacher was the first one to respond.

"It looks like my students are not doing so well," Melanie said. "My top five students all moved during the semester, and they were replaced with five new students all reading below grade level. I know it's not my fault, but I accept responsibility for all of these students. But I know I can't do this alone; I need help."

The discussion then shifted to how we could all help. We shared ideas, planned interventions, and allocated resources. At the end of the year, we again compared data. All but three students in Melanie's class were now on grade level; two were very close. Mike was still the lowest in the class, but he had actually made more progress than any other student. When he transferred to our school in November, he did not even know letters and sounds. By the end of second grade, he was reading on mid–second grade level. With targeted interventions and additional support continuing into third grade, Mike closed the achievement gap and was reading on grade level by midyear of third grade.

Collaborative data analysis is not about pointing fingers at teachers with nonproficient students. It is about trusting in the collective wisdom of the team to collaboratively bring about high levels of learning for all students. Digging deep into data helped Melanie assess the effectiveness of her efforts with Mike; it was key to helping him meet the standard and prepare for future learning.

Collective Inquiry

Collective inquiry is essential for continuous learning for school improvement (Fullan, 1993; Morrissey, 2000). DuFour and Eaker (1998) described collective inquiry as "the engine of improvement, growth, and renewal in a professional learning community. People in such a community are relentless in questioning the status quo, seeking new methods, testing those methods, and then reflecting on the results" (p. 25).

Collective inquiry transforms data into useful information through the collective efforts of a collaborative team. Collective inquiry is about seeking out best practice, experimenting with best practice, and then analyzing the results (Eaker, 2007). The inquiry process begins with a question posed about teaching or learning that leads to action research to find the answer. For example, teachers might ask, "Does a particular instructional strategy help students learn this concept?" The teacher implements the strategy and then assesses the results. Action research is a reflective process of inquiry and discussion among a collaborative team that includes analyzing data to make informed decisions (Ferrance, 2000).

Digging deep into data through inquiry helped us make many informed decisions at Westside. For example, we wondered whether our limited resources would be better spent on 10 minutes a day of targeted individual intervention for struggling half-day kindergarten students *or* on extending kindergarten for 1 hour for those students to receive additional time and support in a small group. We randomly assigned students to both interventions, implemented the interventions, assessed students, and then collaboratively analyzed the results. The students receiving 10 minutes a day of targeted intervention significantly outperformed the other group. We then collaboratively decided that this would be our kindergarten intervention for our school. Our results were tied to our school, with our resources, with our students, with our staff. The results were not generalizable to all schools, but that did not matter. We were improving student learning at *our* school. A professional learning community always uses specific local data within the collective inquiry process to make decisions that will increase student learning.

Statistical Data

Monitoring statistical data is another tool to help schools improve. Data on school demographics, attendance and punctuality, and discipline is another source for informed decision-making.

School Demographic Data

Socioeconomic status (SES), English as a second language (ESL), mobility, and ethnicity data help schools paint a portrait of their students. At Westside we used this data to identify students for supplemental language instruction and support. The demographic data of our Title I–impacted school helped us qualify for grants to purchase supplemental instructional materials for students.

Attendance and Punctuality Data

Attendance and punctuality are critical to a student's educational success. At Westside the principal, counselor, and teachers all worked together to monitor attendance and punctuality data to improve student learning.

Discipline Data

Digging deep into office referral and discipline data helps principals identify problem areas in the school, students who may need behavior interventions, and teachers who may need additional support. For instance, we found the greatest number of discipline referrals came from second grade. In their team collaboration, the second-grade teachers decided to intensify explicit social-skills instruction and then reward students who had no discipline referrals for the week. These students got an additional 15-minute physical education period on the playground to practice new games. At the same time students who had discipline referrals received additional instruction and practice in the social skill they were lacking as evidenced by their behavior choice. The social-skill practice session took place in a room with a large window overlooking the playground. After this intervention, the second-grade discipline referrals virtually disappeared.

Perception Data

In addition to assessment and statistical data, schools can use perception data from opinion and needs surveys to find out what the school community really thinks about their school. At Westside we annually surveyed parents, teachers, staff, and students to learn their perceptions of teacher excellence, parent support, instructional quality, student commitment, administration, safety, and resource accessibility, as measured on a Likert scale that could provide numerical data for analysis. We also collected important qualitative information through these open written-response questions:

- What do you like about our school?

- What do you wish were different about our school?

We found that parents wanted a gifted program, and so we started one. We found parents wanted more music experiences for their children, so we implemented a piano keyboard program and a school choir. By digging deep into perception data, we were able to improve our programming and build community support.

Data Leadership

The challenge for instructional leaders in PLCs is learning first to select data that can improve teaching and learning, and then learning how to use that data effectively for informed decision-making. Numbers alone mean nothing unless we extract useful information through analyzing specifically how this data can help improve teaching and learning. Principals can mentor teachers in data analysis and model how to analyze comparative data by posing probing questions:

- Are there any patterns in the data? What do you notice?

- Where did students do well?

- Where did students have difficulty?

- Was this a bad question or an indicator that reteaching is needed?

- Which specific students need more time and support to master this concept?

- How can the team provide that additional time and support?

Principals can also model using data to improve practice more directly, by collecting and interpreting perception data on their own leadership. At Westside, for example, I asked teachers, staff, administrative colleagues, and district supervisors to complete a survey on my leadership. I modeled what I was asking teachers to do: I collected and analyzed data to see how I could become better at my job as an education professional. My staff saw that I sincerely wanted to improve, and I used their feedback to do it. Digging deep into data is risky; it forces us to confront our current reality, which may cause discomfort. Ultimately, looking at data empowers teachers and principals because it produces positive results—for our students and for us as members of professional learning communities.

References

Black, P., & Wiliam, D. (1998). Inside the black box: Raising standards through classroom assessment. *Phi Delta Kappan, 80*(2), 139–148. Accessed at http://proquest.umi.com.erl.lib.byu.edu/pqdweb?index=9&sid=1&srchmode=3&vinst=PR on January 18, 2006.

Bond, L. A. (1996). Norm- and criterion-referenced testing. *Practical Assessment, Research & Evaluation, 5*(2). Accessed at http://PAREonline.net/getvn.asp?v=5&n=2 on October 29, 2007.

Bryk, A. S., Camburn, E., & Louis, K. S. (1999). Professional learning community in Chicago elementary schools: Facilitating factors and organizational consequences. *Educational Administration Quarterly, 35*(Supplemental), 751–781.

Collins, J. (2001). *Good to great: Why some companies make the leap . . . and others don't.* New York: HarperCollins.

De Pree, M. (1989). *Leadership is an art.* New York: Dell.

DuFour, R. (2004). What is a professional learning community? *Educational Leadership, 61*(8), 6–11.

DuFour, R. (2007). *Confronting hard facts, half-truths, and total nonsense in education.* Keynote address at PLC Institute, August 7, 2007.

DuFour, R., DuFour, R., Eaker, R., & Many, T. (2006). *Learning by doing: A handbook for professional learning communities at work.* Bloomington, IN: Solution Tree.

DuFour, R., & Eaker, R. (1998). *Professional learning communities at work: Best practices for enhancing student achievement.* Bloomington, IN: Solution Tree (formerly National Educational Service).

Eaker, R. (2007). *A focus on learning.* Breakout session at PLC Institute, August 7, 2007.

Ferrance, E. (2000). *Action research.* Providence, RI: Northeast and Islands Regional Educational Laboratory at Brown University.

Fuchs, L. S., Fuchs, D., Karns, K., Hamlett, C. L., Katzaroff, M., & Dutka, S. (1997). Effects of task-focused goals on low-achieving students with and without learning disabilities. *American Educational Research Journal, (34)*3, 513–545.

Fullan, M. (1993). *Change forces: Probing the depths of educational reform.* Bristol, PA: Falmer.

Kruse, S., Louis, K. S., & Bryk, A. (1994). Building professional community in schools. *Issues in Restructuring Schools.* Madison: Center on Organization and Restructuring of Schools, School of Education, University of Wisconsin at Madison.

Morrissey, M. S. (2000). *Professional learning communities: An ongoing exploration.* Austin, TX: Southwest Educational Development Laboratory.

Newmann, F. M., & Wehlage, G. G. (1995). *Successful school restructuring: A report to the public and educators.* Madison: Center on Organization and Restructuring of Schools, School of Education, University of Wisconsin.

No Child Left Behind Act of 2001. Washington, DC: U.S. Department of Education.

O'Neill, J., & Conzemius, A. (2006). *The power of smart goals: Using goals to improve student learning.* Bloomington, IN: Solution Tree (formerly National Educational Service).

Reeves, D. (2004). *Accountability for learning: How teachers and school leaders can take charge.* Alexandria, VA: Association for Supervision and Curriculum Development.

Reeves, D. (2005). Putting it all together: Standards, assessment, and accountability in successful professional learning communities. In R. DuFour, R. Eaker, & R. DuFour (Eds.), *On common ground: The power of professional learning communities* (pp. 45–63). Bloomington, IN: Solution Tree (formerly National Educational Service).

Schmoker, M. (1999). *Results: The key to continuous school improvement.* Alexandria, VA: Association for Supervision and Curriculum Development.

Sebring, P. B., Bryk, A. S., Easton, J. Q., Luppescu, S., Thum, Y. M., Lopez, W. A., & Smith, B. (1995). *Charting reform: Chicago teachers take stock.* Chicago: Consortium on Chicago School Research.

Senge, P. M., Cambron-McCabe, N., Lucas, T., Smith, B., Dutton, J., & Kleiner, A. (2000). *Schools that learn: A fifth discipline fieldbook for educators, parents, and everyone who cares about education.* New York: Doubleday.

Stiggins, R. (2005). Assessment FOR learning: Building a culture of confident learners. In R. DuFour, R. Eaker, & R. DuFour (Eds.), *On common ground: The power of professional learning communities* (pp. 65–83). Bloomington, IN: Solution Tree (formerly National Educational Service).

Stiggins, R. J., Arter, J. A., Chappuis, J., & Chappuis, S. (2004). *Classroom assessment for student learning: Doing it right—using it well.* Portland, OR: Assessment Training Institute, Inc.

Stiggins, R., & Chappuis, J. (2006). What a difference a word makes: Assessment FOR learning rather than assessment OF learning helps students succeed. *Journal of Staff Development, 27*(1), 10–14.

Part Three

LEADING FOR PLC AT THE DISTRICT LEVEL

ERIC TWADELL

An award-winning practitioner, Eric Twadell, Ph.D., has used the Professional Learning Communities at Work model to direct curriculum, staff development, and mentoring programs at Adlai E. Stevenson High School District 125 in Lincolnshire, Illinois. He served as director of the school's social studies division and as assistant superintendent for organizational and leadership development before his promotion to district superintendent. Dr. Twadell's commitment to student achievement reaches beyond the academic setting through his directorship of numerous athletic and adventure education programs. Dr. Twadell works closely with schools and districts nationwide to advance the successful implementation of the PLC model. He has also consulted with both the Illinois State Board of Education and Missouri Department of Education.

TWELVE

Win-Win Contract Negotiation: Collective Bargaining for Student Learning

Eric Twadell

[Great organizations] simplify a complex world into a single organizing idea, a basic principle or concept that unifies and guides everything.

—Jim Collins

Fortunately, schools across North America have begun to make a seismic shift in assumptions; they are reshaping structures and cultures to focus on learning rather than teaching as the fundamental purpose and guiding principle of their work. Schools working as professional learning communities are spending considerable time and effort to ensure that *learning* serves as the "organizing idea" for curriculum, instruction, and assessment. As a result, the way that central office and district-level staff make decisions is also changing. The board of education and central office now play a unique and important role in showing how learning must serve as the "guiding principle" for *all* decisions being made within the district. This chapter will explore how collective bargaining can be re-envisioned so that *learning* serves as the guiding principle in contract negotiations in the professional learning community school.

Traditional Collective Bargaining

Those who are leading school improvement processes understand that one of the biggest levers for change, both positive and negative, is the board of education and faculty negotiations process. In the traditional school, collective bargaining between the board and faculty is as far removed from discussions and questions of learning as New York is from Hong Kong. The *American School Board Journal* painted a clear picture of the conventional model of school board and teacher negotiations:

> During the 1960's and 1970's, the rules for collective bargaining were clear. Each side went to the table with a list of demands and tried to get the most of their demands satisfied without resorting to a strike. That philosophy made for an adversarial relationship between the School Board and the Teachers' Union: Teachers had to be prepared to strike, Boards, to defend against a strike. Each side had to be willing to use all its ammunition to win support. (Bulach, 1991, p. 25)

The traditional negotiations between the board of education and teachers' union usually involve competing interests, heated debate and argument, and nearly always, winners and losers. More often than not, both the board and the teachers' union walk away from negotiations never quite feeling as if they had "got what they wanted." In districts beginning to work as a professional learning community, however, the board of education and teachers' unions have moved beyond the adversarial negotiations of the traditional school and have restructured the collective bargaining process to ensure a positive outcome for the district, the teachers, and most importantly, the students.

A positive and productive relationship between the board of education and the teachers' union is an important ingredient in creating high-performing schools. Consider the following from Linda Kaboolian, author of *Win-Win Labor-Management Collaboration in Education*:

The Union's involvement is both directly and indirectly connected to the success of a school or district. Directly, union-management relations determine the way organizational resources will be used in pursuit of organizational goals. . . . The tenor of labor management relationships will play a large role in determining the value that can be created by available resources and the extent to which more satisfying professional jobs can be created. High-trust, participatory relationships have been shown to enhance organizational effectiveness. Low-trust, conflict-ridden relationships experience attendant costs associated with conflict remediation, absenteeism, and high turnover. (Kaboolian, 2005, p. 11)

Beyond enabling dysfunctional and unhealthy relationships, the traditional collective bargaining model is inconsistent with the basic tenets of a professional learning community: a focus on learning, building shared knowledge, collaborative processes, dispersed leadership, and decisions based on evidence. If districts are trying to create schools with these characteristics and to foster the positive reciprocal relationships that result, they should model those characteristics—even during the negotiations process.

Win-Win Collective Bargaining

In the professional learning community, the positive relationship between the board of education and the teachers' union is built on the assumption that the collective bargaining process is a "win-win" endeavor. Stephen Covey described the win-win relationship as follows:

Win/Win is a frame of mind and heart that constantly seeks mutual benefit in all human interactions. Win/Win means that agreements or solutions are mutually beneficial, mutually satisfying. With a Win/Win solution, all parties feel good about the decision and feel committed to the action plan. Win/Win sees life as a cooperative, not a competitive arena.

Most people tend to think in terms of dichotomies: strong or weak, hardball or softball, win or lose. But that kind of thinking is fundamentally flawed. It's based on power and position rather than principle. Win/Win is based on the paradigm that there is plenty for everybody, that one person's success is not achieved at the expense or exclusion of the success of others. (Covey, 1989, p. 207)

Using Covey's vision of a healthy win-win relationship, John Cassel, John Allen, and Angela Peifer (2007) of the Illinois School Board Association have characterized the win-win collective bargaining process between the board of education and the teachers' unions as one in which neither side enters into "contract negotiations with the assumption that one side will win and the other will lose. If one begins with the assumption that teachers, administration, and Board all have the same end in mind (quality public education), then contract negotiations take on a whole new ethos."

Utilizing win-win collaborative negotiation protocols is an important component of creating strong professional learning community structures and cultures. In Kildeer Countryside District 96 in Buffalo Grove, Illinois, and Adlai E. Stevenson High School District 125 in Lincolnshire, Illinois, the board of education, administrations, and teachers' associations have been working collaboratively for over 15 years to develop a strong collective bargaining process that utilizes win-win negotiations protocols.

Win-Win Negotiations Protocols

Along its journey as a professional learning community, Adlai E. Stevenson High School District 125 in Lincolnshire, Illinois, has established protocols to guide the relationships between the board of education, the administration, and the Adlai E. Stevenson High School Education Association. These protocols represent a deliberate attempt to create a positive, mutually beneficial and mutually satisfying win-win negotiations process.

Prenegotiation Protocols

It is difficult to create a win–win atmosphere for negotiations if neither party has made an effort to work together in the years *between* contract negotiations. Here are some of the steps District 125 has taken to promote a collaborative working relationship.

Mutual commitment to "no surprises." The board of education, administration, and education association have verbally committed to a shared interest in keeping dialogue free from hidden agendas and surprise "gotcha's." Each group has identified open and honest communication as an important component of a positive working relationship. Intentional effort is made to overcommunicate issues of joint question and concern and to engage in joint problem-solving.

Monthly meetings between the education association, the superintendent, and the principal. Each August, the superintendent meets with the president of the education association to establish meeting times and locations for the school year. In addition to monthly meetings with the association's executive board, the superintendent and principal hold a monthly lunch meeting with the education association president, and informal meetings are held throughout the month to address issues of mutual concern and interest.

Regular standing subcommittee meetings to address negotiations issues. Although formal negotiations only occur every 3 to 4 years, standing committees of administrators and faculty meet to discuss ongoing questions and issues. The Benefits Committee, for example, meets quarterly to monitor issues such as changes in the district's health and dental insurance programs, new 403b regulations and guidelines, and changes in the state's retirement system. Rather than waiting for the collective bargaining process, the committee may recommend immediate changes that would benefit the district and its employees.

Development and agreement of negotiations protocols. Prior to the start of the formal negotiation process, the board of education and the education association develop and agree to formal protocols for the collective bargaining process.

Prenegotiation committee meetings to discuss and make recommendations on contractual issues. Eighteen to twelve months before formal negotiations begin, the board of education and the education association collaboratively identify prenegotiation subcommittees to investigate contract "language" issues, questions, and concerns (such as advancement and reimbursement for graduate courses, professional travel policies, part-time teacher guidelines, and so on). Comprised of a broad representation of administrators and faculty, the committees study the issues together, build shared knowledge, and make recommendations to be considered during the formal negotiations process.

Mutual identification of negotiations topics. In addition to the recommendations from the negotiation subcommittees, the board of education and the education association agree to the specific topics to be included in the formal negotiations process. Both the board of education and the education association commit to limiting the collective bargaining process to only the identified topics. As such, they avoid a "laundry list" approach to negotiations and have more time to devote to only those meaningful and significant issues.

Negotiation Protocols

Establishment of a nonthreatening atmosphere. Every effort is made to ensure that the setting and atmosphere for the negotiation meetings are nonthreatening to both groups.

Development of specific agendas for each session. For each formal negotiations meeting, the board of education and the education association agree to a formal agenda that outlines the specific topics and parameters for the meeting. The negotiation teams *only* discuss items identified on the agenda.

Adherence to pre-established meeting times. In an effort to respect the time and energy of the members of each group, the negotiations meetings are limited to 3 hours. The sessions will not be extended beyond the time limit unless all parties agree.

Use of live audio feed for board of education and education association caucus groups. While the board of education and the education association agree to send only three representatives to the negotiation meetings, each team is encouraged to host caucus groups in adjoining rooms. The caucus groups can listen to the meeting through a live audio feed.

Direct communication between board of education and education association members. The board of education and education association agree to communicate directly and openly with each other during negotiation sessions. While the protocols allow each group to have an outside representative (such as association or legal counsel) attend each session, only the three members of each negotiating team may participate in the collective bargaining process.

Publication of minutes immediately following each session. A mutually agreed-upon recorder keeps minutes for the negotiations sessions. Minutes are distributed within 24 hours to all members of the negotiating teams and require the signature of the lead negotiator for each group to become official. Official minutes are immediately released to the full board of education and high school faculty in order to keep open channels of communication and to prevent misunderstanding and misinterpretation at a later date. This transparency contributes to a trusting relationship between all parties and prevents concerns about misrepresentation.

Intentionality in framing discussion and solutions as win-win. The working assumption of the board of education and the education association is that the collective bargaining process is collaborative, designed to find common solutions to common questions and concerns. When offering comments and discussing solutions, participants are expected to frame their responses in terms of how the proposed change is a benefit (win-win) to both the board of education (the district) and the education association.

Serving as advocates for tentative agreement. The board of education and the education association agree that once a tentative agreement is reached, each team has an obligation to serve as an advocate when presenting the proposed agreement to their respective groups. Teams make every effort to work collaboratively to share the tentative agreement and provide information sessions to interested groups.

Win-Win Negotiations At Work

In districts that are moving along the continuum as a professional learning community, creating "wins" in collective bargaining for the board of education and the faculty is not enough. In the professional learning community district, the most important beneficiary of the collective bargaining process must be *students* and their learning. Negotiations that only address salary and benefits, cut organizational costs, secure outsourcing agreements, and so on typically do very little to directly impact student learning and achievement. The following sections will show how districts and education associations have worked together to create these targeted wins for all stakeholders: for the board, the faculty, and most importantly, the students.

Revisiting the Master Schedule

In Kildeer Countryside School District 96 in Buffalo Grove, Illinois, the board of education and the education association have been working hard to develop and practice collective bargaining protocols that bring focus to their shared interest in student learning and achievement. In 2007 the board of education and the education association agreed to a new 4-year contract that rests on the assumption that the purpose of negotiations is to produce win-win outcomes.

For many years, Kildeer Countryside School District 96 followed a fairly traditional elementary and middle school schedule. However, as the district moved further along in its journey as a professional learning community, administrators and teachers found that teachers needed more time for collaborative teamwork. Additionally, many teachers realized that they needed more time to develop and implement intervention programs to respond effectively to students when they were not learning. Both the board of education and the Kildeer Education Association agreed that the collective bargaining process presented an excellent opportunity to resolve the "time problem" in the district.

Entering negotiations, the board and the education association agreed to collaborative negotiations protocols based on the shared belief the primary objective of collective bargaining was to advance student learning. Given the questions and difficulties teachers were having in finding time, both groups agreed to work together to develop a master schedule that created time for teachers to 1) meet in collaborative teams and 2) create and implement intervention programs.

The agreement between the board and the faculty resulted in a competitive increase in salary that enabled the creation of a master schedule that added 1 hour of time to the contractual day—time dedicated to and protected for teacher collaboration and student intervention programs. The extra 5 hours every week allowed District 96 to lengthen the school day by 15 minutes and add 45 minutes of teacher collaboration time after school. The new schedule sets 2 days aside each week so that teachers can facilitate short-cycle student interventions in two 30-minute blocks. An After-School Assistance Program was created for the remaining days of the week; during this time, teachers can provide mid- and long-range interventions and meet with their grade-level and curriculum teams.

The board and faculty agreement in Kildeer Countryside School District 96 is a clear example of how a district that seeks to function as a professional learning community can develop collective bargaining protocols that focus first and foremost on student learning. When we move beyond adversarial negotiations to form collaborative win–win partnerships, we begin to understand the power of collective bargaining to impact student achievement.

Revisiting the Salary Schedule

The District 125 Board of Education and the Adlai E. Stevenson High School Education Association in Lincolnshire, Illinois, have made a conscious effort to think creatively regarding how to recognize and compensate teachers for professional development and advancement and reimbursement along the salary schedule. On a typical salary schedule, movement across the "lanes" and down the "steps" is based on a simple accumulation of graduate school coursework combined with years of teaching experience. As a teacher accumulates continuing education credits (such as B.A. to B.A.+ 15 to M.A. to M.A. + 15, and so on), as well as years of teaching, he or she "moves along" the salary schedule, making more money as time passes. Movement through this kind of salary schedule, however, does not take into account factors such as the quality of the graduate school courses taken, the level of success the teacher had in the courses, or the impact the teacher is having on student learning and achievement. Furthermore, there is no research or evidence to support the notion that simply teachers piling on classes in a race across the salary schedule has any impact on student learning.

While some districts are piloting pay-for-performance contracts and merit-based pay systems, the step-and-lane salary schedule remains ubiquitous in public school systems. Allan Odden of the University of Wisconsin has suggested that "the single salary schedule is so resilient, that one could argue that the 'steps and lanes' of the salary schedule are the DNA of teacher pay" (as quoted in Sennett, 2004, p. 52).

As an alternative to the slow march across the traditional salary schedule, the District 125 Board of Education and the Adlai E.

Stevenson High School Education Association negotiated an agreement that provides alternative routes for teachers to advance across the salary schedule. While the "far right" column of the salary schedule continues to represent the highest possible salary for a teacher (depending upon years of experience), the new salary schedule identifies a teacher who has reached this point as a "Master Teacher." Once teachers have completed their first master's degree, they can follow one of three avenues for attaining Master Teacher status:

1. Completing a second master's degree in education or in their content area

2. Completing National Board Certification

3. Completing University of Stevenson Master Teacher Program

Completing a Second Master's Degree

Teachers who wish to pursue a more traditional model of professional development are free to enroll in an approved master's degree program in education (such as curriculum and instruction, educational leadership, and so on) or in their teaching content area (such as biology, American history, mathematics, and so on). The collective bargaining agreement no longer allows teachers to freely move across the salary schedule by accumulating credit through a patchwork of seemingly random courses. Courses such as "Disenabling the Enabler" and "Microsoft Excel for the History Teacher" are no longer approved for advancement along the salary schedule.

The working assumption of the new contract language is that by enrolling and completing a second master's degree from an approved institution, a teacher will continue his or her learning of the essential knowledge and skills to improve his or her professional practice. By deepening their understanding of their subject area and the knowledge, disposition, and skills of effective teaching, teachers significantly enhance their ability to positively impact student achievement.

Completing National Board Certification

In addition to completing a second master's degree in their content area or education, the District 125 Board/Faculty Agreement allows teachers to achieve Master Teacher status by completing National Board Certification from the National Board for Professional Teaching Standards. The National Board for Professional Teaching Standards (NBPTS) is an independent, nonprofit, nonpartisan, and nongovernmental organization formed to "advance the quality of teaching and learning by developing professional standards for accomplished teaching" (NBPTS, 2007, p. 5). Teachers who seek National Board Certification are evaluated on knowledge, skills, and dispositions that are derived from the Five Core Propositions of the National Board for Professional Teaching Standards:

1. Teachers are committed to students and their learning.

2. Teachers know the subjects that they teach and how to teach those subjects to students.

3. Teachers are responsible for managing and monitoring student learning.

4. Teachers think systematically about their practice and learn from experience.

5. Teachers are members of learning communities. (NBPTS, 2007, p. i)

More than 55,000 K–12 teachers have completed National Board Certification since 1987, and a growing body of research finds that teachers who complete the National Board Certification process are improving their ability to positively impact student learning and achievement.

Teachers who have attained National Board Certification raise achievement among their students. Multiple studies have shown that students who have teachers who achieved National Board

Certification "perform better on standardized tests and other measures than students of non–National Board Certified Teachers" (NBPTS, 2007, p. 5). The findings demonstrate that African-American and Hispanic students perform higher with National Board Certified Teachers (NBCTs); students of NBCTs "make learning gains equivalent on average to an extra month in school," and on year-end exams, students score 7 to 15 percentage points higher with NBCTs (NBPTS, 2007, p. 5).

Teachers who have attained National Board Certification inspire deeper learning in their students. Research has found that students of NBCTs develop higher order and critical thinking skills needed for work in a global economy. Students of NBCTs exhibit stronger "writing abilities and comprehension of the classroom material than students of non-certified teachers" (NBPTS, 2007, p. 5). In addition, students of NBCTs are more likely to develop interdisciplinary writing skills and are able to integrate complex ideas.

Teachers who have attained National Board Certification continually seek to improve their practice. Teachers who have achieved National Board Certification demonstrate stronger content knowledge and teaching skills and "routinely seek educational strategies that better meet students' needs" (NBPTS, 2007, p. 5). Additionally, NBCTs create more challenging curricula and have a higher capacity to evaluate student learning and provide better feedback to students.

Teachers who have attained National Board Certification have an influence on school improvement through mentoring and other leadership activities. Studies have found that NBCTs have a profound impact on the culture of their schools in ways that improve student achievement (NBPTS, 2007). NBCTs are involved in coaching and mentoring younger teachers and work collaboratively to develop programs that serve to increase student learning and achievement.

Although attaining National Board Certification may take considerably less time than a master's degree program or individual courses taken to move across the salary schedule, the significant body of research that demonstrates the positive effect that National Board Certified teachers have on learning made it an easy decision for the board of education to move teachers receiving certification to Master Teacher status on the salary schedule.

Completing the Stevenson Master Teacher Program

For teachers interested in working through a more personalized professional development plan that allows for a deep examination of curriculum, instruction, and assessment within their own teaching at Stevenson, the District 125 Board/Faculty Agreement gives teachers the option of participating in the Stevenson High School Master Teacher Program. The Stevenson administration and faculty jointly developed the Master Teacher Program to allow teachers to explore topics that relate directly to their daily work within the school, in their classrooms, and with students.

The Master Teacher Program requires teachers to develop an individualized professional development plan that explores one of five core areas: assessment, content knowledge, leadership, content-based pedagogy, or technology. While their plans and projects vary, the work of all teachers in the Master Teacher Program must demonstrate a dedication to collaboration, self-reflection, and instructional improvement.

Both the board of education and the education association are excited about the three new opportunities the contract presents for teachers to advance along the salary schedule. Although the new contract language eliminates "shortcuts" across the salary table, its new avenues toward Master Teacher status link salary increases to a meaningful progression more consistent with the characteristics of high-quality professional development and the foundation of a professional learning community: learning.

A Process Guided by Learning

Moving beyond the traditional patterns of collective bargaining is no easy task. In *Good to Great,* Jim Collins (2001) challenges those of us interested in building high-performing organizations to make all our decisions in light of our "guiding principle." In a professional learning community school, *learning* serves as the fundamental purpose and guiding principle. As a result, collective bargaining—once a process filled with mistrust and competing interests—becomes a collaborative endeavor. In this new vision of collective bargaining, there are no "sides" in the negotiation process, and both parties respect and value the other's opinions. Together, the board of education and the teachers' union look past adult autonomy and convenience, and place student learning as the prized outcome of the negotiations process.

References

Bulach, C. (1991). Guidelines for win-win negotiations. *American School Board Journal, 178*(7), 25–26.

Cassel, J., Allen, J., & Peifer, A. (2007). *Thinking win/win.* Accessed at www.aasb.org/BoardStds/7Habits/winwin.html on September 26, 2007.

Collins, J. (2001). *Good to great: Why some companies make the leap . . . and others don't.* New York: Harper Business.

Covey, S. (1989). *The seven habits of highly effective people: Powerful lessons in personal change.* New York: Free Press.

Kaboolian, L. (2005). *Win-win labor-management collaboration in education: Breakthrough practices to benefit students, teachers, and administrators.* Mt. Morris, IL: Education Week Press.

National Board for Professional Teaching Standards (NBPTS). (2007). *A research guide on national board certification of teachers.* Arlington, VA: Author.

Sennett, F. (2004). *400 quotable quotes from the world's leading educators.* Thousand Oaks, CA: Corwin.

JAY WESTOVER

Executive director of the Center for Educational Efficacy and former administrator of Educational Leadership Services at the Riverside County Office of Education in California, Jay Westover applies his knowledge of what it takes to plan, implement, and sustain a professional learning community at local, regional, and state levels. His valued guidance includes practical information gleaned from his own success with the PLC model as a middle school principal. Jay has worked extensively with several school districts across the United States to put into place "loose-tight" structures and processes for implementing the PLC model as well as tools and routines to guide the work of collaborative teacher teams. He works closely with more than 50 schools each year, coaching principals, facilitating school leadership and principal teams, and supporting schools to meet state and federal academic achievement measures.

THIRTEEN

A Framework for Excellence: The Role of the Central Office

Jay Westover

Rick DuFour makes a compelling point in *On Common Ground*: "If schools are to be transformed into PLCs, the educators within them will be required to change many things—including themselves" (2005, p. 26). Transformation is equally critical at the central office level. Without central office support, professional learning communities will continue to exist in a minority of schools as "temporary havens of excellence" whose existence is dependent upon a "temporary collaborative culture" (Fullan, 2005, p. 210). The number of schools embracing the PLC concept has grown substantially since the mid-1990s. In most instances, however; the creation of a PLC has been dependent upon a courageous site administrator willing to buck the traditional education system. And in many cases, an individual administrator's success in sustaining change depends greatly upon his or her ability to prevent external forces from distracting the school's focus and collective efforts. As Linda Lambert has pointed out, "Excellent schools in poor districts implode over time, whereas, poor schools in excellent districts get better" (2003, p. 80). Similarly, in *Inventing Better Schools*, Phillip Schlechty argues, "Only through revitalizing and redirecting the action of district-level operations can the kind of widespread and radical change that must occur be possible" (1997, p. 78). Thus, to realize the full potential of professional learning communities, we must clarify and transform the role of the central office. The central office must become the catalyst for the structural and cultural changes required to implement and sustain a thriving PLC at the site level.

This revitalization and redirection will require the central office to make fundamental shifts: a shift from fragmentation to clarity, a shift from dependence to interdependence, and a shift from resignation to directed empowerment (Sparks, 2007). The shift from fragmentation to clarity requires that the central office align its policies, practices, and procedures with structures and processes grounded in the three big ideas of a PLC—that is, a focus on learning, a collaborative culture, and a results-orientation. Lambert emphasizes that excellent districts "model certain leadership behaviors; abide by certain structures, processes and policies; and focus on student learning" (2003, p. 80). The central office must define a strategic focus, with clear parameters for team and classroom practices as evidenced by team products and student learning results. This results in an academic program supportive of all students' learning, creates a system for monitoring student progress, and establishes structures that accelerate a collaborative culture through job-embedded professional learning.

The shift from dependence to interdependence requires the establishment of widely distributed leadership. This will require the development and cultivation of strategic and analytical leadership practice at all levels: in central office administrators, principals, and teachers. Similarly, the shift from resignation to directed empowerment requires cultivating the collective efficacy of teachers and administrators through job-embedded professional learning. To do this, autonomy must be blended with accountability through the use of tools and routines that guide the work of collaborative teams.

A framework for the central office's role has been established in *Learning by Doing* (DuFour, DuFour, Eaker, & Many, 2006): Identify a limited number of very focused goals, and design tools and routines to drive those goals into every classroom in every school. Engage all members of the organization in clarifying priorities, establishing indicators of progress to be monitored carefully, and embedding continuous improvement throughout the organization. This chapter will provide examples and resources for implementing this leadership framework through *"loose-tight" practices* characterized by *strategic focus*—clear parameters and priorities—that create *collective efficacy* by directly empowering individuals to work within established boundaries in a creative and autonomous way.

A Leadership Framework

Zmuda, Kuklis, and Kline (2004) stated that in a competent school system, thoughts, emotions, and resulting actions become collective. The role of the central office in implementing a professional learning community is to provide the overarching framework that will support this alignment. However, there may be structural and cultural barriers (DuFour, DuFour, Eaker, & Many, 2006), and overcoming these challenges requires a paradigm shift through the enactment of new processes and procedures that support learning for all students. The central office must drive this shift by presenting a clear, consistent, and compelling vision and by cultivating trust through effective collaboration. It does this by building shared knowledge, developing common beliefs, and establishing collective commitments. Figure 13-1 (page 238) shows the leadership framework as a strategic process that addresses each critical area; the following sections will discuss each point of the triangle in turn.

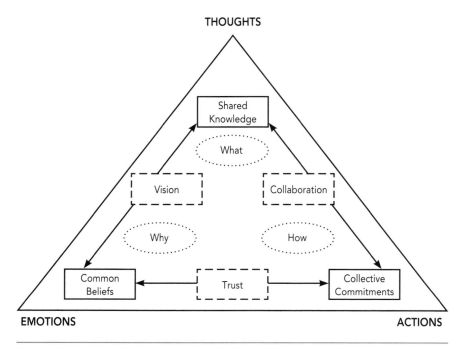

Figure 13-1: A Leadership Framework *(© Jay Westover. Used with permission.)*

Build Shared Knowledge Through Strategic Focus

"What are the intended impacts of team and classroom practice on student learning, as evidenced by team products and student achievement results?"

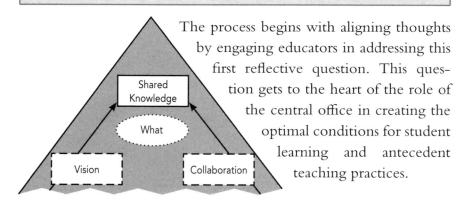

The process begins with aligning thoughts by engaging educators in addressing this first reflective question. This question gets to the heart of the role of the central office in creating the optimal conditions for student learning and antecedent teaching practices.

Building shared knowledge creates a strategic focus with clear parameters for team and classroom practices, as evidenced by team products and student learning results. The central office can then align its policies, practices, and procedures around the three big ideas of a PLC: a focus on ensuring all students learn, a results–orientation, and a collaborative culture. These big ideas translate into critical structural changes: an academic program supportive of all students' learning, a system for monitoring student progress, and job–embedded professional learning. The central office should be "tight" on supporting school sites in making these *structural* changes and "loose" in providing the school sites the autonomy to make the accompanying *cultural* changes.

Structural changes occur as a result of clearly articulating a focus on student learning, and the two vehicles that drive this focus are the master schedule and school site plan. The first is the blueprint for the academic program, and the second is a tool for monitoring progress and designing professional development. Progress monitoring is essential to guide the implementation of the academic program. Monitoring coordinates interventions that accelerate student learning and informs collaborative teams of their respective professional development needs. You can therefore determine the common purpose of the array of central office services by asking very specific questions as outlined in Figure 13-2 (page 240). Your team's responses will reveal the extent to which existing processes and structures support a results-oriented, collaborative culture that ensures all students learn.

Answering these questions will clarify the specific ways in which the central office can create the optimal conditions for implementing a professional learning community at all school sites. The discussion also provides a common process to strategically create systems to monitor, support, and provide feedback to each school site. The central office role will shift from fragmentation to clarity as you use the discussion to bring common purpose to existing initiatives, focus and reduce new initiatives, create a common language, and coordinate services to support PLC implementation.

1. **A Focus on Learning: Academic Program**

   - How are all students placed properly in academic classes?

   - How are all students provided access to a fully implemented, guaranteed, and viable curriculum?

   - How do all collaborative teams refine and consistently follow the agreed-upon pacing of a guaranteed and viable curriculum?

   - How are all students provided necessary interventions during the school day?

2. **A Results-Orientation: Progress Monitoring**

   - What systems and processes are used to frequently provide collaborative teams with timely data on student learning results to guide the implementation of the academic program, provide interventions that accelerate student learning, and inform collaborative teams of their respective professional learning needs?

   - How are results used to provide support, monitoring, and feedback to collaborative teams?

3. **Collaborative Culture: Professional Learning**

   - How is collaboration time embedded in the school day and used effectively?

   - How are support and/or coaching provided to collaborative teams for their professional learning of curriculum, instruction, and assessment?

   - How is professional development job-embedded and guided by student learning results?

   - How do tools and routines guide the work of collaborative teams?

Figure 13-2: Structures to Build Shared Knowledge Around the Big Ideas of a PLC

An Academic Program

In the Moreno Valley Unified School District, for example, the superintendent has created the vision that PLCs will provide the framework to coordinate the services of the central office and guide the work of each school site. The central office and site administrators have focused their efforts to align with the three legs of student achievement: full implementation of the core curriculum, connecting with students, and implementing effective interventions. To ensure that students are properly placed in academic classes and provided necessary interventions, the central office facilitates the creation of a multiple measures grid that is used for initial student placement in both academic courses and interventions. The central office also has worked with teachers throughout the district to create course pacing guides that are revised annually based on teacher input. A data-monitoring system has been implemented to support teachers and administrators by analyzing common assessments using a common data protocol template created by the central office. Every school site has a minimum of 2 hours per month of collaboration time, and many have math and English language arts coaches that provide teams support with analyzing data, developing common lessons, and implementing effective instructional practices. This focus creates a results-orientation and collaborative culture to ensure all students learn.

A System of Monitoring Student Progress

A system of monitoring, support, and feedback linked to a few unifying goals is essential to guide the actions of the central office and each school site through a hierarchy of implementation and achievement of SMART goals. Robert Fritz has said:

> When we build our organization on structural tension, goals have a special function—they are the prime organizing principles of the organization. Every action taken is linked to other goals that are linked still to other goals. And there is a very special way that goals are linked. They move from goals that reflect the overall purpose of the central office, to goals that reflect its strategy, and goals on the local site level supporting the strategy of the central office. (1999, p. 31)

An adaptation of Fritz's model of structural tension seems to best serve this critical aspect of building shared knowledge. To begin, the central office creates a few overarching goals and discerns the current reality for each. Then the central office establishes a few action steps and corresponding implementation and achievement SMART goals to attain each overarching goal. Each school is expected to use the same process within a loose-tight framework in which the central office is tight on the need for schools to support each overarching central office goal and loose on each school's action steps and respective SMART goals. The central office then monitors, supports, and provides feedback based on the SMART goal results, celebrating successes and providing support for continued efforts to attain goals.

An example of this process is provided in Figure 13-3 (page 243). Jurupa Valley USD has created a blueprint to achieve its overarching goals to educate each student to the highest levels of academic achievement and prepare students to succeed in life. Jurupa Valley has chosen five strategies to achieve the overarching goals: Focus fiscal resources, utilize the Academic Program Survey, fully implement standards-based textbooks, utilize PLCs as a model for continuous improvement, and provide district support for implementation. The strategy to utilize the Academic Program Survey could be restated as: *Plan, implement, and evaluate a standards-based curriculum comprised of essential learning outcomes.* The implementation SMART goal might become: *By September, 2008, a standards-based curriculum comprised of essential learnings will be implemented at every school as evidenced by grade-level and course-alike team pacing guides and common assessments.* The achievement SMART goal might become: *By November 2008, 80% of students will score proficient on common assessments administered by each grade-level and course-alike team.* Using the loose-tight framework, the central office is tight on having each school support this strategy of the central office and simultaneously loose on the strategy and SMART goals chosen by the school. The creation of structures by the central office to support the implementation of

PLCs will only impact student learning if there exists widely distributed loose–tight leadership.

Blueprint for Learning

The mission of the Jurupa Unified School District is to educate each student to the highest levels of academic achievement and prepare students to succeed in life.

A "Blueprint for Learning" is being implemented in the Jurupa Unified School District. Research tells us that we must focus on learning. Teaching can only be effective in an environment in which students are motivated and have an opportunity to learn. A five-point plan is outlined below.

1. The Resources

Focus fiscal resources, including categorical monies, on providing tools to sites, including staff development, assessment, support and materials, and human resources. Utilize an evaluation system with administrators to clarify expectations focusing on the implementation of the plan. Provide training and support to teachers.

2. The Structure

Utilize the Academic Program Survey (APS) developed by the California Department of Education for School Assistance Intervention Team (SAIT) schools at every school in the District. This will provide for planning, implementing, and evaluating a standards-based curriculum. Base the instructional program on all State Standards with a focus on the most Essential Standards.

3. The Materials

Continue with full implementation of standards-based textbooks. Purchase standards-based textbooks in English/language arts, math, science and history/social science.

Provide professional development to teachers (AB 466) and to principals (AB 75) on full implementation of standards-based textbooks.

Establish a clear evaluation system for certificated administrators.

(continued)

Figure 13-3: Blueprint for Learning

Blueprint for Learning (continued)

4. The Method

Utilize a model of professional learning communities (PLC) and continuous improvement devised from Quality Systems Theory. Create grade level, cross grade level, and disciplinary (subject area) teams at every school to focus on improving student learning by:

- Utilizing data to drive the instructional process

- Sharing and critiquing instructional strategies

- Looking collaboratively at student work

- Evaluating and modifying the instructional process

- Creating clear expectations in the staff evaluation system

5. The Support

Provide district support for plan implementation. Provide coaches to aid in the implementation of collaborative teams using the PLC model and the application of APS.

Professional Learning

Traditionally, professional learning occurs under the guise of staff development, with models of training and implementation varying from site-based to districtwide initiatives. A need for improvement or change is clarified, a program is chosen, and staff is trained; however, most often what occurs is fragmented implementation due to a disconnect from the daily work of teachers and limited support to augment current practices. In comparison, job-embedded professional learning is interconnected with daily curricular, instructional, and assessment practices; implemented through tools and routines used by collaborative teams; and monitored for effectiveness through student learning results. Job-embedded professional learning requires that collaborative teams collectively clarify essential learning objectives, analyze student learning results, and discern student strengths and weaknesses to be strategic in improving their team and classroom practices. It is critical that the central office shift its focus and resources to be tight on ensuring school sites make *structural* changes to allow for job-embedded professional learning, and loose in providing school sites with the autonomy needed to make necessary *cultural* changes.

Sweetwater Union High School District has begun to make such a shift in their professional development practices to create the optimal conditions for PLCs to thrive at all school sites. The central office has identified a limited number of professional development focal areas directly connected to team and classroom practices. Each school is expected to implement PLC structures and processes as well as focus on academic vocabulary. In addition, each school is expected to implement any two of the nine instructional strategies from *Classroom Instruction That Works* (Marzano, Pickering, & Pollock, 2004). Academic support teams provide continuous support to school sites. These teams serve as a resource to site administrators and teachers by targeting their professional development needs and prompting reflective dialogue as to the effectiveness of instructional, curricular, and assessment practices. In this respect the central office directly empowers school sites within defined parameters. The superintendent commented as follows on this new approach of job-embedded professional learning:

> With the implementation of new academic initiatives at both the district and campus levels, we have strengthened our focus on offering campuses more support. Specifically, we created two Academic Support Teams with subject matter specialists who will work directly with teachers to see that every student achieves at expected levels. On our journey toward 100% student success, our concern is not with who gets to the goal first, but on ensuring that everyone gets there. We know that in order to reach our goals, school sites need to be able to count on continuous support from the district. We are moving in that direction. These two Academic Support Teams, one serving middle schools and one for high schools, are one way that

our energy, effort and expertise are being put toward making every school in the Sweetwater District a high-performing school. (Dr. Jesus M. Gandara, Superintendent of Sweetwater Union High School District, personal communication)

Develop Common Beliefs Through Widely Distributed Leadership

"Why is it critical to align our core values and collective efforts to attain the intended impacts and outcomes on teaching and learning?"

The next steps are to align emotions, as emotions assign a value to our experiences, and formulate our initial plan of action. It is critical that members of the leadership team participate in facilitated dialogue to discern each member's perceptions and create a common set of beliefs and values. This is a necessary step in the process of aligning core values and collective efforts, for changing people's practice is dependent upon changing their beliefs and values.

Rick DuFour (2003) contends that to change beliefs, values, and ultimately practice, the central office must address two critical tasks: 1) Identify and articulate the fundamental purpose of the organization and a few big ideas to achieve that purpose, and 2) encourage individual and organizational autonomy within defined parameters. This ensures the fundamental shift from dependence to interdependence—an essential transition, as administrators and teachers usually perceive their actions as dependent upon directives cast down from the central office. This has been described by Dennis Sparks (2007) as a form of learned helplessness that is a byproduct of school reform initiatives based on mandates and compliance. A component of the central office's work, then, is to create interdependence and collective responsibility by conveying a compelling vision characterized by a collaborative, trust-oriented culture. This can be achieved by developing strategic and analytical leadership practices at all levels: central office, school, and classroom. DuFour, DuFour, Eaker, and Many (2006) have said that developing the capacity of staff to function as a PLC requires the creation of conditions that result in people acting in new ways that lend coherence to those actions through big ideas that give them meaning.

James Spillane suggests that "organizational tools and routines are bundles of possibilities that shape leadership practice but can also be reshaped by that practice" (2006, p. 20). In this respect, the role of the central office is to clarify and deepen the belief that widely distributed loose-tight leadership practice focused on designing, implementing, and refining tools and routines is what guides the work of collaborative teams. Loose leadership practices promote *collegiality* by providing a collaborative team with the autonomy to develop values and beliefs that drive their team and classroom practices; tight leadership practices promote *accountability* by requiring a collaborative team to produce artifacts that articulate their focus on student learning. Collaborative teams become collectively responsible as a result of the questions they ask each other, the student learning results they share, and tools and routines they use to guide their collective work.

This type of leadership transformation is vital for implementing a districtwide professional learning community. To develop loose-tight leadership at all levels, the central office should direct their attention to the site principals, instructional coaches, and school leadership teams. Principal meetings need to be focused so as to create collaborative principal teams that work collectively to establish leadership practices for implementing critical aspects of a PLC, such as the effective use of embedded collaboration time, creation of grade-level and course essential learnings, team analysis of common assessment data, use of assessment data to transform team and classroom practices, and implementation of a system of student interventions. Within this format, the central office is loose on the leadership strategies and actions that collaborative principal teams create and tight on the impact on team and classroom practices and student learning results. As a result of this process, the principals become accustomed to modeling the same loose-tight practices in supporting their collaborative teams to implement these same critical aspects of a PLC. In much the same way, time needs to be dedicated to support instructional coaches and school leadership teams in developing their leadership practice in implementing PLCs. Both of these groups should be given the autonomy to establish values and beliefs to guide their collective efforts to support teacher teams while being held accountable to produce products in the form of tools and routines that support teacher teams and impact student learning.

Establish Collective Commitments Through Collective Efficacy

"How should interactions (tools and routines) be designed, implemented, and refined to cultivate collective responsibility by balancing autonomy with accountability?"

As a result of dialogue around this question, all members of the central office team will understand how they personally contribute to the collective vision of helping each school site implement the professional learning communities model.

The collaborative teacher team is the fundamental building block of a PLC. The team's collective commitments fuel the fire of continuous improvement, but individuals and teams struggle with establishing and collectively committing to action if they lack the confidence in their ability to be successful. The central office must provide resources and support for schools to achieve short-term wins and develop skills at all levels to achieve long-term goals. This can only be achieved in an environment that supports innovation, risk-taking, and learning by doing. To become the catalyst for PLCs, the central office must model job-embedded professional learning by establishing structures, processes, and conditions that require schools and collaborative teams to work together, thus shifting collaborative teams from resignation to directed empowerment by cultivating collective efficacy. This is best accomplished by providing schools with tools and routines to guide the work of collaborative teams that can be framed in the 5Cs of a PLC: collaboration, common curriculum, common assessments, collective prevention and intervention, and confirmed instructional practices. The central office exhibits tight leadership by focusing the efforts of collaborative teams within these defined parameters and simultaneously exhibits loose leadership in allowing the teams to design, implement, and refine tools and routines to collectively engage in continuous improvement of student academic achievement.

The central office of Christina School District has begun to use a 60-day plan as a tool to provide support, monitoring, and feedback to school leadership teams. In this process, each team is asked to formulate a plan to support teacher teams at their site; the central office provides training and resources for facilitating meetings, processes for consensus and decision-making, and protocols for team meetings. Other tools and routines used to guide the work of collaborative teams include templates for designing common curriculum through clarifying essential vocabulary, prerequisite skills, and standards-based outcomes; protocols for creating SMART goals and common assessments and analyzing data and student work; methods for creating student interventions at the classroom, team, and school levels; and access to research-based instructional strategies for teams to consider adding to their strategy banks of best instructional practices. The leadership teams and coaches then devise plans for implementing tools and routines at their school sites as well for monitoring and supporting teacher teams. In so doing, the central office has created a structure and process for directly empowering leadership teams, instructional coaches, and teacher teams to implement the 5Cs of a professional learning community.

Permanent Havens of Excellence

In education, we want solutions that are exotic and easy, but in reality the answers are simple and hard to do. The thought of becoming a professional learning community can be enticing and enlightening to a school as it empowers staff and promotes collegiality. In reality, creating a PLC is hard to do, but the process can be simplified by retaining clarity of focus, developing confidence and belief in our collective ability, and consistently using loose-tight leadership practices. To create thriving professional learning communities at all school sites, the central office must establish a framework of structures and processes that reinforce a collaborative culture focused on results and learning and simultaneously foster a culture that directly empowers school sites to function within these parameters to ensure all students learn.

This chapter has provided an example of such a framework for the central office to become a catalyst for implementing PLCs. By identifying a limited number of very focused goals and creating well-designed tools and routines, the central office can drive those goals into every classroom in every school. Engage all members of the organization in clarifying priorities, establishing indicators of progress to be monitored carefully, and embedding continuous improvement throughout the organization. Create loose-tight leadership practices characterized by clear parameters and priorities to directly empower individuals to work within established boundaries in a creative and autonomous way. Align the thoughts, emotions, and actions of the people in your organization by shifting from fragmentation to clarity, from dependence to interdependence, and from resignation to directed empowerment. In so doing, you can play a powerful role in ensuring that your professional learning communities become permanent havens of excellence with a thriving collaborative culture.

References

DuFour, R. (2003, May). Building a professional learning community. *School Administrator, 60*(5), 13–18.

DuFour, R. (2005). What is a professional learning community? In R. DuFour, R. Eaker, & R. DuFour (Eds.), *On common ground: The power of professional learning communities* (pp. 31–43). Bloomington, IN: Solution Tree (formerly National Educational Service).

DuFour, R., DuFour, R., Eaker, R., & Many, T. (2006). *Learning by doing: A handbook for professional learning communities at work.* Bloomington, IN: Solution Tree.

DuFour, R., Eaker, R., & DuFour, R. (Eds.). (2005). *On common ground: The power of professional learning communities.* Bloomington, IN: Solution Tree (formerly National Educational Service).

DuFour Burnette, R. (2003, May). Central-office support for learning communities. *School Administrator, 60*(5), 13–18.

Fritz, R. (1999). *The path of least resistance for managers: Developing organizations to succeed.* San Francisco: Berrett-Koehler.

Fullan, M. (2005). Professional learning communities writ large. In R. DuFour, R. Eaker, & R. DuFour (Eds.), *On common ground: The power of professional learning communities* (pp. 209–223). Bloomington, IN: Solution Tree (formerly National Educational Service).

Lambert, L. (2003). *Leadership capacity for lasting school improvement.* Alexandria, VA: Association for Supervision and Curriculum Development.

Marzano, B., Pickering, D., & Pollock, J. (2004). *Classroom instruction that works: Research-based strategies for increasing student achievement.* Alexandria, VA: Association for Supervision and Curriculum Development.

Schlechty, P. C. (1997). *Inventing better schools: An action plan for educational reform.* San Francisco: Jossey-Bass.

Sparks, D. (2007). *Leading for results: Transforming teaching, learning, and relationships in schools.* Thousand Oaks, CA: Corwin.

Spillane, J. P. (2006). *Distributed leadership.* San Francisco: Jossey-Bass.

Zmuda, A., Kuklis, R., & Kline, E. (2004). *Transforming schools: Creating a culture of continuous improvement.* Alexandria, VA: Association for Supervision and Curriculum Development.

Make the Most of Your Professional Development Investment

Let Solution Tree schedule time for you and your staff with leading practitioners in the areas of:

- **Professional Learning Communities** with Richard DuFour, Robert Eaker, Rebecca DuFour, and associates
- **Effective Schools** with associates of Larry Lezotte
- **Assessment *for* Learning** with Rick Stiggins and associates
- **Crisis Management and Response** with Cheri Lovre
- **Discipline With Dignity** with Richard Curwin and Allen Mendler
- **PASSport to Success** (parental involvement) with Vickie Burt
- **Peacemakers** (violence prevention) with Jeremy Shapiro

Additional presentations are available in the following areas:

- Youth at Risk Issues
- Bullying Prevention/Teasing and Harassment
- Team Building and Collaborative Teams
- Data Collection and Analysis
- Embracing Diversity
- Literacy Development
- Motivating Techniques for Staff and Students

Solution Tree

304 W. Kirkwood Avenue
Bloomington, IN 47404-5131
(812) 336-7700
(800) 733-6786 (toll-free number)
FAX (812) 336-7790
email: info@solution-tree.com
www.solution-tree.com